Dialogues on Italian Constitutional Justice

A Comparative Perspective

Edited by
Vittoria Barsotti - Paolo G. Carozza
Marta Cartabia - Andrea Simoncini

Dialogues on Italian Constitutional Justice

A Comparative Perspective

Routledge
Taylor & Francis Group
LONDON AND NEW YORK

G. Giappichelli Editore

First published 2021
by Routledge
2 Park Square, Milton Park, Abingdon, Oxon OX14 4RN

and by Routledge
605 Third Avenue, New York, NY 10158

Routledge is an imprint of the Taylor & Francis Group, an informa business

British Library Cataloguing-in-Publication Data
A catalogue record for this book is available from the British Library

This book was published with the support of the research funds from the University of Florence.
Volume pubblicato con il contributo dei fondi di ricerca dell'Università degli Studi di Firenze.

Library of Congress Cataloging-in-Publication Data
A catalog record has been requested for this book

ISBN: 978-88-921-3235-1 (ebk-G. Giappichelli Editore)
ISBN: 978-0-367-50745-9 (hbk-Routledge)
ISBN: 978-0-367-61772-1 (pbk)
ISBN: 978-1-003-05112-1 (ebk-Routledge)

Typeset in Simoncini Garamond
by G. Giappichelli Editore, Turin, Italy

The manuscript has been subjected to the double blind peer review process prior to publication.

CONTENTS

LIST OF FIGURES AND TABLES

Figures

Graph

CONTRIBUTORS

Vittoria Barsotti, University of Florence

Paolo G. Carozza, University of Notre Dame

Marta Cartabia, University of Milan-Bicocca and President of the Italian Constitutional Court

Andrea Simoncini, Director of the Department of Legal Sciences of the University of Florence

Paolo Passaglia, University of Pisa

Marc Verdussen, University of Louvain

Tania Groppi, University of Siena

Anna Maria Lecis Cocco Ortu, University of Aix-Marseille and University of Siena

Maartje De Visser, Singapore Management University

Diletta Tega, University of Bologna

Sarah Haring, IIT Chicago-Kent College of Law

Elisabetta Lamarque, University of Milan-Bicocca

Victor Ferreres Comella, Pompeu Fabra University

Giorgio Pino, University Roma Tre

Jeffrey A. Pojanowski, University of Notre Dame

Marta Infantino, University of Trieste

Patricia Popelier, University of Antwerp

Armin von Bogdandy, Director at the Max Planck Institute for Comparative Public Law and International Law in Heidelberg

Davide Paris, Max Planck Institute for Comparative Public Law and International Law in Heidelberg

Chapter I

INTRODUCTION. DIALOGUE AS A METHOD

Vittoria Barsotti, Paolo G. Carozza, Marta Cartabia and Andrea Simoncini

SUMMARY: 1.1. Relationality as the hallmark of the Italian Style of constitutional adjudication. – 1.2. Relationality revisited. – 1.2.1. Relationality vs. weakness: perception and reality. – 1.2.2. Relationality "unpacked". – 1.2.3. Official vs. Unofficial relationality. – 1.3. Dialogue as a method. – 1.4. Relationality and constitutional pluralism.

The Italian Constitutional Court represents one of the earliest, strongest, and most successful examples of constitutional judicial review established in the last century. Following its delayed implementation in 1956, eight years after the Constitution of the Italian Republic entered into force, the Court immediately took up a strong position among the other Italian political institutions [1] and ever since then it has always been well respected at the domestic level. Beyond national borders, together with the Constitutional Court of Germany it has served as an important forerunner of the "postwar paradigm" [2] and one of the principal prototypes for later constitutional tribunals in other parts of Europe, from Spain and Portugal in the 1970s and 1980s, to Central and Eastern Europe after the collapse of the communist regimes in the 1990s, to the more recent reform of the French *Conseil Constitutionnel* in 2008 [3]. Its value transcends Europe, moreover: it has a fascinating and instructive history for any country seeking to create and consolidate a new constitutional regime including a system of judicial review in its

---

[1] B. ACKERMAN, *Revolutionary Constitutionalism*, Cambridge, Ma., Belknap Press, 2019, 174 (numbers refer to pages of the electronic version of Bruce Ackerman, *The Rise of World Constitutionalism. Volume one: Revolutionary Constitutions)*.

[2] L.E. WEINRIB, *The Post-War Paradigm and American Exceptionalism*, in S. CHOUDHRY (eds.), *The Migration of Constitutional Ideas*, Cambridge, Cambridge University Press, 2006, 89-90.

[3] See generally T. GINSBURG, *The Global Spread of Constitutional Review*, in D. KELEMAN, K. WITTINGTON (eds.), *The Oxford Handbook of Law and Politics*, Oxford, Oxford University Press, 2008, 81-95.

institutional architecture.[4] It belongs to the Continental European tradition of Kelsensian-style constitutional courts, but it is distinctive in its structural, procedural, and institutional dimensions. It produces a sophisticated jurisprudence, with a unique voice distinguishing it among global constitutional actors, on a broad range of topics from fundamental rights and liberties to the allocations of governmental powers and regionalism.

Yet, the Italian experience of constitutional review has been either neglected or misinterpreted in a number of comparative constitutional law studies, especially those which rely primarily on secondary literature available in English. The aim of this book is to offer a deeper understanding of the experience and work of the Italian Constitutional Court, based on primary sources and on examination of certain key features of the Italian system in a comparative perspective.

This book qualifies as a "sequel". In a previous volume,[5] we meant to offer a concise but comprehensive introduction to constitutional adjudication in Italy. Our aim was to make the Italian Constitutional Court and its jurisprudence more accessible and familiar to scholars and judges engaged in comparative constitutional dialogue. We sought to do so by providing a broad introduction to the development of the Court, from its formation and early history to its growing insertion into the regional European constitutional space. The book offered an overview of the Court's structure – a dynamic hybrid of centralized and diffuse judicial review – as well as its judicial processes and its principal patterns of reasoning and methods of interpretation. We also delved into several of the most important substantive areas of the Court's case law: key rights and freedoms; the allocation and interrelationship of powers among the branches of government; and the distribution of authority between the central State and more local entities. In short, the book presented some of the most salient themes that make the Italian Constitutional Court an interestingly distinctive and important contributor to our understanding of constitutional law and politics in the global context in which we find ourselves today. The aim of that book was not in the first instance to be a critical evaluation of Italian constitutional law. Instead, we addressed an audience of readers who were likely to encounter the Italian Constitutional Court for the first time in any detail and we

---

[4] As Bruce Ackerman suggests in his analysis of the rise and consolidation of Revolutionary Constitutional regimes around the world: he describes a pattern common to a number of States where, after some phases in which the Constitution is in the hands of the political actors that lead the fundamental change, the judiciary emerges on the stage.

[5] V. Barsotti, P. Carozza, M. Cartabia, A. Simoncini, *Italian Constitutional Justice in Global Context*, Oxford, Oxford University Press, 2016.

wanted the Court's own voice to emerge. For this reason, the book includes a larger number of longer excerpts from the Court's judgments so that the reader could become acquainted with the Court's own judicial style.

Fifty years after John Henry Merryman introduced the idea of an "Italian style" to comparative law in general,[6] we can see in the Italian Constitutional Court today an "Italian style" of constitutional justice. The core idea that emerges from the previous book is that the "Italian Style" of constitutional adjudication is most centrally characterized by the *relational approach* of the Court both internally in its own structure and methods, and externally in its interactions with other judicial and political actors. The key word, *relationality*, merits some further elaboration.

1.1. Relationality as the hallmark of the Italian Style of constitutional adjudication

In a way, the idea of relationality addresses questions of judicial activity and style that have animated many other studies of the behavior of courts in the past: judicial activism vs. self-restraint or deference;[7] passive and active virtues of courts;[8] strong and weak models of judicial review;[9] classic and romantic judges;[10] heroes, mutes, soldiers, and minimalist judges;[11] and more. The originality of the relational approach to constitutional justice lies in the fact that the focus is both on the types of interactions that the individual justices have inside the Court and also on the interactions that the Court as an institution cultivates with other actors external to it.

Like any judge in well-functioning systems of justice generally, the

---

[6] J.H. MERRYMAN, *The Italian Style: Doctrine,* in 18 *Stanford Law Review* 39 (1965); J.H. MERRYMAN, *The Italian Style: Law,* in 18 *Stanford Law Review* 396 (1966); J.H. MERRYMAN, *The Italian Style: Interpretation,* in 18 *Stanford Law Review* 639 (1966).

[7] R.A. POSNER, *The Rise and Fall of Judicial Self-Restraint*, in 100 *California Law Review* 519 (2012).

[8] A. BICKEL, *The Least Dangerous Branch. The Supreme Court at the Bar of Politics*, New Haven and London, Yale University Press, 1962.

[9] S. GARDBAUM, *Are Strong Constitutional Courts Always a Good Thing for New Democracies?*, in 53 *Columbia Journal of Transnational Law* 285 (2015); R. DIXON, *The Core Case for Weak-Form Judicial Review*, in 38 *Cardozo Law Review* 2193 (2017).

[10] M.A. GLENDON, *A Nation Under Lawyers. How the Crisis in the Legal Profession is Transforming American Society*, Cambridge, Harvard University Press, 1996.

[11] C.R. SUNSTEIN, *One case at A Time. Judicial Minimalism on the Supreme Court*, Cambridge, Harvard University Press, 2001 and *Id., Constitutional Personae*, Oxford, Oxford University Press, 2015.

Constitutional Court is indeed independent from other branches of government. As a body called to exercise a *judicial* review of *legislation*, however, the Constitutional Court also has to come to terms with other judicial and political bodies. They are therefore endowed with a composite character. [12] More than other institutional actors such as legislatures, chief executives, and ordinary courts, specialized constitutional courts are always required to find and preserve their place in the constitutional map in a location equidistant from both the judicial and political branches, so that they are effectively in a position to relate to both audiences.

One of the major challenges for a constitutional court taking its first steps, therefore, is to be both self-assertive and yet cooperative with the legislative branch. Although any court required to review acts of legislation is in a certain sense necessarily in opposition to the legislature, after its inauguration in 1956 the Italian Constitutional Court was not seen to be a true antagonist of the more democratically representative bodies. This was mainly because it spent its initial energy, beginning with its very first decision, on eliminating all the Fascist vestiges from the new constitutional order. In the beginning, the natural target of judicial review was the old Fascist legislation still contained, for example, in the civil code and in the criminal code and patently incompatible with the new Constitution. The activity of the new legislature only came under the Court's scrutiny years later. This made for a vital and constructive initial alliance between the new Parliament and the Constitutional Court against the Fascist legacy, which politically strengthened the legitimacy of the Constitutional Court vis-à-vis the political institutions and in Italian society as a whole. Instead of taking sides in current political disputes, therefore, the Court emerged originally as a defender of the shared values entrenched in the anti-Fascist Constitution and was able to disseminate the new constitutional principles in a legal system that was very much in need of renewal. [13]

If there is an assertive tone in the first expressions of the Constitutional Court's jurisprudence, it was in its clear pronouncements on the binding character of all constitutional provisions as higher law, strengthening the normative force of the Constitution in the context of what had otherwise been a strong Italian tradition of "legislative constitutionalism" – that is,

---

[12] H. KELSEN, *Judicial Review of Legislation: a Comparative Study of the Austrian and American Constitution*, in 4 *The Journal of Politics* 183 (1942), 187; A. STONE SWEET, *Governing with Judges: Constitutional Politics in Europe*, Oxford, Oxford University Press, 2000, 135-137.

[13] See V. BARSOTTI, P. CAROZZA, M. CARTABIA, A. SIMONCINI, *Italian Constitutional Justice in Global Context,* op. cit., 5-39.

constitutional texts amendable by a simple piece of legislation approved by the Parliament.[14]

Over time, the doctrines elaborated by the Court have helped to maintain smooth relations with Parliament. For example, the fundamental "interpretive judgments" doctrine, separating the *norme* from the *disposizioni*,[15] allowed the Court to strike "interpretations" down, while keeping the parliamentary "texts" alive. In many ways even the judgments that add, substitute, or remove something from a statute (*sentenze manipolative*) can be understood as attempts at cooperation with the legislature, given that in those cases the Court preserves the parliamentary act, introducing only the revisions strictly necessary to make that act consistent with the Constitution.[16] All of these techniques contribute to the remarkable absence (especially from an American perspective) of concern over the counter-majoritarian difficulty[17] in Italian constitutional and political debate ever since the Court began its activity.

A particularly noteworthy recent example of a dialogical relation with the Parliament is Order n. 207 of 2018 on assisted suicide.[18] Following the example of Canada[19] and the UK,[20] the Constitutional Court, while recognizing the need to update the existing legislation on end-of-life issues, made a rare use of its procedural powers and postponed a final judgment, in order to allow room for the Parliament to introduce a new regulatory framework through legislation. The one-year delay established by the Court expired and – unlike its British and Canadian counterparts – the Italian Parliament did not pass any legislation. In these types of cases, parliaments and

---

[14] T. GROPPI, *The Italian Constitutional Court: Towards a Multilevel system of Constitutional Review?*, in A. HARDING, P. LEYLAND (eds.), *Constitutional Courts: A Comparative Study*, Wildy, Simmonds & Hill Publishing, 2009, 139.

[15] See V. BARSOTTI, P. CAROZZA, M. CARTABIA, A. SIMONCINI, *Italian Constitutional Justice in Global Context*, op. cit., 82-85.

[16] See V. BARSOTTI, P. CAROZZA, M. CARTABIA, A. SIMONCINI, *Italian Constitutional Justice in Global Context*, op. cit., 82-91.

[17] J.H. ELY, *Democracy and Distrust. A Theory of Judicial Review*, Cambridge, Harvard University Press, 1980.

[18] The order can be retrieved in English at https://www.cortecostituzionale.it/ documenti/download/doc/recent_judgments/S_207_2018_EN.pdf. The Court can issue orders (*ordinanze*) or judgments (*sentenze*). Generally speaking, orders are only briefly reasoned and are similar to *per curiam* opinions, whereas judgments are fully reasoned. It is worth recalling that no separate opinions are allowed: the decision always appears on its face as the decision of the whole Court.

[19] Supreme Court of Canada, Judgment of 6 February 2015, *Carter v. Canada*, 2015 SCC 5.

[20] Supreme Court of the United Kingdom, Judgment of 25 June 2014, *Nicklinson and another*, [2014] UKSC 8.

constitutional courts can sometimes act together as "co-legislators", as Michel Troper puts it,[21] because the court is required to invalidate the piece of legislation that contradicts the constitution, but does not have the power to fill the gap and to create a new positive legislative framework, which is the task of the parliament. In this case, Parliament failed to act and was not able to take advantage of the opportunity offered to it by a *relational* Court extremely respectful of the prerogatives of the legislative branch. Eventually, the Court issued decision n. 242 on September 26, 2019, holding that although the originally contested provision of the criminal code on assisted suicide is still valid, there are some limited cases in which it cannot be applied without breaching the Constitution. The Court pointed out that medical advancements today enable people, like the plaintiff in the underlying case, to survive severely damaging illnesses and events, leaving them dependent upon medical technologies for basic survival, in severe pain, but with their intellects intact. It recalled the existing right of these persons to demand cessation of such treatments to allow death to take its course (a request binding upon third parties), and the right to be heavily sedated during the time between cessation of treatment and death. The Court then held that under these circumstances the law cannot punish those who help mentally competent persons making a free and informed decision to commit suicide, but unable to carry out the act themselves due to their medical state.[22] Not surprisingly, this controversial decision has been both celebrated by some and sharply criticized by others, both because of the outcome mandated by the Court and because the Court ultimately assumed an affirmative legislative role in the matter. Whatever one's overall evaluation of the substance of the judgment, however, it does represent a paradigmatic example of the Constitutional Court's give-and-take engagement with the legislative branch.

Cooperative relations with other national judicial bodies have been equally crucial for the Italian Constitutional Court. On the one hand, the Court firmly discarded the old assumption of the Court of Cassation of 1948 on the programmatic nature of the Constitution that would have deprived the Constitution of any normative force and the Constitutional

---

[21] M. TROPER, *Pour une théorie juridique de l'État*, Paris, Presses Universitaires de France, 1994.

[22] The relational approach of the Italian Constitutional Court in the assisted suicide case recalls closely that of Judge's Calabresi concurrent opinion in *Quill v. Vacco*, 80 F3rd 716, 738 (2nd Cir. 1996). The facts of the two cases are very similar and Calabresi, considering that the New York statute under attack regulating assisted suicide was very old and that on the issue public opinion was particularly sensitive, suggested a "constitutional remand" in order to offer an occasion of dialogue to the legislative branch.

Court's activity of any teeth. On the other hand, the Constitutional Court has not been jealous of its mission as the "guardian of the Constitution" and has encouraged the ordinary judiciary to participate in the implementation of the Constitution. After all, in Italy the main avenue to bring cases before the Court is the incidental referral procedure, where the ordinary courts are gatekeepers of the Constitutional Court, deciding which cases will be referred to the Constitutional Court for judgment and which ones will not. This implies strict cooperation among the courts. It is worth recalling that the participation of ordinary judges in the implementation of the Constitution was spelled out in the 1965 "Gardone National Congress" of the judiciary, and soon became a milestone in the evolution of the judicial function in Italy.[23] In fostering this cooperative relationship, the Constitutional Court has over time shown a great deal of trust in the ordinary judiciary, for example by preserving the latter's competence as the primary interpreter of legislation, and by favouring the ordinary judiciary's use of creative methods of interpretation "in conformity with the constitution" (*conforme a costituzione*) in order to avoid having to refer matters to the Constitutional Court. Most decisions of the Constitutional Court, in fact, presuppose a healthy cooperation with the ordinary judiciary, both with lower courts and with the highest courts (the *Corte di Cassazione* and the *Consiglio di Stato*). Without this interjudicial relationality, the pronouncements of the Constitutional Court would remain ineffective.

As to the relations with the European Courts – the Court of Justice of the European Union and the European Court of Human Rights – and with foreign constitutional courts, the Italian Constitutional Court has dramatically changed its attitude over time. Indifference and formal segregation of jurisdictional authority were the Cartesian coordinates that described the starting position of the Court vis-à-vis its supranational and foreign counterparts. Then, a period of informal and silent reciprocal influence followed, during which the Italian Constitutional Court avoided all formal reference to the jurisprudence of the two European Courts but showed itself implicitly to be well aware of the case law developed in Luxembourg and in Strasbourg.[24] The Constitutional Court currently gives a similarly implicit and silent but influential consideration to foreign law and to comparative sources: whereas in recent years the Italian Constitutional Court has only occasionally referred openly to the case law of other constitutional

---

[23] A. Meniconi, *Storia della magistratura italiana*, Bologna, Il Mulino, 2012, 312 ff.

[24] See V. Barsotti, P. Carozza, M. Cartabia, A. Simoncini, *Italian Constitutional Justice in Global Context*, op. cit., 205-230.

tribunals, the influence of the latter is much deeper than is apparent on the surface.[25] In sum, Italian constitutional justice incrementally entered into an active relationship with European, international, and comparative law, and especially with the judge-made law of the two European supranational courts, in particular in human rights cases. While in some areas the impact of these external sources has induced the Constitutional Court to revise its previous jurisprudence and to develop new principles and standards, in some other cases the Court intentionally takes a position distinct from European or foreign courts, especially when the core values of Italian constitutional identity are at stake. In short, the Court engages now in open and direct relations with external judicial bodies, but those relations are not oriented to an unreasoned importation of judicial solutions from outside; it is rather a two-way relation among peers, a dialogue that triggers constructive convergence but also leaves room for difference and distinctiveness.

If the assisted suicide case is a good recent example of a relational attitude of the Constitutional Court vis-à-vis the national legislative body, the well-known *Taricco* saga may show the virtues of a dialogic relation between the Court and a supranational body and may also show the constructive effects of a conversational posture. Given the importance of the case, it is worth summarizing the sequence of events.

With the judgment handed down in the *Taricco* case on September 8, 2015, the Court of Justice of the European Union (CJEU) established that in criminal proceedings for infringements relating to the value added tax (VAT), national courts should not apply existing national statutes of limitation in two cases: (a) if they lead to impunity in a significant number of cases of serious VAT fraud; and (b) if, in the national legal system, analogous crimes of fraud committed against the Member State concerned are subject to longer statutes of limitation. The CJEU did not consider the "Taricco rule" – as formulated in these terms – to conflict with the principle of legality in criminal matters, because it considered statutes of limitation to be procedural matters. In the Italian legal system, however, according to the broad formulation of Article 25(2) of the Constitution ("[n]o one may be punished except on the basis of a law in

[25] See V. Barsotti, P. Carozza, M. Cartabia, A. Simoncini, *Italian Constitutional Justice in Global Context*, op. cit., 78-82. A judgment making extensive reference to foreign case law is n. 186 of 2017. Interesting notes from "inside" the Court on the issue, among many others, of the use of the comparative method can be found in S. Cassese, *Dentro la Corte: diario di un giudice costituzionale*, Bologna, Il Mulino, 2015. See also P. Passaglia, *Corte costituzionale e comparazione giuridica: una analisi (molto sineddotica), una conclusione (quasi sinestetica)*, in *I rapporti civilistici nell'interpretazione della Corte costituzionale nel decennio 2006-2016*, Naples, Esi, 2018.

force at the time the offence was committed"), this statute of limitation falls within the scope of substantive criminal law because it affects punishability. A statute of limitation thus conforms to the Constitution only if it complies with the rules of specificity and non-retroactivity according to the principle of legality in criminal matters, as the Constitutional Court has held on several occasions. For this reason, Italian scholars perceived the "Taricco rule" as failing to consider a supreme principle of the Italian constitutional order with regard to criminal matters, both because it applies to actions committed before it was pronounced and because of its absolute indeterminacy, which made it unpredictable for society at large and impossible for judges to apply. The doubts fostered by the legal debate were taken up by the ordinary courts, which turned them into subjects of questions of constitutionality that they referred to the Constitutional Court. The Constitutional Court in turn concluded that the "Taricco rule" contradicted the constitutional principle of legality in criminal matters. However, it refrained from expunging the rule from the legal system. The Court rejected the request to declare the law ratifying the Treaty on the Functioning of the European Union (TFEU) unconstitutional insofar as it required application of Article 325 TFEU – as interpreted by the CJEU – and consequently the setting aside of two provisions of the Criminal Code regarding statutes of limitation. In Order No. 24 of 2017, the Constitutional Court chose to refer a set of questions to the CJEU for a preliminary ruling. Without calling into question the CJEU's interpretation of Article 325 TFEU, the Constitutional Court simply underscored the substantive nature of statutes of limitation in the Italian legal system and the fact that, consequently, they fall within the scope of the principle of legality in criminal matters. That principle, which Article 49 of the Charter of Fundamental Rights of the European Union and the constitutional traditions common to several Member States recognize as fundamental and worthy of protection, would be violated by judicial application of the "Taricco rule" because of its retroactivity and lack of determinacy. In *M.A.S. and M.B.*, handed down on December 5, 2017, the CJEU acceded to the Italian Constitutional Court's view and acknowledged the substantive nature of statutes of limitation in the Italian legal system. Furthermore, the CJEU made it possible for national courts to not apply the "Taricco rule" where they deem it to conflict with the principle of legality in criminal matters enshrined in Article 49 of the Charter of Fundamental Rights of the European Union. The *M.A.S.* judgment does not significantly depart from the approach adopted in *Taricco*, but rather recasts it in light of the new information on the national legal system that the Italian Constitutional Court presented to the CJEU in its request for a preliminary ruling. The matter was finally closed when the Italian Constitutional Court handed down Judgment No. 115 of 2018, in which it identified the contradiction between, on one hand, Article 325 TFEU and the "Taricco rule", and, on the other, the Italian Constitution's supreme principle of legality in criminal matters, thereby conclusively rejecting the possibility that criminal courts could set aside the relevant rules on limitation. It must be emphasized that this conclusion was not based on national constitutional law alone, but also on the application of Union law as detailed by the CJEU. In other words, the dialogue between the Italian Constitutional Court and the CJEU made it possible to elaborate a rule shared by the two legal orders, with a view to assuring respect for human rights. After the Taricco cases both the Italian Constitutional Court and the CJEU were enriched by a positive legal experience that makes their relationship stronger and reinforces mutual trust.

Where does this *institutionally relational* mindset of the Italian Constitutional Court originate? Nuno Garoupa and Tom Ginsburg have recently argued that there is a positive correlation between the composition of a constitutional court and its inclination to take a conflictual or cooperative stance with other institutional bodies.[26] Although the final outcome of the research is debatable at least in relation to the Italian case, we agree with the thesis and share the view that the overall external attitude of the Constitutional Court as such is very much dependent on its internal structure.

In the Italian Constitutional Court, the Justices tend to have diverse perspectives because of their different appointment sources – some selected by highest courts of the ordinary judiciary, others by Parliament, and still others by the President of the Republic – and because of their different backgrounds, with career judges working alongside university professors and practicing lawyers. They are all united broadly by a common legal education, but differ completely in their professional trajectories and in their personal cultural formation.[27] This pluralism has always been a great asset for the Court, and it has to a degree compensated for the otherwise deficient diversity of the Court along certain other sociological lines such as age, geography, or – most pointedly – gender.

Notwithstanding these differences, the Justices are nevertheless prompt-

---

[26] T. GINSBURG, N. GAROUPA, *Building Reputation in Constitutional Courts: Political and Judicial Audiences*, in 28 *Arizona Journal of International and Comparative Law*, No. 3, 539 (2011), 539-568.

[27] See V. BARSOTTI, P. CAROZZA, M. CARTABIA, A. SIMONCINI, *Italian Constitutional Justice in Global Context*, op. cit., 43-46.

ed to dialogue and agreement because of the *principle of strict collegiality* that governs the work of the Court. The internal organization and working procedures of the Court are designed to spur the justices to work intensely in common with one another; they are obliged to dialogue with one another. They sit in deliberation chambers for hours and hours and have oral debates over every single word written in every decision of the Court. This fosters reciprocal cross-fertilization among the members of the Court and their respective ideas, political and social backgrounds, cultures, and mentalities, and serves as the principal growth factor in the Court's internal capacity for building interpersonal relations. The absence of separate opinions and the requirement that texts be discussed together in chambers and approved collectively, for instance, fosters a consensual approach and encourages the Justices to incorporate broadly the particular views of their various individual colleagues into the final text.[28]

That inclusive approach that the individual justices are impelled to take internally to the Court, thanks to the principle of collegiality which pervades all the Court's activities, also shapes the *external* posture of the Court as an institution. The Constitutional Court has developed a self-understanding that it is a part of a broader system, and that its mission in the democratic polity is not to take on the entire responsibility of constitutional governance, but instead to cooperate with other actors, according to the specific constitutional role of each one.

In short, a first examination of the Italian Constitutional Court reveals its relational approach in many different dimensions: internal and external; judicial and political; institutional and interpretative; national and transnational.

1.2. Relationality revisited

The first volume – *Italian Constitutional Justice in Global Context* – and its core idea of relationality were presented and discussed in universities such as Notre Dame, Bocconi in Milan, Harvard, the Central European University in Budapest, Berlin, Bologna, and King's College in London. As always happens, we learned much from the debates, which helped us to think afresh about the relational nature of the Italian Constitutional Court. These first discussions made it clear that the idea of relationality as a framework to understand the effective role of a Constitutional Court is

---

[28] See V. BARSOTTI, P. CAROZZA, M. CARTABIA, A. SIMONCINI, *Italian Constitutional Justice in Global Context*, op. cit., 46-49.

promising, helping to capture the overall stance of the institution and to distinguish its position from comparable bodies. Yet, the debates with academics of these different milieus have also emphasized that the idea of relationality requires further clarification and nuance.

1.2.1. Relationality vs. weakness: perception and reality

This relational approach of the Italian Constitutional Court is easily misinterpreted, as it can be perceived as a sign of weakness. In fact, the Italian Court has been often compared to its German sister and a common remark is that the Italian "twin" came to be overshadowed by the *Bundesverfassungsgericht* because it did not speak with the same "assertive" voice.[29] Moreover, the "war" that occasionally broke out between the Italian Supreme Court of Cassation and the Constitutional Court[30] has been misrepresented as a sign of the constitutional tribunal's inferiority or subordination to the older, well established apex judge of the ordinary system. In the same vein, it has been said that "the main source for the difficult relationship between the Italian Constitutional Court and regular courts is the process of submitting legal questions".[31] Similarly, the fact that the Court neither is polarized nor publishes dissenting opinions is considered a sign of its insecurity.[32]

In our view, accounts like this do not reflect the real experience of the Italian Constitutional Court. The fact that there is neither a stable, predictable majority, nor a strong polarization between a majority and a minority in the Court does not imply that it has a weak or undecided stance in the constitutional system. On the contrary, the fact that the majority

---

[29] T.G. DALY, *The Alchemists*, Cambridge, Cambridge University Press, 2017, 68 ff., 81 ff.

[30] J. FEREJOHN, P. PASQUINO, *Constitutional adjudication, Italian Style,* in T. GINSBURG (eds.), *Comparative Constitutional Design*, Cambridge, Cambridge University Press, 2012, 294. To be true, they are not representative of the ordinary relations between the Constitutional Court and the Supreme Court of Cassation in Italy.

[31] Id. 561-562.

[32] T. GINSBURG (eds.), *Comparative Constitutional Design*, op. cit., 543: "Constitutional Courts that are weak vis-à-vis their supreme courts, such as those in France and Italy, take a long time to become polarized; even now France and Italy preserve the façade of unanimous decisions and do not publish dissents". On the story and practice of separate opinions in Europe, see respectively A. DI MARTINO, *Le opinion dissenzienti dei giudici costituzionali. Uno studio comparativo*, Naples, Jovene Editore, 2016 and K. KELEMEN, *Judicial Dissent in European Constitutional Courts*, Abingdon, Routledge, 2018.

that governs the court is variable and unpredictable is a strong feature of the composition of the Court. It encourages consensual decisions and deliberative processes based more on the logic of persuasion than on the law of numbers, and that privileges seeking consensus rather than simply casting votes.

Similarly, occasional divergences with other courts – both national and European – do not indicate that the Italian Court entertains a conflictual or confrontational relation with other judges. In its recent case law the Italian Constitutional Court has engaged in a number of dialogues with the Court of Justice of the European Union,[33] has accepted with some distinctions the jurisprudence of the European Court of Human Rights,[34] and has entertained a relation of mutual respect with the Supreme Court of Cassation, even in a delicate phase in which the Constitutional Court has slightly adjusted its jurisprudence related to the implementation of European law.[35] Like any relationship, even the judicial relationships of the Constitutional Court require understanding, comprehension, mutual respect, and the resolution of conflicts.[36]

Even less true is the statement that the Constitutional Court's incidental procedure undermines its authority vis-à-vis ordinary judges. In fact, as Elisabetta Lamarque demonstrates in her contribution to this volume, it facilitates a cooperative and constructive relationship among the different branches of the judiciary and is less imposing than other forms of direct complaint where the constitutional court plays the role of a judge of final appeal over the decisions of all other judicial bodies.

As Armin von Bogdandy and Davide Paris show in the final essay of this book, there is a paradoxical strength of the Italian Court that becomes evident under the guise of an accommodating attitude. However, in order for the reader to go beyond appearances and to be persuaded that relationality is not equal to weakness, it is necessary to delve deeper into the jurisprudence of the Constitutional Court.

---

[33] The apex of this dialogue is the famous Taricco case, Judgment n. 24 of 2017 described supra at 18 ff.

[34] For example Judgment n. 49 of 2015.

[35] See Judgment n. 117 of 2019 that summarizes an evolution started with Judgment n. 269 of 2017 and continued with Judgments n. 20 and 63 of 2019.

[36] On the conditions for a veritable judicial dialogue see G. LATTANZI, M. CARTABIA, *Dialogue Between Courts and the Taricco Case,* https://www.cortecostituzionale.it/documenti/news/CC_NW_20190404.PDF.

1.2.2. Relationality "unpacked"

Relationality is a very complex, nuanced notion, and can be useful only if it is "unpacked" in different chapters. An institution can be well disposed to open relations in some areas of its activity even while it maintains a defensive position in other ones. In order to appreciate the experience of the Italian Constitutional Court from the perspective of its relational approach, it is therefore necessary to consider separately and independently different aspects of the system.

For instance, although we have shown that the Italian Constitutional Court is deeply relational if we take into consideration its posture toward other national and European courts or the national Parliament, we reach a different conclusion if we examine its posture with respect to public opinion and the social sector more generally. So far, the Court has done little to encourage a more open and transparent participation of civil society. Traditionally, the circle of subjects allowed to officially intervene in the constitutional process was strictly limited to the parties that were able to trigger the process to the exclusion of all others. Nevertheless, on January 11, 2020 a press release was posted on the web page of the Constitutional Court, titled "The Court Opens to Hearing the Voice of Civil Society", announcing that the Court amended its Rules introducing, among other things, the great novelty of *amicus curiae* briefs in the Italian system of constitutional procedure.[37]

More generally, ordinary citizens largely ignore the Constitutional Court and its justices. Among the constitutional institutions of the Italian Republic, it is the one surrounded by an air of mystery: remote, obscure, and inaccessible. In media surveys, the Constitutional Court is often confused with the Supreme Court of Cassation. The function of judicial review of legislation, the core mission of the Court, is inscrutable for most people except jurists and academics specialized in the field of constitutional law. Public opinion perceives the Constitutional Court as a distant institution that speaks an arcane language. The public generally is unfamiliar with the names, faces, and backgrounds of the Justices who compose it. Despite a good start, when the Court took the relation with public opinion very seriously in its early years, over time it has lost contact with the public. It is only in very recent times, when the Court decided to celebrate its 60th anniversary with a conference dedicated to "the decisions that have changed the life of Italians",[38] that things have begun to take a different course. Since then the Court has devoted a lot of energy to being more proactive in

---

[37] T. Groppi, A.M. Lecis Cocco Ortu in this volume, especially the post scriptum.

[38] https://www.cortecostituzionale.it/jsp/consulta/documentazione/convegni_seminari.do.

reaching out transparently to civil society, scholars, and professionals through a number of concurrent channels.[39]

For example, in the past the Court's press releases used to be a sort of preview of the final words of its decisions, written in the same technical language as the legal documents. In recent years, however, the Court has strengthened its press office with professional journalists and now provides the public with a new style of press release on the website and announces the most important decisions with a note that explains the Court's position and its effects in a language capable of being communicated directly through the media. Moreover, in most cases a summary of the reasoning of the Court (in both Italian and English) accompanies the publication of the decision. In addition, the Court continues its traditional habit of holding an annual press conference, but again the style of communication has been modernized in order to reach a broader audience, not only academics and institutional actors and lawyers.

However, the most important initiatives have been the "journeys of the Court".[40] Well aware of the distance that separates the Court from the lives of the people, the Court decided to open the doors of the beautiful building of the Consulta palace in which it is located, not only to let people in but also to have the Justices reach out to all the regions of Italy. Since 2018, the Court has set up a program with the Minister of Education to visit schools in every corner of the Italian territory, especially those in more remote areas, to speak to the students about the values of the Constitution and the role of the Constitutional Court in the protection and implementation of the Constitution. Encouraged by the success of this first venture, the Court decided to sail off into more troubled waters, and began a second journey in a number of prisons. The success of this unprecedented adventure cannot be spelled out only in words; it requires participation. That is why the Court has recorded footage of these encounters between justices, detainees, police officers, and prison administrative staff that will be made into a documentary.[41] These journeys of the Court into different sectors of society are very helpful instruments

[39] For the first time, the Constitutional Court's communication strategy is becoming a topic of scholarly reflection: see for example D. CHINNI, *La comunicazione della Corte costituzionale: risvolti giuridici e legittimazione politica*, in *Diritto e Società*, No. 2, 255 (2018), 255-280.

[40] The first journey in the Italian schools is here below documented: https://www.cortecostituzionale.it/jsp/consulta/viaggioItalia/viaggio_home.do; the second journey in prisons can be followed here https://www.cortecostituzionale.it/jsp/consulta/vic/vic_home.do.

[41] https://www.raiplay.it/video/2019/06/Speciale-Tg1-c24535fb-96d4-428a-90bc-7174abe1163f.html.

for disseminating the values of the Constitution and the role of its custodian among the people.

These are only some examples that confirm the necessity of articulating the relational capacity of the Court to different audiences: the *institutional* relationality of the Court, which in turn can be sub-divided into *judicial* and *political* relationality; the *social* relationality of the Court is another thing. Definitely, relationality as a benchmark for a realistic and effective understanding of the role of the Constitutional Court needs to be disaggregated and unpacked.

1.2.3. Official vs. Unofficial relationality

In the same vein, the relational behavior of the Court can be more fully grasped if the observer takes into account not only its explicit words and activities, but also the implicit signs that appear on the surface and whose meaning needs to be more deeply investigated, decoded, and uncovered. In fact, the relations of the Court can be *official* – such as those taking place institutionally between the Constitutional Court and the ordinary judiciary – and *unofficial*. The latter exists when contacts are through informal and less visible channels.

For example, dialogue between the Italian Constitutional Court and legal scholars seems at first glance to be completely absent in the Italian system. The Court refrains from explicitly quoting any piece of scholarship in its decisions. Nevertheless, it is no mystery that the Court maintains close relations with academics: first, a significant number of justices are university professors (today, 10 out of 15); second, in the files of the Court one can find significant references to scholarly sources; third, when the Court wants to reform some aspects of its practice it often organizes seminars and debates with scholars and experts in the field. These and other forms of relations are dealt with in Paolo Passaglia's chapter where he illustrates these and many other informal avenues through which scholarship filters into the Court's work and opinions. Perhaps, in this case, an informal way of communication is more efficient than a formal one because it allows Justices to take into account scholars' thoughts without showing explicitly their preferences and because it allows Justices not to reveal the theoretical sources of their ideas, thereby avoiding academic jealousies.

Parallel observations can be made regarding the use of comparative law by the Italian Constitutional Court. It is only in the most recent developments of the case law of the Court that some particular references to the jurisprudence of other sister courts have been made explicitly, as happened in Order 207 of 2018 on assisted suicide and in decision n. 141 of 2019 on prostitution.[42] However, the practice of taking into account other constitutional experiences in a comparative perspective dates back to some decades ago. For example, Sabino Cassese[43] has testified that at the time of the first decision on abortion, n. 27 of 1975, the Court was aware of other court decisions including that of the US Supreme Court in *Roe v. Wade*, thanks to the contribution of the Research Office of the Court, the staff of which includes comparative law experts.

In some cases, however, informal relations can have also some costs. If we think about how "closed" the Italian constitutional procedure used to be until the Rule's reform of January 2020, the Court's position presented some problems. The traditionally closed and formal character of the Italian constitutional process seemed to be inconsistent with the richness of the reasoning of the Court. For example, the Court was not inclined to make use of its official investigative powers. Nevertheless, its decisions were generally well documented even in terms of technical knowledge outside of the law (see decision n. 5 of 2018 on vaccinations, for example). Some informal channels of information were probably used by the Research Office, other members of the staff, clerks, and the Justices themselves to develop the necessary fact-finding activity, especially in economic, financial, medical, scientific, and statistical matters. This implies that there was some discrepancy between the Court's closed attitude to official relationality in the *procedural* sphere even when in fact there was some unofficial reliance on other sources in its rich and comprehensive *investigative* activity. Such discrepancy will eventually disappear with the adoption of the 2020 reform.[44]

A slightly different example that recalls the idea of unofficial relationality is the way through which the Court "compensates" for the lack of a direct complaint mechanism.[45] The Court compensates for not having an *official* way for litigants to gain direct access to it by amplifying its ordinary jurisdiction.[46] In any case, there still are some "blind spots" and "dark sides" which remain out of reach, both official and unofficial, of the Italian Court, as Ferreres Comella shows.

For all these reasons we felt the need to test the idea of relationality as the hallmark of the Italian Constitutional Court's attitude toward its powers of constitutional judicial review, and to submit it for a broader discus-

---

[42] See *supra* text and notes 18-21.

[43] S. CASSESE, *Dentro la Corte: diario di un giudice costituzionale*, op. cit.

[44] See T. GROPPI, A.M. LECIS COCCO ORTU in this volume especially the post scriptum.

[45] See the conversation between Lamarque and Ferreres Comella in this volume.

[46] See, for example, Judgment n. 1 of 2014 and Judgment n. 18 of 2019.

sion among a number of Italian and foreign colleagues capable of seeing it in a comparative perspective.

1.3. Dialogue as a method

In the end, the relational approach reflects simultaneously both the substance and the method of the project. This book offers an interpretative key to the Italian experience of constitutional adjudication focused on its dialogical approach; yet, the book itself is the result of an approach based on *dialogue as a method.*

Like the first book, this "sequel" also represents a conscious effort by all four of the coauthors to work in a systematically collaborative way. All the coauthors contributed substantially to the whole enterprise. In this, we have sought to emulate some of the most successful examples of comparative legal scholarship, which so often depend on collaborative efforts to be able to bridge the gaps of understanding across legal traditions. Comparative research is necessarily a cooperative effort. Our labours have brought together two comparatists and two constitutionalists, three Italians and one American, two women and two men, a constitutional judge and three professors – in short, a microcosm of constitutional dialogue to contribute to the macro-dynamics of global constitutionalism.

However, we decided to extend the conversation to other scholars – from Italy, elsewhere in Europe, and the United States, with three main purposes in mind:

a) to elaborate more on the core idea of the book, i.e. relationality as a distinguishing feature of the Italian constitutional court;
b) to fill some gaps left open in the first book, which have been the subject of important Italian scholarly debate on constitutional adjudication; and
c) to put the hypothesis of "relationality" to the test in areas we didn't explore or we didn't explore sufficiently in the first book, including in comparison with the experiences of other constitutional courts.

We decided to adopt the same methodology that we used for the first volume, but also including more actors, who are the contributors to this book. We convened a workshop focusing on six topics that needed a deeper analysis of the idea of relationality and amplifying our method. For each of the six topics we had two main goals: (a) to assess the presence and effectiveness of a relational approach in the work of the Italian Constitutional Court; and (b) to compare the Italian situation with other constitutional systems. To this end, for each topic an Italian scholar first prepared a paper focused on the Italian debate, but with an eye toward engaging in a comparative exchange. A scholar from outside of Italy then assumed the task of responding to the Italian colleague and amplifying the comparative perspective through their dialogue. In the end, we therefore hope to have achieved the result of analyzing *relationality* through a *relational* method: a real experiment in co-operative comparative constitutional law.

The workshop was held in Rome on July 12-13, 2018, thanks to the generosity of the University of Notre Dame. During the seminar the non-Italian scholars presented the Italian papers, each topic was deeply examined collectively, and for each one the discussion was dense and vibrant. The results of the debate were fruitful and somewhat unexpected showing the soundness of the method. All of us learned from one another: some of the ideas we had about the relational nature of the Italian Constitutional Court have evolved as a result of the workshop, and the present volume can be considered a step forward vis-a-vis *Italian Constitutional Justice in Global Context.*

The results of this comparative exercise provided some evidence that the idea of relationality is potentially applicable to a broader spectrum of cases, well beyond the Italian experience, and might be useful as a benchmark to classify different constitutional systems and also as an indicator of new emerging trends in global constitutional justice. Relationality can be adopted as a touchstone in order to measure and classify the various systems of constitutional adjudication along a scale from more relational toward less relational systems. [47]

1.4. Relationality and constitutional pluralism

When our first book was published at the beginning of 2016, the globalization process appeared still to be ascendant. It was (and to some extent still is) a commonplace to recognize that the world was in a dynamic age of transnational constitutional dialogue and exchange, with a rich and growing network of interactions among constitutional norms and systems around the world. Comparative constitutional studies had exploded in scope and grown in sophistication, and tribunals around the world were increasingly acquiring the habit of drawing on the practical experience and jurisprudence of their counterparts in other countries. Both scholars and judges widely read, borrowed, and cited the jurisprudence of the high courts of other legal systems. In that atmosphere a main purpose of our work was to fill an important gap

[47] See V. BARSOTTI, *External Relationality. New Colors for the European Model of Constitutional Justice*, in *Annuario di diritto comparato e studi legislativi*, Part I, Naples, Edizioni Scientifiche Italiane, 2017.

in those global constitutional dialogues, adding the voice of the Italian Constitutional Court to the choir of the other courts. We began from the simple fact that constitutional adjudication in the twenty-first century had acquired an undeniably transnational dimension. The transnational character of constitutional justice had become a structural component of globalization itself. Whatever the reader's normative approach to globalization, it is an observable fact that the transnational dimension of our juridical and political environment in the early twenty-first century is undeniable.

Although these facts are in our view irreversible to some extent, the spirit of the time has quickly changed over the past few years. Today, walls replace bridges; exit overcomes voice; particularities overshadow commonalities; withdrawals are more frequent than new connections; divergences prevail over convergences. Nowadays, especially in Europe, society is shaken by opposing forces. The constant search for European cohesion clashes with the strong desire to protect constitutional identities. The ideal of an inclusive transnational community is often at odds with a rapidly evolving multiculturalism and the various social and political reactions to it. The tension between global and local is becoming dramatically more evident: "the very notion of the 'public' (and public space) has changed. We experience, as never before, being part of a local (at times non spatial) space, a national (still strong everywhere) space, and a transnational and global space". [48] Even at the national level, the overall tonality of political relations are frequently dominated by conflict, anger, resentment, fear, distrust. For the first time in Europe, some systems of constitutional justice appear to be at risk, in terms of their independence and autonomy. [49] Relationality in any form seems to be dimming if not eclipsed.

It has been said that in this context, judicial review is going through a new phase where a number of constitutional courts give voice to "identitarian" challenges and are questioning the legitimacy of a number of international and transnational norms. In a seminal article, Doreen Lustig and Joseph Weiler, [50] borrowing from Mauro Cappelletti's metaphor of the waves of judicial review around the world, [51] argue that we are witnessing a third wave in the development of judicial review. The first wave was marked by

---

[48] D. LUSTIG, J.H.H. WEILER, *Judicial Review in the Contemporary World – Retrospective and Perspective*, in 16 *I-CON*, No. 2, 315 (2018), 370.

[49] One for all: W. SADURSKI, *Poland's Constitutional Breakdown*, Oxford, Oxford University Press, 2019.

[50] D. LUSTIG, J.H.H. WEILER, *Judicial Review in the Contemporary World – Retrospective and Perspective*, op. cit., 318-319, 369-371.

[51] M. CAPPELLETTI, *Judicial review in the contemporary world*, Indianapolis-Kansas City-New York, Bobbs Merrill Co.,1971.

the postwar horizontal spread of judicial review within national legal orders.[52] The second one was characterized by the emergence of transnational orders of higher law (like the ECHR and EU in Europe) that could be used by national courts as a basis for judicial review. Moreover, transnational courts were set up with the power to review national acts and actions directly. The third wave is a reaction to the first two, to some extent a course correction and a backlash against them, and is marked by a visible turn to identity and more local forms of belonging as a consequence of the cosmopolitan impact of international law on constitutional law. In their account, this wave cannot be confused with the old nationalistic or sovereigntist approaches. National courts are becoming an instance of control of transnational and international governance on identitarian grounds, and they introduce an identitarian (vs. sovereigntist) element to constitutional discourse.

Against this background, constitutional courts are called to face unprecedented challenges. More specifically, adjudicatory authorities must find new ways to tame the complexities of the world and to mediate between conflicting values, if not to make "tragic choices",[53] in order to develop a common language for a plural society.

Within this scenario, channels of relationship between institutions, and between institutions and society, are gaining importance. Constitutional courts are often called to solve hard cases and to balance different values, bridging the national and the transnational. If the courts' decisions are not perceived by all the political actors as the "last word" but as part of an ongoing dialogue, then perhaps the decisions, even the hard ones, will be more easily accepted.

In this context, the relational nature of constitutional court activity is becoming an increasingly important resource that we can all benefit from in a number of ways.

First, from a methodological point of view, courts enjoy a number of qualities that make them naturally more receptive to the dynamics of transnational interactions. They resolve issues case by case; therefore, judicial lawmaking is interstitial and smoothly percolates between gaps. Judicial lawmaking is also incremental, proceeding on a trial-and-error basis from one case to the next, and therefore leaves room for changes and adjustments. Courts generally adhere to similar procedural rules, commonly respected: for instance, they hear the parties and give reasoned explanations

---

[52] T. Ginsburg, M Verteeg, *Why do Countries Adopt Constitutional Review*, in 30 *Journal of Law, Economics and Organization* 587 (2014).

[53] G. Calabresi, P. Bobbit, *Tragic Choices. The conflicts society confronts in the allocation of tragically scarce resources*, New York, Norton, 1978.

of their decisions. The relation between constitutional courts, when they communicate and borrow principles and practices, is more horizontal than hierarchical, and courts thus tend to form a sort of network and in fact participate in a number of judicial networks.[54] Courts can also recognize and establish general principles, standards, and doctrines – like proportionality, reasonableness, balancing – that are very broadly applicable and easily transferrable, but also flexible enough to be adjusted according to different contexts and thus adaptable to local realities. Judicial lawmaking can thereby link the local and the global dimensions of justice, the identitarian and the universal, by both appealing to common shared principles and giving plural and differentiated answers to varied situations and demands.

From the point of view of the substantive contents of constitutional adjudication, the globalization of courts' activities is also driven by an increasing number of problems brought to the bench that can no longer be contained merely within the limited horizons of the nation-state.[55] Some issues draw constitutional justice into a transnational space for what might be called "external" characteristics. That is, international or foreign law is implicated because the empirical reality of the problem before the courts necessarily crosses national borders: to name just a few examples, people's mobility and migration, financial flows and foreign investments, or transnational standards in the fields of environmental protection. Other disputes deal with questions that tend toward the global dimension because of their internal characteristics – norms and principles that intrinsically claim a certain universality that transcends borders. Here, human rights claims are paradigmatic. The role of courts as human rights adjudicators has evolved rapidly, along with the amplification of "rights talk"[56] generally, since the final decades of the twentieth century, and today the language of rights is often the primary mode for speaking about new challenging social and legal problems (e.g., non-discrimination issues, or questions arising out of the development of new technologies). This evolution greatly affects the role of judges, not only because it asks courts to become protagonists of social change but also because a rights culture inevitably fuels transnational judicial interactions. Human rights, by virtue of their appeal to a transcendent

---

[54] M. CLAES, M. DE VISSER, *Are You Networked Yet? On Dialogues on European Judicial Networks*, in 8 *Utrecht Law Review* 100 (2012).

[55] This is the thesis by S. BREYER, *The Court and the World: American Law and the New Global Realities*, New York, Vintage, 2016, showing the reasons why even the US Supreme Court, always tempted by the "American exceptionalism", cannot ignore the global context.

[56] M.A. GLENDON, *Rights Talk. The Impoverishment of Political Discourse*, New York, Free Press, 1991.

dignity of all persons, have a natural vocation to trespass beyond the border of any single country. Moreover, as subjective rights belong to individual persons, the rights claims move as their holders themselves move, bringing together the external and the internal factors impelling judicial globalization. It is no surprise, therefore, that human rights are one of the most fertile grounds for transnational judicial dialogue and exchange.

For these and other reasons, constitutional courts still maintain a certain advantage over parliaments in their capacity to adapt to the demands of keeping connections with their peers. In the volatile conditions of the present era "reactive" institutions, such as courts, appear better suited than "active" institutions such as parliaments (to use Mirjan Damaska's well-known distinction[57]) to giving prompt answers to complex problems and to mediating between global and local interests, between unity and diversity. Courts are in a good position to take up these challenges and work as a transmission belt between the local and global, the particular and the universal, the national and the supranational, since they are still deeply entrenched in the domestic legal system, but they also belong to the global space, establishing links with other national, international, and supranational legal orders and with their respective courts. It is worth emphasizing that this observation is not to advocate for a new form of judicial supremacy or juristocracy.[58] Indeed, a relational understanding of the role of constitutional courts necessarily recognizes that they are embedded in, and in some ways dependent on, a network of other actors and relationships in order to accomplish their goals. Their place is not to supplant the democratically accountable political institutions, but to work with them.

Some courts are more reluctant than others to adjust their traditional competences and methods to a wider and more complex legal order, and instead seem inclined to keep the use of transnational law to a minimum level in their own decisions, to decide cases on domestic grounds rather than on European ones, to avoid formal references to supranational law, and to resist engagement with other foreign or supranational courts.[59] Occasionally certain courts have even challenged directly the applicability of a decision of a European or an international court, opening a phase of silent conflict. In most cases, however, national courts (at least in Europe) proac-

[57] M. DAMASKA, *The Faces of Justice and State Authority*, New Haven, Yale University Press, 1986.

[58] R. HIRSCHL, *Towards Juristocracy. The Origins and Consequences of the New Constitutionalism*, Cambridge, Ma., Harvard University Press, 2004.

[59] T. GROPPI, M.C. PONTHOREAU (eds.), *The Use of Foreign Precedents by Constitutional Judges*, Oxford, Hart Publishing, 2013.

tively cooperate with other judges and willingly take part in the global judicial conversation, although with different voices and even more diverse tonalities. In recent years, an increasing number of national constitutional courts have contributed to the development of common legal principles, taking an active role on the European and global stage through their interpretation and enforcement of common transnational standards.

However different the attitudes of the various courts may be, a realistic approach to constitutional adjudication today has to come to terms with a transnational dimension of the role of courts along with their domestic mission. In an age of nationalism and populism, constitutional courts are in a strategic position that allows them to preserve both national self-awareness and transnational connections. The relational capacity of constitutional courts in this context becomes all the more important as a vital instrument to preserve and develop the essential value of constitutional pluralism, which implies that the different components are in a way simultaneously linked and separate: apparently a contradiction, but in fact a sort of paradox of this era of ours, that is not so much to be resolved as it is to be lived through.[60]

[60] N. MACCORMICK, *Questioning Sovereignty: Law, State, and Nation in the European Commonwealth*, Oxford, Oxford University Press, 1999; M. KUMM, *Who is the Final Arbiter of Constitutionality in Europe? Three Conceptions of the Relationship Between the German Federal Constitutional Court and the European Court of Justice*, in 36 *Common Market Law Review*, Issue 2, 351 (1999), 351–386; M.P. MADURO, *Contrapunctual Law: Europe's Constitutional Pluralism in Action*, in N. WALKER (eds.), *Sovereignty in Transition*, Oxford, Hart Publishing, 2003, 502-537; N. WALKER, *The Idea of Constitutional Pluralism*, in 65 *Modern Law Review* 317 (2002), 317-359; A. VON BOGDANDY, *Pluralism, Direct Effect, and the Ultimate Say: on the Relationship Between International and Domestic Constitutional Law*, in 6 *I-CON* 397 (2008), 397-413.

Dialogue I

CONSTITUTIONAL COURTS AND LEGAL SCHOLARSHIP

Chapter II

JE T'AIME... MOI NON PLUS: SOME CONSIDERATIONS ON (AND IMPRESSIONS OF) THE RELATIONSHIPS BETWEEN CONSTITUTIONAL JUSTICE AND LEGAL SCHOLARSHIP

Paolo Passaglia

SUMMARY: 2.1. The difficulties encountered during research. – 2.2. The semi-direct sources. – 2.3. The indirect sources. – 2.4. Implied sources. – 2.5. Reasons (and prospects) for the absence of direct sources. – 2.6. An impression, not a conclusion.

2.1. The difficulties encountered during research

The relationship between constitutional case law and scholarship is always challenging to define, as the real impact of scholars' work on courts is often difficult to ascertain, even when considering those courts that make explicit citations and references. The challenge is obviously greater when dealing with courts that avoid references to scholarship. Italian courts, including the Constitutional Court, belong to the latter category, such that with regard to the Italian legal system, more than others, analyzing the relationships between constitutional case law and scholarship is rather risky. Far from enjoying the benefit of objective findings,[1] researchers are primarily required to select guidelines and indicators, on the basis of which they may then develop an examination that strives to be *as defensible as possible* from a scientific point of view. From the very outset, therefore, this research topic appears to be as stimulating as it is complex and, especially, fraught with the risk of ending without reaching significant results.

---

[1] The very notion of "scholarship" is far from clear, as it can be defined in several different (and diverging) ways. For the purposes of this article, it will be limited to legal scholarship of academic provenance exclusively. For a justification of such a restrictive approach, see P. PASSAGLIA, *La presenza della dottrina all'interno della Corte costituzionale italiana*, in P. PASSAGLIA (eds.), *I rapporti tra la giurisdizione costituzionale e la dottrina / Les rapports entre la juridiction constitutionnelle et la doctrine, Atti delle Giornate italo-franco-belghe di diritto comparato – Pisa, 6 e 7 marzo 2015*, Naples, Editoriale Scientifica, 2015, 29 ff.

In light of this need for caution, this article does not aspire to outline a complete picture of the subject. Rather the scope will be a much more modest, indicative contextualization of the impact that scholarship *presumably* has on the activity of the Constitutional Court.

Even with such a delimitation, the purpose of scholarship remains difficult to ascertain precisely because of the absence of sources of a *direct* nature. As may be known, the Constitutional Court generally does not make express references to scholarship in its judgments.

The foundations of this research are therefore far more elusive. In any case, they may be classified into three "subsidiary" categories: *semi-direct, indirect,* and *implied.* These categories will be described briefly by reference to the findings on the Italian system of comparative research based on papers presented at the *XXXe Table Ronde Internationale sur la Justice Constitutionnelle.* The topic of this conference was "Constitutional Judges and Scholarship", and it was held in Aix-en-Provence on 5-6 September 2014.[2] This basic research was then developed through a more in-depth trilateral comparative effort, the main event of which consisted of the *Giornate italo-franco-belghe di diritto comparato.* Held in Pisa on 6-7 March 2015, the *Giornate* focused on "The relations between constitutional adjudication and legal scholarship".[3]

2.2. The semi-direct sources

The most significant sources available could be called *semi-direct*, in that they provide concrete suggestions – which remain, however, merely *suggestions* – on the Court's use of scholarship to decide a case.

These sources are heterogeneous in nature and enjoy highly variable degrees of reliability. There are three main semi-direct sources: the case files prepared by the judges' assistants, which contain the legal and case-law sources and other material deemed potentially useful in deciding the case; the reports of the constitutional judges' discussions in chambers; and the draft judgments prepared by the judge rapporteurs to be submitted to the entire body of constitutional judges, for their collegial consideration and approval.

---

[2] The proceedings of the Round Table were later published in the *Annuaire international de Justice constitutionnelle*, vol. XXX, 2014, 199 ff.

[3] The proceedings of these *Giornate*, organized within the 2010-2011 PRIN on "Courts, scholarship and inclusive society: the impact of the scholarly legal element on superior courts", were published in P. PASSAGLIA (eds.), *I rapporti tra la giurisdizione costituzionale e la dottrina / Les rapports entre la juridiction constitutionnelle et la doctrine, Atti delle Giornate italo-franco-belghe di diritto comparato – Pisa, 6 e 7 marzo 2015, op. cit.*

This first category of sources is particularly interesting, at least in theory, as scholarly contributions are often included in the case files. Unfortunately, its impact is significantly attenuated by the fact that the case files are not made public. Indeed, the research conducted by the assistants is not published on the Constitutional Court's website; only some of the comparative law research occasionally prepared for particular cases is made available. However, there is no indication of the case for which the comparative research was requested, such that it is only possible to draw a link after actually examining the contents of the research.

In other words, the impossibility to analyse *how* scholarship is included in the case files and to identify the *choices* made in this respect diminishes the significance of semi-direct sources. One may only derive an appreciation of *whether* scholarship plays a part in constitutional adjudication from statements concerning how case files are made. It is harder, if not impossible, to discern the entity of the practice of using scholars' contributions.

The experience of the Italian Constitutional Court does not provide significant examples of the second and third category of semi-direct sources. On one hand, the Court does not record any account of the discussions held in chambers, such that any references that judges may make to scholars or papers are merely oral.[4] On the other hand, the draft judgments generally do not contain (or rather, are said to not contain) references to scholarship, and are therefore irrelevant for present purposes. As discussed by Professor Tega, Italian constitutional judges may not author concurring or dissenting opinions. In other legal systems, this additional avenue for scholarly references is particularly precious, because the judge contesting the majority decision (or the reasoning supporting it) will often support his or her positions with references to authoritative texts.

[4] In other legal systems, such records play a very important role in reconstructing the impact of scholarship. Consider, for example, the case of France, after the reform introduced by Organic Law no. 2008-695, of 15 July 2008, of *ordonnance* no. 58-1067 enabled access to the *Conseil constitutionnel*'s internal documents, including the minutes of sessions, after twenty-five years. Therefore, it is now possible to have a detailed account of the debates, from which it is possible to ascertain the use made of scholarship during the discussions, especially for major decisions. Certainly, the long period of time after which the minutes become publicly available prejudices any possibility for currency; for the purposes of historical examination, however, they are precious documents. The minutes of the sessions are freely available on the website of the *Conseil constitutionnel* (*https://www.conseil-constitutionnel.fr/comptes-rendus-des-seances*; as at 1 February 2020, the most recent minutes published are those relating to the session held on 20 December 1994). The research conducted on the minutes available has been compiled into B. MATHIEU, J.-P. MACHELON, F. MELIN-SOUCRAMANIEN, D. ROUSSEAU, X. PHILIPPE, *Les grandes délibérations du Conseil constitutionnel. 1958 – 1986*, 2nd ed., Paris, Dalloz, 2014.

Beyond the latter observation, semi-direct sources suggest that scholarship is a legal element that, although (presumably) present, is *unexpressed*, in a twofold sense: it is externally unexpressed because there is no documentary evidence to support it; and it is internally unexpressed because even in draft decisions, it remains within the pen of the judge rapporteur, and is therefore not made available – or at most, only orally communicated – to his or her colleagues.

2.3. The indirect sources

The category of *indirect* sources refers to the presence of academic jurists within the collegial body and the constitutional proceedings. This rests on the dual assumption that such a presence cannot fail to generally enhance the impact of scholarship on the decision-making process and that, with regard to the decisions to be made, it may have an important impact upon the scholarly references chosen.

Nevertheless, in this connection, it is necessary to clearly distinguish between *(a)* the academic world's "penetration" into the judicial panel, on one hand, and (*b*) its mere participation in constitutional proceedings, on the other.

(*a*) As for academic jurists within the judicial panel, a salient feature of the Italian Constitutional Court is the remarkable interpenetration it presents between scholarship and constitutional adjudication, a peculiarity that is particularly evident in comparison with the composition of other bodies of constitutional justice.

The composition of the Italian Court may be considered "doubly mixed", in that its judges are chosen by different bodies and may be chosen from among several categories.[5] The Court is composed of "fifteen judges, a third of nominated by the President of the Republic, a third by the Parliament in joint sitting and a third by the ordinary and administrative supreme Courts" (Article 135(1) of the Constitution). The judges of the Court "shall be chosen from among judges, including those retired, of the ordinary and administrative higher Courts, university professors of law and lawyers with at least twenty years practice" (Article 135(2) of the Constitution).

In the practical application of these provisions, university professors are clearly favoured. Professors make up the greatest proportion of judges in

---

[5] On the Court's composition, see V. BARSOTTI, P.G. CAROZZA, M. CARTABIA, A. SIMONCINI, *Italian Constitutional Justice in Global Context*, Oxford, Oxford University Press, 2016, 43 ff.

the Court's history, occupying approximately half of all appointments since 1956.[6]

In choosing the individual nominees, scholarly authority has certainly played a part – however, not as a decisive condition, but rather as a prerequisite to nomination. In other words, the tendency has been (and is) to designate renowned jurists for the Court, who are chosen from a considerably broad pool. In addition, in light of the dynamics underlying the selection process, political considerations also appear to come into play. Although appointees to the Court have rarely been professors who were "organic" to certain parties, it cannot be doubted that the political parties make specific nominations, especially in the case of the judges selected by Parliament. Harboring sympathies for the nominating party is a *de facto* prerequisite to access the *Consulta.*[7]

Despite this political "contamination", the fact remains that the solid presence of judge-professors has fostered a degree of osmosis between academia and the Constitutional Court. Further enhancing this osmosis, with regard to individual decisions, the President of the Court usually assigns the judge rapporteur for particular cases based on his or her specialization in the subject matter of the case. This clearly indicates that the judges' previous scientific research necessarily affects not only their selection as judge rapporteurs, but also on the structure of the inquiry and the decision (because its drafting is normally entrusted to the judge rapporteur him – or herself); however, this occurs with the observance of the collegial nature of the Court's activity and method of deliberation, which preclude excessive personalization.[8] As previously written, if the draft decision is to be approved, it must be read by all judges sitting in chambers together. Therefore, the position of the judge rapporteur authoring the draft is "naturally" subject to discussion, integrations and changes.[9]

---

[6] For an analysis of the data available up to mid-2015, see P. PASSAGLIA, *La presenza della dottrina all'interno della Corte costituzionale italiana*, *op. cit.*, 44 ff. It should be noted that the most recent appointments (since December 2015, of the 7 judges appointed, 5 were professors) have brought the number of judge-professors to 57 out of 114 (the total number of judges in the history of the Court).

[7] An exception to this rule is Professor Franco Modugno, who was elected in December 2015 by the Parliament in joint sitting upon a proposal by the Five Star Movement. The proposal was submitted after a voting session held among the members of the party itself, to choose from among a list of "candidate" figures compiled on the basis of competences, without consideration for their political orientation.

[8] On the importance of the principle of collegiality for the operation of the Italian Court, see V. BARSOTTI, P.G. CAROZZA, M. CARTABIA, A. SIMONCINI, *Italian Constitutional Justice in Global Context*, *op. cit.*, 46 ff.

[9] Actually, such a reading is required only for judgments, which are however the

(*b*) As for the other actors in constitutional proceedings, it is necessary to recognize the important role of judicial assistants. Since the 1980s, judicial assistants have been chosen not only from members of the judicial branch, but also from university professors.

In the last two to three decades, judicial assistants have served as a vital channel of communication between the Court and the university sector. Indeed, the position of judicial assistant is formally entrusted to "judges of the ordinary or administrative jurisdictions, associate professors, researchers and university teaching assistants" (Article 3(1) of the Court's Regulations on services and staff).

Moreover, this channel appears to be experiencing a reflow. Indeed, the tendency to select university staff – which was particularly strong in the 1990s – has gradually ebbed since the beginning of the present century, resulting in a (now overwhelming) majority of assistant-judges. [10]

The presence of academic jurists within the Court's staff does not compensate for the "drying up" of the judicial assistant channel: indeed, within the Court's offices and services, the penetration of scholarship is generally very limited. Scholarship is present mainly thanks to the stipulation of contracts for services, in particular within the Studies Department. Indeed, since 2004 and for a number of years, yearly contracts for services have been offered, which have enabled the Studies Department to benefit from a good number of (relatively young) jurists, some of whom were drawn from the ranks of the judiciary, but who were mostly from the university sector. In fact, these contracts would usually be renewed, even for several years, thus giving rise to some stability in the contracted services. However, in the last eight years, the trend has been to drastically curtail the number of external contract relationships. The aim was (and is) to enhance internal skills as much as possible, with the effect that the remaining contracts are for the performance of specialized activities and research (for example, those pertaining to comparative and international law).

While the Court's structure does not appear to be particularly open to scholarship, scholarship has filtered into the Court on the basis of a functional, and not an organic, means of participation.

Indeed, the Court's decision-making procedure is highly technical. Constitutional proceedings are not open to simply anyone, in that the right to speak with the judicial panel is reserved to lawyers. Pursuant to Article 20(1) of Law no. 87 of 11 March 1953, "in constitutional proceedings, the

---

most important decisions. Orders, which are usually much less elaborate decisions, are distributed to the judges for their individual reading.

[10] On this subject, see, for further details, P. PASSAGLIA, *La presenza della dottrina all'interno della Corte costituzionale italiana*, *op. cit.*, 53 ff.

representation and defence of the parties may only be entrusted to lawyers qualified to appear before the Court of Cassation". Therefore, only the most qualified lawyers may take part in the proceedings. The third paragraph of the same provision establishes specific regulations for the Executive. "[E]ven when it intervenes as the President of the Council of Ministers or as a Minister to which such a purpose has been delegated", they must be "represented and defended by the State Counsel or by a substitute thereof". That which for the central Government is an obligation is, however, merely subject to discretion, for Regions having ordinary status: according to Article 10 of Law no. 103 of 3 April 1979, these Regions may choose whether to avail themselves of the Office of the State Counsel or of other ordinary lawyers (provided that they meet the criteria enunciated in the aforementioned Article 20(1)).[11]

On the basis of the above considerations, it must be noted that, when private parties and (especially) Regions appear or intervene before the Constitutional Court, their legal representation is very often entrusted to lawyers who also hold an academic position.

Scholarship may thus enjoy some attention within constitutional proceedings. Upon this view, lawyer-professors may effectively contribute, by drawing attention to scholarship when the judicial panel forms its views. This may happen especially if the lawyer can directly expound his or her studies in support of the positions submitted, which therefore combine research and legal practice.[12] However, it cannot be denied that the role played by the parties before the Constitutional Court tends to be rather limited, especially in proceedings concerning the constitutionality of laws on an interlocutory basis (which make up more than half of the total number of judgments). In these instances, the case is structured around the questions raised by the referring judge, and the parties can only submit

---

[11] The only derogation to the principle of the necessity of technical defence before the Court is provided in Article 20(2) of Law no. 87 of 1953, according to which "the bodies of the State and of the Regions have the right to intervene in the proceedings". In constitutional case law, this provision has been interpreted as imposing "a rule concerning representation and defence in the context of legal proceedings, such that it is established that for such bodies, no professional defence is needed" (Judgment no. 350/1998, para. 2 of the Considerations on points of law).

[12] On the role of lawyers-professors, and generally on lawyers' contribution to the penetration of scholarship in constitutional proceedings, see B. BRANCATI, *L'influenza della dottrina sulla giurisprudenza costituzionale per il tramite degli avvocati-professori*, in P. PASSAGLIA (eds.), *I rapporti tra la giurisdizione costituzionale e la dottrina / Les rapports entre la juridiction constitutionnelle et la doctrine, Atti delle Giornate italo-franco-belghe di diritto comparato – Pisa, 6 e 7 marzo 2015, op. cit.*, 223 ff, especially the Appendix containing interviews with several scholars who have engaged in proceedings before the Court (241 ff.).

their point of view, at most suggesting further lines of argument (they cannot broaden the question posed to the Court). [13]

On the other hand, the absence of further avenues for communication, such as the amicus briefs that may be submitted to the Supreme Court of the United States, deprives scholarship of a further chance to take an active part in the decision-making process. [14]

2.4. Implied sources

The inconclusiveness of the findings achievable from indirect and semi-direct sources, coupled with the impossibility to glean information (or even mere trends) concerning individual aspects of constitutional case law, compel reference to additional sources, *implied* sources, that act on a more specific level; however, this does not make them easier to verify than the others. These further sources are the *implicit* references made in judgments to scholarship. In an abstract sense, if supported by empirical findings, these elements could significantly corroborate discussions on the relationships between scholarship and constitutional case law. However, for this last observation, the conditional tense must be used, because the quest for implicit references requires such a thorough knowledge of constitutional case law, such a detailed reading of the judgments, and such a mastery of academic production, that finding scholars capable of such a task appears somewhat arduous. At best, this may be possible for limited fragments of the legal system. Indeed, the examples that may be given are nothing more than that, *examples* – and as such are unsuitable to be considered as indicators of general trends.

The research conducted, including in recent years, has provided some remarkable findings. However, the objective can only be to sketch an outline that – beyond certain features evoking general trends and some details on individual fragments of the legal system – essentially resists thorough

[13] For context behind the Court's numerous judgments on its own competences, see V. Barsotti P.G. Carozza, M. Cartabia, A. Simoncini, *Italian Constitutional Justice in Global Context*, *op. cit.*, 49 ff.

[14] In this regard, some changes could soon occur, since the Constitutional Court, by means of a deliberation dated 8 January 2020, adopted a new Article 4-*ter* of the Supplementary Rules on Proceedings before the Constitutional Court, according to which all non-profit social groups and all institutional bodies representing collective or diffuse interestsrelevant to the questions discussed will be able to present brief written opinions, to provide the Court with information that may be useful in understanding and evaluating the case before it.

By the same deliberation, a new Article 14-*bis* was adopted according to which the Court can decide to hear ewnowned experts, when deemed necessary. These experts should not be, in principle, legal scholars, but rather experts in other fields of study.

empirical analysis.[15] For that matter, these examinations incontestably demonstrate that in Italy, as in other legal systems where judgments do not contain express references to scholarship,[16] scholarship is certainly a non-negligible component of the cultural background supporting all constitutional adjudication.[17] Thus, one may conclude that its significance is most likely directly proportional to the complexity of the decision at hand and to the number of possible outcomes.

Beyond these broad observations, a recent examination of implicit references has provided some further general indications.[18] Although conclusive results could not be obtained, a threefold classification for implicit reference was suggested.

The first category includes those implicit references to scholarship used in "judgments in which the interpretative process follows itineraries and reaches conclusions that have already been developed or opposed in scholarship and expressed within individual scientific hypotheses".[19] In this case, scholarship is seen as an interlocutor of the Court – one that assumes particular significance as this type of reference is usually found in judgments relating to issues that have been analysed and debated at length within scholarship, to the extent that it is possible to identify various positions, each of which enjoys adequate supporting arguments. The Court wades into the debate by expressing support for one position or another, or even by setting forth yet another hypothesis – which of course will prevail.

An example is judgment no. 274/2003, in which the Court implicitly re-

---

[15] On implicit references to scholarship, see A. CARDONE, *I riferimenti impliciti alla dottrina nelle decisioni della Corte costituzionale italiana: una proposta di metodo e alcuni esempi di merito*, in P. PASSAGLIA (eds.), *I rapporti tra la giurisdizione costituzionale e la dottrina / Les rapports entre la juridiction constitutionnelle et la doctrine, Atti delle Giornate italo-franco-belghe di diritto comparato – Pisa, 6 e 7 marzo 2015, op. cit.*, 313 ff.

[16] Such as Belgium or France, on which see, respectively, P. NIHOUL, *Les références implicites à la doctrine dans les décisions constitutionnelles: l'expérience belge*, in P. PASSAGLIA (eds.), *I rapporti tra la giurisdizione costituzionale e la dottrina / Les rapports entre la juridiction constitutionnelle et la doctrine, Atti delle Giornate italo-franco-belghe di diritto comparato – Pisa, 6 e 7 marzo 2015, op. cit.*, 277 ff., and C. SEVERINO, *L'influence de la doctrine sur la jurisprudence du Conseil constitutionnel*, *ibidem*, 289 ff.

[17] Cf. T. GROPPI, I. SPIGNO, *Constitutional Reasoning in the Italian Constitutional Court*, in *Rivista AIC*, No. 4, 1 (2014), 9: "We can assume that scholarship strongly contributes to the evolution of jurisprudence, although explicit quotations of authors are not permitted in judgments".

[18] Cf. A. CARDONE, *I riferimenti impliciti alla dottrina nelle decisioni della Corte costituzionale italiana: una proposta di metodo e alcuni esempi di merito*, *op. cit.*, 320 ff.

[19] *Ibid*, 320 (author's translation).

ferred to constitutional scholarship that supported the need to maintain a difference between the State and the Regions with regard to the grounds for invalidity of laws that could be contested in direct appeals before the Court. Despite the changes resulting from the constitutional reform of 2001, the Court confirmed that the State could challenge regional laws for unconstitutionality on any grounds, whereas Regions could challenge the legislative acts of the State only for alleged breaches of their attributions.

The second category of implicit references to scholarship includes "all those cases in which the positions expressed in scholarship are taken into consideration, not so much as proposed interpretations of the individual constitutional or legal provisions that the Court applies within the judgment [...], but rather as implicit theoretical premises that are common to several judgments, which are particularly significant because of the statements of principle that they make".[20] In other words, "scientific reflection is taken into consideration as a logically coherent and generally abstract formulation of a set of definitions and general principles that make it possible to describe, interpret and classify, with varying levels of generalization, various aspects of the law".[21]

Among the examples of this type of use, one could mention the distinction between "provisions" (*disposizioni*, corresponding to the normative text) and "norms" (*norme*, that is, the result of the interpretation of the text). This distinction was first established by constitutional scholars, then the Court began to make widespread use of it.

The third category comprises the implicit references to scholarship made in cases "in which the decisions of constitutional judges appear to be affected by an unexpressed choice (which could barely be defined as 'methodological') that, establishing the perspective from which the decision looks upon the subject matter of the judgment, precedes and guides the adhesion to theoretical premises and individual interpretative solutions that may have already emerged in scholarship, or the elaboration of theories and interpretative arguments that may be used for the purposes of making decisions". Therefore, scholarship is a vehicle "of a 'way of seeing things', of a 'mentality' [...] that are typically representative of the *modus procedendi* of a specific juridical school of thought [...] or capable of crossing the boundaries between scientific sectors".[22] That is, "of a pre-comprehension of the issue addressed that may be considered not only legitimate but also necessary, to clarify the inter-

[20] *Ibid*, 332 (author's translation).

[21] *Ibidem* (author's translation).

[22] *Ivi*, 349.

pretative context in which a specific statement can be considered true and a given truth can be considered as having been comprehended".[23]

A comparison between judgment no. 348 and judgment no. 349 of 2007 can help to explain the meaning of this third category. The two judgments dealt with the same issues and provided the same solution; however, there were some differences in the legal reasoning adduced in each. These differences could probably be explained precisely by the different legal backgrounds of the judges who wrote them: judgment no. 348 was drafted by a constitutionalist, and judgment no. 349 by an internationalist. The different backgrounds of the two judges resulted in the slight differences in terms of content between the two judgments and in the varying significance each accorded to different elements and aspects of the issues.

While this classification, although extremely interesting from a theoretical point of view, may hint at how scholarship is taken into account, the actual practice does not give rise to a rule capable of effectively describing the *impact* of scholarship on the Constitutional Court's activity. Rather, the studies conducted show that the relationship between constitutional adjudication and scholarship – especially with regard to implicit references – is entrusted to the individual persons within the institution, and to the dynamics arising between them and within the relationships with outside parties. For external observers, all of these elements mean that the "unsaid" remains largely inscrutable, and therefore impossible to analyse in any genuinely "scientific" way.

This is not the appropriate venue to focus on one aspect or another of the case law issued by the bodies under examination. Therefore, it is perhaps expedient to draw inspiration precisely from the need to resort to an element as elusive as implicit references: to explore the reasons behind (and the justification for) the absence of *direct* sources – that is, of express references to scholarship in constitutional case law.

2.5. Reasons (and prospects) for the absence of direct sources

The simplest explanation for the complete absence of express references to scholars and/or their work lies, where applicable, in the existence of an express prohibition on making such references. In this vein, Article 118(3) of the Provisions Implementing the Code of Civil Procedure is emblematic: "[i]n all cases, any reference to juridical authors must be omitted".

Against such a linear argument, it may be countered that it is not possible to assume that the above provision is binding on the Constitutional

[23] *Ivi*, 350.

Court. Article 22(1) of Law n. 87 of 11 March 1953, which establishes further sources for the regulation of constitutional proceedings, remands to the regulation of administrative proceedings (which in turn refer to the aforementioned Article 118; see Article 88(3) of the Code of Administrative Proceedings). However, Article 22(2) allows the Constitutional Court to integrate these provisions by means of self-regulation. Therefore, at least in light of the rather extensive use that the Court has made of this power, there is nothing to prevent replacing the prohibition with a provision establishing discretion in this regard.[24] Or even stating that this aspect of civil proceedings simply does not apply to constitutional adjudication.

Regardless of this (albeit non-secondary) aspect, for present purposes, the "devaluation" of the abovementioned Article 118 actually results from its being an effect, and not so much a cause, of the absence of references: specifically, from its being an effect of this refusal, the roots of which go far beyond the mere positivization occurring in the procedural code.

Indeed, the exclusion of references to scholarship could be traced to a certain conception of adjudication, rather than to an individual provision. Although such a conception may now be considered obsolete, it has undeniably become entrenched in continental European systems, especially those that have been most strongly influenced by the French prototype. In particular, this refers to the reconfiguration of the role of the judge within the boundaries of a function consisting in the mere repetition of legislative provisions: "les juges de la nation ne sont [...] que la bouche qui prononce les paroles de la loi; des êtres inanimés qui n'en peuvent modérer ni la force ni la rigueur".[25]

Such a framework implies a certain "automatism" in interpretation and application. This framework thus becomes associated with a depersonalization of the parties called upon to concretely apply, in individual cases, the precepts resulting from political authority, which is legitimated by the popular vote. This depersonalization has several effects, including a repression of the manifestations from which the "cultural background" of the person making the decision may emerge. If the decision is to be the outcome of the most linear syllogism possible, it must also be true that the conclusion must

---

[24] For criticism of this view, see M. NISTICÒ, *I rapporti tra la giurisdizione costituzionale e la dottrina giuridica in Italia. Il ruolo dei giudici-professori*, in P. PASSAGLIA (eds.), *I rapporti tra la giurisdizione costituzionale e la dottrina / Les rapports entre la juridiction constitutionnelle et la doctrine, Atti delle Giornate italo-franco-belghe di diritto comparato – Pisa, 6 e 7 marzo 2015*, *op. cit.*, 176.

[25] "The national judges are no more than the mouth that pronounces the words of the law, mere passive beings, incapable of moderating either its force of rigour": Ch.-L. DE SECONDAT MONTESQUIEU, *De l'Esprit des Lois,* 1748, Livre XI, Chapitre VI.

always be the same, regardless of the person called upon to render it. On the basis of this premise, to admit that the person is expressing his or her individual culture would imply, in itself, a risk of subjectivizing the decision. Indeed, it could be believed that the solution ultimately provided is the result of a syllogism, but of a non-necessary one, in that it was conditioned by the personal knowledge and inclinations of the judge, and therefore it was not predetermined in its development by a "mechanical" approach to interpretation triggered by specific, objective, foundational facts.

Such a conception of adjudicative activity sheds light on what is probably one of the features that most strongly distinguishes civil law systems (especially the ones that were influenced by the French model) from common law systems, in which the personalization of decisions is an unavoidable and indeed a consubstantial fact of adjudication. In these systems, there is nothing to prevent express references to the scholarship that may have contributed to forming the decider's view.

At the same time, it is no coincidence that, in the same legal systems that do not allow for express references to scholarship, individual judges may not express dissenting or concurring opinions. In this regard, the mechanical approach to interpretation noted above is both a cause and an effect of the fact that there can be only one decision. It is a cause in that the automatism in interpretation should lead all judges to identical conclusions, such that a decision articulated according to the contributions of the individual members of the deciding body would translate into an iteration of the same syllogism on behalf of all. However, in some ways, this mechanicity is also a consequence of the monolithic nature of the decision, which in itself accredits the idea that there can be only one solution to a specific case (the solution required by the pronouncement of the law).

Today, it is incontrovertible (and non-controversial) that this vision of the judicial role is no longer tenable. This is all the more true with regard to constitutional adjudication. Even if one does not wish to endorse the radical position of those who consider that "[w]e are under a Constitution, but the Constitution is what the judges say it is",[26] the statement is so obvious as to make any further argument superfluous.

Therefore, the question is whether in the current legal landscape, it still makes sense to invoke the alleged (and disavowed) mechanicity of jurisdictional activity as a foundation for a ban on including, in judgments, refer-

[26] This phrase is attributed to Charles Evans Hughes, the politician who was to become the Chief Justice of the United States. The statement was made during a speech before the Elmira Chamber of Commerce (New York) on 3 May 1907 (*Addresses and Papers of Charles Evans Hughes, Governor of New York, 1906–1908*, 1908, 139).

ences to the opinions and works that have contributed to forging the juridical culture of the deciders – both the sources leveraged to identify the solution and those that were deemed inappropriate and therefore discarded or opposed.

On this view, arguments supporting express references are not so hard to find. For example, it could be considered opportune to ensure that the reasoning and premises of decisions are clear and transparent, especially in light of what this may yield in terms of communication between the institution and public opinion (especially the legal community) and, ultimately, of the legitimacy of the institution itself.

However, these advantages are counterweighed by a number of hindrances. For example, references may be instrumentalized; the authoritativeness of a decision may be impaired because certain references were made and others omitted. On a purely concrete plane, even if references were to be allowed, there would surely be a risk of perceiving the *lack* of references as an indication of the incompleteness of the sources used by the deciding body. This would inevitably lead to an additional workload for the judges (with corresponding repercussions on the times required to deliver judgment), who would have to scan through a scholarly body of work that, especially in some cases, is extremely vast and difficult to select from. There is also a real danger that any selection is seen as arbitrary. The existence of a professional supporting structure (which may also be rather large, such as that surrounding the Italian Constitutional Court), composed principally of qualified jurists, may attenuate these practical inconveniences, although it could certainly not nullify them.

However interesting it may be, exploring the pros and cons of a system in which express references are allowed risks becoming a rather sterile exercise. Indeed, even if the (legislative or custom-based) ban on express citation is overcome, it cannot be said with certainty whether constitutional courts would *actually* proceed to make such references.

This statement seeks to convey nothing more than an impression, which does not appear to be wholly devoid of support. In this respect, an example is Spain. Although the country certainly falls within the civil law family of legal systems, it presents some non-negligible peculiarities regarding the forms through which adjudication takes place. Historically, in the Spanish legal system, there was no rule establishing that there could be only a single decision. Rather, pursuant to the 1489 Ordinance of Medina, the practice of the so-called *votos reservados* was introduced. The *votos reservados* were decisions expounding the judges' individual opinions; however, they were to remain "reserved" unless the decision was appealed. If so, the "votes" would no longer be reserved and would be communicated to the relevant judges and parties. A derogation to this system emerged in the 1930s. The

Tribunal de Garantías Constitucionales was established, the decisions of which could accommodate dissenting opinions. Taking up on this precedent, Article 164 of the 1978 Constitution provides that "The judgments of the Constitutional Court shall be published in the Official State Gazette (*Boletín Oficial del Estado*), with the dissenting opinions, if any".

The acknowledgment of the *votos particulares* (and of the *votos reservados*) clearly suggests that the depersonalization characterizing other civil law systems – especially those in which the French influence is more deeply entrenched, such as the Italian one – has been rejected. On this view, it is unsurprising that there is nothing to prevent the *Tribunal Constitucional* from making express references to scholarship. However, the most interesting aspect is that the court's actual practice shows an extremely sparing use of the power to cite, to the extent that in this regard, the Spanish constitutional judges may be equated with those of France and Belgium, systems in which – as in Italy – express references are absolutely prohibited.[27] This is probably enough to significantly rescale the impact of "anti-citation" laws or traditions on the approach adopted by constitutional courts towards scholarship. Therefore, if bans on citation are not decisive in explaining the absence of references – an absence that continues after such bans are revoked – the search must turn elsewhere.

2.6. An impression, not a conclusion

At this point, one may notice that the results of this research can hardly be said to be satisfactory, if only because they do not present a sufficient degree of 'scientificity'.

Essentially, it only appears possible to confirm a foregone outcome – the absence of *definite* findings on the impact of scholarship on constitutional adjudication – without being able to adduce elements with at least an acceptable degree of objective reliability, and that are capable of shedding light on the relationship between the academic world and constitutional judges.

The inconclusive nature of the findings emerged in full once it was confirmed that there was no evidence of the real reasons for opposing references to scholarship.

The substantive stalemate resulting from this research might justify the inclusion of some brief observations in a sort of "appendix", which – it must be emphasized – does not claim at all to obey the canons of empirical

[27] Cf. P. Passaglia, S. Ragone, *Un attore lontano dalle luci della ribalta: la dottrina nella giurisprudenza costituzionale di Belgio, Francia e Spagna*, in *Annuario di diritto comparato e di studi legislativi*, vol. VI, Naples, Edizioni Scientifiche Italiane, 2015, 63 ff.

verifiability applied to the initial findings and the operational stage. Thus, in closing this article, it is not a conclusion that will be proposed, but rather an *impression*.

When seeking to define the relationships between scholarship and constitutional adjudication, it became increasingly clear that the examination could be conducted on two levels: the "official" level and the "informal" level. In the latter, particular importance is held by that which is not expressed but is, rather, only implied (and perhaps merely suggested).

Thus far, this examination has striven to consider the "official" level. However, there was no real alternative, if not at the cost of *ab initio* foregoing the chance to obtain results that could at least aspire to be demonstrable. Nevertheless, it was precisely this choice that led to the difficulty of combining, on one hand, care to maintain the communication between constitutional courts and the scientific community, on the premise that the latter is important for the development of the Court's case law; and, on the other, the complete refusal to account for such importance by expressing it in explicit terms. This refusal is so absolute that it can explain not only the present, but also predict future developments with some reliability.

Juridical scholarship certainly plays more than a secondary role in constitutional adjudication. In this regard, consider also the search for direct channels of communication between the Court and scholars, an effort that gave rise to several workshops organized by the Court itself (especially in the early 1990s, and that it still organizes today, although maybe less frequently) to enable judges and scholars to debate on crucial subjects coming before the Court. Theoretical bases – which of course are provided by scholarship – are indispensable when conducting research for the cases and outlining the structure of the decisions. This role is commonly acknowledged, even by the constitutional courts themselves.[28] After the decisions have been issued, the commentary made thereupon is equally important, as it is increasingly considered an essential element in the formation of juridical opinion on the individual issues coming before the courts.[29]

These confirmations of the important role of scholarship should not

---

[28] In this regard, see M. Nisticò, *I rapporti tra la giurisdizione costituzionale e la dottrina giuridica in Italia. Il ruolo dei giudici-professori*, *op. cit.*, 157 ff. and the interviews given by current and past constitutional judges at the end of the chapter (179 ff.).

[29] In this connection, the publication on the website of the French Constitutional Council of documentation on the "[*r*]*éférences doctrinales*" relating to each decision (or rather, the decisions for which commentary is available) is emblematic. See also the website of the Italian Constitutional Court, which has recently added a page on "SCHOLARLY commentary". This is a database of scholarly articles that specifically discuss the Court's decisions; it is also possible to search this database by number and year of the decision, by author, by title and by journal name: see *www.cortecostituzionale.it/actionNoteSentenza.do.*

overshadow the marked distinction between theory and *jurisdictio*, a distinction that takes the form of the constitutional judges' consistent denial of the plausibility of applying conceptual schemes without any adaptations. When faced with real-life circumstances (in concrete review) or, in any case, with the impossibility to avoid considering the impact of their decisions, judges must make choices that cannot always correspond to coherent materializations of abstract formulations. Within this gap lies a certain "wariness" of scholarship, especially with regard to the responses that may be elicited by the decisions. Such wariness encompasses a certain degree of "fear" (of being misunderstood) and of "discomfort" (because of the failure to perceive any actual effort to understand on the part of legal commentators).

These barriers to communication between constitutional courts and the academic world tend to remain unexpressed or, at most, are merely hinted at; however, this certainly does not mean that their impact can be ignored. The absence of recent manifest examples to the contrary[30] cannot be taken as proof that the distance between the two fields has closed,[31] because the distance is structural. The tendency to emphasize the dialogue between them may foster mutual understanding, but it cannot nullify a gap that consists in a different approach to issues, in a perception of the dramatic consequences ensuing from certain options, in the unavoidability of certain compromises. In other words, communication between the constitutional jurisdiction and scholarship is certainly sought, as it is felt to be necessary; however, at the same time, it remains elusive because of the necessarily different viewpoints and perspectives from which issues are examined.

Therefore, an ambiguous relationship develops, in which evident manifestations of proximity constantly alternate with reservations and vindications of "otherness" on the part of constitutional courts. From this situation, fluctuations and perhaps even misunderstandings arise, which may be

---

[30] Most paradigmatic in this respect is perhaps the criticism made by the then-President of the Constitutional Court Giuseppe Branca regarding scholarship: cf. G. BRANCA, *Quis adnotabit adnotatores?*, in *Foro italiano*, 1970, V, c. 17 ff., and ID., *Chiosa a chiusa*, *ibidem*, V, c. 145 ff.

[31] A partially different evaluation is made by D. TEGA, *La dottrina come amica curiae. L'esperienza della Corte costituzionale italiana*, in P. PASSAGLIA (eds.), *I rapporti tra la giurisdizione costituzionale e la dottrina / Les rapports entre la juridiction constitutionnelle et la doctrine, Atti delle Giornate italo-franco-belghe di diritto comparato – Pisa, 6 e 7 marzo 2015*, *op. cit.*, 105, who notes that "the mental attitude of the Constitutional Court [...] is one of openness to scholarship, which it is well aware of needing: indeed, long past are the times of President Branca's piqued replies to the criticisms levelled by some scholars" (author's translation); this author agrees with the first part of the quote, but harbours some reservations on the second part, as will be seen below in the text.

explained essentially by the different levels on which the two fields operate and by the misconstructions necessarily engendered by the barriers to communication. Therefore, although the importance of scholarship for the work of constitutional judges is confirmed, the impression is that an underlying ambivalence subsists. An ambivalence that, to adopt a hyperbolic synaesthesia, evokes the title of one of Serge Gainsbourg's most famous songs: *Je t'aime... moi non plus*.

Chapter III

THE WASP AND THE ORCHID: CONSTITUTIONAL JUSTICE AND LEGAL SCHOLARSHIP NEED EACH OTHER *

Marc Verdussen

SUMMARY: 3.1. The influence of legal scholarship on constitutional justice. – 3.1.1. Semi-direct sources. – 3.1.2. Indirect sources. – 3.1.3. Implied sources. – 3.2. The perception of constitutional justice by legal scholarship. – 3.2.1. The perception of the constitutional court itself. – 3.2.2. The perception of constitutional case law. – 3.3. The destinies of constitutional justice and legal scholarship are more intertwined than ever before.

3.1. The influence of legal scholarship on constitutional justice

In his text, Paolo Passaglia shares some considerations and gives some impressions on the influence that Italian scholarship has, or has not, had on constitutional justice. He envisages three types of potential sources of influence, which he describes as "semi-direct", "indirect", and "implied". In so doing, he makes three 'assumptions', even if he does not use that particular word. The considerations advanced concerning these three assumptions are very cautious because they are scientifically unverifiable.

Clearly, these assumptions are transferable to other states employing the European model of constitutional review of legislation, where they remain just as unverifiable by scientific means. Even though no scientific statement can be established based on these hypotheses, each of them lends itself to empirical attempts at confirmation or refutation. While these attempts may not establish a definitive truth value (true or false), they make it possible to assess the degree of credibility of the hypotheses. Note that here we are

* This text is is based on the same definition that Paolo Passaglia gives, in the companion chapter to this one, to the notion of "doctrine" for the purposes of his chapter: "legal scholarship of academic provenance exclusively". This definition certainly can be debated, but that is not the objective of the two contributions. On this question, see, for example, M. FATIN-ROUGE STEFANINI, *Juges constitutionnels et doctrine. France*, in XXX *Annuaire international de justice constitutionnelle* 345 (2014), 345-347; A. RASSON-ROLAND, M. VERDUSSEN, *Juges constitutionnels et doctrine. Belgique*, in XXX *Annuaire international de justice constitutionnelle* 229 (2014), 229-230.

speaking mainly of states based on the European Kelsenian model of constitutional justice, which was designed by a law professor.

3.1.1. Semi-direct sources

Semi-direct sources are essentially three in number: case files prepared by justices' assistants, reports of constitutional justices' discussions, and draft judgments.

Supposing that we can consider legal scholarship to be a source of law (which certainly merits being debated and requires us to examine the notion of a "source of law"), it is clear that legal scholarship is not a compulsory source for constitutional justices. It is an optional source, sometimes recognized by law.[1] Consulting legal scholarship is even inherent to the function of judging. As Professor Michel Hottelier astutely writes: "the constitutional imperative of providing reasons results, in particular, in the obligation that courts establish, through reasoning based on logical, analytical arguments, the structure and content of the judgments they pronounce. The idea is not only to set out the legal foundations of the court decision in question. The purpose of the requirement that reasons be given is also to avoid arbitrariness, and to ensure equal treatment as well as legal security".[2] In this regard, legal scholarship's contribution belongs to the order of evidence.

In a context of pluralistic sources of law and highly abstract, open interpretation of a legal text (the constitution), legal scholarship plays a particularly essential role. Depending on the decision, its contribution will be considered decisive, supporting, or illustrative.

In some states, constitutional justices do not hesitate to cite doctrinal sources directly in judgments or, when they are authorized to do so, in separate opinions (the Federal Constitutional Court of Germany, the Constitutional Court of Portugal, the Federal Supreme Court of Switzerland…). In other states' courts (the Constitutional Court of Belgium, the French Constitutional Council), the doctrinal sources that the justices use are never expressly cited in the final decisions. Instead, they are employed in a manner that we will describe as "furtive". Moreover, in those states, the doctrinal

---

[1] See the third paragraph of article 1 of the *Swiss Civil Code*: "the court shall follow established doctrine and case law". [Our translation.] Compare with article 118 of the implementing provisions of the Italian *Code of Civil Procedure*, which prohibits inserting references to doctrine into judgments (G. ALPA, *La rédaction de la décision de justice en Italie*, in *Revue internationale de droit compare* 853, (1998), 856).

[2] M. HOTTELIER, *Juges constitutionnels et doctrine. Suisse*, in XXX *Annuaire international de justice constitutionnelle* 473 (2014), 484-485. [Our translation.]

sources consulted are generally not revealed at all. Yet, we know that the files compiled during case preparation contain many references to legal scholarship, and it is likely that such sources are cited in draft judgments, but those remain confidential. It is no different in states where the archives of decisions by constitutional courts can be consulted and published.[3] In such cases, a number of years have to go by before they can be accessed. It should nonetheless be mentioned that in France, legal scholarship is cited in the comments that accompany judgments, and those comments are produced based on notes by the Constitutional Council's legal department.

Generally, it seems that "improving transparency would require that some courts demonstrate greater clarity in the way their decisions are written to show what elements were given weight in the final interpretation or in the exercise of oversight to establish the solution".[4]

One may note that constitutional courts cite legal scholarship in the reports established in the framework of international networks: the World Conference on Constitutional Justice, the Conference of European Constitutional Courts and the Association des cours constitutionnelles ayant en partage l'usage du français (ACCPUF).

3.1.2. Indirect sources

Indirect sources are academic jurists within the collegial body of justices and the court's staff, and lawyers who also hold academic positions.

Most European constitutional courts are made up of trained jurists who also have significant professional experience in the legal world. It is therefore not very surprising to find lawyers, magistrates, public servants and law professors among constitutional justices. In some states (Germany, Portugal…), they comprise a significant proportion. However, it should be noted that, sometimes, the fact that the courts are composed in this way can be explained "by the fact that it is in those ranks that it is easiest to find independent people when an authoritarian regime shifts to a democratic regime".[5] Justices with an academic background are able to play a particu-

[3] In France, an organic law establishes a waiting time of 25 years for access to the archives of the Constitutional Council. In 2009, a work was published reporting on the Council's deliberations during its 25 first years of operation: B. MATHIEU, J.-P. MACHELON, F. MÉLIN-SOUCRAMANIEN, D. ROUSSEAU, X. PHILIPPE, *Les grandes délibérations du Conseil constitutionnel 1958-1983*, Paris, Dalloz, 2009.

[4] F. MALHIERE (eds.), *L'élaboration des décisions des cours constitutionnelles et européennes*, Research conducted with the support of the Mission de recherche Droit et Justice, Paris, May 2017, 56. [Our translation.]

[5] L. FAVOREU, *La légitimité de la justice constitutionnelle et la composition des juri-*

larly decisive role in the first years after the creation of a constitutional court, at a time when what is stake for such a court is not only to break away from the constitutional culture of the preceding regime, but also to lay the first stones of constitutional jurisprudence. This phenomenon was observed in Spain, for example.[6] Subsequently, the credit given to university professors, especially those specializing in constitutional law, is sometimes replaced by a degree of distrust of the academic world. On France's Constitutional Council, for example, the presence of university professors specializing in constitutional law has become marginal.

Most justices from academia have an impressive number of publications. Moreover, in some judgments, the fact that a given justice has already expressed an opinion in prior writings makes it possible to think that, while respecting the constraints of collegiality, he or she may have had a determining influence over the judgment's structure or reasoning. However, that remains speculative since, as we have pointed out, there is no reliable indicator for assessing the impact of legal scholarship on constitutional jurisprudence.

Once appointed or elected, are justices from academia authorized to publish works, contributions and articles? Certainly, and they do not hesitate to do so, whether or not they have retained a university position (within the legal limits). However, the opinions published in this way are purely personal: they are those of the justice, not of the court. Moreover, it is considered inappropriate for a constitutional justice to evade the prohibition against separate opinions (concurring or dissenting) – in places where that prohibition exists (the Constitutional Court of Belgium, the French Constitutional Council, the Federal Supreme Court of Switzerland) – by expressing an opinion on judgments in which he or she participated. Justices have a duty of reserve that is not necessarily imposed by law, but which flows from the secrecy of the deliberations and is founded on professional ethics generally integrated into the culture of European courts.

One question merits attention in this regard: in very specific, and thus exceptional, circumstances, can legal scholarship published by a justice be grounds for questioning his or her objective impartiality? Belgian Constitutional Court judgment No. 155/2011 of 13 October 2011,[7] on a request that a justice with university activities recuse himself, notes: "universities

dictions constitutionnelles, in AA.VV., *Legitimidade e Legitimaçao da Justiça Constitucional*, Coimbra, Coimbra Editora, 1995, 239. [Our translation.]

[6] M. Carrillo, *Juges constitutionnels et doctrine. Espagne*, in XXX *Annuaire international de justice constitutionnelle* 291 (2014), 299.

[7] Judgment not published in the *Moniteur belge*. Available on the Constitutional Court website: http://www.const-court.be. [Our translation.]

are special environments fostering academic freedom based on the principle that, in the interest of advancement of knowledge and pluralism of opinions, professors and researchers must enjoy very great liberty to conduct research and express opinions in the performance of their duties [...] the plaintiff does not show concrete elements that compromise the subjective impartiality of the justice whose recusation is being requested [...] and, in particular, has not demonstrated that the said justice openly took a position, at any point in time whatsoever, and in a manner that would be evidence of a reprehensible negative prejudice against one of the parties to the trial, concerning constitutionality issues submitted to the Court". This decision should be compared with the more surprising decision of 28 June 2010 by the Constitutional Court of Spain,[8] which, ruling on the action instituted against the Statute of Autonomy of Catalonia, agreed to remove one of its members on the grounds that, prior to his appointment, he had published an academic study on relations between the Autonomous Community of Catalonia and the European Union.[9] In Germany, the *Federal Constitutional Court Act* states expressly, in section 18(3)2, that a justice's expression of a scholarly opinion on a point of law that may be relevant to the case is not a legitimate reason for debarring the justice from the case. Still, a justice's conscience may lead him or her to prefer to recuse himself or herself if he or she considers that a prior publication could cast doubt on his or her impartiality. For example, in 1982, in the case *Quotas par sexe I*, Georges Vedel decided not to sit[10] since he had published an opinion on the issue before being appointed to the French Constitutional Council.[11]

In every court, justices' assistants (advisors, assessors...) play determining roles in preparing cases and decisions. Whether they are seconded or recruited by competition, they often come from academia. Sometimes they even remain associated with their university and participate in group or individual research projects. In all cases, they are inclined to refer to legal scholarship when carrying out their duties.

In many states with the European model, lawyers who appear regularly before the constitutional court work as professors or assistants in a university, most often in public law. As such, they are the authors of doctrinal works.

---

[8] *Boletin Oficial del Estado*, 16 July 2010, No. 172, Supplement.

[9] J. Tornos Mas, *La sentencia del Tribunal Constitucional español 31/2010 sobre el Estatuto de Autonomía de Cataluña*, in 1 *Istituzione del Federalismo* 13 (2011), 22.

[10] Conseil constitutionnel français, déc. No. 146 DC of 18 November 1982.

[11] L. Favoreu, L. Philip, *Les grandes décisions du Conseil constitutionnel*, Paris, Dalloz, 1999, 556-562.

3.1.3. Implied sources

References to legal scholarship are implied sources in judgments

Constitutional courts are supposed to be familiar with the relevant legal scholarship, especially when they are resolving a specific dispute. They generally have a documentation service or library, or even a legal department. Moreover, scholarly research is part of the mission of justices' assistants, when justices have assistants. Naturally, lawyers do not fail to cite legal scholarship that supports their arguments.

In many states with a European model, constitutional courts have inevitably been influenced by certain legal works considered to be crucial and written by eminent academics, which does not mean that there is a hierarchy of doctrinal sources or authors. The quality of a piece of legal scholarship flows from its intrinsic value, and not from the author's titles and qualifications. Limiting ourselves only to works on constitutional litigation and constitutional justice, there is a work by Professor Eduardo Garcia de Enterria in Spain [12] and another by Professor Gustavo Zagrebelsky in Italy. [13] There are also the publications by Professor Louis Favoreu in France. [14]

Other specific legal works have had an impact on certain decisions in leading cases. For example, [15] there is the work by Santiago Munoz Machado on freedom of the press and defamation trials, [16] and on the interpretation of article 20 of the Spanish constitution in decision STC 6/1988 of 21 January 1988. [17] In France, doctrinal influences are presupposed, even if they are not able to be established. [18]

A constitutional court may also use other scholarly work from the social sciences (history, economics, sociology, anthropology, demographics…). For example, when a constitutional court must render a ruling on the discriminatory nature of a difference in pay between two categories of people, the justices can consider it necessary to adopt an empirical approach and consult numerical data taken from economic studies. The integration of

---

[12] E. GARCIA DE ENTERRIA, *La Constitución como norma y el Tribunal constitucional*, Madrid, Civitas, 1982.

[13] G. ZAGREBELSKY, *La giustizia costituzionale*, Bologna, Il Mulino, 1977.

[14] Some of these publications are reprinted in: L. FAVOREU, *La Constitution et son juge*, Paris, Economica, 2014, 29-335.

[15] M. CARRILLO, *Juges constitutionnels et doctrine. Espagne*, *op. cit.*, 297.

[16] S. MUNOZ MACHADO, *Libertad de prensa y procesos por difamación*, Barcelona, Ariel, 1988.

[17] *Boletin Oficial del Estado*, 5 February 1988, No. 31, Supplement.

[18] M. FATIN-ROUGE STEFANINI, *Juges constitutionnels et doctrine. France*, *op. cit.*, 365-366.

such elements refutes the idea that extra-legal scholarship has only contextual value and is therefore not part of justices' *ratio decidendi*. The question nonetheless arises of whether, when referring to such extra-legal data, justices consider them as doctrinal sources or as expert testimony.

This also raises the question of whether constitutional justices favour direct contact with authors. Informal contact is obviously not publicized, but it probably occurs. Nothing really prevents a constitutional justice from entering into contact with a given eminent author so long as their discussion does not concern a specific case. Such a discussion would be ethically challengeable. Moreover, in such cases, there are reasonable expectations that the consulted academic would demonstrate basic discretion.

There is also formal contact. Constitutional justices frequently participate in scholarly events held by academics, but usually on the initiative of the latter. Sometimes constitutional courts agree to host academic events in their facilities. Lastly, such contact may be initiated by the institution itself. In some states, constitutional courts have more highly developed communications with legal scholarship than in others. They may even have a communications strategy. For example, in Spain, annual seminars are held by the association of legal assistants of the Constitutional Court (*letrados*). In France, on the occasion of the publication of each issue of the *Nouveaux Cahiers du Conseil constitutionnel*, a luncheon is organized by the Constitutional Council, and all of the contributors are invited to it. In Belgium, a symposium was held in 2005 on the relations between the Constitutional Court, the judiciary and the Council of State, bringing together representatives from the highest courts, members of the Bar, and academics, which resulted in a major publication.[19] However, also in Belgium, when a colloquium was held for the thirtieth anniversary of the Constitutional Court, the latter invited representatives of lawyers, parliaments, business, unions, associations, and foreign and European courts; however, no academics representing Belgian legal scholarship were invited.[20]

Direct contact with legal scholarship is sometimes possible in the framework of specific cases. For example, paragraph 22(5) of the *Rules of Procedure of the Federal Constitutional Court* of Germany authorizes the presiding justice of the house that is seized, on the house's initiative or at

---

[19] A. Arts, I. Verougstraete, R. Andersen, G. Suetens-Bourgeois, M.-F. Rigaux, R. Ryckeboer, A. De Wolf (eds.), *Les rapports entre la Cour d'arbitrage, le Pouvoir judiciaire et le Conseil d'Etat – De verhouding tussen het Arbitragehof, de Rechterlijke Macht en de Raad van State*, Bruges, die Keure; Brussels, La Charte, 2006.

[20] A. Alen, J. Spreutels, L. Lavrysen, P. Nihoul, E. Peremans, B. Renauld, J. Theunis, W. Verrijdt (eds.), *Cour constitutionnelle 1985-2015*, Brussels, La Charte; Bruges, die Keure, 2016.

the suggestion of the reporting justice, to "request persons with special knowledge of a specific subject to provide expert opinions on an issue material to the decision". Section 52, paragraph (3) of Act No. 47/1992 on the organization and functioning of the Constitutional Court provides that the presiding justice can invite to the deliberations "persons considered necessary". [Our translation.] There is also the French "narrow gate" process, by which, in the context of *a priori* referral to the Constitutional Council, any physical or corporate person – or group of persons – can address to the Council a brief that may support or contest the constitutionality of the legislation being challenged. Such briefs are generally highly appreciated by constitutional justices. Professor Marthe Fatin-Rouge Stéfanini notes, however, that "quite obviously, when the narrow gate is written by an academic but for a third party (a professional order, association, union…), the opinion expressed by the professor of Law is in service to whoever mandated him or her to write it and who, in principle, paid for the consulting services thus performed […] such that the intellectual freedom supposed by the expression of a doctrinal opinion is not necessarily present".[21]

3.2. The perception of constitutional justice by legal scholarship

In Europe, relations between legal scholarship and constitutional justice are not limited to the influence that the former has over the latter. They also concern the impact that the latter has on the former. Constitutional justice "feeds" legal scholarship, not only with respect to what it represents institutionally, but also regarding what it produces jurisprudentially. In short, the interactions are mutual.

3.2.1. The perception of the constitutional court itself

As a general rule, only constitutionalist scholarship focuses on constitutional courts as institutions – their composition, organization, functioning, duties, ways of being seized and procedure. Across all of Europe, certain criticisms recur, for example, regarding the process for appointing constitutional justices and especially the politicization of that process, as well as the form of the decisions (opaque writing, excessively brief reasons, lack of separate opinions, etc). The criticisms are sometimes more radical, with their authors arguing for a complete change of model of constitutional jus-

[21] M. Fatin-Rouge Stefanini, *Juges constitutionnels et doctrine. France*, *op. cit.*, 362. [Our translation.]

tice, and even, though it is increasingly rare, for the elimination of any constitutional review of legislation.

In every state, the spectrum of analysis can be very different from one author to the next. Whether it is a question of whether or not to integrate a historical dimension, a comparativist vision or interdisciplinary reflection (to limit ourselves to only those), there are clear doctrinal variations.

3.2.2. The perception of constitutional case law

Constitutional case law generates interest, not only among constitutionalists, but also among specialists of the disciplines concerned.

One of the consequences of the increasing penetration of constitutional law into the various branches of law through constitutional jurisprudence is that commentary on such jurisprudence is no longer the purview of constitutionalists alone; it is also the charge of specialists of the discipline concerned. In France, a major sign of this can be seen with the introduction of the question of the precedence of constitutionality (QPC) in 2010. In short, the interest aroused by the jurisprudence of the Constitutional Council (which was at first a veritable craze) has extended far beyond constitutionalists' circles.

The angles of analysis are generally different and should therefore complement one another. For example, when it is a question of commenting on a given constitutional court decision, specialists in the subject matter tend to focus their analysis more on the theme at stake and the decision's impact on it. Constitutionalists are more inclined to investigate the methodological and conceptual aspects of the approach taken by the constitutional court, such as the forms of interpretation used, the degree of material oversight, implementation of the proportionality test, possible intrusion into the legislative realm, and also the quality of the formal reasons. On the last point, constitutionalist scholarship does not fail to criticize ambiguous, approximate, incomplete, excessively brief, etc. decisions. In that respect, it is certainly more attentive to the overall consistency of constitutional jurisprudence.

Moreover, the idea is sometimes defended that non-constitutionalist scholarship is more critical than constitutionalist scholarship. According to Professor Xavier Magnon, "constitutionalist scholarship's natural inclination towards respect for its subject matter can appear as a significant tendency, or at least it is most often perceived as such, whereas it is precisely the distance of other scholarship from that subject matter, which is not their primary focus, which authorizes and favours the critical eye".[22] However-

[22] X. MAGNON, *La doctrine, la QPC et le Conseil constitutionnel: quelle distance?*

ever, this hypothesis needs to be verified. In passing, we call attention to the *Mustafa Erdogan v. Turquie* judgment of 27 May 2014, in which the European Court of Human Rights condemned Turkey for having sanctioned a professor of constitutional law who had strongly criticized a decision by Turkey's Constitutional Court.

Yet, this distribution of doctrinal work does not show systematically divergent assessments, even though differences can sometimes be seen. For example, German civil law and constitutional law experts have different perceptions of personality rights.[23]

The separating line is not necessarily between constitutionalists and other jurists. In a country like Belgium, where there is a deep divide between the French and Flemish extremes, it is not surprising that a cleavage has gradually become clear between French-language legal scholarship and Flemish legal scholarship on the Constitutional Court. The cleavage is certainly not general, and it should in no way be overemphasized. It concerns certain judgments that have also given rise to discussions between justices within one or the other linguistic group. On a more epistemological level, it also, and perhaps above all, concerns the form of the doctrinal approach. For example, speaking only of comparative methodology, there is the feeling (this hypothesis needs to be scientifically proven) that foreign sources of inspiration are not necessarily relevant.

There are other separating lines, confirming that legal scholarship is not monolithic: there are originalists and non-originalists, conservatives and progressives, federalists and sovereigntists, those in favour of the European Union and "Euro skeptics" [...] That said, beyond these lines, it is difficult to establish typologies of approaches or criticisms regarding constitutional jurisprudence, not only within single states, but also and *a fortiori* within the European model of constitutional justice. It is especially difficult with respect to concrete constitutional disputes that require reasons in terms of evaluation, conciliation, weighting, etc.

Works dealing more specifically with constitutional disputes and constitutional justice are written most often by professors,[24] but also sometimes

---

Quelle expertise?, in 1 *Revue du droit public et de la science politique* 135 (2013), 142. [Our translation.]

[23] R. ARNOLD, *Juges constitutionnels et doctrine. Allemagne*, in XXX *Annuaire international de justice constitutionnelle* 217 (2014), 220.

[24] See for example D. ROUSSEAU, P.-Y. GAHDOUN, J. BONNET, *Droit du contentieux constitutionnel*, 11th ed., Paris, L.G.D.J., 2016; G. DRAGO, *Contentieux constitutionnel français*, 4th ed., Paris, P.U.F., 2016 ; P. PEREZ TREMPS, *Sistema de justicia constitucional*, 2nd ed., Madrid, Civitas, 2016; A. RUGGERI, A. SPADARO, *Lineamenti di giustizia costituzionale*, Turin, Giappichelli Editore, 2014. Sometimes the work is published by profes-

by justices or former constitutional justices,[25] justices' assistants,[26] and lawyers.[27] Sometimes, the author has more than one title, such as professor and lawyer,[28] and some such works are written by non-jurists. For example, the sociologist Dominique Schnapper wrote a book on beliefs and impressions inspired by her nine years of experience as a member of the Constitutional Council.[29]

When legal scholarship comments on a decision (or a set of decisions), we expect it to bring added value in relation to the decision itself. Ideally, it views the decision from three perspectives.[30]

Retrospectively. This means situating the decision being commented on in relation to the constitutional court's prior jurisprudence in order to establish continuities or, on the contrary, breaks. It also means measuring the consistency of the reviewed decision in relation to comparable jurisprudence by other courts, whether domestic (Court of Cassation, Supreme Court, Council of State…) or European (European Court of Human Rights, Court of Justice of the European Union…). It is especially important with respect to fundamental rights, where different systems for protecting those rights function in competition with one another.

Introspectively. This means analyzing and criticizing the decision being commented on. The goal is to measure the exact impact of the judgment on the state of law. However, the objective is also, first, to identify the steps in the constitutional justices' reasoning and to pinpoint the assumptions, detours, contradictions, etc. From this perspective, commentators must be attentive to the fundamental difference between their stances, that of observers who have to be accountable only to themselves, and the positions of constitutional justices, who are required to take part in a dialogue and be able to make compromises. Justices must also be realistic and aware of con-

---

sors from other states: see for example D.P. KOMMERS, R.A. MILLER, *The Constitutional Jurisprudence of the Federal Republic of Germany*, Durham, Duke University Press, 2012.

[25] See for example J.-L. DEBRÉ, *Ce que je ne pouvais pas dire*, Paris, Robert Laffont, 2016.

[26] See for example M.-F. RIGAUX, B. RENAULD, *La Cour constitutionnelle*, Brussels, Bruylant, 2009.

[27] See for example R. Zuck, *Das Recht der Verfassungsbeschwerde*, 5th ed., Köln, C.H. Beck, 2017.

[28] See for example M. VERDUSSEN, *Justice constitutionnelle*, Brussels, Larcier, 2012.

[29] D. SCHNAPPER, *Une sociologue au Conseil constitutionnel*, Paris, Gallimard, 2010.

[30] A. RASSON-ROLAND, M. VERDUSSEN, *Juges constitutionnels et doctrine. Belgique*, *op. cit.*, 230.

sequences. Constitutional courts are expected to be attentive to situating their decisions in the context of society as a whole. As Stephen Breyer has shown clearly, the link between the law and life forces justices to be attentive to the consequences of how they interpret the law.[31]

It is through this *introspective stance* that the critical dimension of legal scholarship appears most sharply. In states where constitutional justice was born in a post-dictatorial context of democratic renewal, there is a doctrinal tendency with respect to constitutional justices: they enjoy a period of grace. This was the case in Spain, for example, and in certain Central and Eastern European states. However, a period of grace never lasts forever. Legal scholarship gradually sharpens its critical regard.

Prospectively. This means casting an eye towards the future. Based on the comments on the decision, legal scholarship is inclined to identify new constitutional issues that might arise in the courts of ordinary judges and be submitted to constitutional justices. However, first, the comments must suggest to the legislator actions that could ward off the ominous unconstitutional situations. The essential role played by legal scholarship on this point can be measured all the better given that constitutional courts do not hesitate to address to legislators veritable injunctions to legislate, forcing them, or at least inviting them, to eliminate the possibility of unconstitutionality. For example, if a constitutional court identifies the unconstitutionality of a legislative oversight, and if that failure cannot be repaired by the justice *a quo*, the decision by the constitutional justices must be interpreted as a signal to the legislators, who are then responsible for remedying the situation. Additionally, when the immediate invalidation of an unconstitutional law would create a legal situation (sometimes a legal vacuum) that would be too harmful, the constitutional court can decide to maintain the effects of the rule for a set period, which must be interpreted as a request to the legislators to amend, or even repeal, the unconstitutional requirement before a set date, since they alone are able to choose the measures to be taken to eliminate the unconstitutionality.

Doctrinal comments do not necessarily concern an isolated decision. They can also target a set of decisions. We therefore propose to distinguish between micro – and macro-comments. "Micro-comments" consider a specific judgment in what have come to be known as case notes. "Macro-comments" are on a set of judgments. Sometimes case notes cover a specif-

---

[31] S. BREYER, *Active Liberty – Interpreting Our Democratic Constitution*, New York, Knopf, 2006, 18.

ic period, generally one year, in which case the contribution to legal schol arship lies in the way in which the cases are selected, presented, shown to have similarities, or classified. Sometimes case notes concern a given issue or discipline.

Does legal scholarship place the constitutional justice of its country in context? Part of the constitutionalist literature on constitutional justice views this from a comparative perspective. Works have been published on comparative constitutional justice.[32] Some of them focus on a specific geographic area[33] or a specific problem;[34] others instead study "models" of constitutional justice.[35] There are also law reports, such as those that the *Annuaire international de justice constitutionnelle* has been publishing since 1985.[36]

3.3. The destinies of constitutional justice and legal scholarship are more intertwined than ever before

Constitutional justice and legal scholarship are inextricably linked.

The objective of constitutional justice is to provide oversight of norms that have an especially high level of abstraction and therefore require highly dynamic interpretation. This is particularly true of constitutional norms embodying fundamental rights. As Pierre Moor writes, "the pyramid structure in which human rights appear as norms at the summit has the paradoxical configuration of having less normative density the higher one rises in the hierarchy".[37] Consequently, "the exercise of judicial review [...] is

[32] See for example L. FAVOREU, W. MASTOR, *Les cours constitutionnelles*, 2nd ed., Paris, Dalloz, 2016; J.J. FERNANDEZ RODRIGUEZ, *La justicia constitucional europea ante el siglo XXI*, Madrid, Tecnos, 2002; M. FROMONT, *Justice constitutionnelle comparée*, Paris, Dalloz, 2013; L. PEGORARO, *Giustizia costituzionale comparata*, Turin, Giappichelli Editore, 2015.

[33] See for example N. DANELCIUC-COLODROVSCHI, *La justice constitutionnelle dans les pays de la CEI: évolutions et perspectives*, Paris, Fondation Varenne, 2012.

[34] See for example J. BELL, M.-L. PARIS (eds.), *Rights-Based Constitutional Review – Constitutional Courts in A Changing Landscape*, Cheltenham, Edward Elgar Publishing, 2016.

[35] See for example V. FERRERES COMELLA, *Constitutional Courts and Democratic Values – An European Perspective*, New Haven, Yale University Press, 2009; G. TUSSEAU, *Contre les modèles de justice constitutionnelle – Essai de critique méthodologique*, Bologna, Bononia University Press, 2009.

[36] Paris, Economica, Aix-en-Provence, Presses universitaires d'Aix-Marseille.

[37] P. MOOR, *Pour une théorie micropolitique du droit*, Paris: P.U.F., 2005, 70. [Our translation.]

rather different from the usual judicial function of applying the law. Modern Constitutions do not limit themselves to a fixed definition of what the law is, but contain broad programs for future action. Therefore, the task of fulfilling the Constitution often demands a higher sense of discretion than the task of interpreting ordinary statutes".[38] This singularity of constitutional justice explains why, for constitutionalists, the jurisprudential interpretations of constitutional justices are necessary.

Even better, constitutional justice has produced a movement favouring the constitutionalization of the different branches of law, the respective spaces of which have gradually been penetrated by the now jurisprudentialized constitutional law. The jurisprudentialization of law has developed above all in disputes concerning fundamental rights and has been strengthened by theories such as that of the horizontal effect of rights ("*Drittwirkung*"). All branches of law are concerned by these constitutional emanations, which require all jurists to question the implications of constitutional law on their disciplines and, by the force of circumstance, contributes to an elimination of boundaries, in particular between public and private law. The consequence of this change in paradigm is that legal scholarship in general can no longer overlook the jurisprudence of constitutional justices and the conditions in which it is produced. Constitutional jurisprudence has become a pivotal point in legal scholarship, contributing to the strengthening of changes in constitutional law.[39]

In contrast, interpreting the constitution is not confined to constitutional courts because "there is no *numerus clausus* of interpreters of the Constitution".[40] As Gustavo Zagrebelsky wrote, constitutional courts, like other state bodies, are not "*padroni del diritto*", since the very existence of such a "ruler of the law" in a constitutional state would be radically incompatible.[41] This is at the heart of democracy, the special nature of which is to always leave the question of rights open, especially the question of constitutional rights, "since one of its axioms is precisely that it does not recognize any power or authority whose legitimacy cannot be challenged".[42] This is what makes Jürgen Habermas say that, in the institutional framework of

---

[38] M. CAPPELLETTI, *Judicial Review in the Contemporary World*, New York, Bobbs-Merrill, 1971, 62-63.

[39] See M. VERDUSSEN, *Un droit constitutionnel métamorphosé*, in 75 *Annales de droit de Louvain*, No. 3-4, 291 (2015), 295-296.

[40] P. HÄBERLE, *L'Etat constitutionnel*, trans., Paris, Economica; Aix-en-Provence, P.U.A.M., 2004, 126. [Our translation.]

[41] G. ZAGREBELSKY, *Il diritto mite*, Turin, Einaudi Editore, 1992, 213.

[42] D. ROUSSEAU, P.-Y. GAHDOUN, J. BONNET, *Droit du contentieux constitutionnel*, *op. cit.*, 833. [Our translation.]

democracy, "no one can claim to have special access to the truth on constitutional issues" and "no one can know with certainty whether someone's understanding is the right one or, supposing there were one, who has it".[43] This is why constitutional justices must be attentive to constitutional interpretations from other places so as to inform their own interpretations and thereby contribute to the constitutional dialogue. According to Barry Friedman, the constitution is interpreted on a daily basis through an ongoing dialogue in which all segments of society participate and in which justices play a special interpretive role: most often, they are the ones who trigger and shape the dialogue.[44] Justices "are not supposed to be, as in a system, passive agents of a legal order but, on the contrary, actors in a never-ending exchange".[45] There is no such thing as social responsibility borne by a justice enclosed in a courtroom as in an ivory tower.

By disseminating constitutional jurisprudence, but also by criticizing it, legal scholarship contributes to establishing the legitimacy of constitutional courts. While in all modern states there is tension between democracy and constitutionalism, it is the Americans who have best understood that the legitimacy of justices' interventions lies in that very tension. In other words, the livelier the discussions on legitimacy are, the less legitimacy is in danger.

Among the many plant metaphors that the French philosopher Gilles Deleuze imagined, there is that of the orchid and the wasp.[46] The orchid is a flower that has the peculiarity of being able to reproduce only if others help to carry its pollen. This is where the wasp comes in. Attracted by the visual and olfactory signals of the orchid, the wasp lands on the flower and, brushing against the plant's structures, covers itself in pollen, which it later deposits on another orchid, which is thereby fertilized. Scholarship is to constitutional justice what the wasp is to the orchid. Scholarship is attracted to constitutional justice, which in turn needs scholarship to spread into the legal order.

---

[43] J. HABERMAS, *Une époque de transitions – Ecrits politiques 1998-2003*, trans., Paris, Fayard, 2005, 200-201. [Our translation.]

[44] B. FRIEDMAN, *Dialogue and Judicial Review*, in 91 *Mich. L. Rev.*, No. 4, 577 (1993), 580-581. [Our translation.]

[45] J. ALLARD, A. GARAPON, *Les juges dans la mondialisation – La nouvelle révolution du droit*, Paris, Seuil, 2005, 7.

[46] G. DELEUZE, F. GUATTARI, *Mille plateaux*, Paris, Minuit, 1980; G. DELEUZE, F. GUATTARI (Translated by B. MASSUMI), *A Thousand Plateaus*, Minneapolis, University of Minnesota Press, 1993.

Dialogue II

OPEN AND CLOSED FORMS OF CONSTITUTIONAL ADJUDICATION

Chapter IV

OPENNESS AND TRANSPARENCY IN CONSTITUTIONAL ADJUDICATION: *AMICI CURIAE*, THIRD-PARTY INTERVENTION, AND FACT-FINDING POWERS

Tania Groppi and Anna Maria Lecis Cocco Ortu *

During the constitutional review of legislation, factual information (especially on "legislative facts") is not irrelevant. It is normally gathered by courts by relying both on *amici curiae* and on third-party briefs, or by using their evidence-gathering powers.

Notwithstanding the growing importance of the topic, the taxonomies concerning the different constitutional justice systems fail to consider this aspect of constitutional review. Neither the openness (or closure) to third-parties and *amici curiae* nor the way courts use their fact-finding powers are taken into account by comparative constitutional scholars.

Despite this gap in the literature, we would like to suggest that this is an important feature of constitutional justice, strongly influencing its relational approach. Far from being confined to the realm of experts of constitutional proceedings, it can contribute to better understanding the relational attitude of a court, bringing to light its relations with the surrounding environment and especially with experts, civil society and public opinion.

Furthermore, these also exert a significant influence on the Court's judgments, since openness leads normally to a more transparent and developed reasoning, which, in turn, can enhance the legitimacy of the court.

In Italy, *amicus curiae* briefs are not taken into consideration. Nonethe-

* This chapter is the result of a joint work of both authors. Nonetheless, in the drafting, Tania Groppi wrote the introduction and the fourth section, Anna Maria Lecis Cocco Ortu wrote the second and third sections, while the final section was written by both authors.

less, experts and civil society can give their contribution as "friends of the Court" through third-party intervention or fact-finding power. Through the first channel, a person can voluntarily address its observations to the Court, which will decide on their admissibility; if admitted, the individual becomes party to the process. Through the second channel, experts can be consulted by the Court through the exercise of its fact-finding powers; this method recalls the original notion of the *amicus curiae*.

We will analyse the mechanisms of third-party intervention and fact-finding powers in order to understand if, and to what extent, the Court uses them to open its proceeding to external contributions and thus implement its relational approach. We will focus only on the incidental system of judicial review (or *incidenter* judicial review), considering it as the core of the Italian system of constitutional justice.

This chapter is divided into three sections. In the first section, we will present the legislative and autonomous framework on third-party interventions and fact-finding powers. In the following two sections, we will examine the case law and the scholarly debate on, respectively, third-party interventions and fact-finding powers.

We conclude that the Constitutional Court's approach to third-party intervention and to the fact-finding powers is highly "flexible", with the Court normally preferring to use informal channels to gather information. Finally, we will present some critical remarks asking the Court to re-think its attitude – to reinforce the "relational approach" that characterizes many aspects of its activity [1] – by entering into an open and formal dialogue with interest groups and experts.

4.1. The legislative and autonomous framework

An analysis of the legal framework concerning third-party intervention and fact-finding powers of the Court clearly demonstrates the specificity of the Italian "constitutional procedural law", [2] i.e. its flexibility because of the combination of "rules and regularity". [3]

---

[1] V. BARSOTTI, P.G. CAROZZA, M. CARTABIA, A. SIMONCINI, *Italian Constitutional Justice in Global Context*, Oxford, Oxford University Press, 2015, 234 ff.

[2] For the scholarly debate on the notion of "diritto processuale costituzionale", see G. ZAGREBELSKY, *Diritto processuale costituzionale?*, in AA.VV., *Giudizio "a quo" e promovimento del processo costituzionale*, Milan, Giuffré Editore, 1990, 105 ff.

[3] A. RUGGERI, *Giudizi di costituzionalità tra riforma delle norme integrative e autoriforma della giurisprudenza* in A. PIZZORUSSO, R. ROMBOLI (eds.), *Le norme integrative per i giudizi innanzi alla Corte costituzionale dopo quasi mezzo secolo di applicazione*, Turin, Giappichelli Editore, 2002, 403.

One important feature of the system of constitutional justice operating in Italy is that, unlike the procedural rules and practices of Italian ordinary courts, which are regulated in detail by the Civil and Criminal Procedure Codes, the procedural rules of the Constitutional Court are more flexible.

Very concise legislative provisions have been integrated through autonomous rules developed by the Court, which play an important role in the definition of the constitutional proceedings in Italy. Nevertheless, significant scope remains for the practice of the Court, which has been developing and tailoring its powers on a case-by-case basis.[4]

Concerning the fact-finding powers, legislative provisions for the Constitutional Court, i.e. Law no 87/1953, only address the acquisition of information under Article 13 and the preliminary stage of investigation (i.e. *fase istruttoria*) under Article 26.

According to Article 13, "The Court may decide the hearing of witnesses and, also by derogation to the prohibitions established in other laws, the request of acts or documents".

Article 26 provides that "[t]he President of the Court nominates one judge in charge of the preliminary investigation and the report on the case". We will refer to him/her as the "judge rapporteur".

As for intervention in the process, the only intervention mentioned by the law – in the incidental proceeding – is that of the President of the Council of Ministers in proceedings concerning national laws and that of the President of a Regional Government, when regional laws are reviewed for constitutionality (Art. 25.3).

The law does not mention third-party interventions.

Detailed rules on the application of these provisions can be found in the Court's internal rules of procedure, called the "Supplementary Provisions Concerning Proceedings before the Constitutional Court" (hereinafter, S.P.). In. fact, these internal rules complete the legal framework for the proceedings before the Court according to Art. 22 of Law no. 87/1953. These rules represent the autonomous framework of the Court's procedural rules, through which the Court can tailor them to the specificity of the constitutional proceedings. A first version of the Supplementary Provisions was approved in 1956. Over time, these rules have been amended, with an important revision taking place in 2004. A new, updated version was then approved in 2008.

The fact-finding powers are regulated by Articles 12 to 14 of the S.P., which were subject only to marginal amendments in 2004.

---

[4] See T. Groppi, *The Constitutional Court of Italy: Towards a Multilevel System of Constitutional Review?*, in A. Harding, P. Leyland (eds.), *Constitutional Courts: A Comparative Study*, London, Wildy, Simmonds and Hill Publishing, 2009, 125 ff.

Art. 12 provides that "The Court decides with an order the means of proof that it deems appropriate and establishes the terms and procedures for their taking".

Article 13 provides that the recording of evidence and facts must take place 10 days after the parties have been notified. This process occurs under the supervision of the judge in charge of the preliminary investigation, with the assistance of the Registrar who draws up the report.

Under Art. 14, the evidentiary report is filed with the registry, and the clerk gives notice of the filing to the parties at least 30 days before the public hearing ("*udienza pubblica*") or the hearing in chambers (in Italian, "*camera di consiglio*").

The main novelty (introduced in 2004) is now included in article 7, paragraphs 2 and 3. According to Article 7, "2. The documents that, by order of the President, following the proposal of the judge rapporteur, are admitted as evidence in the proceedings are filed with the registry. 3. The registry notifies the parties of the filing".

This reform may be considered a direct reaction to criticism that scholars had voiced against the practice of the Court.[5] As we shall see further *infra*, the Court seldom applies the rules on formal fact-finding provided by the Law and the S.P., and it actually prefers to follow an informal fact-finding procedure carried out by the judge rapporteur. One of the problems raised by this informal fact-finding procedure, however, is the lack of transparency, since the information collected cannot be accessed by the parties and remains classified to the public. The new provision aims to address this first point of criticism by giving the parties the possibility of accessing the information; however, scholars have deemed this amendment insufficient to solve the problem. Despite continued criticism, the new S.P. adopted in 2008 did not introduce additional rules.

In reference to the third-party interventions, despite the lack of any legislative basis, the Court first introduced them in its case-law.

The jurisprudence of the Court concerning third-party interventions would identify two phases: a first phase, lasting from 1956 to 1990, of absolute closure based on the principle of the "formal coincidence between parties in the *principaliter* proceeding and parties in the *incidenter* proceeding"; a second phase, beginning in 1991, in which the Court started to admit third-party interventions on a case-by-case basis.

During the first phase, from the beginning of its activity to approxi-

---

[5] T. Groppi, *I poteri istruttori della Corte costituzionale nel giudizio sulle leggi*, Milan, Giuffré Editore, 1997.

mately three decades later, the Court consistently decided against the admissibility of such interventions.[6]

The first exception to this practice was made in 1982, when the Court allowed the intervention of a third-party whose interest in the constitutional review proceedings arose from the question of constitutionality raised by the Constitutional Court itself, as an "*a quo* judge".[7] This case was later defined as an "exception" by the Court,[8] which then confirmed for almost ten more years its closure to third-party interventions.

Starting in 1991, the Court partially overruled its previous jurisprudence, formulating some other exceptions on the basis of Article 24 of the Constitution (the right to defense).[9] The admissibility of third-party interventions thus responds to the need to correct possible mistakes in the proceedings or gaps in the legal system which would prevent a person from protecting his/her relevant right. The Court indicated that, pursuant to Article 24 of the Constitution, a right holder whose right could be affected by the constitutionality judgment must be allowed to present his/her reasons and to defend such rights in the constitutional proceedings.[10]

In a subsequent decision issued that same year, the Court confirmed the rule on the inadmissibility of interventions, but it also identified the three possible exceptions recognized until then which were grounded in the right to defense.[11] Despite this decision, the following year the Court started to admit some third-party interventions filed by professional orders and other groups. The Court admitted these interventions on the basis of interests other than those previously enumerated. In the meantime, though, it rejected applications for intervention submitted by a number of interest groups and advocacy groups, especially trade unions and civil rights groups.

---

[6] See critically on this phase, M. D'Amico, *Parti e processo nella giustizia costituzionale*, Turin, Giappichelli Editore, 1991.

[7] Judgment 20/1982.

[8] Judgment 1/1984.

[9] Judgments 429/1991 and 314/1992.

[10] Judgment 314/1992.

[11] See the three exceptions listed in the Judgment 315/1992: "a) A matter is raised whose resolution is relevant for determining the possibility, for the subject who petitioned to intervene in the constitutional proceedings, to intervene in these proceedings; b) the legitimacy to intervene in the constitutional review proceedings arises from the order referring the case to the Constitutional Court, through which the Court itself raised an issue of constitutionality before itself (on its own motion); c) the right held by the subject, even if formally extraneous to the precautionary proceedings, is directly connected to the substantive relationship upon which – should the referring judge actually raise the issue of constitutionality – a possible declaration of unconstitutionality would exert a direct influence and would cause an irreparable harm to the right that was exercised".

This fluctuating case-law has been widely criticized by scholars who seek greater clarity in the eligibility criteria for third-party interventions.[12]

In order to address those critics, in 2004 the Court amended the S.P., explicitly recognizing the possibility of third-parties intervention in Article 4, paragraph 3, according to which "possible interventions of other [other than the President of the Council of Ministers or the President of the Region] subjects, firm the competence of the Court to decide on their admissibility, must take place with the same formalities".

Therefore, the reform did not introduce any procedural rules, and it refrained from establishing any admissibility criteria. As before, the decision on the admissibility of the intervention was made by the Court in the very moment of the substantive decision, by the way of an order published as an annex to the judgement and it remained fully discretional.

Far from ending the debate, the recognizance of third-party interventions in the S.P. actually rekindled it. The jurisprudential approach following the reform continued to generate issues. This was reinforced by the fact that the Court did not amend the rules on interventions when the new S.P. were adopted in 2008.

4.2. Third-parties and *amici curiae*: case-law and scholarly debate

The reform of Art. 4 S.P. has been defined as "an empty shell",[13] as it neither improves nor clarifies the legal framework concerning interventions. Actually, this reform did not bring any consequences for the praetorian approach to third-party interventions: as the Court explains, "the admissibility of interventions [...] has not been affected by the amendments to the Supplementary Provisions in 2004".[14]

Those waiting for a more transparent approach to the interventions following the modification of Art. 4 have been disappointed,[15] since neither the number of interventions filed nor the number of interventions admitted

---

[12] See for example the debate on "*Il contraddittorio nei giudizi davanti alla Corte*" retranscripted in A. Pizzorusso, R. Romboli (eds.), *Le norme integrative per i giudizi innanzi alla Corte costituzionale dopo quasi mezzo secolo di applicazione*, *op.cit.*, 302 ff.

[13] A. Pugiotto, *Sul crocifisso la Corte costituzionale pronuncia un'ordinanza pilatesca*, in *Diritto&Giustizia*, No. 3, 80 (2005).

[14] Ord. June, 21st 2005, joint to Judgment 345/2005.

[15] See P. Carozza, R. Romboli, E. Rossi, *I limiti all'accesso al giudizio sulle leggi e le prospettive per il loro superamento*, in R. Romboli (eds.), *L'accesso alla giustizia costituzionale: caratteri, limiti, prospettive di un modello*, Naples, Jovene Editore, 2006, 738.

has increased.[16] Despite the small number of interventions admitted, the debate on third-party intervention requests is not without interest.

In light of the practice implemented before the Court, as seen through the lens of comparative law, two types of interventions can actually be distinguished.

On the basis of the interest to intervene and the scope of the intervention, scholars have distinguished between a "third-party intervention" in the strict sense, based on a personal interest, and "interest group interventions", based on a collective interest, often called "*amicus curiae* briefs". Even if the latter is not regulated under the Italian legislative framework and the constitutional jurisprudence, one may argue that it exists in practice. In fact, despite their inadmissibility, some kinds of interventions continue to be filed with the Court.

Therefore, we will first examine the case-law on third-party interventions, as established after the reform of the S.P.; then, we will focus on the academic debate concerning a particular type of third-party intervention that could be classified under the definition of "*amicus curiae*".

4.2.1. The established case-law on third-party interventions

The "intervention" mentioned by Art. 4 S.P. is reserved for "third-parties holding a special interest directly concerned with the *principaliter* case and thus susceptible to be directly and immediately affected by the judgment".[17]

However, the Constitutional Court constantly rejects instances of intervention from third-parties who are parties in a proceeding similar to the *principaliter* proceeding, even if their litigation has been suspended in order to wait for the decision on the constitutionality. A well-established case-law declares these interventions inadmissible "because the opposite solution would represent a substantial suppression of the *incidenter* character of the constitutional review" as it would allow access to the parties of another proceeding "without previous assessment of the relevance (it. *rilevanza*) and not manifestly unfounded character (it. "*non manifesta infondatezza*") of the issue of constitutionality".[18] For the same reasons, constitutional jud-

---

[16] See R. ROMBOLI, *Aggiornamenti in tema di processo costituzionale (2005-2007)*, Turin, Giappichelli Editore, 2008, 96 ff.; R. ROMBOLI, *Aggiornamenti (2008-2010)*, Turin, Giappichelli Editore, 2011, 97 ff.

[17] See among others: ord. attached to Judgment 2/2016.

[18] These are the two conditions that must be met in order for the referring judge to legitimately be able to raise the question of constitutionality. See, among others: Judgments 32/2013; 71/2015; ord. July 5th, 2016 attached to Judgment 173/2016.

ges have also rejected interventions submitted by third-parties who intervened in the *principaliter* proceeding after the referral of the question of constitutionality, with the clear aim of participating in the *incidenter* proceeding.[19]

Exceptionally, the Court recognizes the right to intervene for those third-parties whose interest is grounded on the general effects of the constitutional review decision, but only if this would specifically and directly affect them.[20]

Besides this exception, the Court constantly rejects those interventions from third-parties whose interest is based on the general effects of the constitutionality judgment because this would be founded on merely factual interests. The range of groups whose interventions have been rejected includes professional orders[21] and trade unions,[22] professional representative groups,[23] civil rights groups,[24] and other advocacy groups defending the rights of their members.[25]

Their representative role and their engagement to defend the collective interests of a category of people are not taken into account: whenever these groups try to intervene in the defense of a collective interest, the Court rejects their interventions because "they do not hold a legal interest that could be immediately and irreparably affected by the judgment".[26]

Interest groups' and advocacy groups' interventions are thus subject to the same eligibility criteria as any other third-party intervention, namely those filed by individuals or legal persons in defense of their personal rights.

For the Court, the only interest to intervene that deserves to be taken into account derives from the right to defense and, therefore, is linked to the protection of a specific right that could be directly affected by the deci-

---

[19] See, among others: ord. February 24, 2015, attached to Judgment 37/2015; ord. no. 24/2015, attached to Judgment 236/2015. However, recently see Judgment 124/2017; 106/2019.

[20] Judgments 237/2013; 178/2015; 200/2015; 115/2016; 180/2018.

[21] Judgments 352/2006; 43/2009; 272/2012; 156/2013; 237/2013.

[22] See among others Judgment 159/2019; 173/2019.

[23] Judgments 279/2006; 411/2006; 414/2007; 76/2008; 96/2008; 94/2009; 312/2010; 118/2011; 119/2012; 59/2013; 85/2013; 116/2013; 134/2013; 231/2013; 178/2015; 187/2016; 195/2016; 206/2016; 214/2016; 220/2016; 227/2016; 16/2017; 144/2019; 213/2019.

[24] Judgments 369/2006; 151/2009; 214/2009; 138/2010; 150/2012; 85/2013; 162/2014; 170/2014; 221/2015; 2/2016; 76/2016;84/2016; 194/2016; 286/2016; 275/2017; 50/2019; 141/2019.

[25] Judgments 293/2011; 296/2012; 220/2014; 2/2016.

[26] Judgments 411/2006; 76/2016.

sion. Hence, the Court does not consider interventions for the protection of other rights and interests that could be impaired by the broader effects of the constitutional review.

Despite this well-established case-law which refuses to admit any intervention on behalf of interest and advocacy groups, these groups continue to file third-party briefs with the Court when the rights they represent are at stake. These interventions constitute a practice that deserves to be examined and that reiterates the longstanding question concerning the introduction of *amicus curiae* procedures.

4.2.2. The scholarly debate on *amici curiae* briefs

Originally developed in the common law,[27] the term "*amicus curiae*" defines a subject who is not a party to the litigation. The subject, an individual or a group, volunteers or is invited by the court to give expertise on some matter(s) concerning the case. While this was the original role of an '*amicus curiae*,' today the notion refers to the voluntary filing of briefs concerning some facts or questions of the pending case. In many proceedings before national, international or constitutional courts, it thus allows some form of participation to the proceedings for third-parties, even if, through the submission of an *amicus curiae* brief, the third-party does not become technically a party to the proceedings.

Despite the fact that *amicus curiae* interventions are not allowed before the Italian Constitutional Court, it is worth noting that a form of *amicus curiae* procedure seems to exist, at least informally; on the other hand, scholars continue to suggest the introduction of a formal procedure for submitting *amicus curiae* briefs.

Even if briefs submitted by third-parties in defense of the collective interests affected by the decision are formally rejected, third-parties are still allowed to access the proceeding for a while. The procedure concerning the submission of third-parties' observations actually leaves some space for them to be taken into account. In fact, briefs submitted by third-parties include their observations both on the admissibility of their intervention and on the matter pending before the Court (i.e. the constitutionality or unconstitutionality of the provision at stake). Therefore, until the intervention is

[27] *Bouvier's Law Dictionary* indicates that "*amicus* cannot be traced in its origin, but it is immemorial in the English Law". Some studies traced its foundations back to Roman Law, but experts in the fields question this conclusion: see L. CREMA, *Tracking the Origins and Testing the Fairness of the Instruments of Fairness: Amici Curiae in International Litigation*, in *Jean Monnet Working Papers*, No. 9, 1 (2012), 6.

declared inadmissible, the conclusions written in the brief can be read and informally taken into account, even if the subject who drafted such brief does not acquire any formal procedural status.

This means that even rejected interventions can serve as information sources, despite their formal non-admission.[28] The Court, in the part reserved for the factual considerations within the motivation of its judgment, refers to arguments submitted by third-parties even if, because those interventions have been rejected, those arguments are not recalled in the legal reasoning founding the decision. Arguably, third-parties' conclusions are sometimes taken into account even more than it would appear as the Court's assessment implicitly recalls some arguments submitted by third-parties.

Current Constitutional Court Justice Marta Cartabia appeared to confirm that third-party arguments receive some attention, despite their formal inadmissibility. In a recent article, she recalls that the Italian Constitutional Court, unlike several foreign courts, cannot receive studies and research from experts as *amicus curiae*. However, she points out that actually the Court cannot *officially* receive this kind of informative contribution, as "third-parties briefs cannot be files to the records, which means that they can neither be part of the official records or be discussed at the public hearing".[29]

Third-party briefs submitted by interest and advocacy groups can thus be *unofficially* taken into account in the proceeding, even if their author is not admitted to participate as an intervener.

Since the institutionalization of third-party interventions in the S.P. in 2004, interest or advocacy groups, interested by the general effects of the judgment, submitted almost half of the overall intervention requests received by the Court.[30] The fact that the Court receives those interventions only in a small number of cases compared to the total number of judgments issued, then, does not preclude the conclusion that third-parties are significantly interested in intervening. This is actually a result of the progressive concretization of the Italian constitutional review, so the Court often deals with very specific and precise questions of constitutionality which do not

---

[28] See A. Cerri, *Azione, difesa e partecipazione nel giudizio incidentale, nei conflitti e in alcune recenti proposte di riforma,* in AA.VV., *Giudizio "a quo" e promovimento del processo costituzionale*, Milan, Giuffré Editore, 1991, 257; P. Bianchi, *Dal «processo senza parti» alla «rappresentanza processuale degli interessi»,* in *Giur. Cost.* (1994), 3045 ff.

[29] M. Cartabia, *Qualche riflessione di un giudice costituzionale intorno al problema dell'intreccio tra diritto, scienza e tecnologia*, in *BioLaw Journal – Rivista di BioDiritto*, No.1, 9 (2017), 11.

[30] See A.M. Lecis Cocco Ortu, *Les interventions des tiers porteurs d'intérêts collectifs dans les contentieux constitutionnels incidents français et italien*, Paris, LGDJ, 2018, 302 ff. and the tables of cases.

attract great attention to their general effects. However, every time the Court considers a general issue concerning some provisions whose possible declaration of unconstitutionality would affect a large number of persons, and whenever an ethical issue or a public interest question is discussed, interest or advocacy groups regularly submit interventions.[31]

Interestingly enough, the Court's closure towards third-party interventions filed for the protection of a collective interest did not have the effect of discouraging such parties from filing an application for intervention. Conversely, the diffusion of "strategic litigation" practices and the growing attention towards lobbying initiatives targeting the judiciary seem to have inverted the trend: in fact, while interest and advocacy groups' interventions represented a minority until 2008,[32] in the last decade they have become the majority of the overall third-party interventions.[33]

Some scholars have questioned the Court's established closed approach, especially towards collective interest interventions. Essentially, they have been voicing three critiques.

First, they criticize the fact that the scope and meaning of the interventions provided in Art. 4 S.P. are not clearly identified. Scholars further point out that the Court gave up the opportunity to clarify them when the new Supplementary Provisions were adopted in 2008, especially with regard to their possible contribution on fact-finding.[34]

Secondly, they regret the closure towards collective interest interventions.[35] Some have argued that the Constitutional Court should adjust the

---

[31] See for example the questions of constitutionality concerning: in vitro fertilization (Judgments 151/2009; 150/2012; 162/2014), same-sex marriage (Judgments 138/2010; 76/2016), electoral law (Judgment 35/2017).

[32] They represented, at best, one-forth or one-third of the total amount of third-parties interventions per year: A.M. Lecis Cocco Ortu, *Les interventions des tiers porteurs d'intérêts collectifs dans les contentieux constitutionnels incidents français et italien, ibidem*.

[33] *Ibidem*.

[34] Recently M. D'Amico, *La Corte costituzionale e i fatti: istruttoria ed effetti delle decisioni*, in *Rivista del Gruppo di Pisa*, No. 1, 1 (2017), 2.

[35] See especially L. D'ANDREA, *L'intervento dei terzi interessati e la tutela di interessi pubblici, collettivi e diffusi nel giudizio incidentale*, in V. ANGIOLINI (eds.), *Il contraddittorio nel giudizio sulle leggi*, Turin, Giappichelli Editore, 1998, 87 ff.; A. RUGGERI, *In tema di contraddittorio e processo costituzionale, ovvero del "pluralismo" nei giudizi sulle leggi quale condizione della "costituzionalità" del processo*, in V. ANGIOLINI (eds.), *Il contraddittorio nel giudizio sulle leggi, op.cit.*, 555 and Id., *Note minime in materia di «accesso» ai giudizi di costituzionalità (dal punto di vista del rapporto tra Costituzione e politica ed avuto particolare riguardo all'oggetto ed agli effetti delle decisioni della Corte*, in A. Anzon, P. Caretti, S. Grassi (eds.), *Prospettive di accesso alla giustizia costituzionale*, Turin, Giappichelli Editore, 2000, 644; A.M. LECIS COCCO ORTU, *L'intervento del terzo*

debate in the *incidenter* proceedings to allow information and arguments that are useful to the interpretation of both the provision at stake and the constitutional norm allegedly violated. Arguments presented in favor of the opportunity to admit collective interest interventions filed by groups reflect the need of a more dialogical system of constitutional review. In fact, some authors advocate for group intervention in order to "democratize" constitutional review proceedings.[36] Some scholars outline the representative function that third-parties may perform in the proceedings, a function that may become essential when the Court balances rights and interests at stake.[37] Others emphasize the argumentative contribution of third parties,[38] which can answer the need for information on the legislative facts regarding the context in which the rule is applied. The different arguments in favor of third-party interventions filed by groups, then, converge in recognizing that these interventions can contribute to reinforcing the Court's legitimacy through a more open and dialogical approach in constitutional interpretation.

Thirdly, scholars have proposed the introduction of two different types of third-party participation: a true third-party intervention and the *amicus curiae*. Through this distinction, the Court would be able to admit various third-party briefs on the grounds of the usefulness of their contribution,

---

portatore di interessi collettivi nel giudizio incidentale, tra funzione collaborativa e legittimazione del giudice costituzionale. Una comparazione tra Italia e Francia, in *DPCE* 347 (2013).

[36] A. Ruggeri, *In tema di contraddittorio e processo costituzionale, ovvero del "pluralismo" nei giudizi sulle leggi quale condizione della "costituzionalità" del processo*, *op.cit.*; L. D'Andrea, *L'intervento dei terzi interessati e la tutela di interessi pubblici, collettivi e diffusi nel giudizio incidentale*, *op.cit.*, 1998.

[37] P. Bianchi, *Dal «processo senza parti» alla «rappresentanza processuale degli interessi»*, *op. cit.,* 3045; M. Bignami, *L'Ordine dei medici 'espugna' il processo costituzionale*, in *Giur. Cost.* (1995), 1293; L. D'Andrea, *Verso una democratizzazione del contraddittorio nel giudizio costituzionale incidentale*, in *Giur. cost.* (1994), 559 ff.; R. Romboli, *L'intervento nel processo costituzionale incidentale: finalmente verso un'apertura del contraddittorio?*, in *Giur. cost.* (1992), 2605.

[38] A. Cerri, *Azione, difesa e partecipazione nel giudizio incidentale, nei conflitti e in alcune recenti proposte di riforma*, *op.cit.* and A. Cerri, *Corso di giustizia costituzionale*, V ed., Milan, Giuffré Editore, 2007, 227; F. Caporilli, P.P. Sabatelli, M.G. Sbrana, *Il contraddittorio nei giudizi in via incidentale e principale*, in A. Pizzorusso, R. Romboli (eds.), *Le norme integrative per i giudizi innanzi alla Corte costituzionale dopo quasi mezzo secolo di applicazione*, 75; M. D'Amico, *La Corte costituzionale e i fatti: istruttoria ed effetti delle decisioni*, *op.cit.*; A.M. Lecis Cocco Ortu, *L'intervento del terzo portatore di interessi collettivi nel giudizio incidentale, tra funzione collaborativa e legittimazione del giudice costituzionale. Una comparazione tra Italia e Francia*, *op. cit.* and A.M. Lecis Cocco Ortu, *Les interventions des tiers porteurs d'intérêts collectifs dans les contentieux constitutionnels incidents français et italien*, *op. cit.*; M. Vicario, *I fatti nel giudizio incidentale di legittimità costituzionale*, in *Rivista del Gruppo di Pisa*, No. 3, (2017).

while still protecting the role of parties participating in the defense of their own rights. The third-party intervention would be reserved for third parties possessing a right that can be affected by the decision, while the *amicus curiae* brief would be reserved for groups or public establishments whose interest to intervene lies in the general effects of the decision on the rights and interests they represent.[39]

The Court, therefore, should admit interventions fitting the first channel in order to protect the right to defense. As for the latter, the Court could decide to admit it in order to acquire useful arguments and information on the issue at stake. This distinction would permit the Court to find a balance between the advantages and disadvantages of *amicus curiae*, submitting the two types of intervention to different procedural rules. In order to avoid an excessive workload for the Court and a consequent decrease in efficiency, some scholars suggested excluding *amicus curiae* from participating in the hearing[40] or allowing them to participate only as long as they present new arguments.[41]

All the propositions made by scholars have been, to date, ignored by the Court, which has reiterated its well-established jurisprudence on third-party admissibility criteria.

In short, third-party intervention, as it is currently conceived by the Court, does not constitute a formal interaction with groups and civil society nor does it formally represent a fact-finding instrument. Information on facts are acquired by the Court through its formal or informal use of its fact-finding powers.

4.3. Case law and scholarly debate on fact-finding

The relevance of legislative facts or other non-legal arguments for the judicial review of legislation is fully recognized by Italian scholars, dating at least as far back as the seventies.[42]

---

[39] A. CONCARO, M. D'AMICO, *Proposte di modifica delle norme integrative*, in A. PIZZORUSSO, R. ROMBOLI (eds.), *Le norme integrative per i giudizi innanzi alla Corte costituzionale dopo quasi mezzo secolo di applicazione*, *op.cit.*, 454 ff. especially 460. See also A.M. LECIS COCCO ORTU, *Les interventions des tiers porteurs d'intérêts collectifs dans les contentieux constitutionnels incidents français et italien*, *op.cit.*

[40] A. CONCARO, M. D'AMICO, *Proposte di modifica delle norme integrative*, *op.cit.* See also G. COINU, A. DEFFENU, *Altri aspetti procedurali*, in *Proposte di modifica delle norme integrative*, in A. PIZZORUSSO, R. ROMBOLI (eds.), *Le norme integrative per i giudizi innanzi alla Corte costituzionale dopo quasi mezzo secolo di applicazione*, *op. cit.*, 236 ff.

[41] A. CERRI, *Corso di giustizia costituzionale*, *op.cit.*, 226-227.

[42] See among the first contributions on the topic, A. BALDASSARRE, *I poteri conosciti-*

Scholars tried to categorize those arguments and the role they play in constitutional review. Several categories of facts (natural, social, economic, scientific, political, administrative) have been examined,[43] as well as several aspects of the constitutional adjudication that they can affect (the standard of review, the object, the typology of the decision, etc.).[44]

Special attention was given to scientific facts due to the growing number of cases affecting life sciences and thus involving new technologies, medicine, and bioethics.[45] The emphasis on scientific facts was also due to increased legislative activity in those fields. For example, in the last decade, the Court has been called upon several times to review the constitutionality of the assisted reproduction law: in these decisions, the lack of a transparent scientific expertise has been highly criticized.[46]

The economic consequences and financial obligations that may arise from Constitutional Court decisions have also attracted the attention of scholars. Although the majority of commentators, and the Constitutional Court itself, have pointed out that the constitutional rules on a balanced budget[47] are not applicable to judicial decisions, the prevalent interpretation still allows the Court, in deciding on constitutional challenges, to take

---

vi della Corte costituzionale e il sindacato di legittimità astratto, in *Giur. Cost.* (1973), 1497 ff.; A. CERRI, *I poteri istruttori della Corte costituzionale nei giudizi sulle leggi e sui conflitti*, in *Giur. Cost.* (1978), 1335 ff.; M. CHIAVARIO, *Ordinanze interlocutorie della Corte costituzionale nei giudizi di legittimità promossi in via incidentale*, in *Scritti in onore di Crisafulli*, Milan, Giuffré Editore, 1986, I, 232 ff.; M. LUCIANI, *I fatti e la Corte: sugli accertamenti istruttori del giudice costituzionale nei giudizi sulle leggi*, in AA.VV., *Strumenti e tecniche di giudizio della Corte costituzionale* Milan, Giuffré Editore, 1988, 521 ff.; G. BRUNELLI, A. PUGIOTTO, *Appunti per un diritto probatorio nel processo costituzionale: la centralità del "fatto" nelle decisioni della Corte*, in AA.VV., *Annali dell'Università di Ferrara*, 1995, 185 ff.

[43] M. AINIS, *Sul rilievo dei «fatti» nel giudizio di legittimità costituzionale. Appunti per una ricerca*, in AA.VV., *Studi in onore di Franco Modugno*, I, Naples, Editoriale scientifica, 2011, 2.

[44] G.A. FERRO, *Modelli processuali ed istruttoria nei giudizi di legittimità costituzionale*, Turin, Giappichelli Editore, 2012,153 ff.

[45] M. CARTABIA, *Qualche riflessione di un giudice costituzionale intorno al problema dell'intreccio tra diritto, scienza e tecnologia*, *op.cit.*, 12, according to which "of course, the Court is not blind to medical-scientific problems and procures documentation whenever necessary. However, it cannot be denied that the characteristics of current scientific research pose the problem of updating the procedural evidence available to the courts".

[46] Recently see A. IANNUZZI, *Istruttoria e valutazioni tecnico-scientifiche*, in *Rivista del Gruppo di Pisa*, No. 1, (2017).

[47] The balanced budget principle has been introduced in Articles 81, 97, 117 and 119 of the Italian Constitution by Constitutional Law no. 1/2012.

into account the financial consequences of its decisions. This raises the question of the adequacy of the tools the Court has to know the possible financial impact of its decisions. This issue has been deeply debated by scholars, especially in the context of the Great Recession.[48]

The Court itself refers to non-legal arguments in many decisions,[49] especially to assess the "reasonableness" (r*agionevolezza*) of a legislative provision (that is, to measure the proportionality of the regulation to the factual situation) or to assess in advance the impact of its decisions (especially in terms of financial impact). As a result of this assessment, the Court can decide which type of decision to adopt, taking into account the different consequences.

However, the factual arguments are formulated very generically, without any reference to the source of the information and without using the formal fact-finding provisions contained in the rules on Constitutional Court proceedings. The factual basis according to which the Court refers to the "situation of environmental emergency", to the "employment emergency", to the "loss of many thousands of jobs", or to the "macroeconomic impact of the repayment of taxes" (to quote a few examples) remains mysterious.

Sometimes, the Court relies on information provided by the parties. Nevertheless, the Court's rejection of third-party interventions and *amici curiae* prevents the Court from gathering information from a wider range of sources, and ultimately enhances the role of the government as the main provider of information to the Court.

As for its own *ex-officio* fact-finding, in the vast majority of cases the Court acquires facts or other non-legal arguments informally during the preliminary investigation carried out by the judge rapporteur and by his clerks.[50] The Court does not mention this activity in the text of the decision – not even in the "in fact" section. In order to formally regulate this infor-

---

[48] T. GROPPI, I. SPIGNO, N. VIZIOLI, *The Constitutional Consequences of the Financial Crisis in Italy*, in X. CONTIADES (eds.), *Global Financial Crisis and the Constitution. A Comparative Analysis*, Farnham, Ashgate, 2013, 89 ff.

[49] T. GROPPI, I. SPIGNO, *Constitutional Reasoning in the Italian Constitutional Court*, in A. JAKAB, A. DYEVRE, G. ITZCOVICH (eds.), *Comparative Constitutional Reasoning*, Cambridge, Cambridge University Press, 2017, 516 ff.

[50] See M. CARTABIA, *Qualche riflessione di un giudice costituzionale intorno al problema dell'intreccio tra diritto, scienza e tecnologia*, *op.cit.*, 12, according to which "[a]ctually, the in-depth preliminary studies that the clerks of the judge rapporteur conduct in relation to each case that is assigned to the judge include, in addition to all the relevant legal materials – laws, jurisprudence and academic literature – also relevant scientific and technical data".

mal activity, in 2004 (as we indicated above) the S.P. were amended to allow the documents acquired to be made available to the parties, but this rule does not seem to have had any impact on the use of arguments.

In 1994, the Court established, because of several very widely discussed financial decisions on "spending", a special section of the Court's Studies and Research Department to "investigate the cost of the decisions". This was clearly a step in the right direction, since it allowed the Court to assess the financial consequences of its decisions independently. This meant that the Court did not have to rely exclusively on the claims of the parties or on data provided by the government, which, in most cases, has a concrete stake in the dismissal of the case by the Court.[51] However, after just a few years, that office was abolished (in 2000), and today the Court, as it did before 1994, bases its decisions on information obtained through informal requests presented by the judge rapporteur to the public administration.

The Court has made use of its formal fact-finding powers, requiring a collegial deliberation and an evidence-gathering order, in very few cases.[52] The analysis of those cases does not show any coherence, with regard to both the circumstances that prompted the Court to start a formal fact-finding proceeding, the documents requested, and the recipients of the requests. The haphazard nature of the evidence-gathering orders has generated doubts, repeatedly raised by scholars, that these orders may likely be used by the Court in order to postpone complex decisions or to give notice to the legislature of a possible forthcoming declaration of unconstitutionality.

In addition, once the Court has received the information requested in the order, only rarely has it referred to the order and to the evidence gathered in the actual judgment addressing the question of constitutionality. It

---

[51] For further analysis *see* T. GROPPI, *La quantificazione degli oneri finanziari derivanti dalle decisioni della Corte costituzionale: profili organizzativi e conseguenze sul processo costituzionale*, in P. COSTANZO (eds.), *L'organizzazione e il funzionamento della Corte costituzionale*, Turin, Giappichelli Editore, 1995, 274 ff.

[52] See T. GROPPI, *I poteri istruttori della Corte costituzionale nel giudizio sulle leggi*, *op.cit.*, according to which, until 1996, the evidence-gathering orders were 55, up to 11,802 decisions of the Court. From 1987 the evidence-gathering orders are neither numbered nor published in the Official Journal (Gazzetta Ufficiale), unlike the other decisions of the Court. Therefore, they can be acceded only by filing a request to the Registry. Between 1997 and 2016, 38 orders were adopted, out of 8,268 decisions. In total, the evidence-gathering orders were 93. Only 68 were adopted in the judicial review of statutes. Among them, 47 were adopted in *incidenter* proceedings: M. NISITICÒ, *Le problematiche del potere istruttorio nelle competenze della Corte*, in *Rivista del Gruppo di Pisa*, No. 1, (2017). The Author underlines that the Court never adopted an evidence-gathering order in one of its leading cases. Our previously mentioned research fully supports this argument.

may happen that no reference to the order is made in the judgment, either in the "facts of the case" (*fatto*) or in the "conclusions on points of law" *(diritto)*. This makes it even more difficult to understand the role played by the formal fact-finding procedure.[53]

The reluctant attitude of the Court towards the use of its formal fact-finding powers, or, at least, towards a more transparent use of its informal powers, has been repeatedly criticized by scholars, who have underlined the political, more than judicial, behaviour of the Court.[54] The issue of a fair acquisition of the facts remains currently open for the Italian constitutional adjudication.

4.4. Conclusion

In conclusion, the Italian constitutional proceedings can be qualified – as far as the third – party interventions, the *amici curiae,* and the Court's fact-finding powers are concerned – as a formally "closed" form of constitutional adjudication.

This feature of the "Italian-style constitutional justice" is only determined in part by the rules on constitutional proceedings. It is mainly due to the attitude of the Court, developed over time through its case-law.

The Court prefers to avoid or minimize any formalized contact with interest groups and experts. It favors informal solutions that could enhance its discretion in the use of arguments, at the expense of transparency of the proceedings and of the reasoning.

Although some pragmatic concerns (like the risk of being overwhelmed by a large number of briefs or lengthening the duration of the proceedings, especially taking into account the public hearing) cannot be underestimated, the underlying reasons behind this attitude remain unclear.

Those reasons can be explored by considering other features – both normative and empirical – of the Italian system of constitutional justice, including: the prohibition of explicit quotation of scholarship; the fact that separate opinions are not allowed in judgments and that the personal views of individual judges are kept secret; the absence of explicit references to foreign precedents: a clear preference for domestic rather than supranational standards; the lack of a direct individual complaint mechanism as an avenue to trigger constitutional review.

---

[53] See M. TROISI, *Attività istruttoria, conseguenze finanziarie e modulazione degli effetti temporali delle decisioni*, in *Rivista del gruppo di Pisa*, No. 1, (2017).

[54] G.A. FERRO, *Modelli processuali ed istruttoria nei giudizi di legittimità costituzionale*, *op.cit.*, 300 ff.

All these distinctive features of the Italian Constitutional Court encourage an "unofficial (or informal) relationality". The attitude of the Court towards external contributions can be described as "Informal, Implicit, Indirect" (III attitude), in the sense that the Court acquires information on facts informally and reads the brief submitted informally, just as it does with scholarship, foreign case-law, and supranational courts decisions.

The picture that emerges is one of a court willing to keep some distance from society (from both facts and people), almost expressing a preference for relying on some mediation instances. This picture corresponds to the Italian model of judicial review as an indirect model (lacking a direct individual complaint), in which the Court turns primarily to ordinary judges, who are the main gatekeepers and implementing actors of its decisions.

If we consider that courts always talk to their "supposed" audience, we can understand why the Italian Constitutional Court adopts an approach to external contributions which is consistent with the tradition of civil law judges.

However, this approach is challenged oftener and oftener by the evolving attitude of ordinary judges themselves and by the Court's compelling need to preserve its legitimacy in an increasingly polarized political context.

In our view, the time has come for a "true" relational approach, which not only implies a positive and constructive dialogue, but it also requires accepting the challenge of confrontation in a more open and transparent manner. In conclusion, it is now time to move from the "triple I attitude" to the "FED (formal, explicit, direct) approach".

4.5. *Post Scriptum*: "The Court Opens to Hearing the Voice of Civil Society"

On January 11, 2020 a press release was posted on the web page of the Constitutional Court, titled "The Court Opens to Hearing the Voice of Civil Society", announcing that on January 8 the Court approved some amendments to the Supplementary Provisions. The amendments were published on the Official Journal some days later and then they entered into force. They completely changed the legal framework we discussed in our Chapter.

In particular, the new Article 4-*ter* introduces the great novelty of *amicus curiae* briefs in the Italian constitutional procedural law. It states that all non-profit social groups and all institutional bodies representing collective or diffuse interests relevant to the questions discussed can submit by email a brief (no more than 25,000 characters). The President, after consulting the judge rapporteur, may admit them, if he/she considers they offer useful information to understand and evaluate the case, given its complexity.

In addition, with regard to incidental proceedings, the Court amended Article 4, codifying the case-law we mentioned in our Chapter (para 4.2.1). The range of potential third-parties intervenors is extended – in addition to the parties to the case and the President of the Council of Ministers (and the President of the relevant Regional Council, if a regional law is concerned) – to other subjects provided that they have a valid and directly and immediately relevant interest in the decision. Prospective third-parties may, when appropriate, be also authorised to access the case files of the constitutional proceedings prior to the hearing before the Court, as stated by Article 4-*bis*.

The Court also amended Article 14-*bis* on facts-finding, introducing the possibility of calling renowned experts to the Court, when it deems it necessary to acquire information on specific areas of knowledge. The experts will be heard in chambers, in the presence of the parties to the case.

Those provisions represent an important step (we could say a real "revolution of openness and transparency") towards that "true" relational approach in constitutional adjudication we auspicated in our Chapter.

Chapter V

PROCEDURAL RULES AND THE CULTIVATION OF WELL-INFORMED AND RESPONSIVE CONSTITUTIONAL JUDICIARIES

Maartje De Visser

This chapter considers the ability of constitutional courts to obtain information held by persons or entities not involved in the litigation at hand, notably including extra-legal facts and arguments. It does so with the help of a comparative perspective, thereby making it the companion chapter of that written by Groppi and Lecis, who inquire into the approach adopted by the Italian Constitutional Court (ItCC) in this regard.

It would be easy to characterise inquiries along these lines as of interest primarily to those actually litigating cases before the ItCC or constitutional scholars with a strong legal-technical bend to their work. This would, however, be misguided. Understanding a court's willingness to accept submissions by those who are not a party to the proceedings and use extra-legal facts is important for at least two related reasons. First, it provides insights into a court's self-perception of its place within the constitutional order and the perceived propriety of engaging with civil society, experts, and public interests in the context of constitutional proceedings. Second, the approach vis-à-vis non-party interventions and extra-legal facts implicates the quality and accuracy of judgments for the court's audiences – their legitimacy, in other words.

These two rationales undergird the analysis presented in this chapter. I will begin by exploring the contribution that non-party interventions and other fact-finding endeavours can make to constitutional adjudication, while also identifying attendant risks and challenges. Assuming that there is value in allowing this type of input, I will next consider the procedural designs available to facilitate the participation of persons or entities that are not a party to the main proceedings and the collection of extra-legal facts from a comparative perspective. At the same time, a court's decision to make use of external sources in adjudicating a given constitutional issue is unlikely to be fully regulated let alone prescribed by its rules of procedure. This is also the case for the ItCC, which has shown itself reluctant to fetter its own discretion in this regard even as it has embarked on repeated reforms of its procedural regime. This chapter will accordingly end with some brief reflections on the methodological implications of this reality. My main argument is that judicial receptiveness to additional input beyond that provided by the litigants should no longer be seen as merely helpful, but rather as required to ensure that the court truly grasps the increasingly complex real-life context in which the legal issues before it manifests themselves. Its procedural framework should accordingly provide a clear basis to allow for the collection of materials that are relevant in this regard. This, I suggest, should ideally extend to measures that cultivate a court's internal ability to identify and make sense of extra-legal considerations. At the same time, insistence on a court's responsiveness to extra persons, entities and sources cannot be taken too far. Constitutional adjudication is designed for the peaceful resolution of the legal dimension of an intra-party dispute or controversy. Losing sight of this fundamental feature could transform the turn towards opening proceedings to other parties and considerations from a boon to a bane for the court's legitimacy.

5.1. Benefits, risks and challenges of 'open' constitutional adjudication

When thinking about why constitutional judges may, or even should, take into account arguments and information beyond those put forward by the main parties to the proceedings, two reasons readily present themselves. These are linked, respectively, to the nature of the text to be applied and the identity of its principal interpreter. On the one hand, constitutions differ from ordinary legislation in that they are more than a supreme, positive, binding law; they also purport to give expression to political, moral and philosophical aspirations. Compared to ordinary statutes, constitutions include more provisions couched in open-ended language that permit multiple interpretations not strictly determined by one's legal imagination. Limitation clauses of fundamental rights that refer to such notions as 'public interest',[1] 'public morality',[2] or 'public order or safety'[3] are a classic example. Sometimes the relative vagueness of constitutions reflects

[1] E.g. Dutch Constitution, Art 14; Czech Constitution, Art. 11(4).

[2] E.g. Italian Constitution, Arts. 19 and 21; Polish Constitution, Art. 45(2).

[3] E.g. German Basic Law, Art 13(4), Spanish Constitution, Section 16(1).

the drafters' inability to agree to more precise and prescriptive terminology. More often, it is a deliberate decision to give the constitution sufficient flexibility to speak to the myriad of existing and future social problems that it is expected to address.[4] It is by now trite that these increasingly involve technical or specialist questions that require knowledge of fields beyond the law such as biology, accounting, artificial intelligence, physics, or econometrics.

Even for problems that are not quite so scientific in nature, former justice of the German Federal Constitutional Court Hoffmann-Riem astutely cautioned that "In order to interpret and apply constitutional norms in a meaningful way, it is important to take into account empirical facts, historical experiences, prevailing paradigms, and the distribution of societal and political powers".[5] It cannot be assumed that those who have invoked the court's jurisdiction and their opponents will always canvass the full suite of "empirical and prescriptive premises".[6] They may fail to realise that the judgment in their case affects other constituencies that hold different views or concerns; and if they are conscious of such a broader impact, they may lack the resources or incentives to tailor their submissions accordingly.

Why should we be concerned about this? This brings us to the elusive notion of legitimacy. Hoffmann-Riem captures the essence of this point well when he remarks that "Constitutional provisions very often concern fields where various interests clash and political controversies arise. Therefore, it is important to attempt to ensure that the interpretation and the application of the norm are acceptable not only to the parties to a dispute, but also to the general public, to political and economic actors, to lawyers, and to the scholarly community".[7] If a court hands down judgments that are, or are perceived to be, out of tune with societal expectations or regu-

---

[4] Flexibility and generality have been identified as possible factors to boost a constitution's longevity: Z. ELKINS, T. GINSBURG, J. MELTON, *The Endurance of National Constitutions*, Cambridge, Cambridge University Press, 2009, 81-92.

[5] W. HOFFMANN-RIEM, *Constitutional Court Judges' Roundtable: Comparative Constitutionalism in Practice*, in 4 *International Journal of Constitutional Law* 556 (2005), 559.

[6] Ibid., 558.

[7] Ibid., 557. See also the fascinating account by Georg Vanberg on the influence of public support on the attitude of Germany's constitutional judges: G. VANBERG, *The Politics of Constitutional Review in Germany*, Cambridge, Cambridge University Press, 2005. One of those interviewed explained that "there cannot be a long-running divergence between the views of the public at large and the jurisprudence of the court. The court must be carried by a consensus of the citizens. … Every citizen has certain ideas about what the Basic Law is supposed to guarantee, and you can't depart too far from that. The decisions have to be understandable and acceptable".

larly misaligned with economic-political realities, it can lose the respect of its audiences who may decide not to give full effects to its rulings or ignore these altogether. Put differently, a court's authority is bolstered when it is seen as responsive to the wider context in which constitutions operate.

Yet, it is clear that real judges fall short, sometimes significantly, of the ideal Herculean model described by Dworkin: superhuman, omniscient adjudicators possessing infinite competence, intelligence and resourcefulness.[8] While Hercules would have had the internal knowledge to supplement any omissions in parties' submissions or correct any mistakes, real judges are likely to require assistance to approximate a complete understanding of the case and its likely ramifications. This is amongst others evident in the growing prevalence and acceptance of judges engaging with their foreign counterparts and case law to improve their understanding of the legal issues at stake.[9] This perspective is essentially based on a 'many minds argument': infusing multiple perspectives helps to expand the argumentative legal terrain.[10] This, it is hoped, should enable the court to produce 'better' decisions supported by more convincing reasoning. In a similar vein, the justification for a broad approach to the (non-legal) sources that feed into the judicial deliberative process ultimately boils down to the positive effect these can have for a court's legitimacy.

There is an important procedural dimension to the apparent value of and need for interventions by non-parties and extra-legal factors that we should be sensitive to. Courts with a constitutional mandate can be accessed through a variety of avenues, including for the purpose of querying the validity of statutes. Professors Groppi and Lecis analyse the ItCC's approach in the context of incidental review, a limitation that they justify by pointing to the fact that "it is the core of the Italian system of constitutional justice".[11] This procedure is also known as the preliminary reference procedure, and involves constitutional questions being identified and litigated during an ordinary lawsuit before a regular court. When the validity of the legislation to be applied is deemed dubious, this issue is certified to the

[8] R. DWORKIN, *Hard Cases*, in 88 *Harvard Law Review* 1057 (1975), 1083; R. DWORKIN, *Law's Empire*, Cambridge, Harvard University Press, 1986.

[9] Amongst many others, see T. GROPPI, M.C. PONTHOREAU (eds), *The Use of Foreign Precedents by Constitutional Judges*, Oxford, Hart Publishing, 2013; M. BOBEK, *Comparative Reasoning in European Supreme Courts*, Oxford, Oxford University Press, 2013.

[10] For versions of this argument, see e.g. A. VERMEULE, *Many-Minds Arguments in Legal Theory*, in 1 *Journal of Legal Analysis* 1 (2009); C. SUNSTEIN, *A Constitution of Many Minds*, Princeton, Princeton University Press, 2009.

[11] See T. GROPPI, A.M. LECIS COCCO ORTU, in this book.

constitutional court in recognition of its role as the country's authoritative interpreter of the constitution. The preliminary reference procedure is by no means unique to Italy. On the contrary, countries that subscribe to the centralised model of constitutional adjudication, usually provide for this access route. [12] At the same time, there can be other ways to get a court to review legislation for its constitutionality. Abstract challenges are a particularly popular alternative option. [13] As their name suggests, these do not require an actual case or controversy: they can, and often are, brought before the statute is promulgated or shortly thereafter.

Importantly, the various procedures to impugn a statute feature different types of parties and do not presume a single, uniform context for constitutional problems to rear their head. In evaluating the merits of inviting additional parties or soliciting more information, we should accordingly be clear about the identity of the parties directly involved in the proceedings and the considerations they can be expected to advance. In other words: what interests will they represent that may need to be counter-balanced, supplemented or contextualised by other views?

Under the preliminary reference procedure, a central role is played by regular judges and private parties. The former are officially the constitutional court's interlocutors and act as gatekeeper by deciding *when* to certify the constitutional issue and *how* the challenge to the statute's validity is formulated, thereby shaping the parameters of the inquiry. The regulatory framework governing the initiation of preliminary reference proceedings typically does not specify at what point the constitutional court must be engaged. [14] The only logical prerequisite is that this must happen before the regular judge hands down her judgment. It is, however, commonly required that the regular judge must have real concerns about the constitutionality of the legal norm or that the constitutional question is a serious one. [15] This makes it prudent to only make the referral once the proceedings are quite advanced and detailed submissions have been made on this

---

[12] Within the EU Member States, this includes Austria, Belgium, Bulgaria, Croatia, the Czech Republic, France, Germany, Hungary, Latvia, Lithuania, Luxembourg, Poland, Romania, Slovakia, Slovenia and Spain.

[13] For a more detailed discussion, see M. DE VISSER, *Constitutional Review in Europe – A Comparative Analysis*, Oxford, Hart Publishing, 2013, 99-128.

[14] But see Organic Law 2/1979 on the Spanish Constitutional Tribunal, Art 35(2) ("The judicial body may raise the question only on completion of the proceedings and within the prescribed deadline for delivering its judgment").

[15] This is the case, amongst others, in Spain (Organic Law 6/1985 on the Judiciary, Art 5(3); Germany (Law on the German Federal Constitutional Court, §80(2) and BVerfG, 2 BvL 3/02 (2009)) and France (Ordinance no 58-1067 on the French Constitutional Council (as amended), ss 23-2 and 23-4).

point. In cases that call for the use of experts, it would be sensible to wait until they have been consulted so that their views can be taken into account and reflected in the file that will accompany the reference. In such situations, there would be less of a need for the constitutional court to also use its own power (where this exists) to appoint experts.

In addition, the focus of preliminary questions will be on the manner in which a statute is applied to identified persons or entities. In their submissions, the parties will accordingly place the alleged constitutional defect within its social, real-world context rather than emphasise considerations of political desirability or abstract points of a legal-theoretical nature. The setting of an ordinary dispute further increases the likelihood of there being specific individuals or corporate entities who are not a party to the proceedings, but whose rights or interests may be affected by the judgment. These are third parties in the way the term is understood in typical private or administrative adjudication. To the extent that the (civil, criminal or administrative) procedural framework governing the main dispute allows such parties to make representations to the deciding regular judge, it would seem both logical and fair to extend their right to do so to the constitutional portion of the proceedings.

It should be noted here that the government is not systematically a party to preliminary reference cases, as many of these will involve two (or more) private individuals or corporations. In these situations, there are, however, good reasons for a constitutional court to invite the government and other public institutions to make representations. The government's role in the preparation of the statute under scrutiny means that it has a unique understanding of the impetus for the statute's adoption, the mischief it is intended to address, and the political and financial considerations that explain why solution A rather than solutions B through E was chosen. Furthermore, if the regime on *locus standi* before the regular courts is generous, cause lawyers and interest groups can strategically use litigation to mount constitutional challenges and in so doing, vindicate the interests of certain segments of society. They will, naturally, champion these particularistic concerns in their presentation of the issue. As Owen Fiss has pointed out, using the example of entitlements to welfare benefits in the US context, "the Court's perspective must be systematic, not anecdotal: The Court should focus not on the plight of four or five or even twenty families but should consider the welfare system as a whole – a complex network embracing millions of people and a host of bureaucratic and political institutions".[16] Extending a right to be heard to the government and other stake-

[16] O. Fiss, *The Law as It Could Be*, New York, New York University Press, 2003, 218-219.

holders with a public mandate ensures that the constitutional judges adjudicating preliminary reference questions remain attentive to the larger picture and are not swayed too easily by the dramatic circumstances of a specific case.

In contrast, abstract constitutionality challenges are usually brought by a range of public institutions, such as the (federal and federated) government(s), a qualified parliamentary minority or the prosecutor general. The government will always be involved, either initiating the constitutional litigation or defending the statute's validity against an attack mounted by another State organ. The dominant role of public institutions means that submissions in the course of abstract review proceedings will be coloured by party concerns and political beliefs. They can be expected to refer to the generalised, empirical, non-legal data that has been collected in support of the statute as it made its way through the legislative process. Put differently, abstract constitutionality challenges are not designed to draw the court's attention to the social circumstances in which legislation operates and the impact it has on the lives of individuals in the same way that preliminary reference procedures are. This is all the more so when countries allow such challenges to be filed *a priori*, so before the statute is promulgated and can generate effects 'on the ground', as is possible in France, Hungary and Poland. Matters are admittedly somewhat different in countries that allow institutions with a clear public interest function to trigger abstract review, such as the Ombudsman (e.g. Spain, Portugal, Hungary) or trade unions and professional associations (e.g. Poland, Slovenia).

It should further be remembered that most constitutional courts carry out functions other than keeping the legislature in check by verifying the constitutionality of statutes. Their additional powers can range from resolving competence disputes between different echelons or branches of the State to ruling on the impeachment of key officials to supervising the integrity of elections to deciding to ban political parties. [17]

In short, the different tasks involve different types of parties to the dispute, different kinds of constitutional questions, and different constitutional provisions that are likely to take centre stage. To concretise: when a court is asked to rule that the central level has encroached upon the powers of the subnational entity, the matter will be litigated by the federal and relevant federated executives, who will argue their claim on and provide evidence pertaining to the requirements of the constitution's vertical competence catalogue, rather than say, the bill of rights which in contrast tends to feature prominently in constitutional complaint proceedings or preliminary

[17] A good overview is offered by T. GINSBURG, Z. ELKINS, *Ancillary Powers of Constitutional Courts*, in 87 *Texas Law Review* 1431 (2008).

reference questions.[18] The assumption will be that individuals or groups representing a collective interest have no obvious role to play in the context of such competence allocation litigation. In the same way, their participation would not be expected to make a helpful contribution to the judicial deliberations when a court is asked to determine that the president has forfeited her office due to unbecoming conduct. Relatedly, the information needed to decide whether the president has engaged in 'high treason' (e.g. Italy, Czech Republic) is of a qualitatively different nature than that required to determine whether someone has been validly elected to parliament (e.g. Germany, France). The implication that the reality of the multi-purpose court has for the procedural regime for extrinsic submissions and extra-legal considerations should be clear: those studying this dimension of constitutional adjudication should neither expect nor encourage a one-size-fits-all framework.

Finally, we should be mindful of the possible risks attendant on opening constitutional proceedings to a wide spectrum of parties and insights. First, the court will need resources to work through the additional submissions and information. This may require it to hire more supporting personnel if its budget would allow for this or, more likely, re-allocate existing staff to the possible detriment of the court's other needs. The judges will need to set aside more time to study the supplementary briefs and materials, which probably means a longer interval between submissions and hearings and the delivery of the judgment. Those having prepared the interventions would also expect the court to engage with the argument and data put forward therein. When the court heeds such expectations, the length of decisions will increase and so does the workload of those in charge of editing and translating (again: a resource issue); when it would not, the social acceptability of its decisions could suffer.

Second, the court might be 'captured', or perceived to be, by certain groups or interests. This connotes the situation in which entities or collectives whose concerns may be affected, but not directly determined by the judgment can make submissions during the adjudication of a constitutional issue with general societal relevance. Although the possibility to intervene will typically be open to all constituencies with a potential interest in the matter, we cannot assume that each and every one of these will do so or do so effectively.[19] Yet again, this is a question of resources, combined with

---

[18] In France, the rules governing this procedure even explicitly limit the grounds of review that can be used to challenge statutes through the preliminary question mechanism to those parts of the *bloc de constitutionnalité* that guarantee fundamental rights and liberties.

[19] Cf. K.J. LYNCH, *Best Friends? Supreme Court Law Clerks on Effective Amicus Cu-*

variations in the degree of institutionalised representation of interests. Corporations, for instance, have sufficiently deep pockets to prepare high-quality interventions in all cases that may impact the business environment. Moreover, they are typically united in industry associations which allows them to more effectively convey their concerns and preferences to different State organs – the courts included. Likewise, professions such as accountants, doctors, lawyers and the like are regulated in most countries. This means that there will be a national association that can claim the mandate to speak with a single voice on behalf of these practitioners and which moreover will have developed considerable experience in doing so.[20]

This may be different for more vulnerable constituencies like consumers, migrants, or minorities. Their rights are often championed by a multitude of smaller advocacy groups whose focus and arguments need not point in the same direction. Their budgets are often smaller as well, consisting mainly of voluntary donations rather than compulsory membership fees. Thus, the external submissions that the court receives may not cover the full spectrum of views on the constitutional issue before it or exhibit the same level of internal cohesion and calibre in the way arguments are presented.

To be fair, the common requirement that would-be interveners need the court's permission before filing briefs (more on this below) is intended to attenuate the resultant risk of judges unintentionally or unconsciously privileging certain interpretations of the general interest over others.[21] Having said that, this requirement cannot satisfactorily address the point about the cogency and persuasiveness of submissions by auxiliary parties. Furthermore, there is nothing to prevent advocacy groups and other interested constituencies from sending in unsolicited briefs despite not having received judicial permission to do so.

5.2. Designing for participation-friendly constitutional litigation and well-rounded judicial deliberations

There is, I suspect, no contemporary constitutional or supreme court whose

riae Briefs, in 20 *Journal of Law & Politics* 33 (2004), 46 ("One of the dominant themes to emerge from the interviews is that close consideration of amicus briefs is highly dependent on quality").

[20] Ibid., 50-51 ("Sixteen per cent of clerks specifically cited the briefs of the American Medical Association, the American Psychological Association, and American Bar Association as consistently trustworthy").

[21] See e.g. UK Supreme Court Practice Directions, Rule 8.8.1; Rules of the Canadian Supreme Court, Rule 55; US Supreme Court, Rule 37(2).

procedural regime completely forecloses the use of outside assistance. Rather, there is a sliding scale in the extent of openness to interventions by auxiliary parties and the degree to which the collection of non-legal information is explicitly catered for. Space constraints prevent a detailed *tour d'horizon* of practices elsewhere. My aim here is simply to place the criticism directed at the ItCC's approach in the Italian discourse, notably that the court's proceedings are not sufficiently receptive to input from outside parties or sources within a broader frame. In so doing, it will become apparent that its attitude is arguably not as uncommon, and perhaps not as problematic as it is sometimes made out to be.

Taken at its broadest level, the parties that are external to the original litigation and whose involvement could be justified with reference to the arguments canvassed earlier, can be subdivided into four sub-categories. These are: i) the government, ii) court-appointed experts, iii) those with a direct stake in the outcome (Groppi and Lecis refer to these as 'third parties'), and iv) those interested in the issue from a more general societal or professional perspective ('amicus curiae' in Groppi and Lecis' account). The right of a government to make its views known in cases where it is not already involved is uncontroversial and typically clearly recognised in the rules of procedure, including in those of the ItCC. The same goes for experts whose assistance has come about at the court's invitation, a category to which we shall return below. The treatment of the remaining two categories is more varied.

A quick glance at the procedural regimes in place at several other constitutional courts in Europe shows that private parties can only participate in proceedings that already envisage a leading role for individuals in identifying possible breaches of the constitution and hence triggering the court's jurisdiction. More particularly, this covers preliminary reference procedures, as in Italy, as well as the constitutional complaint mechanism, which allows individuals to seek redress for alleged violations of their fundamental rights at the hands of a public authority.[22] Some courts operate under a stricter regime than that governing the ItCC as far as preliminary references are concerned: in Germany and Spain, for instance, only the parties to the controversy before the ordinary court which raised the preliminary ques-

[22] At first blush, Belgium appears to be an exception, as any party "declaring a justifiable interest" is entitled to make submissions during abstract challenges as well as during preliminary reference proceedings, Special Act of 6 January 1989 on the Belgian Constitutional Court, Art 87 §1 and 2. This, however, is in line with Art 142 of the Belgian Constitution, which is quite unusual in allowing private individuals who are personally and directly affected by legal provisions to bring such abstract challenges, alongside public institutions.

tion are entitled to submit statements and make oral submissions.[23] Others approximate the ItCC's case law allowing interventions by those third parties on whom the court's ruling would "exert a direct influence and would cause an irreparable harm to the right that was exercised".[24] Thus, the French Constitutional Council too can allow observations prepared by "a person with a special interest".[25] In a similar vein, when adjudicating constitutional complaints, individuals who were involved in or benefited from the behaviour that is the subject of the complaint can typically make their views known to the court. In Spain and the Czech Republic, amongst others, standing to do so is also granted to "persons with a legitimate interest",[26] respectively to those with "a legal interest in the outcome of the proceeding".[27]

Against this backdrop, there is merit in the objection voiced in Italian academic discourse to the current elusive formulation used in the ItCC's judicially-devised framework, which merely proclaims that it can "decide on the admissibility of interventions".[28] To better satisfy the value of legal certainty, the rules of procedure should codify the eligibility criteria present in the case law, which appear to mirror those operated by several of its peers. In doing so, it also ought to be clearly indicated that once a party meets the 'special legal interest' threshold, its participation in the proceedings is a matter of right and no longer subject to the exercise of judicial discretion, which should only govern the initial determination of whether that interest indeed exists.

The other prong of the scholarly criticism directed at the ItCC's approach is more value-laden: should its proceedings be pried open further by granting professional or other advocacy groups the opportunity to make submissions? Seen from a comparative perspective, there is a significant distinction between countries that practice centralized constitutional review and those that subscribe to the decentralized model of constitutional adjudication. At least in continental Europe, there is no trend of constitutional courts formally being receptive to amicus curiae briefs when verify-

[23] Act on the German Federal Constitutional Court, § 82; Organic Law 2/1979 on the Spanish Constitutional Tribunal, Art 37(2).

[24] Judgment no 315/1992.

[25] Ordinance no 58-1067 on the French Constitutional Council (as amended), s 23-8(2).

[26] Organic Law 2/1979 on the Spanish Constitutional Tribunal, Art 47.

[27] Act on the Czech Constitutional Court, § 76(2).

[28] Supplementary Provisions Concerning Proceedings before the Italian Constitutional Court, Art 4.

ing the validity of legislation. The procedural frameworks tend to explicitly regulate which additional parties can intervene. As explained earlier, this roughly boils down to representatives of the principal public institutions (government, houses of parliament) if they are neither petitioner nor defendant in abstract review proceedings; and individuals who are personally and directly affected by the constitutional defects brought to the court's attention, either through a preliminary reference or a constitutional complaint. As such, the ItCC might even be somewhat of an outlier in having a self-authored procedural rule that at least on its face provides a legal basis for accepting amicus curiae briefs.

Such briefs are more typically associated with common law systems in which the supreme court ultimately settles constitutional disputes. The US Supreme Court, the Canadian Supreme Court and the UK Supreme Court all can accept submissions prepared by general interest groups and concerned citizens. There are a couple points of note in relation to the conditions under which this happens that may be instructive for the Italian debate. First, besides securing the court's permission to submit unsolicited briefs, the parties to the case must typically also give their consent to the proposed intervention in due recognition of their leading role in presenting the constitutional issue and their stake in its resolution. That having been said, their refusal to grant consent need not be fatal. In the U.S., the would-be amicus curiae can file a motion for leave with the court,[29] whereas under the more lenient UK rules the intervener must file a notice indicating that it has served its application to intervene on the parties and briefly set out the reasons for the latter's refusal of consent.[30] The UK rules further stipulate that if the court grants permission to the would-be amicus, its written submissions must be shared with the appellant and respondent at least four weeks before the oral hearing, presumably to give the latter the opportunity to engage with the points raised in the intervention.[31] It could be interesting for Italian scholarship to consider whether similar procedural safeguards ought to be included in the ItCC's rules, notably given the latter's professed concern with the right of defence in demarcating the range of individuals and entities that it is willing to accept submissions from.

Second, the various procedural frameworks prescribe that judicial decisions to allow an intervention should be made with reference to the expected content of the brief, not the identity or other attributes of the pro-

---

[29] US Supreme Court, Rule 37(2b).

[30] UK Supreme Court Practice Directions, Rule 6.9.2.

[31] ibid., Rule 6.9.4.

spective amicus curiae. The threshold criterion here is one of originality. This can be pitched at a rather generic level, as in the U.S. rules, which stipulate that the submission "brings to the attention of the Court relevant matters not already brought to its attention by the parties".[32] Likewise, in deciding to grant leave to intervene, the UK Supreme Court is guided by "the expectation that [the would-be interveners'] fund of knowledge or particular point of view will enable them to provide the [Court] with a more rounded picture than it would otherwise obtain".[33] The Rules of the Canadian Supreme Court impose a higher burden on would-be interveners by requiring that the motion for intervention already sets out the "relevance [of the submissions] to the proceedings and the reasons for believing that the submission will be useful to the Court and different from those of the other parties".[34] The inclusion of relatively stringent admissibility criteria can perform an important signalling function in that it may deter prospective amicus curiae from sending in poorly drafted submissions or ones that merely repeat points already argued by the parties. This would clearly be a welcome outcome for the judges (in particular the reporting judge and her clerks), who would not need to waste time reading through briefs that would not add anything valuable to the court's knowledge base. At the same time, we should realise that 'usefulness' is very much in the eye of the beholder. Groppi and Lecis note on several occasions that the principal argument in favour of a more detailed regime on interventions, notably the inclusion of eligibility criteria, is to reduce the flexibility that presently characterises the ItCC's approach which scholars "often label as arbitrary" and consider as an "element of weakness in the Italian constitutional system".[35] It may legitimately be asked, however, whether the inclusion of requirements akin to those found in the U.S., UK, or Canada would actually fetter the ItCC's discretion to the extent apparently hoped for.

Let us now turn to the issue of access to non-legal facts. Various avenues are available to courts to collect such information. One is to rely on external sources, including through the submission of amicus curiae briefs by professional associations or advocacy groups that are well-versed in or have ready access to pertinent scientific, economic or social science data. Whether a court can indeed avail itself of this possibility is dependent on

---

[32] US Supreme Court, Rule 37(1).

[33] Lord Hoffmann's opinion in *E v The Chief Constable of the Royal Ulster Constabulary (Northern Ireland Human Rights Commission intervening)* [2008] UKHL 66, [2009] 1 AC 536, as quoted in the UK Supreme Court Practice Directions, Rule 8.8.2.

[34] Rules of the Canadian Supreme Court, Rule 57(2)(b).

[35] See T. GROPPI, A.M. LECIS COCCO ORTU, in this book.

the governing procedural framework and its interpretation thereof, as explained above. It appears that there are voices within Italian scholarship that agitate in favour of opening constitutional adjudicatory proceedings to amicus curiae precisely for the improved access to non-legal information their briefs can provide. While there is merit in this view, we ought to bear in mind that deciding *whether* to intervene in a given case as well as the *type of information* to include is the preserve of the would-be amicus, and not of the court. Further, interveners are not neutral in their approach; their objective is to convince the court to embrace a particular position and this guides their selection and presentation of non-legal facts. As was commented in a study of the use of amicus curiae briefs by former U.S. Supreme Court law clerks: "[p]rofessional groups are considered to be more reliable than ideological groups".[36]

An alternative route is for the court to take the lead and solicit what it deems to be pertinent information from parties external to the litigation. A quick glance across the borders confirms that there is no unified or even largely similar approach in procedural regimes in this regard. In several countries (e.g. Belgium,[37] Germany,[38] the Czech Republic[39]) the appointment of independent experts is explicitly provided for in the legal framework alongside further specifications as to when and how expert opinions should be communicated to the court. A somewhat different tack is taken in the UK: while the Supreme Court can be assisted by "specialist advisors", their appointment can only come about at the behest of a request by one of the parties. Once approved, however, the rules stipulate that such advisors must conduct themselves in a manner "strictly independent of the parties to the appeal".[40] In other jurisdictions (e.g. Spain), the procedural framework simply grants the court a general power to take evidence, without any further particulars as to manner or form.[41]

It is interesting to note that procedural regimes elsewhere regularly impose an obligation on other State organs to provide the court with documents or other information if and when the latter so requires. By way of example, the Czech Constitutional Court Act insists that "All courts, public administrative bodies, and other state institutions shall, at the request of

---

[36] K.J. LYNCH, *Best Friends? Supreme Court Law Clerks on Effective Amicus Curiae Briefs*, *supra* note 19, 51.

[37] Special Act on the Belgian Constitutional Court, Art 91.

[38] Law on the German Federal Constitutional Court, § 27a.

[39] Act on the Czech Constitutional Court, § 49(1) and §50(2).

[40] UK Supreme Court Practice Directions, Rule 8.13.

[41] Organic Law 2/1979 on the Spanish Constitutional Tribunal, Art 89.

the [constitutional] court, grant it assistance in procuring evidence to assist in its decision-making".[42] In a similar vein, all German courts and administrative authorities are tasked to "provide the German Federal Constitutional Court with legal and administrative assistance".[43] The Spanish Constitutional Tribunal may "request the public authorities and any organ of public administration to furnish records, reports and documents concerning a decision or act that is subjected to a constitutional proceeding".[44] The ItCC too appears to place heavy reliance on information provided by the government, a habit that Groppi and Lecis seem quite critical of, since the latter "in most cases, has a concrete stake in the dismissal of the case".[45] This is undoubtedly a valid point that could bolster the case to grant the ItCC the explicit power to seek input from other quarters, notably independent experts in non-legal fields.

At the same time, there are reasons that can be marshalled in support of the status quo. The privileging of the government writ large as a supplier of facts and other materials allows the judges to capitalize on the former's superior capacity vis-à-vis private entities or individuals in compiling nationwide data sets and providing them with financial information not (yet) in the public domain. In addition, the judicial practice of emphasizing government-generated information underscores that the court is part of a larger State structure and dependent on other State institutions (Parliament, government, regular courts, administrative agencies) for the faithful execution of its rulings. Seen from this angle, the ItCC's behaviour is accordingly neither surprising nor unusual, although a compelling comparative case can again be made to place it on a sturdier legal footing.

Finally, a court could ensure that its in-house levels of non-legal expertise are of an acceptable standard. Doing so should not be thought of as obviating the need to rely on external input. Rather, it would be a complimentary strategy, enabling the court to better assess the quality of the data provided and inferences drawn therefrom by experts and particularly amicus curiae, for the reasons set out earlier. Realizing adequate intramural capacity can take various forms. The rules governing appointments of new judges to the French Constitutional Council, for example, do not set out any eligibility criteria. This has enabled the appointment of individuals who were trained in fields other than law. Its current president and one of the other members hold qualifications in (modern) literature and political sci-

[42] Act on the Czech Constitutional Court, § 48.

[43] Law on the German Federal Constitutional Court, § 27.

[44] Organic Law 2/1979 on the Spanish Constitutional Tribunal, Art 88.

[45] See T. Groppi, A.M. Lecis Cocco Ortu, in this book.

ence as well as a degree from the National School of Administration; none of these members received a formal legal education. In a related vein, half of the 12 judges on the Belgian Constitutional Court should have at least five years of political experience and these members are not required to hold law degrees.[46] As has been observed, their familiarity with government administration means that such judges "are well equipped to judge whether the [non-legal] arguments advanced by the government are really compelling".[47] The Belgian framework, and even more so that in France, are, however, outliers in Europe. The clear trend for countries that have a constitutional court is to insist that candidates for appointment to the constitutional bench are legally trained and have worked for a substantial period as a legal professional in the regular judiciary, as a prosecutor, lawyer, or law professor. This makes it more difficult to 'front-load' the court with expertise in other disciplines. Matters are better in the U.S. and other jurisdictions where law is studied at the postgraduate level. While all justices on the U.S. Supreme Court hold law degrees and have had extensive legal careers prior to their judicial appointment, they have been exposed to sociology, history or economics during their undergraduate studies and should accordingly feel comparatively more comfortable interpreting data, methodologies and arguments derived from those fields.

Given the strictures in place for judges, a more promising approach would be to focus on disciplinary diversification among judicial support staff: clerks, research judges, or personnel of internal research institutes. A good non-European example is offered by the South Korean Constitutional Court, which established a Constitutional Research Institute in 2011 that, amongst others, is tasked with preparing "for potential constitutional disputes [regarding] global constitutional issues that emerge as a result of rapid scientific and technological advances through active research and communication with various academic fields".[48] The topics that it has studied to this end include withdrawal of life-sustaining treatment, the collection and use of electronic information, monitoring and protection of privacy, and equal protection of sexual minorities and sexual orientation.

It should however be admitted that the regulations governing the ap-

---

[46] Special Act on the Belgian Constitutional Court, Art 34(2). In France too, the composition of the Constitutional Council is strongly tied to the political establishment: more than two-thirds of its membership to date has consisted of former politicians, either cabinet ministers, members of Parliament or direct advisors to leading politicians.

[47] V. FERRERES COMELLA, *Constitutional Courts & Democratic Values – A European Perspective*, New Haven, Yale University Press, 2009, 41.

[48] Korean Constitutional Court, *CRI Brochure*, 3 (available on the court's website).

pointment of support staff and the actual hiring decisions made by courts normally place a premium on engaging clerks and researchers with a legal background that are well-versed in constitutional law in particular. Any change in this regard will require a shift in the internal legal culture of constitutional courts, which seems unlikely to come about in the short term.

In view of this reality, should we lament generic references to extra-legal information, as practiced by the ItCC, and their subordination to legal reasoning or simply accept this as inevitable and even sensible? Constitutional courts are conceived – and themselves eager to emphasize and cultivate their character – as judicial institutions, deciding issues that are presented as legal problems by making use of legal reasoning and judicial decision-making techniques. While the disputes brought before them will have political, ethical or economic overtones, many courts with a constitutional mandate put in considerable effort to "sound like judges rather than legislators or cabinet members".[49] The perceived need to do so can be linked to the counter-majoritarian difficulty and societal expectations of proper judicial behaviour. Even in the U.S., where economic and social-scientific references are commonplace in submissions by counsel and third parties, the vast majority of decisions by the U.S. Supreme Court are steeped in legal-technical jargon.[50] Even as measures are taken to ensure greater or qualitatively better input of non-legal facts and arguments into the constitutional proceedings, it may very well be the case that their visibility in judicial opinions will remain largely unchanged. In my view, this is not overly problematic for the reasons just canvassed. At the same time, I do not want to suggest that improving the availability of extra-legal materials is therefore a futile exercise. Doing so could improve the quality of judges' internal deliberations and the likelihood of the court reaching the 'right' outcome, which will positively impact on its social legitimacy.

5.3. Of hermeneutics and legal formants

Groppi and Lecis' examination suggests a discrepancy between the ItCC's rules of procedure pertaining to third party submissions and actual judicial

---

[49] A. JAKAB, A. DYEVRE, G. ITZCOVICH, *Introduction: Comparing Constitutional reasoning with Quantitative and Qualitative Methods*, in A. JAKAB, A. DYEVRE, G. ITZCOVICH (eds.), *Comparative Constitutional Reasoning*, Cambridge, Cambridge University Press, 2017, 19.

[50] H. SCHWEBER, J. BROOKHART, *The Supreme Court of the United States*, in A. JAKAB, A. DYEVRE, G. ITZCOVICH (eds.), *Comparative Constitutional Reasoning, supra* note 49, 746.

practice. The legal framework remains silent as to interventions by non-parties, which the ItCC originally took as warranting a hostile attitude to such interventions. It relented in the early 1990s, judicially carving out three situations in which it would accept third party submissions.[51] The ItCC has however not been consistent in the application of the criteria that it has devised in its case law, sometimes accepting interventions by groups that would appear to fall outside of the exceptions and on other occasions refusing requests to participate emanating from bodies that could be brought within these.[52] Even more interesting than this fluctuating case law is the fact that, their formal inadmissibility notwithstanding, the arguments advanced in own-initiative third party briefs "receive some attention" within the ItCC. This is so "even if their author is not admitted to participate as an intervener",[53] according to the extra-judicial observations of one of the court's justices.

These findings confirm that the formal regime regulating submissions by parties not directly involved in the litigation and governing the collection of extra-legal information tells only part of the story. There is no reason to suspect that this will be markedly different for courts whose rules of procedure do address these matters in greater detail, if only because the relevant provisions are typically couched in discretionary language. By way of example, the fairly comprehensive framework governing the Belgian Constitutional Court stipulates that its judges "*may* hear any person [they] *deem useful* to hear; *may* assess the situation on site; and *may* appoint experts".[54] If the latter option is used, the rules demand that the precise terms of reference for expert evidence are "decide[d] by order", but do not lay down any further constraints or conditions.[55]

Truly understanding and evaluating a court's receptiveness to input from third parties, amicus curiae or extra-legal arguments accordingly requires the study of materials beyond the written law, from constitution to statute to internal rules of procedure. This is a well-accepted prescription for general comparative scholarship.[56] Ran Hirschl has forcefully advocat-

---

[51] Judgment no. 315/1992.

[52] See T. GROPPI, A.M. LECIS COCCO ORTU, in this book.

[53] See T. GROPPI, A.M. LECIS COCCO ORTU, in this book.

[54] Special Act on the Belgian Constitutional Court, Art 91(3) through (5). Emphasis added.

[55] Ibid., Art. 94.

[56] See, among many others, J. HUSA, *A New Introduction to Comparative Law*, Oxford, Hart Publishing, 2015, chs. 6 and 7; M. SIEMS, *Comparative Law*, Cambridge, Cambridge University Press, 2014, Part II – *Extending the Methods of Comparative Law*

ed the same within the specific sub-domain of comparative constitutional law, although his concern is primarily to foster the use of insights derived from the social sciences.[57] Comparatists interested in court procedures can usefully look to methodological matrixes in social psychology and behavioural economics to identify what another Italian scholar, Rodolfo Sacco, has famously referred to as 'legal formants'. This term denotes the plurality of legally relevant elements that together and through their interaction produce a particular legal outcome.[58] The discovery process that yields the legal formants at play in a given legal or judicial setting must extend to their unformulated elements. These are what Sacco refers to as 'crypotypes', and these formants allow us to make sense of why a decision differs from what we would expect on the basis of explicit rules and standard patterns. It is evident from Professors Groppi and Lecis' account, as summarised above, that the ItCC's approach to third party submissions is characterised by the presence of several such formants and crypotypes. Again, the open-ended language used in the official rules of constitutional procedure elsewhere all but guarantees that the same holds true in other jurisdictions.

The legal formants with the greatest hermeneutical value in this context, I would suggest, are the justifications that are seen as valid and proper for judges to invoke in favour or against the use of outside assistance and extra-legal information. These may not be discussed openly or extensively in the judgment; yet as we know, the text of judicial decisions is not a complete or necessarily accurate reflection of what has gone on within the court during the judicial conferences and preparatory stages.[59] There have been credible suggestions that arguments regarding the propriety of using non-legal materials and auxiliary interventions are in turn shaped by what can be called the 'secondary legal formants' of a judge's background and training as well as her professional relationship with the other groups in their larger epistemic community of reference, to wit, regular judges, lawyers and jurists.[60] A judge appointed to the constitutional bench who has spent a

("a rule-based comparison gives no consideration of the real-world sense in which these rules operate", 95).

[57] R. HIRSCHL, *Comparative Matters – The Renaissance of Comparative Constitutional Law*, Oxford, Oxford University Press, 2014, ch. 4.

[58] R. SACCO, *Legal Formants: A Dynamic Approach to Comparative Law*, in 39 *American Journal of Comparative Law*, No. 1, 1 (1991) and 39 *American Journal of Comparative Law*, No. 2, 343 (1991).

[59] Consider notably the work of M. de S.-O.-l'E. LASSER, *Judicial Deliberations: A Comparative Analysis of Transparency and Legitimacy*, Oxford, Oxford University Press, 2009, on the French judiciary.

[60] See the references in R. HIRSCHL, *Comparative Matters – The Renaissance of Com-*

significant part of her prior career in government service or politics may be more comfortable with non-legal facts and arguments than her colleague who joined the regular judiciary immediately upon graduating from law school before being elevated to the constitutional bench. In a related vein, a judge with a scholarly background may give more serious consideration to the theoretical and normative principles regarding the constitutional issue at hand,[61] whereas a judge who used to work in legal practice may privilege the practical arguments pertaining to the same issue deployed by lawyers.

The relative weight ascribed to each legal formant within a given constitutional court would, arguably, be the most interesting crypotype to uncover. In particular, the possible existence of a time dimension seems relevant. Here what I have in mind is the evolving composition of the court: whether changes in the internal judicial reasons that are considered legitimate vis-à-vis reliance on third-party or amicus curiae interventions and extra-legal facts coincide with the appointment of new judges or the election of a new president. Since there are great variations in the selection of justices and the length of their tenure across jurisdictions, a study of the legal formants mentioned above can help us understand why the growing convergence in the types of polycentric and scientific constitutional questions that come before courts may not translate into convergent judicial approaches to their resolution.

5.4. Concluding thoughts

Transparency has become a powerful rallying cry within the constitutional realm and a favoured yardstick to measure the behaviour of the full suite of State institutions against. The courts have not escaped this development. What is more, many have taken it in their stride, embarking on outreach efforts that would have been scarcely imaginable a few decades ago, from appointing special media judges to hosting 'open days' for the public to speaking engagements to professional and other communities to the live streaming of proceedings. Soliciting the involvement of parties not directly involved in the litigation and collecting extra-legal information can be seen as specific manifestations of this broader trend. Allowing a wider range of

---

parative Constitutional Law, *supra* note 57, 166-168; T. GROPPI, M.C. PONTHOREAU (eds.), *The Use of Foreign Precedents by Constitutional Judges*, *supra* note 9, 413-414; A. JAKAB, A. DYEVRE, G. ITZCOVICH, *Introduction: Comparing Constitutional reasoning with Quantitative and Qualitative Methods*, *supra* note 49, 16-25.

[61] By way of example, US Supreme Court Justice Ruth Bader Ginsburg, who spent considerable time in academia before being elevated, has been quoted as "always ask[ing her] law clerks, in addition to reading all the briefs, including all the amici briefs, that if there's a good law review article, they should bring it to [her]".

interested parties to offer their views for consideration in judicial decision-making can democratise constitutional adjudication. It simultaneously ensures better-informed and hopefully more responsive courts. Put in language that is similarly *en vogue*, accepting interventions by non-parties and considering extra-legal factors strengthens the dialogic qualities of constitutional review, as Groppi and Lecis also acknowledge in their conclusion.

Extrapolating from the Italian context, their account underscores the important role that a court's procedural regime plays in cultivating openness and engagement, including the role of the protagonists themselves in fashioning and interpreting such rules. There is considerable force in the plea from Groppi and Lecis, echoed by several of their colleagues in the Italian constitutional discourse, for the ItCC to move away from the procedural 'closed-ness' that it currently practises, notably in relation to the use of amicus brief and experts. Having looked at how the relevant rules are couched elsewhere, it would indeed seem apposite for the ItCC to embark on a further update of its procedural framework to make it more prescriptive and detailed. At the same time, as much as the focus in the Italian discourse is on the ItCC's internal regime and implementation thereof, we should not overlook the role that the legislature can play. Any changes to the ItCC's internal rules ought to be accompanied by a legislative reform of its governing statute along similar lines, as it sets the parameters within which the judges can exercise their internal rule-setting competences.

In closing, though, a cautionary note seems warranted. The almost intuitive appeal of notions like transparency, engagement and dialogue should not cause the pendulum to sway too far in their direction. Judges are neither trained nor should be expected to behave as political theorists, economists or scientists; and court deliberations should not approximate parliamentary proceedings in their focus and scope. In the pursuit of openness, court reformers should aim for a calibrated approach that accommodates interpretative room for manoeuvre, while recognizing that the judge remains a legal professional, primarily using formal legal reasoning and legal methodologies to ply her trade. A failure to do so would excessively hamstring constitutional adjudication and would, in the long run, carry greater risks for a court's stature than an enduring closedness in attitude.

Dialogue III

THE PRINCIPLE OF COLLEGIALITY

Chapter VI

COLLEGIALITY OVER PERSONALITY: THE REJECTION OF SEPARATE OPINIONS IN ITALY

Diletta Tega

SUMMARY: 6.1. The meaning of the collegiality principle and its repercussions on separate opinions. – 6.2. The Constitutional Court's position: preservation of the *status quo*. – 6.3. Pros and cons: the debate among scholars. – 6.4. Conclusion.

6.1. The meaning of the collegiality principle and its repercussions on separate opinions

The Italian Constitutional Court (ItCC) has highlighted many times, through its Presidents, that collegiality[1] is one of its essential features. This collegial character is evident during the decision-making process, but it also has a deeper meaning for the Court, well beyond mere respect for procedural rules. The Court speaks in the public arena with a single voice – that of its rulings. The judgments are the result of a deliberative process, which redresses the potential (alleged) political biases of single judges. Gustavo Zagrebelsky, President of the ItCC in 2004 and a very influential constitutional lawyer and scholar, stated, "Italian constitutional judges do not vote, they deliberate". This pinpoints the fact that judges make an effort to con-

[1] This principle is enshrined in Articles 16 and 18, Law no. 87 of 1953 (On the establishment and functioning of the Constitutional Court), and in Article 18 of the Additional rules for proceedings before the ItCC (Norme integrative per i giudizi davanti alla Corte costituzionale, adopted by the Court itself on 16 March 1956). Among other literature, see: V. BARSOTTI, P.G. CAROZZA, M. CARTABIA, A. SIMONCINI, *Italian Constitutional Justice in Global Context*, Oxford, Oxford University Press, 2016, 46 (and 239, on the "relational mindset" of the ItCC); G. ZAGREBELSKY, *La Corte costituzionale italiana*, in P. PASQUINO, B. RANDAZZO (eds.), *Come decidono le Corti Costituzionali (e altre Corti)*, Milan, Giuffrè Editore, 2009, 59-83. According to Gaetano Silvestri (interviewed just after his Presidency of the Court), the ItCC expresses its collegiality within a symphony of many voices, with Presidents playing the role of conductors, able to find and distill a unitary position. For this reason, the President expresses their personal opinions after all their other colleagues, in order not to unduly influence the discussion (see D. TEGA, *La Corte costituzionale vista da vicino Intervista di Diletta Tega a Gaetano Silvestri*, in 3 *Quaderni costituzionali* 757 (2014), 758-759).

vey a sort of uniform consensus[2] particularly concerning the most sensitive constitutional issues. The ItCC moves following a horizontal and inclusive logic, intended to account for every possible constitutional argument and to unify diverging viewpoints, without casting and tallying individual votes. This – provided that the deliberation process is animated by effective participation and genuine dialogue among the judges – is an important facet of the ItCC's relationality in its internal dimension.

In recent years, Court Presidents have repeatedly highlighted this feature in answer to the claims – made by the center-right coalition – that constitutional judges have a precise partisan alignment and that the Court is politically over-exposed. The ItCC had, and continues to have, an impact on important parts of the Governments' agenda. For example, judgment 466/2005 on Law no. 189/2002 amended legislation concerning immigration and asylum. It also dismantled pieces of legislation passed specifically to favor the President of the Council of Ministers (e.g. judgment 24/2004 on Law no. 140/2003, which suspended prosecution of the President while he was in office).[3] The ItCC has attained a conspicuous position since the late 1990s, becoming central to both the form of the government and the form of the state in Italy. This is because the ItCC scrutinizes legislative choices made by Parliament and Government (through legislative decrees and decree-laws) while they are still in office, and the Court resolves conflicts among State powers, between the State and the Regions, and between Regions. To draw again from Gustavo Zagrebelsky, "the Court is in itself in-politica" (in-politics).[4] In other words, it is embedded in a constantly fermenting body politic because its powers

---

[2] G. Zagrebelsky has expressed this position several times, for example in G. ZAGREBELSKY, *Intorno alla legge. Il diritto come dimensione del vivere comune*, Turin, Einaudi Editore, 2009, 305, 309-310. He recalls the majority opinion by Justice Robert Jackson in *West Virginia State Board of Education v. Barnette*, 319 U.S. 624 (1943): "One's right to life, liberty, and property, to free speech, a free press, freedom of worship and assembly, and other fundamental rights may not be submitted to vote". Note that this passage refers to political elections, while Zagrebelsky extends it to judicial deliberations.

[3] See P. PEDERZOLI, *La Corte costituzionale*, Bologna, Il Mulino, 2008, 219. On the transformation undergone by the political parties, see *Italian Politics: a review*, New York-Oxford, Berghahn, 1985-2016; D. TEGA, *The Italian way: a blend of cooperation and hubris,* in *the Heidelberg Journal of International Law* 3/2017 in 77 *Zeitschrift für ausländisches öffentliches Recht und Völkerrecht* 685 (2017). This over-exposure was expressly mentioned in the 2012 *Annual Report* (Relazione sulla giurisprudenza costituzionale) by President Franco Gallo, available at *www.cortecostituzionale.it.*

[4] G. ZAGREBELSKY, *Intorno alla legge. Il diritto come dimensione del vivere comune*, cit., 303 ff.

affect the functioning of the political system – the Court is able to halt or adjust the choices made by Parliament, the Government, and the President of the Republic – without belonging to the political system. In light of this, the ItCC must be regarded as the guardian of the *pactum societatis*.

How does collegiality *à l'italiénne* work? The President of the Court, with the assistance of the *Ufficio del ruolo*, distributes pending cases among the judges. The judge appointed as rapporteur (*relatore*) has the duty to study the case, in order to open public discussion about it in case of a public hearing, and, more importantly, to bring it before the convened ItCC when it gathers in the privacy of the Conference Room (*Camera di consiglio*). Secrecy envelops both the discussion among the judges and any voting when it takes place.[5] The decision is usually written by the judge rapporteur, following the suggestions made during the discussion. If the rapporteur disagrees with the outcome, he or she may decline to write the decision, and another judge will be appointed as drafter (*redattore*).[6] The decision's heading reports the name of the judge rapporteur, and, if he or she has relinquished the task of writing, the final part of the text will indicate a different judge as the drafter. Since 1987, decisions have been signed by both the President and the drafter (previously, all the judges signed).

Thus, decisions tend to incorporate the Court's prevailing line of reasoning, while *obiter dicta* are often inserted to take into account minority views. Zagrebelsky[7] reports that when he was on the Court, an attempt was made to write down all the various opinions within a single judgment, but it was not successful because the minority felt misinterpreted.

The content of a decision remains secret until the written text has been approved, deposited, and published. During the last ten years, the press office has published very brief press releases on the Court's website regarding the outcomes of the most important or popular cases. Only very recently, the same press office has begun to publish longer summaries, once the full decision is made public, intended to "speak" to public opinion (and particularly to journalists).

---

[5] After the expiration of their term, several judges have commented publicly on how certain decisions were made, occasionally revealing previously unknown details.

[6] This discrepancy occurred for the first time in order 52/1988. These occurrences are episodic, but still current: they happened approximately 80 times between 1988 and 2019.

[7] G. ZAGREBELSKY, *La Corte costituzionale italiana*, *cit.*, 77.

The option to introduce separate opinions[8] would be quite a dramatic change within a system shaped around the principles of collegiality and secrecy.[9] Separate opinions would break the secrecy, subjecting to public scrutiny topics and discussions that are currently confined to the Conference Room. The Italian aversion to separate opinions stands out as an unusual feature in the comparative landscape of continental Europe. Although with strong differences regarding sources, structure, style, and practice of law, separate opinions are allowed in almost every constitutional justice system, with the notable exceptions of Italy and France.[10]

And yet, separate opinions represent a topic that continues to emerge periodically not only in the general legal debate, but also within the Court itself and in Parliament.

In this paper, I critically assess the official position of the ItCC and of several of its judges, as well as the outcomes of the doctrinal debate. I strongly agree with Di Martino's approach to the question of whether separate opinions may be introduced: she identifies different periods in the Court's history – specifically in terms of its relationships with constitutional organs and public opinion – to contextualize the issue.[11]

Many bills have contemplated the issue in Parliament, but almost none of them were ever discussed. It is worth briefly revisiting the seven noteworthy times the topic was considered. The first time took place as a part of the discussion on the legislation regarding the foundation and functioning of the ItCC (Law no. 87/1953). The possibility of dissents was rejected for fear that judges would be subjected to partisan political influence and

---

[8] Here I have used the expression "separate opinions" to refer to both concurring and dissenting opinions, without taking into consideration the different types within both categories. Hereinafter, I will refer to dissenting opinion only, as historically this has been the focus of Italian speculation on this subject.

[9] See V. DENTI, *Per il ritorno al «voto di scissura» nelle decisioni giudiziarie*, in *Le opinioni dissenzienti dei giudici costituzionali ed internazionali* (Scritti raccolti a cura di Costantino Mortati), Milan, Giuffrè Editore, 1964, 1-20, for a broader history of the Italian tradition concerning judicial deliberations (which shifted in favour of providing a single line of reasoning in the eighteenth century). See also, A. DE NITTO, *In tema di opinioni dissenzienti nell'esperienza delle corti italiane*, in A. DE NITTO, *Diritto dei giudici e diritto dei legislatori*, Lecce, Argo, 2002, 50 ff.

[10] See the analysis by A. DI MARTINO, *Le opinioni dissenzienti dei giudici costituzionali: uno studio comparativo*, Naples, Jovene Editore, 2016, and K. KELEMEN, *Judicial Dissent in European Constitutional Courts. A Comparative and Legal Perspective*, London, New York, Routledge, 2018. The latter, in particular, offers a valuable perspective on East-Central European constitutional courts, 120 ff.

[11] A. DI MARTINO, *Le opinioni dissenzienti dei giudici costituzionali: uno studio comparative*, *cit.*, 319-320 ff.

that the autonomy and prestige of the newly created organ would be diminished. Second, in 1981, Stefano Rodotà (professor of private law and an influential progressive intellectual who became a member of Parliament as a left-wing independent) presented a legislative proposal to introduce dissenting opinions.[12] The issue was brought up twice more: during the 1983-1985 discussions of wider constitutional reforms, when the so-called 'Bozzi Commission' was established; and in 1997, in the text developed by the 'D'Alema Commission.' On the latter occasion, the Commission's majority gathered around the idea that the formal introduction of dissenting positions would emphasize judges' responsibility and enhance the clarity and consistency of decisions. None of these initiatives met with any degree of success. The issue resurfaced again in 2004, when a former President of the Republic, Francesco Cossiga, presented a constitutional bill (XIV Legislature, A.S. no. 2690) as a reaction to the aforementioned judgment 24/-2004.[13] In 2008, six bills concerned dissenting opinions were introduced (XVI Legislature, AC nos. 446 and 1598; AS nos. 200, 216, 1030,1158). The last bill was presented in 2015 (XVII Legislature, AS no. 1952) by Linda Lanzillotta, a senator of the Democratic Party. This bill, too, had the somewhat inappropriate appearance of being a polemical reaction by Parliament against the much-contested decision no. 70/2015 (which struck down a rule that severely limited the annual automatic increase for retirement pensions, a move urgently imposed by the Monti Government in 2011 during the acute phase of the financial crisis). Neither of these bills was ever discussed.

6.2. The Constitutional Court's position: preservation of the *status quo*

Within the Court, it is possible to identify diverging ideas regarding the introduction of separate opinions. We will first address the official position of the Court and then the stances of the various judges. The Court discussed this topic right at the beginning of its activity, when, in 1956, it laid down its own Additional rules (*Norme integrative per i giudizi davanti alla*

[12] On the Rodotà proposals, see S.C. PANZA, A. REPOSO, *Le "dissenting opinions" ancora alla ribalta*, in 3 *Quaderni costituzionali* 595 (1981), 596-597. On a previous constitutional law proposal which, in 1973, was withdrawn almost immediately, see K. KELEMEN, *Judicial Dissent in European Constitutional Courts. A Comparative and Legal Perspective*, cit., 97.

[13] See S. PANIZZA, *L'introduzione dell'opinione dissenziente nel sistema di giustizia costituzionale*, Turin, Giappichelli Editore, 1998, 485 and A. DI MARTINO, *Le opinioni dissenzienti dei giudici costituzionali: uno studio comparativo*, cit., 370.

Corte costituzionale) and Judge Mario Bracci, professor of administrative law, made a concerted effort to convince his colleagues to introduce that tool. [14] It bears remembering that, at the outset, things were not easy for the ItCC: its establishment was a crucial novelty, introduced by the Constitution. It is not by chance that the ItCC started its work only in 1956.

In the 1960s, Costantino Mortati, one of the most important constitutional scholars of all time and Vice-President of the Court, engaged in the most active campaign in favor of the introduction of separate opinions ever seen within the Court. [15]

The Court held two other Seminars on the topic, in 1993 and 2009. We will come back to the first of the two in the next paragraph. The most recent one opened with a general report by Sabino Cassese, who was an ItCC judge at that time, followed by two addresses, by judges Maria Rita Saulle and Franco Gallo. [16] Whilst Cassese made an insightful analysis of the arguments both in favor and against separate opinions, as well as of the different legal and cultural systems that use dissenting opinions, the other judges remained quite skeptical. Cassese made the following points: there are different types of dissenting opinions; dissenting opinions as such are only seventy years old (he marks 1940 as the start of contemporary debate on the topic); the theoretical debate is deeply influenced by context and might be overblown compared to the concept of dissent itself and its practice due to the cultural environment (mostly that of the US) in which the debate has taken place.

Concerning the judges' individual positions, a *caveat* is necessary. Judges usually reveal their opinions after the end of their term: Aldo Corasaniti, Ugo Spagnoli, and, very recently, Gaetano Silvestri followed this practice. [17] Yet there have been exceptions to this practice. Several judges have taken open positions, even during their terms. These include Costantino Mortati, Francesco Paolo Casavola (who was President of the Court at the time), Giuseppe Branca and Francesco Paolo Bonifacio (both professors of Roman Law), [18] Sabino Cassese, and Franco Gallo. [19] In particular, the diary

---

[14] See A. Di Martino, *Le opinioni dissenzienti dei giudici costituzionali: uno studio comparativo*, *cit.*, 321.

[15] The campaign also lead to a book, *Le opinioni dissenzienti dei giudici costituzionali ed internazionali* (Scritti raccolti a cura di Costantino Mortati), cit. and several other writings.

[16] Texts are available on the Court's website, at http://www.cortecostituzionale.it/

[17] Ugo Spagnoli also implied his position in favor before the end of his term. See his words in A. Anzon, *L'opinione dissenziente*, Milan, Giuffrè Editore, 1995, 121-127.

[18] See U. Spagnoli, *La Corte della Crisi*, Turin, Einaudi Editore, 1996, 121-127.

[19] Concerning the positions expressed by judges, I cannot omit an insightful remark by

written by Sabino Cassese and published just after the end of his term as constitutional judge came close to lifting the veil of secrecy. The publication of Cassese's diary was the first time that a past constitutional judge decided to make public several of the Court's *interna corporis.*[20] Sabino Cassese, as we will discuss in the next paragraph, can be listed among the supporters of separate opinions. Interestingly, there is also one case of a scholar who was in favor of dissents, but he changed his mind after being appointed judge and later President of the ItCC: Gustavo Zagrebelsky.

After the ItCC had been active for eight years and had built up a positive constitutional experience in enhancing pluralism and guaranteeing rights, Mortati believed that secrecy should be abandoned with regard to both the decision and its grounds (to avoid improper uses of dissenting opinions, Mortati proposes either withholding the authors' names or publishing them on condition that at least two judges join the opinion).[21] According to Mortati, the ItCC had gained such widespread prestige – thanks to the total independence of its decisions – that worries about separate opinions (expressed when Law no. 87/1953 was passed) had to be considered obsolete. Indeed, in those years, the ItCC drew acclaim not only for having struck down illiberal fascist regulations, but also for having held that all constitutional dispositions were legally binding, and not just a political manifesto.

Mortati envisioned several positive outcomes from the use of the dissent: more profound analysis of the cases, more consistent reasoning within the majority opinion, and general enrichment of the topics on the table. Dissenting opinions can be useful both to referring judges, and to Parliament. If the majority opinion rejects a question of constitutionality, dissents can help to frame a new referral of the same question and, therefore, to update case law to keep pace with the development of social customs. If the majority opinion affirms the unconstitutionality of a piece of legislation, dissents can provide Parliament with a clearer understanding of how to realign it with the Constitution and also with some hints about how to enact further legislation on the issue. Mortati rejected the assumption that the in-

Alessandro Pizzorusso: a convention has developed, permitting the judges to express *de facto* dissent through informal statements made within seminars, public speeches, and interviews. A. PIZZORUSSO, *Intervento*, in N. OCCHIOCUPO (eds.), *La Corte Costituzionale tra norma giuridica e realtà sociale. Bilancio di vent'anni di attività*, Bologna, Il Mulino, 1978, 138, also mentioned in S.C. PANZA, A. REPOSO, *Le "dissenting opinions" ancora alla ribalta, cit.*, 599.

[20] S. CASSESE, *Dentro la Corte*, Bologna, Il Mulino, 2015.

[21] Mortati abandoned the idea of anonymity in the amendment to the Additional rules of the Court he wrote in 1965, see *Proposta del Giudice prof. Mortati di "emendamenti dell'art. 18 «Norme integrative»" Relazione illustrativa*, in *Il dibattito sull'introduzione della c.d. "opinione dissenziente" nel sistema italiano di giustizia costituzionale*, edited by L. IANNUCCILLI and I. NORELLI, 85.

troduction of separate opinions could diminish the judges' independence and autonomy or the strength of their judgments. First, he argued that the rules on judges' nomination and election, together with the prohibition of re-appointment,[22] are sufficient to defend their full autonomy *vis à vis* political influence. Second, Mortati believed that public awareness of constitutional law would be better served by the clear and precise expression of different and divergent rational arguments than by a lame and illusory unanimity.

During the very first years of the Court's existence, rejection of separate opinions could be justified by the necessity to prevent any potential challenge to the moral strength of constitutional judgments. Since the ItCC was charged with radically new tasks and powers, such as limiting Parliament's will or adjudicating conflicts among the supreme State powers, such challenges would have been serious threats to the court's reputation.

Mortati developed his stance starting from two basic assumptions. First, certainty of law can only be attained in glimpses and through repeated iterations. Dissenting opinions are useful for this purpose. Second, the Italian Constitution is a living organism, the vitality of which depends upon its adherence to social awareness as well as upon its capacity to evolve. Hence, judges have the creative function of elucidating and adapting constitutional principles.

In Mortati's view, the Italian Constitution arose from a society in the process of transformation. He proposed that dissents could help attenuate the risk that case-law might crystallize and become rigidly anchored to precedents. This rigidity would deprive the basic law of its deep bond with popular sentiment – the true foundation for the authority of the Constitution – in the long term, according to Mortati.

Judge Aldo Sandulli, in a public debate also attended by Mortati, drew attention to the risk that organized political parties could take advantage of dissents in a society that remained deeply ideologically divided.[23] The same concern was raised by judge Leopoldo Elia in 1981[24] and by Ugo De Siervo in 2007.[25]

---

[22] According to Article 135 of the Constitution, judges of the Constitutional Court are appointed for nine years, beginning in each case from the day of their swearing in, and may not be re-appointed.

[23] A. SANDULLI, *Intervento*, in G. MARANINI (eds.), *La giustizia costituzionale*, Florence, Vallecchi, 1966, 365 ff.

[24] Leopoldo Elia had a deep knowledge of the role of political parties in shaping the form of government in Italy: his work *Governo, forme di* (published in 1970 in *Enciclopedia del diritto*) is still an essential reading on the topic. See S.C. PANZA, A. REPOSO, *Le "dissenting opinions" ancora alla ribalta, cit.*, 598. Later, Elia changed his mind, in L. ELIA, *Intervento*, in P. PASQUINO, B. RANDAZZO (eds.), *Come decidono le Corti Costituzionali (e altre Corti)*, cit., 128 ff.

[25] U. DE SIERVO, *Intervento*, in P. PASQUINO, B. RANDAZZO (eds.), *Come decidono le*

During a seminar in 1970 Judge Giuseppe Branca, a committed supporter of the value of collegiality, stated that collegiality and dissent were not necessarily opposed to one another, and that the latter could prevent judges from dodging their responsibilities when deciding, particularly on liberal reforms.[26]

Judge Francesco Paolo Casavola, during a 1993 seminar, considered dissent a useful tool to redress the indifference and ignorance that, at the time, were still intertwined with respect for and knowledge of the Court. It is quite telling that he considered dissent to be a "peaceful search for the right decision guided by reason and not by prejudice or passion".[27] On the same occasion, Judge Renato Granata,[28] without taking a position for or against them, expressed his concern that separate opinions would inhibit the efficacy of the principle of collegiality.

Sabino Cassese, in his diary, said he voted in 2010 to introduce dissents in the simplest way: through a modification made directly by the Court to its own internal regulations. He proposed implementing this novelty progressively, in three phases: inserting the different positions into the decision; indicating to which group of judges these opinions are related; and, last, indicating the names of judges and publishing both dissenting and concurring opinions.[29] Cassese believes that making separate opinions transparent would benefit public debate. Although the public conversation on constitutional topics can be highly conflictual, he claims that the different opinions would enrich and not necessarily stir up the debate. He also sees a downside: certain judges might become more influential than others. This was previously a reality of the United States Supreme Court, with "Justice Kennedy...considered the *supreme* judge...because he represent(ed) the *swing voter* among four conservatives and four liberals".

The Court has voted on the topic two times.[30] On July 20th, 1995, the

---

Corti Costituzionali (e altre Corti), cit., 131-133, stressed that political parties and the press would likely use dissents as a tool to put pressure on judges.

[26] Branca did not hide his socialist beliefs. see A. DI MARTINO, *Le opinioni dissenzienti dei giudici costituzionali: uno studio comparativo*, cit., refers to Branca's position, 338, 339-340. Branca (together with Alessandro Pizzorusso, later) edited the most important commentary to the Italian Constitution: G. BRANCA, A PIZZORUSSO, *Commentario della Costituzione*, Bologna-Rome, Zanichelli, published in several volumes since 1975.

[27] F.P. CASAVOLA, *Prefazione*, in A. ANZON, *L'opinione dissenziente*, cit.

[28] In A. ANZON, *L'opinione dissenziente*, cit., 52-54.

[29] S. CASSESE, *Dentro la Corte*, cit., 134 and 50.

[30] Secrecy does not cover non-judicial decisions such as this one, published by the Court itself in *Il dibattito sull'introduzione della c.d. "opinione dissenziente" nel sistema italiano di giustizia costituzionale*, cit., 23 and 25.

Commissione studi e regolamenti (Commission on research and regulations), composed of three judges,[31] rejected a proposal drafted by Mortati in 1965. The question was whether to add a disposition to the Additional rules of the Court allowing for dissent both on the decision and its grounds. The report attached to the proposal advocated a full disclosure of dissents and authors. A few months later, on September 6th, the *plenum* of the Court again entrusted the Commissione studi e regolamenti with a comprehensive new study and a set of proposals. On April 21st, 1997 the Commissione studi e regolamenti[32] agreed unanimously on a proposal adding to the Additional Rules a disposition allowing for anonymous dissent. The proposal was voted five years later, on May 9th, 2002. Only two Judges, Cesare Ruperto (President at that time) and Valerio Onida (later President of the ItCC and of the Italian Association of Constitutional lawyers), were in favor.[33] The majority ruled against it for three reasons: doubts regarding the advisability of anonymous dissents; again, attachment to collegiality and lingering doubts on the opportunity to let internal divisions appear outside the Court; and unsuitability of the Additional Rules as a legal source for such a novelty. Sabino Cassese reported in his *memoir*[34] that a third vote was held in 2010 (no public record is available): only four judges voted for the introduction of dissenting opinions. In all these occasions, the *status quo* prevailed.

As previously mentioned, Gustavo Zagrebelsky changed his mind on the issue after serving as a constitutional judge. In particular, he has argued that it would be impossible to foresee the effects that the alteration would produce. Zagrebelsky fears that separate opinions might foster both attention-seeking behavior by the judges and a deleterious pursuit of public and political party support.[35] Furthermore, he believes that how the innovation would perform over time would be linked, at least partially, to the perception that judges have of themselves, a perception that does not seem to be consistent. Zagrebelsky thinks that the pluralistic essence of the Italian

---

[31] Vassalli, President of the Court, Guizzi and Santosuosso.

[32] Composed by Ruperto, President of the Court, Chieppa and Onida.

[33] See *Il dibattito sull'introduzione della c.d. "opinione dissenziente" nel sistema italiano di giustizia costituzionale*, *cit.*, 25. For an analysis of it, see K. KELEMEN, *Judicial Dissent in European Constitutional Courts. A Comparative and Legal Perspective*, cit., 100; S. PANIZZA, *L'opinione dissenziente e il sistema italiano di giustizia costituzionale: una questione davvero chiusa?*, in *Scritti dei dottorandi in onore di Alessandro Pizzorusso*, Turin, Giappichelli Editore, 2005, 476 ff.; A. DI MARTINO, *Le opinioni dissenzienti dei giudici costituzionali: uno studio comparativo*, cit., 365.

[34] S. CASSESE, *Dentro la Corte*, cit., 134.

[35] G. ZAGREBELSKY, V. MARCENÒ, *Giustizia costituzionale*, Bologna, Il Mulino, 155.

Constitution – which implies the presence of many, coexisting different souls,[36] – should be reflected in the judgements. Hence, separate and (especially) dissenting opinions would weaken this pluralistic vocation.

Unlike Zagrebelsky, Gaetano Silvestri, another influential constitutional lawyer and past President of the Court, has never changed his mind on the topic. He was, and still is, in favor of publishing both dissenting and concurring opinions. He recalls the two 'natures' of ItCC decisions. From an institutional perspective, they perform the 'removal of doubt,' as Carl Schmitt stated (in the well-known debate with Hans Kelsen about the role of the constitutional judge). At the same time, from a cultural standpoint, decisions are messages which explicate the reasons why judges have decided in a certain way, especially to the public. The public should be made aware of different opinions emerging within the ItCC in a given case so that the discussion can continue in society.[37] According to Silvestri, the dissent would 'purify' the majority reasoning, and the minority judges would have the chance to write their opinion.[38] He believes that Parliament would do well to enact this novelty through an ordinary law; however, internal rules adopted directly by the Court could take the place of such a law, should Parliament act too slowly. Currently, the general feeling is that the Court has no intention of changing the *status quo* and letting dissenting opinions come to the surface.

6.3. Pros and cons: the debate among scholars

At the level of doctrine, Italian commentators have discussed both the desirability of introducing separate opinions and the appropriate regulatory instrument for introducing them. It has almost never been debated that the Constitution did not and does not preclude this option.

Seminal considerations have been presented by the following books: *Le opinioni dei giudici costituzionali e internazionali*, edited by Costantino Mortati in 1964 (to which we have already referred); *L'opinione dissenziente*, edited by Adele Anzon in 1995 (collecting the most influential scholarly posi-

---

[36] G. ZAGREBELSKY, *La Corte costituzionale italiana*, cit., 79.

[37] He recalls that the nature of constitutional norms itself implies a consistent margin of oscillation in the interpretation, D. TEGA, *La Corte costituzionale vista da vicino Intervista di Diletta Tega a Gaetano Silvestri*, *cit.*, 757-758.

[38] Here he considers one of the common criticisms of the lack of separate opinions: they would make clearer the majority decision because the judges who disagree with the decision, shared by the majority, would not need to insert their arguments into the reasoning of the Court.

tions expressed during the seminar held at Palazzo della Consulta in 1993); *L'introduzione dell'opinione dissenziente nel sistema di giustizia costituzionale*, by Saulle Panizza, published in 1998; *Le opinioni dissenzienti dei giudici costituzionali: uno studio comparativo*, by Alessandra Di Martino, published in 2016. Within the literature in English, it is worth mentioning the recent works by Katalin Kelemen, *Judicial Dissent in European Constitutional Courts. A Comparative and Legal Perspective*, published in 2018; by Nicolò Zanon[39] and Giada Ragone (edited by), *The dissenting opinion. Selected essays*, published in 2019. Their books also discuss the Italian experience.

The 1993 seminar attempted to examine whether any principle or disposition barred this innovation and, consequently, to establish which would be the most appropriate legal instrument for introducing separate opinions. The seminar proceedings, together with the two books by Panizza and Di Martino, singled out the various points for and against dissent, showing that the doctrinal debate leaned in favor of the prospective introduction of dissenting opinions. This conclusion relied on two theories: the so-called discursive theory (law develops in the dialogue between the parties, and between the parties and the judge), and the-so called deliberative theory[40] (since law is a discussion enlightened by arguments, a richer discussion leads to better law).

These sources listed the following advantages of separate opinions: the enhancement of the independence and autonomy[41] of judges; a deeper analysis and study of the case; a more transparent reasoning, because a separate opinion would allow its authors to disclose the logical process[42] followed and the dialectical[43] foundation of the decision, ultimately bolstering both the authority of the decision itself and the public debate; a clearer and more coherent decision, because there would be no need to

---

[39] Nicolò Zanon was appointed constitutional judge by the President of the Republic in 2014.

[40] Dissenting interpreted as a sort of «marketplace of competing ideas», cited in R. POST, *The Supreme Court Opinion as Institutional Practice: Dissent, Legal Scholarship, and Decision making in the Taft Court*, in 85 *Minn. L. Rev.* 1267 (2001).

[41] For the unforgettable, renowned intellectual, civil lawyer, professor, and writer Piero Calamandrei, the secrecy of the *Camera di Consiglio* was «the institutional consecration of conformism; a typical example of State unanimity, able to save appearances to the detriment of consciences», P. CALAMANDREI, *Elogio del giudice*, III ed., 1955, 274 ff.

[42] A. BALDASSARRE, *L'«opinione dissenziente» e l'intervista di Amidei*, in *Democrazia e diritto* 238 (1981).

[43] A. ANZON, *L'opinione dissenziente*, *cit.*, 434, and before M. CAPPELLETTI, *Questioni nuove (e vecchie) sulla giustizia costituzionale*, in *Giudizio a quo e promovimento del processo costituzionale: atti del Seminario svoltosi a Roma, Palazzo della Consulta, nei giorni 13 e 14 novembre 1989*, Milano, Giuffrè Editore, 1990, 39 ff.

consider minority objections, leading to better understanding of the decision both by Parliament and by ordinary judges; an increase in the case law's dynamism and capacity to evolve and to adapt to the concrete needs and requests coming from society; the chance for a minority opinion to later become the foundation of a future overruling;[44] a suggestion and incentive to ordinary judges to raise new questions and participate in the evolution of the case law.

On the contrary, two fears lie at the heart of Italian skepticism toward separate opinions. On one hand is the fear that social commitment to the values enshrined in Constitution is not yet strong enough, while fractures in public opinion are still highly problematic. On the other hand, some fear an undermining both decisions' moral value and the authority of the ItCC because dissenting opinions would foster uncertainty, conflict, and controversies that could threaten the leading role of the ItCC for *iuris dictio* in general.

It has been argued that the existence of dissenting opinions would make each judge more vulnerable to political pressures, thus making it more difficult for the judges to decide to follow their own consciences.[45] Dissenting opinions would also unduly increase the personalization of the decisions and even some polemical excesses – pushing the judicial body itself away from the principle of collegiality. Dissent would also increase the amount of work for the judges, entailing a general slowing of the Court's pace.[46] Finally, since a dissenting judge would not renounce any potential influence on the majority decision, the decision would not really gain clarity.

Regarding the best suited instrument to introduce that novelty, the options on the table continue to be five: auto-regulation by Court, either by *i*) introducing a specific provision (an Art. 18-*bis*) in the Additional rules for the proceedings before the ItCC (revised in 2008), or *ii*) through an entirely new internal regulation; an amendment to *iii*) ordinary or *iv*) constitutional legislation, enacted by Parliament; *v*) introduction directly through the case law of the ItCC. The first solution received support (in the seminar of 1993 and also later on) from, among others, Mortati, Pizzorusso, Romboli, and

[44] C. MORTATI, *Considerazioni sul problema dell'introduzione del "dissent" nelle pronuncie delle Corte costituzionale italiana*, in G. MARANINI (eds.), *La giustizia costituzionale*, cit., 163; V. ONIDA, *Intervento*, in P. PASQUINO, B. RANDAZZO (eds.), *Come decidono le Corti Costituzionali (e altre Corti)*, cit., 151.

[45] A. ANZON, *L'opinione dissenziente*, cit., 434; A. SANDULLI, *Intervento*, cit., 365.

[46] R. Romboli recommended adopting detailed regulation of separate opinions to prevent delays: R. ROMBOLI, *L'introduzione dell'opinione dissenziente nei giudizi costituzionali: strumento normativo, aspetti procedurali e ragioni di opportunità*, in A. ANZON, *L'opinione dissenziente*, cit., 83.

Panizza. Cassese[47] is for the second option. On the contrary, Zagrebelsky,[48] Anzon, Bartole, and Ruggeri (whose opinions are collected in the book by A. Anzon) support the instrument of constitutional legislation. Stefano Rodotà, as member of Parliament, proposed an ordinary law, and Gaetano Silvestri supports modifying the ordinary law no. 87/1953 (or an internal regulation, as an alternative). The last option was considered to be feasible in the seminar held in 1993 by Romboli, although it was not recommended.

6.4. Conclusion

It is evident that this topic continues to be present in scholarly debate. Many influential constitutional lawyers have weighed in on it. It is possible to affirm that most scholarship falls in favor of instituting the possibility to dissent. Against this trend, there is the telling case of Gustavo Zagrebelsky who, after becoming a constitutional judge, changed his mind on the subject.

The ItCC has debated this issue since the very beginning of its existence. Eminent constitutional judges have spoken openly in favor of dissents, but the principle of collegiality, as developed by the Court, has been one of the strongest obstacles to the introduction of separate opinions. This obstacle is amplified by a reluctance to abandon the *status quo*.

Both without and within the Court, the possibility of separate opinions is not considered to be particularly compelling when compared with other constitutional law topics. The chief reason for this is because the ItCC has performed extremely well compared to other republican powers, and in the last twenty-five years, it has shown a remarkable capacity to keep up with transformations of both political parties and society at large.

There are many variables at work in this process of innovation: there are many unknowns, and their resolution is uncertain; cultural factors play a significant role, and examples taken from experiences elsewhere do not offer a clear point of comparison; finally, there is very little hope of accurately predicting ultimate impacts.[49]

We also assessed the well-developed phenomenon which could be labeled 'internal dissent.' It reflects only a marginal facet of the separate opinions' complex significance: it allows rapporteurs to abstain from drafting judgments they strongly oppose, and only incidentally also allows dissenting

[47] S. CASSESE, *Dentro la Corte*, cit., 134.

[48] G. ZAGREBELSKY, *La Corte costituzionale italiana, cit.,* 77.

[49] G. ZAGREBELSKY, V. MARCENÒ, *Giustizia costituzionale*, cit., 156.

rapporteurs to reveal their opposition. From time to time, judges have also indulged in publicly commenting on decisions they did not support.

In my opinion, the introduction of separate opinions is surely not a pressing concern for the Italian system of constitutional justice, which has historically performed well. Nevertheless, this innovation would have its advantages. Above all, it would pave the way for a better general understanding of current and future rulings, and it would heighten the level of engagement of each individual judge in each individual decision. Fears that dissenting opinions could critically endanger the Court's collegiality, or be exploited by partisan politics, are exaggerated: the Court has proven to be one of the most mature and sound bodies within the Italian constitutional order.

In any case, the Italian debate has brought one clear fact to light: this debate is not merely technical. It is intertwined with the very idea of constitutional justice which a legal system opts for.[50] From a constitutional point of view, the positions both in favor and against separate opinions are legitimate. But, as Zagrebelsky[51] has wisely stated, the ItCC is a body that is radically different from those of common law systems – in which the culture of precedents is deeply rooted[52] – and, in addition, the quality of the public debate in Italy is different from that of other countries.[53] The ItCC was described in 1970 by Franco Modugno (currently sitting as a constitutional judge) as "the island of reason amidst a chaos of opinions".[54] Even if this description might sound a bit overemphatic, the prevailing idea in Italy is that constitutional justice is a function carried out by a body, not by fifteen persons. No pre-fixed majorities or minorities exist. Decisions are ascribed to the Court, not to particular judges or groups of judges. The cru-

[50] More generally, what is at stake is the peculiarity of Italian civil law tradition, as J.H. Merryman masterfully addressed in J.H. MERRYMAN, *The civil law tradition: an introduction to the legal systems of western Europe and Latin America*, Palo Alto, Stanford University Press, 1969. Merryman recalls that a legal tradition is «a set of deeply rooted, historically conditioned attitudes about the nature of law, about the role of law in the society and the polity, about the proper organization and operation of a legal system, and about the way law is or should be made, applied, studied, perfected, and taught. The legal tradition relates the legal system to the culture of which it is a partial expression. It puts the legal system into cultural perspective», 2.

[51] G. ZAGREBELSKY, *La Corte costituzionale italiana*, *cit.*, 76.

[52] V. VARANO, *A proposito dell'eventuale introduzione delle opinioni dissenzienti nelle pronunce della corte costituzionale: considerazioni sull'esperienza americana*, in A. ANZON, *L'opinione dissenziente*, cit., 129 ff.

[53] On this, see the useful points made by S. CASSESE, *Una lezione sulla cosiddetta opinione dissenziente,* in *Quaderni costituzionali*, No. 4, 973 (2009), 977-980.

[54] F. MODUGNO, *L'invalidità della legge*, I Milan, Giuffré Editore, 1970, XI.

cial factor is understanding how the Court decides: this influences the structure of the decisions and, consequently, the opportunity to dissent. To come back to what I said at the beginning of this article, Gustavo Zagrebelsky has written that the ItCC does not follow a vertical line of deductive reasoning, or a logic that divides and demands the casting and tallying of individual votes.

Chapter VII

"COLLEGIALITY" IN COMPARATIVE CONTEXT

Sarah Harding

Professor Dilletta Tega's paper reviews the various arguments for and against "collegial" decision-making on the Italian Constitutional Court. In this context "collegial" decision-making is defined as decisions arrived at in secrecy, published as one single opinion with no concurrences or dissents. The author of the opinion, typically the rapporteur, is not anonymous. While separate opinions are not permitted, there is no requirement that decisions actually be unanimous. [1] Since voting is private and secret there is no indication of the internal tally aside from knowing that a majority of judges were able to accept the written opinion. Professor Tega's primary focus is the richness of the debate regarding this unique element of Italian constitutional decision-making. The "collegiality" requirement has been a focus of robust debate since the creation of the Court in the 1950s and has continued to play out within the judiciary, the legislature, and among constitutional scholars. [2]

While the debate is no doubt complex, one comes away from Professor Tega's paper with two straightforward conclusions. First, the arguments for or against a "collegiality" requirement have been relatively static over time. As Professor Tega notes, constitutional scholars and judges were actively arguing for the introduction of separate opinions within the first ten years of the Italian Constitutional Court's establishment. Proponents of the change argued that separate opinions would lead to deeper analysis, more consistent majority decisions and a "general enrichment" of constitutional law. On the other hand the most consistent arguments for continued "collegiality" were and continue to be concerns about the reputation of the

[1] Rules on the Constitution and the Functioning of the Constitutional Court Law 11 March 1953, n. 87 Art. 16.

[2] *See* K. KELEMEN, *Dissenting Opinions in Constitutional Courts*, in 14 *German L.J.* 1345 (2013), 1369 (noting that the debate regarding the value of dissenting opinions has been particularly robust in Italy despite the lack of separate opinions).

Court, in particular judicial independence, and the benefits of reaching a consensus.

The second clear conclusion is the consistent alignment of the arguments. On the one hand the arguments for "collegiality" focus on the reputation of the Court as a whole. Both the secretive process of arriving at a single, collective decision and publishing that decision as a reflection of the position of the Court as a whole is justified as necessary to preserve the legitimacy of the Court as an impartial, non-partisan institution. This argument, as Professor Kelemen notes in her study of dissenting opinions, is based on the "external aspect of judicial independence". [3] The publication of a single Court decision, while inhibiting internal judicial independence, arguably limits opportunities for external political pressure. Separate opinions risk exposing judges to external political influence, thus undermining "the moral strength of constitutional judgments" and the reputation of the Court. Whatever one might think of these arguments, single majority decisions at the very least make it difficult to *consistently* critique the politics of the Court or of any one judge.

There are some references in Professor Tega's paper to the importance of reaching consensus as an argument in favor of "collegiality". The idea that decisions are reached not by vote but by deliberation – and through that deliberation, some sort of consensus – is particularly prominent in the commentary of Justice Gustavo Zagrebelsky. But in the history of the debate over "collegiality" that Professor Tega details, the value of consensus seems secondary. Concerns about the legitimacy of the Court and its justices appear to be the primary focus of arguments in favor of retaining the "principle of collegiality".

On the other hand, most of the arguments against "collegiality" or for permitting separate opinions tend to focus on the development of constitutional law and legal principles. The arguments articulated in the 1960s, particularly by Justice Costantino Mortati, are similar to arguments made more recently in favor of separate opinions: "public awareness of constitutional law would be better served by the clear and precise expression of different and divergent rational arguments". As Professor Tega notes, both discursive and deliberative theories of law and legal development support separate and independent decisions as a means to more fully encourage and enhance debates about constitutional law.

Finally, by way of summary, Professor Tega herself seems to prefer a shift towards permitting separate opinions. Following the traditional fault lines of the arguments for and against "collegiality", she rejects concerns

---

[3] K. KELEMEN, *Dissenting Opinions in Constitutional Courts*, *supra.* note 2, 1359.

that permitting dissents would unduly affect the reputation of the Court, and argues that separate opinions would have a positive affect on legal development.

Professor Tega recognizes from the outset that "collegiality" on the Italian Constitutional Court is very much a contextual issue. Concerns about the legitimacy and reputation of the Court as a new legal institution were central at the moment of its creation, thus providing much support for the "principle of collegiality". As Professor Tega notes, "It bears remembering that, at the outset, things were not easy for the Italian Constitutional Court: its establishment was a crucial novelty ...". While the Court has cemented its reputation, indeed its performance outshines other branches of government, for some this provides more support for maintaining the status quo rather than moving to a different model. In short, while greater institutional maturity encourages some to argue for innovation, the strong reputation of the Court leads others to resist rocking an otherwise stable and secure boat. Furthermore, one cannot ignore the broader political chaos in Italy that obliges the Italian Constitutional Court to continue performing as an "island of reason".

Given these important contextual limitations, it is with some hesitation that I wade into a broader discussion about "collegiality". My background is firmly rooted in the common law tradition and the benefits of comparing Italian Constitutional Court rules and processes with those of common law supreme courts are, at best, limited. Even without factoring in the unique contextual aspects of the operation of the Court, the institutional and historical distinctions between European constitutional courts and common law supreme courts make comparison difficult.[4] But with this difficulty firmly recognized, a general exploration of collegiality might at a minimum add some interesting color to the Italian debate and suggest some additional lines of analysis.

Two broad points might be gleaned from a review of the decision-making processes and constraints of other courts. First, there is a wide variety of decision-making options, from a system of completely independent seriatim, signed decisions to unanimous, *per curiam* or "by the court" unsigned decisions. Identifying the various models and determining when courts with options choose one approach over another might provide a richer set of ideas for discussing the "principle of collegiality". The second

[4] In the context of decision-making norms, some of these broader systemic distinctions are detailed in K. KELEMEN, *Dissenting Opinions in Constitutional Courts, supra.* note 2, and in her recent book, K. KELEMEN, *Judicial Dissent in European Constitutional Courts: A Comparative and Legal Perspective*, Abingdon and New York, Routledge, 2018.

broad point is that the fault lines so clearly evident in Professor Tega's summary of the pros and cons of "collegiality" might not be so clear in other contexts. It might not be the case that the strongest arguments for "collegiality" stem from broader concerns about the independence of judges and the general reputation of the court. Indeed, it might be the case that single decisions, whether unanimous or reflecting a mere majority of judicial votes, are important tools for legal development, without necessarily limiting the dialogic and discursive benefits presumptively connected with separate and dissenting opinions.

The following commentary will explore some of these broader considerations regarding "collegiality". The next section will look briefly at a spectrum of decision-making options identifying examples of each approach. Following that the paper explores the arguments frequently utilized for opting for more or less collegial decisions. A very brief final part will look at other significant factors that influence perceptions about the legitimacy of a court, factors that Professor Tega briefly references.

There are two important things this commentary will not explore. First, Professor Tega's paper addresses, albeit briefly, the various regulatory means available for instituting changes in the Italian Constitutional Court system of decision-making. I will not address this aspect of her paper.

Second, and much more broadly, there is a significant civil law/common law divide underlining much of this discussion. Most of the examples I introduce to fill out the collegiality discussion come from common law systems, in particular Canada and the United States. Needless to say, and as already noted, common law supreme courts are different from European constitutional courts in a wide and complex variety of ways. And, of course, common law supreme courts have historically embraced a tradition of separate – both concurring and dissenting – opinions. While this is true of all common law systems, the U.S. Supreme Court has become most infamous for the independent decision-making of each Justice leading to what some argue is a "cult of personality". [5] This may indeed be one of the most interesting (not necessarily admirable) distinguishing features of the U.S. Supreme Court. [6] But the purposes of this commentary are very lim-

---

[5] See, *e.g.* T. KOPAN, *The Not So Reclusive Justices*, Politico, 28 June 2013. Available at https://www.politico.com/story/2013/06/supreme-court-justices-public-appearances-093583 last visited February 20, 2020.

[6] One can hardly imagine anything like the current popularity of the documentary about Ruth Bader Ginsburg, happening anywhere outside of the United States. *See Documentary 'RBG' Explores the Cult of Personality Around Ruth Bader Ginsburg*, Radio Boston, 11 May 2018. Available at http://www.wbur.org/radioboston/2018/05/11/rbg-documentary-film last visited February 20, 2020. Nor could one imagine anything like the intense public and political scrutiny over the confirmation hearings of Justice Brett Ka-

ited and there is no space for taking account of broader systemic differences between the opinion writing of common law supreme courts and European constitutional courts. In any event, the vast majority of European constitutional courts already permit dissents and separate opinions, so it's not clear that the common law/civil law divide in this area really matters as much as it might have previously.[7]

7.1. A spectrum of collegiality

The "principle of collegiality" or just "collegiality" is put in quotes throughout this paper when referring to the unique approach to decision-making on the Italian Constitutional Court. It is utilized as a term of art reflecting a form of decision-making that requires collective decisions without concurrences or dissents, giving the appearance of unanimity. But as noted in the introduction, it does not require unanimous or anonymous decisions. The author of an opinion, typically the assigned judge-rapporteur, is clearly noted and recognized in the decision and in the identification of the case on the Court's website. So while the requirement of reaching a decision in secrecy and publishing a single decision of the Court lends a "black box" element to the Court's decision-making, the recognition of an author provides at least a tiny and very important window into an otherwise entirely secret and collaborative process.

I call attention to this because it suggests another element in a range of discrete and interchangeable elements when it comes to the process of crafting, writing, and publishing decisions. There are choices beyond the basic separate opinions or no separate opinions dichotomy. In terms of analyzing collegiality more generally we can look at the process of choosing which cases to hear, the process of arriving at a legal conclusion, the rules or norms regarding writing decisions, the identification of the opinion writer, and the rules regarding the publication of those decisions.[8] All of these

vanaugh that were ongoing when this paper was written, occurring in a European constitutional court system.

[7] K. Kelemen, *Dissenting Opinions in Constitutional Courts*, *supra.* note 2 at 1351.("The comparative overview … shows that the publication of dissents is not limited anymore to the practice of common law judges. Today it is a widespread practice even in continental Europe".) It's also worth noting that even the traditional abstract v. concrete decision-making divide is less pronounced than in the past with many constitutional courts providing for avenues of concrete decision-making and many arguing that much of the work of the US Supreme Court is really abstract constitutional reasoning. *Id.* 1355.

[8] *See* F.B. Cross, E.H. Tiller, *Understanding Collegiality on the Court,* in 10 *Journal*

elements can contribute more broadly to questions or concerns about the collective decision-making of a constitutional court. In combination they can be placed on a loose spectrum of collegial decision-making. The chart below (*Fig.1*) captures only a small segment of these elements.

Least Collegial					**Most Collegial**
Seriatim opinions Publicly authored Without conferencing or collaboration	**Seriatim opinions** Publicly authored With conferencing and collaboration	**Majority/ Plurality opinions** Attempt to reach a single majority decision through conferencing and collaboration Publicly authored Separate opinions permitted	**"By the court" or *per curiam* opinions** Majority decision is anonymous Separate publicly authored opinions permitted	**Single majority opinions** Publicly authored majority decision No additional independent decisions permitted ("Principle of Collegiality")	**"By the court" or *per curiam* opinions** Single opinion No authorial attribution

Let's begin at the end of the spectrum furthest from the "principle of collegiality" – a system of independent seriatim decisions that are the product of equally independent, non-collaborative analysis. To my knowledge, there is no current supreme or constitutional court that operates without some form of collaborative discussion and analysis, but there is a wonderful historic example of this in the early Supreme Court of Canada. That court produced seriatim non-collaborative opinions partly from tradition, but also as a matter of convenience. The justices were drawn from different regions and only rarely met together as a single bench. They operated completely "independent of each other rather than holding conference".[9] According to the authors of a recent book on, among other things, collegiality in the Supreme Court of Canada, "The fact the court did not harmonize in its judgments may partially explain its lack of legitimacy at the time".[10] The

of Constitutional Law 257 (2008), 259 (detailing some elements that lead to greater or lesser collegiality among judges).

[9] D.R. Songer, S.W. Johnson, C.L. Ostberg, M.E. Wetstein, *Law Ideology, and Collegiality: Judicial Behaviour in the Supreme Court of Canada,* Montreal, McGill-Queen's University Press, 2012, 20.

[10] *Id.* 19.

early years of the Supreme Court of Canada are generally considered to be a failure.[11]

It's worth noting that the U.S. Supreme Court also began in the tradition of seriatim opinions, with no process of conferencing or collaborative analysis. In 1801 Chief Justice John Marshall single-handedly altered this tradition, arguing that the Court would be stronger if it issued plurality opinions, speaking with one voice as much as possible.[12] Both of these examples provide interesting comparative support outside the constitutional court tradition for the "principle of collegiality" in the early years of the Italian Constitutional Court.

Moving through the spectrum, the UK Supreme Court provides a high-profile example of a court that still frequently follows the tradition of seriatim opinions, although with the added benefit of conferencing. Certainly there is more collective discussion and collaboration than might have been the case in previous generations, and the Justices are encouraged to publish plurality or majority decisions when appropriate.[13] But an emphasis on the individual responsibility of each Justice and a desire to produce the widest possible range of legal ideas has kept the UK Supreme Court firmly on the left side of this spectrum. Although it should be noted that the proliferation of separate opinions does not necessarily mean there is a higher level of dissent. Indeed, the UK Supreme Court frequently has a higher rate of unanimous outcomes than other common law supreme courts. So the justices more frequently agree on the final judgment, but regularly write separate opinions expressing their agreement.[14]

The majority of supreme and constitutional courts sit in the middle of this spectrum, most of the time. They operate with no formal limitations on the publication of separate opinions and most opinions are publicly autho-

---

[11] *Id.* 18-20.

[12] R. ROTUNDA, *The Fall of Seriatim Opinion and the Rise of the Supreme Court*, Verdict: Legal Analysis and Commentary from Justia, 9 October 2017. Available at https://verdict.justia.com/2017/10/09/fall-seriatim-opinions-rise-supreme-court, last visited February 20, 2020. *See also*, M.T. HENDERSON, *From Seriatim to Consensus and Back Again: A Theory of Dissent*, in *John M. Olin Law & Economics Working Paper*, No. 363, 1 (2007), 21-24.

[13] Lady HALE, *Judgment Writing in the Supreme Court*, UK Supreme Court Blog, 25 October 2010, available at http://ukscblog.com/judgment-writing-in-the-supreme-court-brenda-hale/ last visited February 20, 2020 (noting a trend toward more "plurality or effectively plurality judgments" but endorsing the tradition of separate opinions provided there is no "grandstanding or self-indulgence").

[14] *See Dissenting Opinions in the UKSC*, UK Supreme Court Blog, 19 August 2010, available at http://ukscblog.com/dissenting-opinons-in-the-uksc/ last visited February 20, 2020 (detailing a comparative study of dissents in common law jurisdictions).

red. Both dissents and concurrences are permitted.[15] Clear majority decisions are preferred, but plurality decisions in which there is no single clear legal opinion are not unusual, at least that is certainly the case in the United States.[16] While the absence of rules prohibiting separate opinions, combined with a preference for unanimous or at least clear majority decisions when possible, provides a shared set of norms across the U.S./European divide, European constitutional courts are different in that they rarely make public the internal voting on the court[17] and they "exert more effort to reach unanimity" than their American counterpart.[18]

There is a strange tension between the next two categories along the spectrum. First is the category of anonymous majority opinions that permit authored dissents and concurrences – an approach that has been used in some high-profile American cases. *Bush v. Gore*[19] was a *per curiam* decision but it included one concurrence by Chief Justice Rehnquist and four separately authored dissents. The "Pentagon Papers Case"[20], was a narrowly crafted *per curiam* decision but each of the nine justices wrote separate opinions – six concurrences and three dissents – articulating different reasons. Authored dissents actually occurred in almost 50 percent of all *per curiam* decisions of the Supreme Court from 1946 to 2011.[21] This puzzling category can be juxtaposed to the approach of the Italian Constitutional Court that requires authored, as opposed to anonymous, collective decisions, but prohibits separate opinions, an approach also followed by a small handful of other European constitutional courts. Given the controversy generated by a decision like *Bush v. Gore,*[22] the Italian approach is evident-

---

[15] It is worth noting that at times these separate decisions push more toward the seriatim end of the spectrum where there is no clear majority opinion. In the U.S. *See, e.g., Van Orden v. Perry* 545 U.S. 677 (2005) The case concerned the constitutionality of a large display of the Ten Commandments outside the Texas State Capitol. The Court concluded that the Establishment Clause did not prohibit the display but the six different opinions – an opinion of the court, three concurrences and two dissents – led Chief Justice Rehnquist to quip when announcing the decision "I didn't know we had that many people on our court". R. ROTUNDA, *The Fall of Seriatim Opinions and the Rise of the Supreme Court, supra.* note 12. There is no clear majority decision in that case.

[16] *See* J. SPRIGGS II, D.R. STRAUSS, *Explaining Plurality Decisions*, in 99 *Georgetown L.J.* 515 (2011).

[17] K. KELEMEN, *Dissenting Opinions in Constitutional Courts, supra.* note 2 at 1362.

[18] *Id.* 1365.

[19] 531 US 98 (2000).

[20] *New York Times v. U.S.* 403 U.S. 713 (1971).

[21] *See* M.C. GIZZI, S.L. WASBY, *Per Curiams Revisited: Assessing the Unsigned Opinion*, in 96 *Judicature* 110 (2012), 112.

[22] In a Time magazine survey of 50 law professors, "many professors were critical of ...

ly more collegial than anonymous opinions with dissents and concurrences, but the *per curiam* status of the majority decision does give it a gloss of baseline agreement.

At the far end of the spectrum is a single unanimous anonymous decision "by the court". This is a category the Canadian Supreme Court uses with some regularity when it wishes to emphasize the importance of a decision. Such decisions were rare prior to Chief Justice Bora Laskin in the 1970s and increased dramatically after the passage of the Canadian Charter of Rights and Freedoms in 1982.[23] Since that time they have served as an important decision-making tool in very high-profile cases. Indeed some of the most important Charter cases have been "by the court", including cases regarding minority language rights, fetal rights, Quebec secession, gun control, extradition when execution is a possible penalty, torture, same sex marriage, physician-assisted suicide, and a range of aboriginal rights cases.[24] It's interesting that the Court chooses this approach when it feels it's in the spotlight. This is in contrast to the US Supreme Court that typically opts for unanimous *per curiam* decisions with no dissents or concurrences when the matter is simply "judicial housekeeping", routine, or unimportant.[25]

More broadly speaking the Canadian Supreme Court has a relatively high level of unanimity in its decision-making, hovering around 60 percent of all cases[26] compared to approximately 40 percent in the U.S. Supreme Court. There are a range of possible structural and procedural reasons for these differences between two otherwise similar common law supreme courts, but many argue that the Canadian Supreme Court is indeed "more oriented towards consensus in decision-making".[27] In a series of interviews with justices in the McLachlin Court, "[s]everal justices indicated that the

---

Bush v. Gore (2000) ..." A. SACHS, *The Worst Supreme Court Decisions Since 1960,* Time, 6 October 2015. Available at http://time.com/4056051/worst-supreme-court-decisions/ last visited February 20, 2020.

[23] Canadian Charter of Rights and Freedoms, Part I of the Constitution Act, 1982, being Schedule B to the Canada Act 1982 (UK), 1982, c 11.

[24] For a full list of these cases since 1980 to the present *see* https://en.wikipedia.org/wiki/By_the_Court_decisions_of_the_Supreme_Court_of_Canada.

[25] *See* M.C. GIZZI, S.L. WASBY, Per Curiams Revisited: Assessing the Unsigned Opinion, *supra.* note 21, 110, 112-114.

[26] B. ALARIE, A. GREEN, *Should They All Just Get Along? Judicial Ideology, Collegiality, and Appointments to the Supreme Court of Canada*, in 58 *U. New Brunswick L.J.* 73 (2008), 78; *See also* Supreme Court of Canada Statistics 2007-2017. Available at https://www.scc-csc.ca/case-dossier/stat/pdf/doc-eng.pdf last visited February 20, 2020.

[27] *Id.* 78.

current chief justice prefers to have the court speak with one voice and encourages justices who express initial differences to try to work them out if possible" [28]. Collegiality rather than ideology appears to be an important decision-making influence.

The Canadian reliance on more frequent unanimous and "by the court" decisions may be connected to the power-sharing dynamics of the Court. [29] The arbitration function of the Court, deciding matters that reflect the underlining divided nature of the country's broader institutional and consociational democratic model, requires a model of decision-making that embraces consensus. [30] Unlike other stronger power-sharing courts, for example the Constitutional Court of Belgium, the Canadian Court is not required by its governing rules to reach consensus in its decision-making, but the tendency to do so is a strong internal norm, central to its desire to achieve a high level of legitimacy. [31]

The purpose of providing a quick glance at all these options is to introduce a few more ideas and examples into the discussion. The debate in Italy, as Professor Tega has chronicled, seems to focus first and foremost on permitting separate opinions. But it would be interesting to hear more about some of the finer details regarding, for example, authorship and publication. If the introduction of separate opinions raises concerns about external independence and the personal perspective of judges eclipsing the status of the court, might anonymous dissents remedy this? Professor Tega mentions in passing that anonymity in dissents has been an important part of the Italian Constitutional Court debate going back to the early proposals by Costantino Mortati. Additionally, it was part of the proposed rule changes that were voted down by the Court in 2002 and 2010. According to Professor Tega's presentation of her chapter at a 2018 workshop, there is no real precedent for anonymous decisions in Italian judicial decision-making, and yet the idea was important enough to appear in these proposed rule changes. It would be interesting to know more about the impact of suggested anonymity on the "collegiality" debate. The use of anonymous decisions, whether in dissents, [32] majority decisions, or in opinions of the

---

[28] D.R. SONGER, S.W. JOHNSON, C.L. OSTBERG, M.E. WETSTEIN, *Law Ideology, and Collegiality: Judicial Behaviour in the Supreme Court of Canada*, *supra.* note 9 at 91.

[29] *See* S. GRAZIADEI, *Power Sharing Courts*, in 3(1) *Contemporary Southeastern Europe* 66 (2016).

[30] *Id.* 86.

[31] D.R. SONGER, S.W. JOHNSON, C.L. OSTBERG, M.E. WETSTEIN, *Law Ideology, and Collegiality: Judicial Behaviour in the Supreme Court of Canada*, *supra.* note 9 at 153-157.

[32] Anonymous dissents have been a tradition in the Greek courts. K. KELEMEN, *Dissenting Opinions in Constitutional Courts*, *supra.* note 2 at 1349.

court as a whole, adds an interesting twist to discussions about court legitimacy and the weight of particular legal decisions.

Similarly, might the publication of dissents at another time, in something like a yearly chronicle of additional opinions address some of the concerns about destroying the current benefits of "collegiality?" This is the approach of a handful of Central and Eastern European constitutional courts.[33] It also appears to be happening in an ad hoc fashion on the Italian Constitutional Court with some judges opting to make public their views about specific legal decisions either after the end of their term on the Court, or in some cases even during their tenure.[34] Reactions to some of these secondary considerations in the debate over "collegiality" might add more complexity to the overall analysis.

7.2. Dialogue and legal development

Professor Tega's paper suggests that controversies regarding opinion writing on the United States Supreme Court have been an important influence in the debate over the "principle of collegiality". The highly politicized nature of the U.S. Supreme Court and what some might argue is excessive grandstanding by individual Justices in their opinions continue to draw attention to the pitfalls of permitting separate opinions. While the influence of the experiences of the U.S. Court is secondary to the influence of the rules and traditions of other European constitutional courts, the American tradition with all its pros and cons looms large. And in many ways that tradition supports the basic fault lines in the Italian debate.[35] Separate opinions have been an important tool of legal development throughout the history of the U.S. Supreme Court. As noted above, single *per curiam* decisions are utilized primarily in inconsequential cases, and in the somewhat rare instance where the Court opts for a *per curiam* decision on a very important matter, separate opinions, both dissents and concurrences are common. Unanimous signed decisions on high profile matters are rare.[36] While all of this might affect the

---

[33] *Id.* 1351.

[34] Even the UK Supreme Court has shifted its approach to publishing judgments, leading with the majority or plurality decision when it exists or as Lady Hale calls it the "donkey-work" judgment, rather than publishing decisions in order of seniority. Lady HALE, *Judgment Writing in the Supreme Court*, *supra.* note 13.

[35] For a thorough treatment of the history of the U.S. debate on these issues *see,* M.T. HENDERSON, *From Seriatim to Consensus and Back Again: A Theory of Dissent*, *supra.* note 12.

[36] An interesting and important counter example is *Brown v. Board of Education of*

legitimacy of the Court, or at least cast doubt about the weight of decisions for which there are multiple separate opinions, this historically has been a marginal concern for the U.S. Supreme Court.[37]

But it's worth looking a little more closely at what occurs north of the American border. The habits and preferences of the Canadian Supreme Court are, as noted above, inverted. The more important the case, the more they strive for unanimity and even anonymity. It would be easy to argue that this too follows the basic fault line in the Italian Constitutional Court debate – a single decision is utilized in exceptional cases out of concern about institutional and judicial legitimacy,[38] while separate opinions in the interest of legal development are the norm. But in fact, the justifications for single decisions are frequently framed in terms of legal development, not institutional legitimacy. Most importantly single decisions are frequently used to promote certainty, clarity, and ongoing collegiality.[39]

Similarly, the arguments encouraging the UK Supreme Court to strive for more majority or plurality opinions, without a confusing series of additional opinions, are primarily rooted in legal development, not institutional legitimacy. Avoiding the appearance that justice and legal interpretation is a matter of individual opinion is an important consideration, but equally important are concerns about clarity and certainty. These concerns are a significant challenge for the UK Supreme Court with its more robust tradition of seriatim opinions.[40] In short arguments focused on limiting separate opinions in both the Canadian and UK context are rooted in concerns about the development of legal norms, not just concerns about institutional and judicial legitimacy.

Topeka 347 U.S. 483 (1954). This was a rare unanimous decision on a highly political and divisive issue, authored by Chief Justice Earl Warren.

[37] Indeed we appear to be at a point in time where the politics of the Supreme Court matter more to people than what goes on in congress or the executive branch, leading many to support an otherwise unpopular president because he promised to appoint conservative justices. *See* J. COASTON, *Polling Data Shows Republicans Turned Out for Trump in 2016 because of the Supreme Court*, Vox, 29 June 2018. Available at https://www.vox.com/2018/6/29/17511088/scotus-2016-election-poll-trump-republicans-kennedy-retire last visited February 20, 2020.

[38] An example where this might be a particularly convincing argument is the Quebec Secession case. *Reference Re Secession of Quebec* [1998] 2 SCR 217.

[39] D.R. SONGER, S.W. JOHNSON, C.L. OSTBERG, M.E. WETSTEIN, *Law Ideology, and Collegiality: Judicial Behaviour in the Supreme Court of Canada*, *supra.* note 9 at 153-164.

[40] *See* Lady HALE, *Judgment Writing in the Supreme Court*, *supra.* note 13 (recognizing that there is a high level of support for separate opinions but drawing attention to some of the downsides in terms of legal development and clarity for both lower courts and potential litigants).

The idea that a single decision, unencumbered with dissents and concurrences, tends to generate more legal certainty is self-evident. But certainty is not the same as productive and meaningful legal development, particularly if it comes in the form of limited narrow opinions. Indeed, reaching better outcomes or more just and responsive legal conclusions requires a more robust set of ever-evolving ideas, not just certainty. Dialogue, which is at the heart of the deliberative and discursive theories that Professor Tega notes provide the theoretical foundations for arguments permitting separate opinions, is central to the development of law, particularly constitutional law. And dialogue as a productive principle supports the idea of more, not fewer, legal ideas. But separate, including dissenting, opinions are not the only way to ensure a robust dialogue. It is entirely possible that single plurality decisions of a court also encourage dialogue, or at the very least do not stifle important debate about the intricacies of legal interpretation, in at least two important ways.

First, the need, or in the Italian context the requirement, to come to agreement on a single opinion necessarily requires greater internal dialogue and debate. If the justices themselves reflect a range of political and legal traditions,[41] and if we assume they are some of the best legal minds of their time within their legal system, this internal dialogue is arguably the most important of all possible legal dialogues. The process of internal deliberation and "unifying diverging viewpoints, without casting and tallying individual votes" is not only important on a case-by-case basis, it leads to a deliberative collegial relationship between the justices that ensures ongoing robust debate about constitutional norms. Justices, even those who have shorter term-limits than the lifetime appointment of U.S. Supreme Court justices, are repeat players who must find ways to get along and produce meaningful outcomes. They are "locked into intricate webs of interdependence"[42]. Requiring a single collective decision concentrates and enhances interdependence and internal dialogue.[43] Permitting separate opinions would not necessarily short-circuit this internal dialogue, but it would certainly affect its intensity and significance.

---

[41] This opens up another significant line of comparative inquiry into diversity or variety in judicial appointments. For the present purposes it is sufficient to note that the rules regarding judicial appointments in the Italian context have the potential to create a court with a broad variety of legal experience and representation from the bench, the academy and politics. *See* V. BARSOTTI, P.G. CAROZZA, M. CARTABIA, A. SIMONCINI, *Italian Constitutional Justice in Global Context*, Oxford, Oxford University Press, 2016, 239.

[42] F.B. Cross, E.H. Tiller, *Understanding Collegiality on the Court*, *supra.* note 8 at 259.

[43] *See* V. BARSOTTI, P.G. CAROZZA, M. CARTABIA, A. SIMONCINI, *Italian Constitutional Justice in Global Context*, *supra.* note 41 at 239-240.

Second, single court opinions may also encourage external dialogue precisely because of their limited nature. While some might find narrow conclusions unsatisfactory or reflecting "lame and illusory unanimity", it's possible they provide more space for ongoing cross-institutional interpretation, which is of course its own form of dialogue.[44] In this way the decisions that are the result of the "principle of collegiality" call to mind the work of Cass Sunstein on "minimalism". Cass Sunstein argues that "minimalism", a judicial style most closely associated in the United States with retired Justice Sandra Day O'Connor, more effectively "leaves room for democratic debate and experimentation".[45] Like standards, versus rules, narrow minimalist decisions "permit a kind of continuing dialogue within the polity, and between the Court and other institutions, in a way that promotes learning".[46] Sunstein goes on to argue that minimalist decisions are also "democracy-forcing in the particular sense that they work to ensure that decisions are made by the democratically preferred institution of government".[47]

While the single majority decisions of the Italian Constitutional Court are not necessarily "minimalist" in the Sunstein or Justice O'Connor sense, compromise typically creates more limited or "fudgier" decisions.[48] The core of the argument against "collegiality" is the fact it restricts the publication of a variety of legal arguments. In other words, it limits the Court to the publication of fewer legal avenues of analysis that are frequently the product of much internal compromise. While this may not necessarily generate "minimalist" decisions in the American sense, the single majority decisions of the Italian Constitutional Court must by their limited nature share some of the dialogue and democracy-forcing features. In this way, the "principle of collegiality" may in fact contribute to the "institutional relationality" of the Court.[49]

---

[44] This cross-institutional dialogue may be particularly important in the Italian system with the existence of strong and reputable ordinary and administrative courts. *Id.* 237.

[45] C. SUNSTEIN, *Problems with Minimalism*, in 58 *Stanford L. Rev.* 1899 (2006), 1915. For a longer and more complete discussions of judicial minimalism, *see* C. SUNSTEIN, *One Case At A Time: Judicial Minimalism on the Supreme Court,* Cambridge, Harvard University Press, 1999.

[46] *Id.* 1916.

[47] *Id.* 1916.

[48] *See* D.R. SONGER, S.W. JOHNSON, C.L. OSTBERG, M.E. WETSTEIN, *Law Ideology, and Collegiality: Judicial Behaviour in the Supreme Court of Canada*, *supra.* note 9 at 92; F.B. CROSS, E.H. TILLER, *Understanding Collegiality on the Court*, *supra.* note 8 at 162-163.

[49] V. BARSOTTI, P.G. CAROZZA, M. CARTABIA, A. SIMONCINI, *Italian Constitutional Justice in Global Context*, *supra.* note 41 at 235-237.

This is an entirely different, but quite important take on decision-making and dialogue. Instead of looking to the varied and separate opinions of judges to enhance debate over constitutional norms, it suggests dialogue might be the product of more limited judicial opinions. According to Professor Sunstein, a narrow, minimalist approach may be particularly important in "frontier" cases – areas of legal interpretation that are relatively new and uncharted territory: "In the most difficult and sensitive cases, at the frontiers of constitutional law, the Court usually does best if it proceeds narrowly"[50]. By implication, although this is also made explicit in Sunstein's scholarship, judicial minimalism is not always preferable. Broad constitutional decisions and more varied normative reasoning may play an important role in well-established areas of constitutional law.

This brief analysis is not intended to be an argument against the dialogic benefits of separate opinions. Having a robust open dialogue in the form of separate opinions accessible to all clearly generates ongoing debate about constitutional norms and interpretation. My point is it would be a mistake to view separate opinions as the only way to promote effective dialogue or to see single majority decisions as not, in their own way, encouraging the development of legal norms. Both the internal dialogue of the court and the external dialogue that is generated from being limited to a single decision are important avenues for legal development. Furthermore, when one factors in the argument that single decisions are important tools for clarity and certainty it may be the case that such decisions play a greater role over time in legal development, effectively balancing dialogue and certainty.

7.3. Institutional legitimacy

The first section in this paper set out a simple spectrum of decision-writing options with full seriatim decisions at one end and anonymous unanimous decisions at the other. The point of this discussion was to introduce some complexity into the debate about collegiality. The next section then explored whether the arguments that seem most prominent in the Italian context for separate opinions, arguments focused primarily on legal development, can be used in support of the current "principle of collegiality". The aim of this section wasn't to challenge the arguments for separate opinions but rather to see the development of legal ideas as a complicated mix of internal and external dialogue, with the internal aspect being particularly well supported by the "principle of collegiality".

This final section will draw attention briefly to a few considerations re-

[50] C. SUNSTEIN, *Problems with Minimalism*, *supra.* note 45 at 1918.

garding institutional legitimacy. I want to begin by relying on a distinction drawn by Wojciech Sadurski between "input legitimacy" and "output legitimacy".[51] "Input legitimacy" refers to the pedigree of a constitutional court, including the process for appointing judges. "Output legitimacy" refers to the impact of a court's case law.

Institutional legitimacy concerns focused on judicial independence stemming from the possible introduction of separate opinions clearly relate to "output legitimacy". Rules and traditions relating to authorship and publication are arguably the most important factors contributing to the public image of a court with respect to its decisions – and thus to "output legitimacy". This may be even more so in the European constitutional court context where jurisdiction is limited to constitutional matters. Needless to say, what courts say in their decisions and how they say it matters. But concerns about institutional legitimacy that focus mostly on "output legitimacy" are incomplete. If those arguing for the status quo in the Italian context do so based on concerns about legitimacy, perhaps there should be, if there isn't already, broader consideration of "input legitimacy" factors.

"Input" factors are first and foremost rules and processes relating to judicial selection and appointment, matters that relate to the pedigree of a court. These matters loom large in the U.S. and Canadian context. The judicial nomination and confirmation process of Supreme Court Justices in the United States has had a significant impact on perceptions about the Supreme Court as a decidedly political institution.[52] The intensely partisan tone of the nomination hearings for Brett Kavanaugh, including the nominee's own testimony, is an obvious case in point.[53] In the Canadian context there has been much debate about the appointment process in the past decade.[54]

---

[51] W. Sadurski, *Constitutional Courts in Transition Processes: Legitimacy and Democratization*, in *Sydney Law School Research Paper* No. 11/53 (2011), available at http://ssrn.com/ abstract=1919363.

[52] *See, e.g.,* G. Dickinson, *One Justice, Two Justice, Red Justice, Blue Justice: Dissecting the Role of Political Ideology in Supreme Court Nominations*, in *U. Ill. L. Rev.* 345 (2017); E. Hamilton, *Politicizing the Supreme Court*, in 65 *Stanford L. Rev. Online* 35 (2012).

[53] *See* R. Brownstein, *Brett Kavanaugh is Patient Zero: President Trump's Nominee Would Bring a Virus of Illegitimacy and Partisanship to the Supreme Court,* The Atlantic Monthly, 1 October 2018, available at https://www.theatlantic.com/politics/archive/2018/10/kavanaughs-partisanship-threatens-supreme-court/571702/ last visited February 20, 2020 ("Since Kavanaugh declared his hostility to the Democratic Party and the left so openly and with such ferocity, it has seemed inevitable that tens of millions of Americans will never see him as an impartial judge").

[54] *See, e.g.* P. Russell, *Selecting Supreme Court Justices: Is Trudeau's Sunny Way a Better Way*, in 68 *U. New Brunswick L.J.* 3 (2017).

But matters that relate to the pedigree of a decision, including rules governing how cases are assigned, debated, written, shared and edited, might also be part of "input legitimacy". These aspects of opinion writing must surely have an impact on the relationships between justices and their level of collegiality.[55] These elements in turn affect how a court presents itself to the public. For example, the Supreme Court of Canada under Chief Justice Beverley McLachlin adopted a conferencing norm in which the most junior members of the Court spoke first, lending a greater egalitarian tone to internal discussions. This was one of a handful of traditions developed under her tenure as Chief Justice that lent the Court an air of openness, fairness, and collegiality.[56] These are all elements that I would argue contribute to input legitimacy.

Secrecy, a central aspect of the Italian "principle of collegiality" is clearly associated with the pedigree of a decision and thus "input legitimacy". But this is not a particularly important distinguishing factor since almost all common law supreme courts and European constitutional courts deliberate in relative secrecy. Aside from oral arguments, the decision-making process of the U.S. Supreme Court is "largely opaque" and entirely behind closed doors.[57] The outcome of secret deliberations may be more public in common law courts, but there is still an important shroud of secrecy over how majority and plurality decisions are reached and crafted. Indeed, there is a greater level of secrecy in unanimous "by the court" decisions of the Supreme Court of Canada than in decisions of the Italian Constitutional Court.

Questions about "input legitimacy" take us well beyond the scope of the "principle of collegiality" and the focus of Professor Tega's paper. But if one of the primary arguments in support of maintaining the "principle of collegiality" is the institutional legitimacy of the Court and the independence of its judges, it would be useful to fill out the picture with other "input" aspects of the operation of the Court. These internal aspects may not be well known by the general public, but to the extent they contribute to

[55] For a discussion of a wide range of these features and their effect on collegiality in their US context *see* F.B. CROSS, E.H. TILLER, *Understanding Collegiality on the Court*, *supra.* note 8, 259.

[56] D.R. SONGER, S.W. JOHNSON, C.L. OSTBERG, M.E. WETSTEIN, *Law Ideology, and Collegiality: Judicial Behaviour in the Supreme Court of Canada*, *supra.* note 9 at 87-93. *See also,* S. FINE, *How Beverley McLachlin Found Her Bliss: Where She Came From and What She Leaves Behind,* The Globe and Mail, 12 January 2018. Available at https://www.theglobeandmail.com/news/national/beverley-mclachlin-profile/article37588525/, last visited February 20, 2020.

[57] T. JOHNSON, *The Supreme Court Decision Making Process*, in *Oxford Research Encyclopedia of Politics* (2016), 2, 16.

the overall scholarly analysis of the Court's operation and the perception of the judges themselves they are important elements of an analysis about legitimacy.

7.4. Conclusion

The "principle of collegiality" sets the Italian Constitutional Court apart from common law supreme courts as well as the vast majority of European constitutional courts. The persistent justification for this unique mode of operation is to preserve the good reputation of the Court and its judges. Many of the scholars and judges discussed in Professor Tega's paper implicitly, and in some cases explicitly, take the position that if there was some way to ensure separate opinions would not negatively affect the reputation of the Court, there would be no debate – separate opinions, clearly beneficial to the development of constitutional norms, would be permitted.

The primary purpose of this brief look at how traditions and rules relating to opinion writing play out in a handful of other jurisdictions has been to simply suggest that the clearly drawn fault lines in the "principle of collegiality" debate may not tell the whole story. Other factors, particularly input factors, may play an important role in the legitimacy of the Court. On the flip side, single unanimous or majority decisions with no concurrences or dissent can be defended on the basis of their contribution to the development of legal principles through their influence on both internal (within the Court) and external (cross-institutional) dialogue.

Dialogue IV

ACCESS TO CONSTITUTIONAL ADJUDICATION

Chapter VIII

DIRECT CONSTITUTIONAL COMPLAINT AND *ITALIAN STYLE* DO NOT MATCH. WHY IS THAT?

Elisabetta Lamarque

SUMMARY: 8.1. The fairy tale of the Constitutional Court in the Italian Constituent Assembly: *Aesop's sheep* or *Cinderella?* – 8.2. Constitutional Court and the judiciary: *it takes two to tango.* – 8.3. The direct complaint according to the Constitutional Court: a superfluous instrument? – 8.4. The direct complaint within constitutional literature. A rarefied yet not a sterile debate.

8.1. The fairy tale of the Constitutional Court in the Italian Constituent Assembly: *Aesop's sheep* or *Cinderella*?

Comparative law scholars have developed a large number of criteria in order to classify and study the various systems of constitutional adjudication, and this is certainly not the appropriate place to examine them.

Nevertheless, all scholars acknowledge that the performance of a centralised system of constitutional review, which is characterised by the existence of a dedicated court capable of ruling laws unconstitutional, is linked to the features and nature of the bodies that have the power within that legal system to involve the constitutional court. Kelsen himself warned that "the question concerning the manner in which proceedings may be launched before the constitutional court is of fundamental importance: the extent to which the court may comply with its task of upholding the constitution is principally dependent upon the solution to this question".[1]

In fact, according to some authors, the mechanism of referral is the essential variable which must be considered when classifying systems of constitutional justice featuring a 'Kelsenian' court. For example, John Ferejohn and Pasquale Pasquino consider three different actors – namely, a parliamentary minority, individual citizens, and the ordinary courts – in order to describe three different "ideal types" of European constitutional tribunals. These three types are, respectively, the French one (which operates – or,

[1] H. KELSEN, *La garantie jurisdictionelle de la Constitution (La justice constitutionelle)*, in XXXV *Rev. dir. publ. et sc. pol.* (1928), para. 5.

better, operated – as "the judge of government"), the German one (which acts as "the judge of the judges") and the Italian one, which functions as "the judge of the law".[2]

Indeed, it is crucial to establish the type of access to centralised constitutional tribunals, especially when one starts from the idea that every court, including the constitutional one, is a "passive" body. A court is "passive" in the sense that its activity is entirely dependent upon the subjects who are able to launch proceedings before it. The great Italian scholar, Mauro Cappelletti, taught that "procedural passivity" is the principal characteristic that sets apart courts from the legislature and political bodies. According to Cappelletti, the judiciary (unlike political bodies) is by definition "a power on demand". It is a power that is only activated when requested and, above all, which only operates within the bounds of that request.[3] So, the answers provided by a constitutional court – and thus its role within the system – ultimately depend on the identity and characteristics of the persons or bodies entitled to put questions before it.

Whereas these claims may be true, it is important to acknowledge that, while providing for the establishment of a dedicated Constitutional Court (*Title VI, Constitutional Guarantees*, Articles 134-137 It. Const.), hereafter ItCC, the text of the Italian Constitution of 1948 is almost entirely quiet about that fundamental issue. For this reason, the situation of Italy is unique within the European panorama.[4]

In fact, the issue of access to the ItCC is only considered in Article 127 It. Const., which is dedicated to the regional form of the State (*Title V, Regions, Provinces, Municipalities*). The Constitution asserts that the Government may challenge regional laws, while regions may challenge any state law, any other act with the force of a state law, or any law of another re-

---

[2] J. FEREJOHN, P. PASQUINO, *Constitutional Adjudication: Lessons from Europe*, in 82 *Tex. L. Rev.* 1671 (2004), 1682-1683.

[3] M. CAPPELLETTI, *Giudici legislatori?*, Milan, Giuffrè Editore, 1984, 63 ff.; this aspect has been stressed by M. CARTABIA, *Mauro Cappelletti: one of the "precious few" of our generation*, in 14 *ICON*, No. 2, 464 (2016), 471.

[4] P. CARROZZA, R. ROMBOLI, E. ROSSI, *I limiti all'accesso al giudizio sulle leggi e le prospettive per il loro superamento*, in R. Romboli, (eds.), *L'accesso alla giustizia costituzionale. Caratteri, limiti, prospettive di un modello*, Naples, Edizioni Scientifiche Italiane, 2006, 685; R. ROMBOLI, *Le oscillazioni della Corte costituzionale tra l'anima "politica" e quella "giurisdizionale". Una tavola rotonda per ricordare Alessandro Pizzorusso ad un anno dalla sua scomparsa*, in *Rivista Aic*, No. 3, 1 (2017), 27. Another distinguishing feature of the Italian system of constitutional review is that there are only two ways to challenge a law before the ItCC. In this respect recently T. GROPPI, *La Corte e 'la gente': uno sguardo 'dal basso' all'accesso incidentale alla giustizia costituzionale*, in *Rivista Aic*, No. 2, 408 (2019), 409, made-up the word "parchitudine" (we can translate it into "soberness", "frugality", or something like that).

gion. This involves a form of *direct access to constitutional justice* typical within federal and regional systems,[5] usually referred to as *giudizio di legittimità costituzionale in via principale* or *di azione*. The Founding Fathers introduced this mechanism into the Constitution without any discussion, as a logical consequence of the choice to structure the Italian Republic into multiple regional political entities and to vest each of them with the power to enact laws applicable within their own territories. This was in accordance with criteria governing the allocation of legislative powers between the State and the regions set out in the Constitution itself (Article 117 It. Const.). For many years after the ItCC started to operate (1956), the mechanism was used in a relatively limited capacity. It only served three out of the four, and later (from 1963) four out of the five, regions governed by special statute (because Sicilian statutes were subject to a different form of governmental control) and became fully operational only when the fifteen ordinary regions were finally created in the 1970s. The institution has enjoyed considerable – and for some commentators, excessive – success in recent years, as a consequence of the constitutional reform of the powers of the regions introduced in 2001.

Leaving aside this aspect, the Constituent Assembly which drafted the Italian Constitution did not formalize a certain method of access to constitutional justice because the access to the ItCC was considered a marginal issue at that time. The Founders, indeed, did not even seriously reflect on this issue, but rather they stopped much earlier than this stage. This occurred both due to time constraints and a lack of vision. When the Assembly ended up discussing what would subsequently become the articles dedicated to the ItCC, only a few days were left in order to approve the entire Constitution in view of its planned entry into force on 1 January 1948.[6] More importantly, though, none of the delegates had a particularly clear idea of how the new body would work and what role it would perform.

Throughout the drafting process, the delegates clearly regarded few certainties. The delegates wanted the new Italian Constitution to be hierarchically superior to the law (unlike the previous document, the Albertine Statute, which was in force from 1848 until 1947). For this reason, it was considered necessary to introduce a form of judicial review of legislation. The delegates wanted this review to consider the contents of the law and not only the procedure adopted for its enactment. They also wanted some form

---

[5] G. VOLPE, *L'accesso alla giustizia costituzionale: le origini di un modello*, in R. Romboli, (eds.), *L'accesso alla giustizia costituzionale. Caratteri, limiti, prospettive di un modello*, Naples, Edizioni Scientifiche Italiane, 2006, 9.

[6] V. BARSOTTI, P.G. CAROZZA, M. CARTABIA, A. SIMONCINI, *Italian Constitutional Justice in Global Context*, Oxford, Oxford University Press, 2016, 17-18.

of legal review on a technical level, rather than a political review or a consideration of the suitability of the choices made by the legislature. Above all, almost all delegates did *not* want this review power to fall into the hands of the (already existing) ordinary courts, because they believed the ordinary courts would end up abusing such a power. The delegate thought that ordinary courts would draw on constitutional rules in order to apply the law in an excessively creative manner, resulting in an unconstrained judiciary with the ability to cripple the representative bodies.

In other words, a body named the 'Constitutional Court' was incorporated into the Constitution *according to a process of elimination.* The Founding Fathers deemed it necessary to charge 'somebody' with the task of reviewing the constitutionality of laws, and they did *not* want this entity to be the existing judiciary. Accordingly, the delegates who called for the introduction of this new organ of constitutional justice could assert with certainty only what it was *not*, or rather what they did *not* want it to be: one of the existing ordinary courts.[7] Therefore, they were at most able to make provisions concerning the composition of the body and to list its powers (which they did in Articles 134-136 It. Const.).

Everything else – including the particular manner in which the ItCC would be engaged, its operation, and the relations between the ItCC and the other branches of state – fell far beyond the vision of the vast majority of delegates and, consequently, at that time, in 1947, still needed to be conceived.

The fact that a considered reflection concerning the question of access was not possible became apparent in the first instance from the wide variety of proposals. None of these were ever discussed in substantive terms. Finally, on 2 December 1947 (only twenty days before the final vote on the entire Constitution), the delegates decided to put off all decisions regarding this matter. On the basis of the famous "Arata Amendment", which takes its name from the delegate who tabled it, Article 137(1) It. Const. still asserts that "a [future] constitutional law shall establish the conditions, forms, terms for proposing judgements on constitutional legitimacy [...]".

The amendment was approved against a backdrop of widespread disinterest and probably thanks to the absence of the delegates who were most sensitive to the issue. The next day some of the delegates discovered what had happened and expressed great concern. In particular, Piero Calamandrei, one of the greatest Italian jurists, voiced his concern that this deferral would thwart the very possibility of effective constitutional review in Italy. Drawing a parallel which he himself defined as *Aesopian*, he argued that to charge the future parliament with the task of choosing the manner of access

---

[7] E. LAMARQUE, *Corte costituzionale e giudici nell'Italia repubblicana*, Rome-Bari, Editori Laterza, 2012, 5-20.

to the ItCC was akin to commissioning the wolves (i.e. the majority) with building the fence around the sheep (i.e. putting in place guarantees for minorities against the overwhelming power of the majority).

Hence, there was a tangible danger that the ItCC might never become fully operational or that it might be designed by the republican legislature in such a manner as to render it essentially ineffective.

Another great jurist within the Constituent Assembly, the constitutional scholar Costantino Mortati, also acknowledged this danger and did his best to avoid it. He sought a hurried compromise concerning the manner of access to the ItCC with the Provisional Government (which was led by Alcide De Gasperi, a Christian Democrat like Mortati), forced the hand of the Constituent Assembly, and took advantage of his tired colleagues in order to secure its approval by the Assembly shortly before it was dissolved. It is important to note that the Constituent Assembly continued to work throughout January 1948 – after the Constitution had already entered into force – because, as the only democratically representative body operating at that time, it was still necessary to attend to several fundamental tasks before the election of the first republican parliament after more than twenty years of fascist dictatorship. Naturally, these tasks included the approval of electoral laws for the Chamber of Deputies and the Senate along with a law on the press, which would be fundamental in order to ensure a free electoral campaign, and the ItCC was not mentioned within these tasks.

Nevertheless, on 31 January 1948 Mortati went for the last time from the Palazzo Montecitorio, where the Assembly was in session, to the Palazzo Chigi. (apparently using an underground tunnel between the two buildings). He presented a single sheet of paper to De Gasperi on which he had noted the bodies which he proposed should be entitled to bring future proceedings before the ItCC: the ordinary courts, the government, and a parliamentary minority. De Gasperi stated his desire that the political actors be removed and that only the ordinary courts be left.[8] Upon his return to Montecitorio, Mortati did not even have time to illustrate his proposal. He only stated that De Gasperi agreed with the text, and it was approved by the Assembly.

Thus, at 8:05PM, on the very last day of the Constituent Assembly, the Italian system of constitutional review was born. Constitutional Law 1/1948 was approved at the time and has not been amended since. It provides that any judicial authority that must resolve a dispute that requires the application of a legal provision, where there is a doubt as to that provision's constitutionality, has both the power and the duty to refer that question to the ItCC.

What happened at the end of the mandate of the Constituent Assembly

[8] P. PASQUINO, *Controllo di costituzionalità e forma di governo in Italia*, in *Giornale di storia costituzionale*, No. 11, 309 (2006), 312 ff.

is akin to a magician pulling a rabbit out of a hat. The ItCC and the judiciary suddenly and unexpectedly became undisputed co-protagonists within the Italian system of constitutional review. Each would play its own unique role in operating the justice system.

In an article written the following year, Mortati himself referred to the ItCC as the *Cinderella* of the Constitution. The ItCC came onto the scene right at the end, as discussions were winding down. It was subject to a hasty and superficial examination due to pressure from the impending deadline, and in the end, it was uncertain how and when the ItCC could start operating.[9] So, now we can say that the ordinary courts performed the role of the inevitable *knight in shining armour*. They 'rode in' to save it before it was too late, and thus before its destiny could be left in the hands of the body – i.e. the Parliament – that had every interest in preventing its birth.

8.2. Constitutional Court and the judiciary: *it takes two to tango*

It's clear that a sort of 'sleight of hand' was used to implement the ItCC. The rarefied legislation establishes the two actors – the ItCC and the judiciary as a whole – as distinct authorities. Despite this, the constitutional and ordinary legislation which still governs the Italian system of constitutional review (Constitutional Law 1/1948, mentioned above, was followed by the ordinary Law 87/1953) also creates a link between the courts that renders them totally interdependent. In fact, if it were not to receive any referral orders, the ItCC would be unable to perform its task of judicial review; similarly, the ordinary courts would also be unable to fully perform their tasks without the involvement of the ItCC. This is because ordinary court proceedings where the constitutionality of legislation is challenged are suspended until the ItCC adopts a ruling which resolves the doubt.

This interdependence between the ItCC and the judiciary, which is a typical characteristic of the incidental system, has historically prevented the establishment of a rivalry between the two bodies. We can say, indeed, that – apart from some isolated incident – they cooperated from the outset to ensure that the system operates properly.[10]

---

[9] C. MORTATI, *La Corte costituzionale e i presupposti per la sua vitalità*, in *Iustitia* (1949), 69.

[10] P. CALAMANDREI, *Corte costituzionale e autorità giudiziaria*, in *Rivista di diritto processuale* 1 (1956), 8-9; E. LAMARQUE, *Corte costituzionale e giudici nell'Italia repubblicana*, *op. cit.*, 5 and *passim*; P. PASSAGLIA, *Making a Centralized System of Judicial Review Coexist with Decentralized Guardians of the Constitution: The Italian Way*, in 2 *The Italian L.J.*, No. 2, 405 (2016), 417.

Thus, over the first forty years – between 1956 and 1996 – the two protagonists of the Italian system of constitutional review engaged in an extended process of 'fine tuning.' They adopted a step-by-step approach according to the watchword '*whatever works.*' Initial misunderstandings were resolved and the ItCC and the ordinary courts established a relationship of loyal cooperation. Over time, this cooperative spirit has become increasingly close, up to the point of morphing into a kind of fraternal endorsement of the same objectives, pursued by different means.

In this way, while remaining structurally distinct from each other, the ItCC and the ordinary courts have progressively given rise to a kind of *Wider Judiciary,* within which they are distinguished "only by their different functions" (Article 107(3) It. Const., which, however, textually refers only to the ordinary courts). The residual distinction between their functions is extremely clear: the function of ruling legislation unconstitutional with effects *erga omnes* is vested exclusively in the ItCC, while such a power is denied to the ordinary courts; on the other hand, the function of the definitive resolution of concrete disputes is by contrast vested in the latter and denied to the former.

Despite this fundamental distinction, today the ItCC and the ordinary courts share the task of ensuring that the legislative framework remains at all times aligned with the Constitution and that the disputes thrown up by everyday life can be resolved in accordance with both ordinary law and the Constitution.[11] Thanks to the increasingly frequent judicial application of the Constitution – as a result both of the direct application of the Constitution as well as the interpretation of the law in a manner consistent with the Constitution – the ordinary courts have ended up sharing with the ItCC the role of 'guardian of the Constitution.' On the other hand, the ItCC has turned into a 'judge among judges' over time, taking care to ensure that constitutionally-valid outcomes of specific cases that come before the courts. The ItCC also ensures cooperation with the other Italian supreme courts (i.e. the Court of Cassation, the Council of State, and the Court of Accounts) in order to enable them to perform in an optimal manner their function as a guide for the lower courts. Furthermore, the two actors now complement each other, as the ItCC defends the interpretative powers and role of the ordinary courts and the ordinary courts, for their part, commit that the full effects of the decisions of the ItCC are achieved. Within external relations with the European courts in Strasbourg and Luxembourg, the

[11] L. ELIA, *L'esperienza italiana della giustizia costituzionale. Alcuni nodi critici*, in M. OLIVETTI, T. GROPPI (eds), *La giustizia costituzionale in Europa*, Milan, Giuffrè Editore, 2003, 146.

ItCC and the other Italian supreme courts form a substantially united front as the primary representatives of the Italian judiciary as a whole.[12]

8.3. The direct complaint according to the Constitutional Court: a superfluous instrument?

It is evident from what it has been already said that the Italian legal system ultimately charges the ordinary courts with the task of upholding rights: individuals may only seek recourse to the ordinary courts (and not to the ItCC), and only the ordinary courts can ultimately provide protection against other private parties or against a public body. The system also provides that, where the violation of an individual right can be attributed to a law which is unconstitutional, that right must be guaranteed (also) with the involvement of the ItCC, but the ItCC only becomes involved at a later stage, indirectly following the intermediation of the court to which the individual applied.

The most distinctive characteristic of the Italian system of incidental constitutional review of legislation thus lies in the exclusive requirement for intermediation by the ordinary courts in order for a specific case involving the violation of a fundamental right to come before the ItCC for examination. Unlike in most other legal systems, this mechanism has never been supplemented by an individual right of appeal by the individual to the ItCC.

Over its more than sixty years of operation (since 1956), the system has been endorsed unconditionally by the ItCC itself, which has never attempted to remove the requirement of intermediation by the ordinary courts. By contrast, the ItCC has at all times incentivised and promoted such a system.

Two aspects of constitutional case law are of particular significance in this regard.

A) In the first place, the ItCC has repeatedly firmly rejected any attempts by individuals to 'jump over' the intermediate stage of ordinary proceedings.

Attempts to achieve such an outcome have been made by making inappropriate usage of the instrument used to settle jurisdictional disputes between branches of state (*conflitto tra poteri dello Stato*).[13] The mechanism is as follows: the individual classifies himself/herself as a branch of state. For example, the individual may be a citizen vested by the Constitution with the power to elect representatives in Parliament or to file an application for

---

[12] E. Lamarque, *Corte costituzionale e giudici nell'Italia repubblicana, op. cit., passim.*

[13] See V. Barsotti, P.G. Carozza, M. Cartabia, A. Simoncini, *Italian Constitutional Justice in Global Context, op. cit.*, 155 ff.

a referendum concerning the repeal of legislation, or as a barrister or a notary performing a public function, etc. Then he/she challenges before the ItCC an act carried out by a branch of state. The applicant purports that his/her own constitutional rights were breached by the state.

Whenever this has occurred, the ItCC has found such an operation to constitute an attempt to introduce surreptitiously a direct complaint through a method that is not provided for in the Italian legal system. The ItCC has always reacted by blocking access to constitutional proceedings with arguments that do not leave any scope for subsequent reconsideration.

The ItCC has in fact asserted, in a peremptory manner, that "the procedure applicable to jurisdictional disputes between branches of state cannot be used as a general instrument for the protection of constitutional rights in addition to those available under the judicial system" (Orders 359/1999 and 101/2000). The ItCC has held that the citizen "has not been granted, as an individual, any power of constitutional significance" (*inter alia*, see Orders 256/2016, 277/2017 and 164/2018). In summary, according to the ItCC, "the individual citizen cannot in any case consider himself/herself to have been charged with a constitutionally significant function that is capable of granting him/her authority to raise a jurisdictional dispute before the ItCC" (Orders 57/1971, 296/2006, 189/2008, 367/2008, 434/2008, 85/2009, 121/2011 and 284/2008).

It is interesting to note that the ItCC arrived at an identical conclusion in a case in which a complaint had been received by persons associated within a political party. In these cases, the ItCC has asserted that "political parties must be regarded as civil society organisations, which are charged under ordinary legislation with certain public functions, and not as branches of state pursuant to Article 134 It. Const". (Orders 79/2006 and 120/2009).

Ultimately, neither individual citizens nor political parties are able to access the ItCC directly. The only possibility left within constitutional case law relates to the possibility of a direct appeal – again, as a jurisdictional dispute between branches of state – by a Member of the Chamber of Deputies or by a Senator. In fact, until Order 177/1988, the ItCC stated that its rulings were "without prejudice" to the question of whether any specific "situation" "involved the individual grant of any constitutional power, in order to protect which the individual Member of Parliament is entitled to initiate a jurisdictional dispute between branches of state" (see also Judgment 225/2001 and Orders 222/2009, 149/2016, 277/2017, 280/2017, 163/2018 and 181/2018, in which it has still declined to state its position regarding this issue).[14] A "situa-

---

[14] As far as the scholars are concerned, see almost N. ZANON, *Il libero mandato parlamentare*, Milan, Giuffrè Editore, 1991, 308 ff.; R. BIN, *L'ultima fortezza. Teoria della Cos-*

tion" of that kind finally arose, and in Order 17/2019 the ItCC acknowledged for the very first time the standing of every Member of Parliament, even if only in case of "manifest" violation of his/her own rights and powers as guaranteed under the Constitution, when the violations are "evidently identifiable already within a summary consideration". In the ItCC's opinion, indeed, "the constitutional status of a member of Parliament embraces a complex body of powers including the right to speak, the right of initiative and the right to vote, which are vested in him or her individually as a representative of the Nation, may be exercised autonomously and independently, and cannot be revoked or amended on the initiative of another parliamentary body" (see subsequently Orders 274/2019 and 275/2019).

B) Secondly, the the ItCC's commitment to defend the system of incidental review has also manifested itself through its endless search within the system, and not elsewhere, for instruments that can enable it to protect fundamental human rights more effectively.

In fact, as will be noted below, in the past the Italian literature has called for the enactment of constitutional legislation establishing a new access route to the ItCC precisely to satisfy the need to protect fundamental rights that have been left 'uncovered' by the incidental system itself.

One may assert, however, that all of the most serious 'shortcomings' and all of the most evident gaps within the system of incidental review that have been objected to in the past have gradually been filled by ItCC's case law. In other words, the ItCC itself has creatively remedied the existing system of incidental review by itself.

Constitutional case law has followed a variety of paths, and the overall result achieved is extremely interesting. I shall consider here only three of these paths.

a) It has been argued in the past that the system of incidental review operates according to a timescale that is incompatible with the effective defence of fundamental rights. If a law violates a human right, the individual may indeed apply to an ordinary court. But before it can guarantee that right, that court must raise a question of constitutionality, stay the proceedings, and wait for the ItCC to declare the law unconstitutional. Under the best-case scenario, even if the ItCC is operating without any backlog, there will be a six-month delay. The mere passage of time could cause irreparable detriment

---

tituzione e conflitti di attribuzione, Milan, Giuffrè Editore, 1996, 140 ff.; A. CERRI, *Corso di giustizia costituzionale plurale*, Milan, Giuffrè Editore, 2012, 412; M. MANETTI, *La tessera mancante: il conflitto di attribuzione promosso dalle minoranze parlamentari in materia di procedimento legislativo*, in *Giurisprudenza costituzionale* 1107 (2016), 1107 ff.

to individuals. According to these commentators, only by introducing the possibility of direct complaint to the ItCC by individuals, along with the possibility to apply for urgent interim relief from the ItCC, could the ItCC ensure the effective defence of the fundamental right that is in danger.

However, the ItCC has been able to resolve this malfunction on its own through case law. In fact, it has rendered any provision for direct complaints superfluous. Without entering into excessively technical detail, it is sufficient to note that the ItCC has held that doubts concerning the constitutionality of legislation may be raised by a civil, criminal or administrative court even when it has been seized on an interim basis. Secondly, the ItCC has held that when such a court refers a question of constitutionality, it may nonetheless adopt a measure granting urgent provisional protection to the right that has been violated and go so far as to set aside, again on an interim basis, the law that is suspected to be unconstitutional, with concomitant provisional direct application of the Constitution. This is evidently an exceptional instance of decentralised review of the law, which the ItCC itself has authorised in order to ensure that the guarantee of individual rights is not neglected pending a definitive ruling on the constitutionality of a law.

The case law of the ItCC concerning this issue has been consolidated for a number of years. The major achievement, which has been obtained thanks to cooperation between the ItCC and the ordinary courts, is that the Italian system of incidental constitutional review is overall already capable of guaranteeing timely and effective protection to all persons of any rights that have been violated by an unconstitutional law, even if no provision has as yet been made for direct constitutional complaints to the ItCC.

b) It has also been asserted that it would only be possible to rule on the constitutionality of decree-laws by a dedicated form of direct complaint, given that it is difficult to bring proceedings before the ItCC before such decrees cease to have effect (i.e. within sixty days). [15]

Here too, the ItCC has remedied the defect within the mechanism of constitutional review simply by altering its own case law. It ruled that the constitutional deficiency of the (manifest) failure by a decree law to fulfil the prerequisites of extraordinary necessity and urgency cannot be remedied by Parliament; on the contrary, it 'infects' the conversion law, which may therefore be brought before the ItCC by a judge and then ruled un-

[15] Article 77 It. Const. in fact provides *inter alia* that, "when the Government, in case of necessity and urgency, adopts under its own responsibility a temporary measure, it shall introduce such measure to Parliament for transposition into law", and that "such a measure shall have no effect from the beginning unless it is transposed into law by Parliament within sixty days of its publication".

constitutional on this basis (from Judgments 171/2007 and 128/2008 onwards).

c) Finally, it had been unanimously asserted and reiterated within the literature that the system of incidental constitutional review did not cover certain areas of the legal order (which, according to Italian scholars, constituted "free-for-all areas", *zone franche*, not covered by constitutional justice), or did not cover certain areas in a comprehensive manner (referred to in the literature as "shadow zones", *zone d'ombra*).

The most serious of these shortcomings, according to critics, was related to the fullness of the electorate's right to vote in relation to elections to the national Parliament. In fact, that right did not benefit from judicial protection. Article 66 It. Const. holds that "Each House" – and not the ordinary or administrative courts – "shall verify the credentials of its members and any grounds for disqualification that may arise at a later stage". Hence, it appeared that there were no proceedings and no courts – either ordinary or administrative – that could raise a question concerning the constitutionality of electoral legislation for Parliament.

The gap was filled by Judgment 1/2014. In that case, a voter brought a highly singular type of action before an ordinary court, seeking a 'declaratory judgment' concerning the right to vote.[16] The voter aimed to establish the scope of the right which was considered to be uncertain. The case was appealed up to the Supreme Court of Cassation, which raised the question to the ItCC.

The response from the ItCC was very clear:

> "It may be inferred that the questions of constitutionality raised within those proceedings are admissible precisely due to the special nature and constitutional significance on the one hand of the right to which the action seeking a declaration judgment relates, and on the other hand of the law which, owing to its suspected unconstitutionality, renders its scope uncertain. The admissibility of the question is also the inevitable corollary of the principle that protection must be afforded to the inviolable right to vote, which – according to the referral order – has been prejudiced by electoral law that does not comply with principles of constitutional law, irrespective of the manner in which it has been applied, since the uncertainty as to the scope of the right itself constitutes legally significant harm. Thus, due to the need to guarantee the principle of constitutionality, it is

[16] C. PADULA, *La tutela diretta dei diritti fondamentali. Il* preenforcement constitutional challenge *contro le leggi negli Stati Uniti e le questioni incidentali «astratte» in Italia*, Turin, Giappichelli Editore, 2018, compares that action to the "preenforcement constitutional challenge" in the U.S.

> essential to conclude that the review power of the ItCC – which "must cover the legal system as fully as possible" [...] – must also apply to laws, such as that relating to elections to the Chamber of Deputies and the Senate, "which would be more difficult to subject to [the Court's scrutiny] in any other manner". In the light of those principles, the questions of constitutionality raised are admissible, having regard also to the requirement that laws such as those relating to elections to the Chamber of Deputies and the Senate, which set out the rules governing the composition of constitutional bodies that are essential for the proper operation of a representative democratic system, and which therefore cannot be immune from such review, must not be subtracted from constitutional review. Any other conclusion would end up creating a free-for-all [*zona franca* in the Italian text] within the system of constitutional justice, precisely in an area which is closely related to the democratic framework as it involves the fundamental right to vote; for this reason, it would end up causing intolerable harm to the overall constitutional order".

It is apparent that the effect of this judgment on the electoral law was to cover a significant, and perhaps the largest, area that would otherwise have been exempt from constitutional review. The contrivance worked thanks to an effective teamwork between the Supreme Court of Cassation, which resolved the serious preliminary procedural problems precisely with the aim of addressing the ItCC, and the ItCC itself, which ruled on the question despite the heavy doubts as to its admissibility. The exceptional nature of the aforementioned procedural mechanism has been highlighted within scholarship on the topic, which has referred to a 'semi-incidental' mechanism of constitutional review. By this, scholars claim that the mechanism is situated half-way between standard incidental review and direct access by private individuals to the ItCC.[17] This 'semi-incidental' has been endorsed by some commentators while attracting harsh criticism from others.[18]

The possibility for voters to seek a 'declaratory judgment' concerning the right to vote before the ordinary courts was subsequently confirmed by Judgment 110/2015, again in relation to the law governing elections of members of

---

[17] M. BIGNAMI, *La Corte costitizionale interviene in via "semi-incidentale" sulla legge elettorale: un approccio prudente per un caso eccezionale*, in M. D'AMICO, S. CATALANO (eds.), *Prime riflessioni sulla "storica" sentenza 1 del 2014 in materia elettorale*, Milan, FrancoAngeli, 2014.

[18] The debate is described by G. REPETTO, *Il canone dell'incidentalità costituzionale. Trasformazioni e continuità nel giudizio sulle leggi*, Naples, Editoriale Scientifica, 2017; G. D'AMICO, *Azione di accertamento e accesso al giudizio incidentale*, Naples, Editoriale Scientifica, 2018; C. PADULA, *La tutela diretta dei diritti fondamentali. Il* preenforcement costitutional challenge *contro le leggi negli Stati Uniti e le questioni incidentali «astratte» in Italia*, *op. cit.*

the national Parliament.[19] Despite this confirmation, it was refused in Judgment 165/2016 concerning the law governing elections to the European Parliament. The reasons provided in support of the latter judgment are of particular interest for our present purposes. In that judgement, the ItCC justified the adoption of a different solution compared to the previous two cases by recalling that the difficulty in securing access to the ItCC regards only the elections of the national Parliament (due to Article 66 It. Const.), while the legislative provisions governing the election of the European Parliament may be subject to constitutional review according to the ordinary incidental mechanism.

A contrivance similar to that used in order to arrive at national electoral legislation has also been experimented with on other occasions. Particularly, several years ago the ItCC was finally able to consider the Penitentiary Law, which had previously appeared to be immune to challenge because there was no court to which prisoners could apply in order to object to right-violating measures adopted by the prison administration during the period of detention. Some of these rights include the right to meet with their defence counsel, the right to receive correspondence, and so on. In that case, a 'supervisory judge' [*Magistrato di Sorveglianza*], who, despite the name, did not have the characteristics typical of a judicial body, nonetheless considered himself entitled to refer a question concerning the constitutionality of the Penitentiary Law. Following this referral, the ItCC considered the merits of the question. The ItCC argued that the reference by the 'supervisory judge' amounted to "the only remedy" available to a convicted prisoner seeking to object to a violation of a fundamental right under the legal system. For this reason, "the procedure in question must be deemed to have the status of 'proceedings', within which a question of constitutionality may be referred" (Judgment 212/1997).

In both cases, the ItCC was confronted with laws on which it had not previously been able to rule – the Law on Elections to the National Parliament and the Penitentiary Law – simply because no 'proceedings' and no 'judge' or 'court' had been identified under Italian law from which the relative incidental questions of constitutionality could be referred. In these and in similar cases, it was necessary to fill the systematic gaps within the protection of rights. Some commentators had called for the introduction of a new form of access to the ItCC involving the filing of direct complaints by private individuals against those laws. Instead, as we have already seen, thanks to the cooperation of the ordinary courts the ItCC was able to fill the gaps *while continuing to operate according to a logic of incidental review*.

---

[19] On that law see also Judgment 35/2017 and Order 63/2018.

8.4. The direct complaint within constitutional literature. A rarefied yet not a sterile debate

Since the adoption of the republican Constitution, there have been sporadic debates between Italian scholars concerning the issue of direct complaint. The brief periods during which authors have contributed to the debate in large numbers have been followed by extended periods of silence, in which the issue has been entirely ignored. So, the direction of the debate has been compared to that of an underground river, which disappears for long stretches, re-emerging only to disappear once again shortly afterwards.

The principal periods during which the river has re-surfaced have coincided in temporal terms with the proposed constitutional amendments that have called for the introduction of new forms of access to the ItCC.[20] In particular, at the end of 1965, a group of scholars discussed the possibility of direct complaints during a seminar held to mark the tenth anniversary of the establishment of the ItCC.[21] The seminar was parallel to the tabling of a first constitutional bill sponsored by the Deputy Francesco Cossiga (the future President of the Republic). In 1989 another constitutional bill was tabled and, in response, the ItCC itself organised a seminar to study the issue.[22] In 1997, the issue was broached once again in Ferrara during commemorations to mark the two hundredth anniversary of the creation of the first chair of constitutional law in Europe. At the same time, the 'bicameral commission', which had been established to present a project for far-sweeping constitutional reform, introduced the possibility of direct complaints into the project. This was followed by a number of academic initiatives,[23] in addition to various sporadic individual articles on the issue.

The scholarly debate has not only been discontinuous but may also ap-

---

[20] For an overview see P. CARROZZA, R. ROMBOLI, E. ROSSI, *I limiti all'accesso al giudizio sulle leggi e le prospettive per il loro superamento*, *op. cit.*, 759 ff. and G. GENTILI, *Una prospettiva comparata sui sistemi europei di ricorso diretto al giudice costituzionale: suggestioni e spunti per la Corte costituzionale italiana*, in *Revista de Estudios Juridicos*, No. 11, 1 (2011), 25 ff.

[21] The acts of the seminar were published in G. MARANINI (eds.), *La giustizia costituzionale*, Florence, Vallecchi, 1966.

[22] The acts of the seminar were published in Corte costituzionale (eds.), *Giudizio "a quo" e promovimento del processo costituzionale. Atti del seminario svoltosi in Roma Palazzo della Consulta nei giorni 13 e 14 novembre 1989*, Milan, Giuffrè Editore, 1990.

[23] Including the volume *L'accesso alla giustizia costituzionale*, published in 2006 on the occasion of the fiftieth anniversary of the ItCC, along with the acts of a seminar organised by the Pisa Group Association in 1999, which were brought together in the volume *Prospettive di accesso alla giustizia costituzionale*, published in 2000.

pear to be substantially sterile, given that the proposals for constitutional amendment have never been acted upon.[24] However, a closer consideration reveals that the debate has in fact brought some results.

Over the last thirty years, discussion within the literature has aimed to advise constitutional lawmakers to be cautious. Scholars have pointed politicians (whenever this was necessary) to the the costs of introducing a mechanism for direct complaints, which they argue would exceed the benefits.[25]

Moreover, when pointing to the shortcomings of the system of incidental constitutional review (which the possibility of direct complaints could eliminate), the literature has often simultaneously suggested ways in which these shortcomings could be remedied through case law, even in the absence of a mechanism for direct review.[26] From this point of view, it is significant that the very same contrivance used in 2014 in order to review the constitutionality of electoral legislation (discussed above) had been proposed sixty years before by the far-sighted Italian scholar, Mauro Cappelletti, in his famous book entitled *La giurisdizione costituzionale delle libertà*.[27]

In a nutshell, only three authors – Cappelletti, Paladin and Mezzanotte – asserted that the lack of a mechanism for direct complaints in Italy negatively impacts the very *nature* of the ItCC, by preventing it from being classified as a court charged with the task of defending human rights and classifies it, instead, only as a "judge of the law". All of these opinions were adopted independently of any political proposals to reform the procedure, at times when the issue was not being widely discussed.

The first of these arguments was put forward by Mauro Cappelletti, precisely in *La giurisdizione costituzionale delle libertà*. He complained that Italy had not made provision for any "way" to effectively invoke fundamental human rights that was "differentiated" and "reinforced" compared to ordinary judicial instruments. Consequently, the ItCC could not be said to be a "consti-

---

[24] R. TARCHI (eds.), *Patrimonio costituzionale europeo e tutela dei diritti fondamentali. Il ricorso diretto di costituzionalità*, Turin, Giappichelli Editore, 2012, 64.

[25] See *inter alia* regarding this issue F. TIRIO, *"Maschera" e "volto" del ricorso individuale di costituzionalità*, in P. COSTANZO (eds.), *Percorsi attuali della giustizia costituzionale*, Milan, Giuffrè Editore, 1995, 127 ff. and G. BRUNELLI, *Una riforma non necessaria: l'accesso diretto delle minoranze parlamentari al giudizio sulle leggi*, in A. ANZON, P. CARETTI, S. GRASSI (eds.), *Prospettive di accesso alla giustizia costituzionale*, Turin, Giappichelli Editore, 2000, 188 ff.

[26] See *inter alia*, for example, L. CARLASSARE, *I diritti davanti alla Corte costituzionale: ricorso individuale o rilettura dell'art. 27 L. n. 87/1953?*, in *Diritto e società* (1997), 445 ff.

[27] M. CAPPELLETTI, *La giurisdizione costituzionale delle libertà. Primo studio sul ricorso costituzionale (con particolare riguardo agli ordinamenti tedesco, svizzero e austriaco)*, Milan, Giuffrè Editore, 1955, 12.

tutional court of freedoms" in a strict sense (a '*giurisdizione costituzionale delle libertà*', as Cappelletti said[28]). On the other hand, according to the author, the mechanism of direct constitutional complaint recognised within other legal systems is not only an instrument that is capable of giving effect to fundamental rights but is, above all, "an effective instrument for ensuring a balance between branches of state". It thus represents the "capstone of the rule of law".[29]

The second argument was presented by Livio Paladin, an important constitutional scholar and ItCC judge who also served as its President. Paladin revisited Cappelletti's argument a number of years later in order to reiterate the point that, within the Italian system, "it cannot be asserted that there is a '*giurisdizione costituzionale delle libertà*' in the technical sense of the term; and this is not because the ItCC does not provide any guarantees in this area, but because the guarantee is indirect or – better put – is implemented insofar as is made possible by the achievement of other purposes".[30] According to the author, the lack of any *Verfassungsbeschwerde* and *amparo* in Italy has resulted in "noticeable" and "negative" consequences for Italian constitutional case law. In particular, the ItCC has taken on the status of "a court charged with reviewing the reasonableness of legislative choices" more than with protecting fundamental human rights. It has, in fact, very often been the case that proceedings concerning the constitutionality of legislation, which have arisen on an incidental basis, "have been conducted and concluded with reference to a highly peculiar principle of constitutional law, such as that resulting from Article 3 It. Const. (the constitutional principle asserting the equality of citizens, and individuals in general, before the law). This has ended up interfering with the very functions of the ItCC, which had originally been conceived of as the guarantor of a specific schedule of values directly enumerated and coordinated within the Constitution. Instead, the ItCC is now called upon – from the perspective of equal treatment – to resolve a range of problems which do not ultimately have constitutional status, applying criteria which at first sight might appear immune to any attempt at prior definition".[31]

---

[28] M. CAPPELLETTI, *La giurisdizione costituzionale delle libertà. Primo studio sul ricorso costituzionale (con particolare riguardo agli ordinamenti tedesco, svizzero e austriaco), op. cit.*, 6.

[29] M. CAPPELLETTI, *La giurisdizione costituzionale delle libertà. Primo studio sul ricorso costituzionale (con particolare riguardo agli ordinamenti tedesco, svizzero e austriaco), op. cit.*, 134.

[30] L. PALADIN, *La tutela delle libertà fondamentali offerta dalle Corti costituzionali europee: spunti comparatistici*, in L. CARLASSARE (eds.), *Le garanzie giurisdizionali dei diritti fondamentali*, Padua, Cedam, 1988, 12-13.

[31] L. PALADIN, *La tutela delle libertà fondamentali offerta dalle Corti costituzionali europee: spunti comparatistici, op. cit.*, 18-19.

Finally, it is necessary to mention the stance taken by Carlo Mezzanotte, also an authoritative constitutional scholar and judge of the ItCC. For Mezzanotte, as had been argued previously by Paladin, the Italian experience provides evidence that a system of constitutional justice that is focused on incidental review is capable of giving effect to the individual values and rights enshrined in the Constitution. Nevertheless, the author does not believe that the incidental system and the direct complaint are "equally efficient and thus fungible" for the purposes of the protection of constitutional rights. In other words, he does not believe that "for a citizen who considers that a law has violated one of his/her constitutional rights, it is really the same thing to apply directly to the ItCC or to pass through the filter of ordinary proceedings".[32] According to Mezzanotte, the assertion that the two remedies are equivalent is not only problematic in theoretical terms but is also not corroborated by the historical record in Italy, as the Italian courts "are much more than a filter for objections of unconstitutionality raised by the parties; they are essentially the exclusive holders of the power to apply to the ItCC. In Italy, an unconstitutionality action is increasingly an action brought by a judge on the assumption that he/she is fully empowered to interpret also the Constitution".

Except for these three opinions, the majority of the authors does not consider it necessary to introduce a mechanism for direct complaints by citizens precisely because it takes the view that the Italian system of constitutional justice has proven and continues to prove its worth in both objective terms (the guarantee of the constitutional integrity of the legal order) and in subjective terms (the guarantee of individual rights).

Only a few commentators take the view that the possibility of direct complaints would perfect the system, meanwhile assessing the efficacy of incidental review in highly positive terms. This has been the essence of the arguments of constitutional scholar Valerio Onida, one of which was presented in his official capacity as President of the ItCC during the customary annual press conference with journalists. Onida identified certain areas in which it is *de facto* difficult for the ItCC to engage in review according to the incidental mechanism – such as the review of spending legislation and laws with organisatory content – and asserted that the ItCC could more easily operate in these areas if the possibility for direct complaints existed. He argued that, in some cases, the ItCC would operate more effectively if it were able to 'tailor' its decision specifically to the concrete facts invoked directly by the injured party. He went on to assert that individual constitutional

[32] C. MEZZANOTTE, *Il problema della fungibilità tra eccezione di incostituzionalità e ricorso diretto alla Corte costituzionale*, in *Giustizia e Costituzione*, No. 2, 77 (1991), 77 ff.

complaints could also be used in order to "avoid errors or defects in the application of the law by the ordinary courts, operating on a preventive basis – at least in some cases – compared to the indirect and only compensatory relief offered by the European Court of Human Rights in Strasbourg".[33]

However, it is highly significant that two of the most prominent supporters of direct complaint as a necessary complement to the system of incidental review – Cappelletti and Paladin – changed their mind at a time when there were real prospects of the constitutional reform they had called for. It is thus important to examine in detail the arguments that convinced them to change their stance.

In 1989, during the seminar held at the *Palazzo della Consulta*, the seat of the ItCC, Cappelletti stated that his "youthful enthusiasm" had given way to "a prudent scepticism", which led him to question whether it would be "wise" to add this further task to the current system of constitutional justice. He offered three considerations in support of his remarks, each of which is particularly significant.

First and foremost, he commented that the system of incidental review had worked, in historical terms, to render "possible a form of constitutional review that lacks any substantial gaps" because whenever any gaps arose the ItCC had been able to fill them.[34]

Secondly, he considered that the understandable desire of every citizen to be able to object directly and without intermediation before the ItCC could be considered to be satisfied by the possibility of applying directly to the European Court of Human Rights.[35] This second argument became even more convincing when, ten years after his comments, Protocol 11 to the ECHR altered the system governing appeals by individuals to the ECtHR by removing the intermediary stage of the committee.

Thirdly, Cappelletti noted that over the years there had been a "deepening" and "reinforcement" of the links between the ItCC and other courts.

---

[33] V. ONIDA, *Relazione di sintesi*, in Corte costituzionale (eds.), *Giudizio "a quo" e promovimento del processo costituzionale. Atti del seminario svoltosi in Roma Palazzo della Consulta nei giorni 13 e 14 novembre 1989, op. cit.*, 303; V. ONIDA, *La giustizia costituzionale nel 2004*, in *www.cortecostituzionale.it*, 2005; see also E. CRIVELLI, *La tutela dei diritti fondamentali e l'accesso alla giustizia costituzionale*, Padua, Cedam, 2003, *passim*.

[34] M. CAPPELLETTI, *Questioni nuove (e vecchie) sulla giustizia costituzionale*, in Corte costituzionale (eds.), *Giudizio "a quo" e promovimento del processo costituzionale. Atti del seminario svoltosi in Roma Palazzo della Consulta nei giorni 13 e 14 novembre 1989, op. cit.*, 32; the example provided by the author may be added to those mentioned above and concerns the constitutional review of criminal laws that are favourable to the accused.

[35] M. CAPPELLETTI, *Questioni nuove (e vecchie) sulla giustizia costituzionale*, *ibidem*, 32-33.

The ordinary courts had acquired a significant "constitutional awareness", and therefore the interpretation of the law in a manner consistent with the Constitution is now commonplace throughout all courts. He argued further that "all courts are to some extent also constitutional courts, which are empowered – and in fact obliged – to apply the Constitution when interpreting the law". Consequently, "while in the 1950s it might have appeared preferable to concentrate within the ItCC all powers of constitutional review, now by contrast it is advisable to extend them, as far as permitted by the fundamental structures of the centralised system, to all courts throughout the land".[36]

Paladin, on the other hand, revisited his position drawing on the experiences of other European legal systems that provide for the possibility of direct complaints.[37] According to the author, the need for caution results from the fact that in Spain and Germany the number of complaints is "innumerable, and in the vast majority of cases are not accepted". The situations in which the mechanism has proven its worth in those countries are, according to Paladin, "isolated, as against on the other hand a plethora of disputes which the court tends to dismiss in a summary manner, with the result that the guarantee of fundamental rights, which may apparently have been emphasised, in actual fact ends up being deprived of any substance".

Over the last thirty years the reasons why scholars have called for extreme caution in relation to the institute of direct complaints to the ItCC have all centred on the arguments set out above.

The greatest perplexities relate to the high number of complaints which would be expected in Italy were this mechanism to be introduced and the consequent risk of paralysis of the ItCC. This is based on a comparative law perspective and has been expressed from all sides, including by those scholars who recognise the benefits of direct complaints.[38]

Moreover, it must be considered that the two undisputed benefits of the Italian system are the timely manner of responses obtained from the ItCC, and the collegial nature of its work. The ItCC deals with all applications received each year and essentially works without any backlog, and all fifteen members work together on all questions without any need to divide the ItCC into sections or committees. Both of these appreciable character-

---

[36] M. CAPPELLETTI, *Questioni nuove (e vecchie) sulla giustizia costituzionale*, *ibidem*, 33-34.

[37] L. PALADIN, *Corte costituzionale: aumentano le funzioni ma il futuro potrebbe portare la "paralisi"*, in *Guida al diritto*, No. 43, (1997) 64-66.

[38] For example, A. ANZON, *Per una più ampia garanzia dei diritti costituzionali dinanzi alla Corte: il ricorso indivduale diretto*, in V. ANGIOLINI (eds.), *Libertà e giurisprudenza costituzionale*, Turin, Giappichelli Editore, 1992, 28.

istics could evidently be jeopardized following an exponential increase in the workload resulting from the new access route.

Furthermore, given that the ItCC would be forced to make selections if confronted with very high numbers, the mechanism of the direct complaint would only be capable of offering occasional – and not timely – relief to the vast majority of complainants. It would thus turn out to be essentially a demagogic instrument of propaganda, which would not be genuinely conducive to achieving enhanced protection for fundamental individual rights.

Further detailed considerations have been offered by Roberto Romboli, who, drawing on the Spanish experience, has shifted attention to the systemic consequences which the provision for direct access by individuals to the ItCC following the exhaustion of ordinary forms of judicial redress would entail. When construed in these terms, the direct complaint process would operate as a fourth istance judgment, and it would enable the permanent control of the judiciary's actions by the ItCC. This would also negate another peculiarity of the Italian incidental system, which is perhaps the most important: the relationship of mutual trust which has been painstakingly built up over time between the ItCC and the judiciary. The two bodies share a great sense of responsibility, working to achieve shared objectives, as mentioned above. Romboli in fact asserts, in an entirely plausible manner, that, "while incidental proceedings lie in the hands of the ordinary courts, direct complaints are made 'against' the courts". Consequently, adding a direct form of access could mean breaking the "virtuous link" between the ItCC and the ordinary courts and thus destroy the good level of performance achieved by the incidental system over the years.[39]

---

[39] E. MALFATTI, S. PANIZZA, R. ROMBOLI, *Giustizia costituzionale*, Fifth edition, Turin, Giappichelli Editore, 2016, 362; however, see also, among the numerous contributions by this author, R. ROMBOLI, *"Torniamo alla Costituente?": considerazioni in ordine all'introduzione di un ricorso diretto del singolo e delle minoranze parlamentari alla Corte costituzionale*, in A. BARBERA, A. LOIODICE, M. SCUDIERO, P. STANZIONE (eds.), *Scritti in memoria di Fulvio Fenucci*, Soveria Mannelli, Rubbettino, 2010 and R. ROMBOLI, *Le oscillazioni della Corte costituzionale tra l'anima "politica" e quella "giurisdizionale". Una tavola rotonda per ricordare Alessandro Pizzorusso ad un anno dalla sua scomparsa, op. cit.*, 29.

Chapter IX

THE POTENTIAL VIRTUES AND RISKS OF ABSTRACT CONSTITUTIONAL CHALLENGES AND INDIVIDUAL COMPLAINTS: SOME REFLECTIONS FROM SPAIN

Victor Ferreres Comella

SUMMARY: 9.1. Constitutional challenges: a powerful weapon. – 9.2. Constitutional challenges: problems with time. – 9.3. Constitutional challenges and the risk of politicization. – 9.4. Constitutional complaints to safeguard fundamental rights. – 9.5. Conclusion.

In her interesting chapter on the Italian Constitutional Court, Elisabetta Lamarque discusses the fundamental question of 'standing:' who has access to the Court to contest the validity of certain acts by public institutions? In particular, who is empowered to challenge a law (a statute or a norm of equivalent rank or force) on constitutional grounds?

Lamarque explains that the Italian system relies on the cooperation between the ordinary judiciary and the Constitutional Court. At the heart of the Italian model is the constitutional question procedure, which ordinary judges can set in motion whenever they entertain doubts about the constitutional validity of the law that applies to the case in question. The Court can only perform its central function if ordinary judges are willing to present questions to it. The ordinary judges, in turn, can only do their job correctly if the answers provided by the Constitutional Court help them decide the cases in conformity with the Constitution. Hence, a symbiosis between the judiciary and the Court characterizes the Italian institutional arrangement.

Lamarque further describes the debate that has developed in Italy over the desirability of amending the system of constitutional review in order to introduce "direct complaint" procedures. She explains that when the constitutional text was being written in 1947, the drafters paid very little attention to the question of standing. In fact, the Constitution was "almost entirely silent" about the procedures to trigger the jurisdiction of the Court. Only when dealing with the regional form of the State was a passing reference made to constitutional procedures. The Constitution delegated to a specific constitutional law the task of specifying who should have standing to bring cases to the Court. As professor Costantino Mortati explained, the Court was the "Cinderella of the Constitution" because it came onto the scene right at the end of the discussions at the Constitutional Assembly. Indeed, it was not until the very last day, on 31 January 1948, that the specific constitutional law was adopted. Professor Mortati himself, in his capacity as a Christian Democratic member of the Assembly, had met that day with President de Gasperi at Palazzo Chigi to talk about the issue. De Gasperi refused Mortati's proposal to entitle the government and a parliamentary minority to commence proceedings before the Court. Accordingly, the text that was finally passed by the assembly excluded political actors, so that only ordinary courts would be empowered to ask the Court to review the validity of legislation.

Over the course of a number of years, Lamarque also tells us, debates have taken place about the pros and cons of enabling private persons to lodge complaints before the Constitutional Court, namely for violations of fundamental rights. No reform of the system has been adopted, however, to incorporate such complaints.

Italy is relatively exceptional in Europe when it comes to the issue of standing.[1] In many European countries, political actors are allowed to challenge laws in the abstract. In particular, it is possible in some nations for a qualified minority of members of parliament to impugn a statute that the majority has passed. A few countries also permit individuals to file abstract challenges against laws. Let us group this variety of possibilities under the category "constitutional challenge".

A different type of procedure that some European countries have also instituted enables private individuals to file a complaint before the Constitutional Court. Individuals may attack specific decisions made by public authorities in concrete cases on the grounds that they violate fundamental rights. Normally, the persons who claim to be victims of rights violations must first exhaust the ordinary judicial remedies. We can call this procedure "constitutional complaint".

As a constitutional scholar coming from Spain, I am familiar with a system of constitutional justice that encompasses both "constitutional challenges" (*recursos de inconstitucionalidad*) and "constitutional complaints" (*recursos de amparo*). The Spanish experience illustrates the potential advantages,

---

[1] For an overview of the European landscape, see M. OLIVETTI. T. GROPPI (eds.), *La giustizia costituzionale in Europa*, Milan. Giuffrè Editore, 2003; V. FERRERES COMELLA, *Constitutional Courts and Democratic Values. A European Perspective*, New Haven, Yale University Press, 2009, 7-8; and M. DE VISSER, *Constitutional Review in Europe. A Comparative Analysis*, Oxford, Hart Publishing, 2013.

as well as the risks and problems, of incorporating such procedures. As I will argue in this contribution, the case in favor of introducing the first type of procedure in a country like Italy is stronger, all things considered, than the case for introducing the second type. I will divide my discussion in two parts, to treat each procedure separately.

9.1. Constitutional challenges: a powerful weapon

Under the Spanish Constitution, certain public organs are allowed to file an abstract constitutional challenge before the Constitutional Court.[2] By means of this procedural instrument, those organs can attack the constitutional validity of a particular provision or set of provisions that figure in a statute (or in a norm of equivalent rank or force). The list of institutions (or fragments of institutions) that have standing to submit a challenge consists of the President of the Government, the Ombudsperson, 50 members of Congress, 50 Senators, the regional governments, and the regional parliaments.[3] Other countries (such as Germany, France, Austria, Belgium, and Portugal), have designed a similar procedure, although there is considerable diversity when it comes to the issue of who is authorized to use this mechanism.

What reason can one advance to justify the establishment of this procedural arrangement? If ordinary judges often raise questions to the Constitutional Court, as is the case in Italy, why should an additional procedure be created to trigger constitutional review of legislation?

The answer, I submit, is that adjudicatory gaps may otherwise emerge in the system, at least for a long period of time. Indeed, it is not always easy to articulate a controversy for ordinary judges to resolve in a context which enables the constitutionality of a particular statute to be questioned. Of course, the legal system may be very flexible when laying down the conditions under which someone can bring a case to the ordinary courts. Lamarque refers to a very interesting jurisprudential precedent in Italy that has facilitated voters, for example, to have access to courts to seek a declar-

[2] For a description and discussion of this procedure, see M.L. Balaguer Callejón, *El recurso de inconstitucionalidad*, Madrid, Centro de Estudios Políticos y Constitucionales, 2001; F. Caamaño Domínguez, Á.J. Gómez Montoro, M. Medina Guerrero, J.L. Requejo Pagés, *Jurisdicción y procesos constitucionales*, Madrid, McGraw-Hill, 2000; J.L. Requejo Pagés (eds.), *Comentarios a la Ley Orgánica del Tribunal Constitucional*, Madrid, Tribunal Constitucional y Boletín Oficial del Estado, 2001; F. Rubio Llorente, J. Jiménez Campo, *Estudios sobre jurisdicción constitucional*, Madrid, McGraw-Hill, 1997; and I. Torres Muro, *La legitimación en los procesos constitucionales*. Madrid, Reus, 2007.

[3] See article 162 of the Spanish Constitution.

atory judgment simply in order to activate questions to the Constitutional Court. The latter has functioned to eliminate areas of immunity, under the correct assumption that no *zona franca* should exist within the system. There are arguably limits to this flexibility, however. In many instances, moreover, it may take some time for a controversy to arise that will set in motion constitutional review. To the extent that adjudicative gaps may appear, there is much to be said for the availability of the constitutional challenge procedure as a complementary device. If the legal system incorporates it, we do not need to wait for someone to be harmed by the application of a given statute to get the Court to speak.

A number of examples, among many that could be drawn from the Spanish experience, illustrate this point. In 1985, the Spanish Constitutional Court had to review the validity of an abortion law recently passed by Parliament.[4] The new law partially de-criminalized abortion: it introduced certain exceptions to the general rule that abortion was a crime. The question arose whether the law was valid, given that the Spanish Constitution protects human dignity and the right to life in articles 10 and 15. Some people opined that the Constitution should be read to establish limits to the liberalization of abortion. According to them, the constitutional protection of human dignity and life requires the legal system to punish those who destroy the fetus. It is hard to see how this kind of objection could have been addressed in the context of a concrete controversy, at least in Spain. Might a prosecutor bring criminal charges against someone who has clearly not committed a crime under the new abortion statute, and ask the judge handling the case to raise a question to the Constitutional Court concerning the validity of the statute? This course of action would be quite shocking. The principle of legality in criminal matters cannot be disregarded so easily. In the context of the abortion controversy, an abstract challenge is the right mechanism to trigger the jurisdiction of the Court. That was, indeed, the procedural avenue that was taken: a qualified minority of the members of Congress impugned the law. This provided the Court with the opportunity to speak. The Court actually found the statute to be constitutionally flawed in various respects, and the legislature had to amend it accordingly. Twenty-five years later, in 2010, a similar discussion developed concerning a new law that further liberalized abortion. Again, it was the parliamentary opposition that instituted proceedings against the law. (The Court has yet to issue its decision on the matter).

Another example: in 2005, the Spanish legislature amended the Civil Code to allow same-sex marriage. The constitutionality of the new law was con-

[4] See STC 53/1985.

troversial, in light of article 32 of the Spanish Constitution, which provides that "a man and a woman" have a fundamental right to get married. The parliamentary opposition decided to file a challenge against the statute. A divided Court reasoned that article 32 should not be read to deny the ordinary legislature the authority to extend the reach of the matrimonial regime to cover same-sex couples. The Court thus concluded that the law was valid.[5] It would have been difficult for the Court to address this controversial issue in the context of a concrete case. Even if judges in Spain often intervene in administrative procedures to formalize marriages, they cannot refer questions to the Constitutional Court when they do so. Under Spanish law, the constitutional question can only be posed when the judge is exercising "jurisdiction", with all the attributes of judicial independence. According to the Constitutional Court, when judges handle the matrimonial proceedings, they act as administrative organs that are subject to the instructions of the executive branch. So the Court refused to examine the constitutional questions that several judges had formulated in that capacity.[6] Moreover, once two persons of the same sex have entered into marriage, it is hard to see who would have standing to challenge its validity before the ordinary courts on the grounds that the statute authorizing same-sex marriage is constitutionally infirm.

An additional consideration worth reflecting upon is that the abstract nature of constitutional challenges permits the Constitutional Court to focus on the objective question concerning the validity of a law and to disregard the factual details of different cases. Because abstract review is not connected to a particular controversy, the Court is detached from the immediate interests of specific litigants. Abstraction thus serves as a "veil of ignorance" technique, to use a Rawlsian expression. This kind of procedure is also likely to encourage constitutional judges to bring a systematic perspective to the legal problems under examination. The judges need to take into account the interests of the many individuals who are involved in complex legal and institutional structures. Concrete review, in contrast, may turn the attention of the Court to the plight of the particular litigants, and thus underestimate the weight of other private or public interests.

---

[5] See STC 198/2012.

[6] See, for example, ATC 508/2005. Probably, the Italian Constitutional Court would have been more flexible than its Spanish counterpart in similar circumstances. Elisabetta Lamarque mentions a case where the Italian Constitutional Court agreed to examine a question referred by a "supervisory judge" in charge of prison affairs, in spite of the fact that such a judge did not have all the institutional features that characterize ordinary courts.

9.2. Constitutional challenges: problems with time

If abstract challenges are included in the constitutional toolkit, certain problems need to be addressed. In this connection, we can draw some lessons from the Spanish experience.

A first set of questions concerns time. Should there be a deadline for filing a challenge? Should the Court be authorized to suspend the operation of the statute until it rules on the merits? Alternatively, should the challenge be registered before the statute is promulgated and thus enters into force?

When thinking about the answers to these questions, it is important to realize that constitutional challenges are very powerful weapons. The organ that is entitled to lodge the challenge is not limited in its attack: it can question any provision of the relevant statute that it finds problematic from a constitutional point of view. The challenger certainly has the burden to argue its case: it has to make explicit the reasons it relies upon to launch the attack. But since the challenge is not linked to any specific controversy, there is no limitation concerning its reach. Therefore, the decision the Court will render may have a very destructive effect. In a single decision, the Court can dismantle many statutory provisions. In contrast, the process through which statutes are tested under the Constitution by way of references sent by ordinary judges is more gradual: even if the Court´s decisions have general effects, only the provisions that apply to the specific cases are scrutinized by the Court.

Because of this feature, it is reasonable for the law to establish a deadline for challenges to be submitted: given how devastating such actions can be, the legal system will suffer less if they can only be filed before a certain period of time has elapsed, after which only "softer" instruments (such as constitutional questions raised by ordinary judges) can be used.

Interestingly, the Spanish Constitution does not establish a deadline for these purposes, but the organic statute that regulates the structure and functions of the Court does: the statute provides that the challenge must be brought within a three-month period after the official publication of the targeted law.[7] There has never been any serious discussion about the constitutionality of this provision, which fixes a quite restrictive deadline that does not figure in the Constitution. By way of justification, one may point to the need to ensure a certain degree of stability in the legal system, while protecting, at the same time, the supreme character of the Constitution.

---

[7] See article 33.1, *Ley Orgánica 2/1978, de 3 de octubre, del Tribunal Constitucional* (LOTC).

A related question is whether the Constitutional Court should be authorized to adopt interim measures before rendering its final decision on the merits of the case. The Spanish system exhibits some flaws in this regard. On the one hand, the Constitution explicitly empowers the President of the Government to require the Court to suspend the operation of a regional law or regulation if the President files a challenge against it.[8] The Court has no discretion at this juncture: it must suspend the effects of the norm, if the President so requests. The Constitution also provides that the Court must decide whether to lift the suspension within a five-month period. The Constitution is otherwise silent concerning the possibility of suspending laws (whether regional or national) in other cases. The legislature, in turn, seems to have read this silence to mean prohibition: the organic statute that regulates the Constitutional Court explicitly provides that the admission of a challenge shall not suspend the effects of the law that is being contested.[9]

The Constitutional Court has been divided on this issue, however. The majority of the judges are of the view that it is indeed impossible to suspend the application of a law that is the target of a constitutional challenge. They consider the organic statute to be clear enough, and not inconsistent with the Constitution. Some dissenting judges, however, have maintained that it is perfectly legitimate for the Court to suspend the effects of a law by means of interim measures. To this end, they distinguish, quite persuasively, between the privilege that the President of the Government is granted, on the one hand, and a request for interim measures, on the other. While the President can simply require the Court to suspend the operation of a law, other challengers need to prove, under relatively strict standards, that there is *fumus boni iuris* and *periculum in mora*. The fact that only the President of the Government is granted the privilege to force the suspension of a law does not mean that other actors cannot request the Court to issue interim measures.

A few years ago, for example, the government adopted a law-decree establishing a sort of fiscal amnesty. The parliamentary opposition instituted an abstract challenge before the Court, on the grounds that the duty to pay taxes that the constitutional text announces in article 31 was being violated. They also argued that the law-decree exceeded the domain that the Constitution carves out for this legal instrument. The Court finally struck down the law-decree. Unfortunately, the Court held that its decision would have no retroactive effects, for reasons of legal certainty.[10] Hence, the decision

[8] See article 161.2 of the Spanish Constitution.

[9] See article 30, LOTC.

[10] See STC 73/2017.

invalidating the fiscal amnesty did not have much practical impact. If interim measures had been adopted, of course, the Court´s decision would have had greater legal repercussions.

In her piece, Lamarque explains that the Italian Constitutional Court has worked out a good system of interim measures in the context of concrete review. If abstract review were inserted into the Italian constitutional regime, I suggest that interim measures should also be made available to guarantee the efficacy of the Court´s final judgments.

An alternative arrangement is to establish *a priori* review, so that a law can be impugned in the abstract before it is promulgated. In France, for example, this procedure has played a key constitutional role. In Spain, such a mechanism was introduced in 1979, when the Constitutional Court was created, even though the Constitution does not make any reference to it. It was designed to contest the validity of organic statutes, as well as Statutes of Autonomy (which regulate the structure and competences of the seventeen regional communities that have been created in Spain). This procedure of *a priori* review was later eliminated in 1985 and re-established in 2015. In its current form, it can be used to question the validity of Statutes of Autonomy. [11]

The reason why this mechanism was re-introduced in 2015 is tied to the controversy surrounding the Catalan Statute of Autonomy that was enacted in 2006. This Statute had been approved by the Catalan people in a referendum and was later referred to the Court by the parliamentary opposition in the Spanish parliament. After a long process of deliberation, the Court finally struck down a few provisions of the Statute, subjected others to an interpretation in conformity with the Constitution, and upheld the rest. [12] There was disappointment and anger in large sections of Catalonian public opinion. Soon after the Court´s decision was released in the summer of 2010, a large demonstration took place in Barcelona in protest. Regardless of one´s view about the consequences of this critical moment of Spanish constitutional history, there is consensus among experts that a delicate situation arises when a court is asked to pass judgment on the constitutionality of a norm that has been ratified by citizens in a referendum. Against this background, it is understandable that the Spanish legislature decided in 2015 to reinstitute the procedure of *a priori* review. In the future, therefore, it will be possible to challenge a new Statute of Autonomy (or an amendment) before the final text is submitted to popular referendum.

---

[11] See *Ley Orgánica 12/2015, de 22 de septiembre*. Article 79 of the LOTC regulates the new procedure.

[12] See STC 31/2010.

9.3. Constitutional challenges and the risk of politicization

Opponents of abstract review challenges often object that such challenges may politicize the Court. While constitutional questions raised by the ordinary judiciary are detached from the political game, constitutional challenges are not: they are brought by public institutions, most of which are political in character. In particular, if a qualified minority of members of parliament is empowered to commence this kind of proceeding, the political fights between the governmental majority and the opposition can simply continue before the Constitutional Court. The latter finds itself in the middle of a political battle, which can only harm its prestige. The Court´s decision will be read by public opinion through political eyes. Prominent Spanish scholars have made such objections, including Francisco Rubio Llorente, who was Vice-President of the Constitutional Court. [13]

There is no doubt that the risk of politicization exists. But one should be careful before concluding that it would be better to eliminate this procedure altogether.

First of all, constitutional review of legislation is itself "political" in some sense, no matter who has standing to trigger it. The question whether a statute is in conformity with the Constitution is often deeply contested. Constitutions tend to speak in rather abstract terms, especially when it comes to fundamental rights and liberties. In addition, the Constitution occupies a central place in the life of the political community: it expresses the basic values and principles that the community shares. The statute that needs to be checked under the Constitution, moreover, is not an insignificant legal piece. It has a special democratic dignity owing to its parliamentary source: it has been produced by an institution whose members are periodically elected by the people. So it is a very delicate issue, most of the time, whether a statute is or is not constitutional. Not surprisingly, in many European countries, the way members of Constitutional Courts are selected differs from the way ordinary judges are appointed: a relatively more democratic method is employed. Verifying the conformity of legislation with the Constitution is still a judicial activity, but it is morally and politically charged to a higher degree than ordinary adjudication is. So the question is whether the institutional choice of allowing public organs to bring challenges to the Court will dramatically transform the conception that the political community holds about the Court´s nature. Arguably, even if additional doses of politicization will be injected into the system as a

[13] F. RUBIO LLORENTE, *Seis tesis sobre la jurisdicción constitucional en Europa*, in F. RUBIO LLORENTE, *Las formas del poder*, Madrid, Centro de Estudios Políticos y Constitucionales, 1997.

result of that institutional choice, the changes in public perception should not be radical.

Secondly, when political institutions are empowered to file constitutional challenges, is it true that they simply continue their political battles in the judicial terrain? We should pay attention, in this connection, to the differences between the kinds of arguments that are made in the political sphere and those that are advanced before the Court. While a wide variety of reasons can be offered in the political forum, only legal arguments can be articulated in court. Not everything that is said politically can be said in constitutional language. There is a constitutional text, as well as a body of jurisprudential precedents and doctrinal commentary, that channels the legal reasons that can be submitted in support of a constitutional challenge, or in defense of the validity of a statute that has been attacked. In actual practice, there is a qualitative difference between the political and legal argumentative modalities in Spain.

There are links between the two argumentative modalities, of course. During the legislative debates, political actors build constitutional arguments to support their position. They sometimes refer to the Court´s case law. And the relevant parliamentary minority is apt to announce that it will go to the Court to impugn the law the majority wishes to approve. This is not problematic, however. The existence of a Court that can be reached by the parliamentary opposition casts a shadow over the legislative discussions. Members of parliament are prone to take the Constitution more seriously as a result of this.

When considering the extent to which constitutional challenges tend to politicize adjudication, we should also take into account the other procedures that are in place. If the Court already possesses jurisdiction to adjust controversies between various constitutional organs of the state, for example, or between the state and the regions, as is true in Italy, there is already a significant "political" element in the system. It is unlikely that introducing constitutional challenges would unbalance things too much in the direction of politicization.

9.4. Constitutional complaints to safeguard fundamental rights

I now turn to the other procedure I described in the introduction. Spain followed the German steps when it decided to establish a procedure that allows private persons who claim to have suffered a violation of their fundamental rights to file a complaint before the Constitutional Court. [14] The

[14] See articles 53.2, 161.1 and 162.1 of the Spanish Constitution. There is a large

German *Verfassungsbeschwerde* inspired the Spanish *recurso de amparo*. Normally, the case must first be referred to the ordinary judiciary. The doors of the Court are only opened when the ordinary judicial remedies have been exhausted. The *recurso de amparo* can be filed by private persons who invoke a legitimate interest, by the Ombudsperson, and by prosecutors. In practice, however, only private persons bring such complaints to the Court.

Historically, the constitutional complaints procedure has served the Spanish legal system well. The Constitutional Court was a new institution that embodied the values of the liberal and democratic order founded by the Constitution of 1978, and it was eager to bring those values to social and political reality. Since the Court was authorized to scrutinize the decisions rendered by ordinary judges, it could strongly shape judicial practices in the name of fundamental rights invoked by private persons. The Court performed a "pedagogical" function when it carefully explained in its opinions how the laws had to be interpreted and applied in ordinary adjudication in order to secure the protection of fundamental rights.

The Court´s success in attracting constitutional litigation, however, led to serious problems. As had already happened in Germany, the Spanish Court became overloaded with cases. Eventually, the Court was unable to effectively carry out the other important functions it is entrusted with – in particular, reviewing the constitutionality of legislation. So a reform was adopted in 2007, to grant the Court a large measure of discretion to decide which constitutional complaints to adjudicate.[15] One can draw a straightforward lesson from the Spanish experience: if this procedure to safeguard fundamental rights is to be made part of the constitutional portfolio, the Court should be conferred wide discretion to select the cases, so that it can focus its attention on a small set.

Lamarque correctly emphasizes two undisputed benefits of the current Italian system: the Court answers in a timely manner the questions that ordinary judges frame; and the judgments are made by the Court as a whole, not by specific sections or committees. These are important virtues. If the constitutional complaints procedure were ever to be instituted in Italy, the Court should be accorded great leeway to be very selective, in order to preserve those features.

Another problematic feature of the *recurso de amparo* is that it makes it more likely that the Constitutional Court and the Supreme Court (as well

---

body of scholarly literature on this procedure. For a comprehensive treatment, see G. Fernández Farreres, *El recurso de amparo según la jurisprudencia constitucional*, Madrid, Marcial Pons, 1994; and P. Pérez Tremps, *El recurso de amparo*, Valencia, Tirant Lo Blanch, 2015.

[15] See *Ley Orgánica 6/2007, de 24 de mayo.*

as other ordinary courts) will clash. The ordinary judges may dislike having their decisions overturned by the Constitutional Court. Hence, a good institutional relationship is vital to reduce these potential tensions. Lamarque is right, in this regard, when she endorses Roberto Romboli´s observation that the introduction of constitutional complaints in Italy might disrupt the cooperative spirit between the ordinary judiciary and the Constitutional Court.

It is actually not easy, from a purely doctrinal point of view, to determine the allocation of adjudicative power between the Constitutional Court and the ordinary courts when the jurisdiction over complaints is introduced. Some fundamental rights, in particular, guarantee that public organs will act in accordance with ordinary law. The constitutional right to the legality of crimes and penalties, for instance, guarantees that a person cannot be punished for an action or omission that is not defined as criminal by the legislation that existed at the relevant time. This fundamental right stems from article 25 of the Spanish Constitution, and the *recurso de amparo* protects it. If ordinary courts make a mistake when interpreting the law, and they therefore wrongly convict someone of a crime he is innocent of, can the latter file a complaint before the Constitutional Court? This scenario points to a serious dilemma. If the Court holds that there has been a violation of the right to legality in such a case, it becomes the supreme court in criminal matters. If, instead, it holds that interpretive mistakes are constitutionally irrelevant, the fundamental right that is at stake is deprived of much of its force. The Spanish Constitutional Court has tried to construct an intermediate solution between these two extremes, so that its task is to control for clear interpretive errors, but such a solution is rather unstable. [16]

It is sometimes argued in Spain that the constitutional complaints procedure should be eliminated altogether. It is said that the Constitutional Court has already performed the pedagogical function that was so necessary during the first stages of Spain´s constitutional enterprise. Ordinary judges should now simply cooperate with the Court by means of constitutional questions and be sensitive to fundamental rights when they adjudicate cases. Judges have this sensitivity, it is maintained, for law schools regularly educate and train future judges as constitutionally-minded adjudicators.

Such a proposal to eliminate the constitutional complaints procedure is too radical, though. There is still room for constitutional complaints to play a critical role in Spain. The Court needs to refine its case law as new problems arise. Complaints brought by private citizens are an important source

[16] See, for instance, STC 111/1993, and STC 150/1997.

of raw material for the Court to develop its jurisprudence. Of course, ordinary judges can provide the Court with the opportunity to address new issues, through the referral mechanism. But judges in Spain are less eager to raise questions than their Italian counterparts. While the latter have acquired an intense "constitutional awareness" ("all courts are to some extent also constitutional courts", Mauro Cappelletti asserted), Spanish judges have done so to a lesser degree.

This connects with a further observation. The centralized model of constitutional review that prevails in Europe exhibits a certain asymmetry; it distinguishes between decisions that consider a statute to be constitutionally invalid, on the one hand, and decisions that consider it to be valid, on the other. Whereas the Constitutional Court holds a monopoly over the former function, it possesses no monopoly over the latter. Indeed, only the Constitutional Court can disregard a statute as invalid on constitutional grounds, while any court can uphold the validity of a statute against constitutional contestation. This asymmetry can be more or less deep. If ordinary judges, for example, are required by the existing rules to send questions to the Court simply because one the parties expresses doubts about the constitutionality of the applicable law, the asymmetry is less pronounced than under a legal system that asks judges to raise questions to the Court only if they are convinced that the applicable law is unconstitutional. Many intermediate possibilities can be conceived. Regardless of the degree of the asymmetry, a fair question is whether a system based on this fundamental distinction between validity and invalidity is tenable, all things considered.

Arguably, the asymmetry is acceptable, insofar as ordinary courts are as sensitive to constitutional values as the Constitutional Court is. If this condition is met, the fact that an ordinary judge considers a law to be constitutionally valid, and therefore chooses not to refer it to the Constitutional Court for its review, is not problematic. If, in contrast, ordinary judges are less constitutionally thoughtful than the Constitutional Court is, their key role as gatekeepers of the Court becomes objectionable. The private party that has failed to convince the ordinary judges in a particular case to refer the issue to the Constitutional Court may believe that the latter would have deemed the statute to be unconstitutional, if it had had the chance to rule upon its validity. In this scenario, the possibility for private persons to bring constitutional complaints to the Court, after the ordinary judicial remedies have been exhausted, should be welcome. The procedure operates as a desirable escape-valve to safeguard fundamental rights in a system that cannot fully rely on the judgments of ordinary courts.

9.5. Conclusion

The Italian system of constitutional review, as portrayed by Elisabetta Lamarque, appears to be a very balanced one. The Constitutional Court has found ways to expand its capacity to scrutinize legislation under the Constitution. In many respects, other countries (including Spain) envy the sophisticated cooperation between ordinary judges and the Constitutional Court that regularly takes place in Italy. Because of the success of this system, it is controversial whether it would be a good idea to introduce additional procedures to trigger the jurisdiction of the Court.

If the Spanish experience is used for comparative purposes, there seem to be good reasons to consider the establishment of an abstract review procedure in Italy. The main advantage of this procedure is that it helps eliminate potential adjudicative gaps.

There is less to be said, in contrast, in favor of constitutional complaints to safeguard fundamental rights. Adopting this mechanism might jeopardize the collaborative spirit between ordinary judges and the Constitutional Court that has characterized the Italian system. In any event, if this procedure were introduced, the Court should be afforded discretionary jurisdiction to select the cases. The Spanish Constitutional Court suffered greatly until a reform was implemented in 2007. We should never forget that the central reason why Constitutional Courts were created in Europe was the need to put constitutional review of legislation in the hands of a special constitutional tribunal. This reason should still be at the heart of the system.

Dialogue V

JUDICIAL REASONING AND INTERPRETATION

Chapter X

FORMS AND METHODS OF CONSTITUTIONAL INTERPRETATION – ITALIAN STYLE

Giorgio Pino

10.1. Constitutional interpretation in contemporary Italian legal culture

Constitutional interpretation has received an extensive and extremely sophisticated treatment by Italian scholars. To be sure, legal interpretation *in general* has always been a point of thorough and intense scholarly debate in contemporary Italian legal culture.[1] But constitutional interpretation has attracted additional interest in its own right, in virtue of the fact that it is widely perceived as a sui generis kind of legal interpretation, different in character from 'ordinary' (i.e. statutory) interpretation.[2] Moreover, constitutional interpretation has gradually become an extremely pervasive issue. Indeed, at least in the last three decades the Italian legal culture has firmly embraced the idea that constitutional principles may be relevant for any kind of legal question, and may exert their normative force on any

---

[1] To name just two Italian classics, E. BETTI, *Interpretazione della legge e degli atti giuridici (teoria generale e dogmatica)*, Milan, Giuffrè, 1949 (a torch-bearer of the hermeneutic approach to legal interpretation); G. TARELLO, *L'interpretazione della legge*, Milan, Giuffrè, 1980 (an outstanding example of analytical and legal realistic jurisprudence). More recent, and comprehensive, primers to legal interpretation are P. CHIASSONI, *Tecnica dell'interpretazione giuridica*, Bologna, Il Mulino, 2007, and R. GUASTINI, *Interpretare e argomentare*, Milan, Giuffrè, 2011.

[2] See L. PALADIN, *Le fonti del diritto italiano*, Bologna, Il Mulino, 1996, 110 (the Constitution "*paves the way for a new theory of interpretation*").

branch of the law. The Constitution, as a consequence, steadily appears in the legal reasoning of Italian jurists – constitutional interpretation is business as usual for Italian jurists, judges and academics alike.[3] Moreover the ItCC, while originally designed by the Constitution to play the role of just a "negative legislator," has gradually evolved also, and prominently, into an "interpretive agency". In other words the ItCC, in addition to issuing declarations of unconstitutionality, pure and simple, consistently produces also "interpretive decisions", which avoid a declaration of unconstitutionality insofar as it is possible to interpret the "suspect" statute in a "constitutionally compatible way".[4]

This essay will highlight some issues that feature prominently in the Italian debate on constitutional interpretation. To be sure, "constitutional interpretation" is not just a single issue, but rather a cluster of different and tightly interwoven issues, such as: the choice of interpretive canons that best fit the Constitution, the nature of constitutional norms, the relation between constitutional interpretation and statutory interpretation – just to mention a few. I will try to untangle at least some of these issues, and to relate them to the underlying conceptions of the Constitution at work in contemporary Italian legal culture, as well as to similar debates in other countries.

10.2. The nature of constitutional norms

A preliminary issue that needs to be addressed concerns the very the nature of constitutional norms. Are constitutional norms properly *legal* norms, or should they be considered more akin to policy directives or political programs?[5]

---

[3] Hereinafter, I will use "Constitution" (with a capital C) in order to refer to a particular constitution (such as, and most frequently, the Italian one), and "constitution" (with a lowercase c) in order to refer to the constitution as an abstract object.

[4] According to a long-standing doctrine of the ItCC, ordinary judges should not even refer a question of constitutionality, if the suspect statute can be interpreted in a way that is compatible with the Constitution (see e.g. Judgment 356/1996). See V. Barsotti, P.G. Carozza, M. Cartabia, A. Simoncini, *Italian Constitutional Justice in Global Context*, Oxford, Oxford University Press, 2016, 82-91.

[5] I use "policy" here in roughly the sense stipulated by R. Dworkin, *Taking Rights Seriously*, London, Duckworth, 1978, 22 ("*I call a "policy" that kind of standard that sets out a goal to be reached, generally an improvement in some economic, political, or social feature of the community*"); see also M. Atienza, J. Ruiz Manero, *A Theory of Legal Sentences*, Dordrecht, Springer, 1998, 5, 11. For a more general view on this topic, see L. Weis, *Constitutional Directive Principles*, in 37 *Oxford Journal of Legal Studies* 916 (2017).

10.2.1. Constitutional norms vs. constitutional programs

This issue has been heatedly debated in the Italian legal culture especially during the hiatus between the entry into force of the Republican Constitution (1948), and the first ruling of the ItCC (1956). Back then some scholars, as well as the Supreme Court (*Corte di Cassazione*), maintained that substantial parts of the Constitution should be understood as "programs" or "policies" rather than as full-blown, mandatory legal norms. These would include the "Bill of Rights" part of the Constitution (articles 1 to 54) almost in its entirety, and possibly also some articles of the "Frame of Government" part. Under this view, arguably shared even by the Framers themselves, the Constitution is to be regarded more as a *political* document, rather than a properly *legal* one. It does not really qualify as *law*, but rather as a sort of political statement. As such, it is not apt for judicial application – its function, instead, is to serve as a point of reference in the political debate and the legislative process. [6]

Now, the idea that the Constitution (or ample portions thereof: hereafter I will leave this qualification aside) is better conceived just in terms of a set of policy directives has clear implications on constitutional interpretation. For one thing, under this view the legislature becomes the sole "master of the constitution:" implementing the Constitution is up *only* to the legislature. It is only through legislation that constitutional policies become legal norms (*interpositio legislatoris*). [7] Courts, on the other hand, in their ordinary adjudicative functions, will not be able to resort directly to the Constitution – the Constitution, as such, is not justiciable.

Interestingly, the merely programmatic character of the constitution, and particularly of the provisions on fundamental rights and liberties – an

---

[6] C. MEZZANOTTE, *La Corte costituzionale: esperienze e prospettive*, in AA.VV. *Attualità e attuazione della Costituzione*, Bari, Laterza, 1979. For a discussion of the theory of the "programmatic" character of the Constitution, see L. PALADIN, *Le fonti del diritto italiano*, n. 2, 135; M. LUCIANI, *Dottrina del moto delle costituzioni e vicende della Costituzione repubblicana*, in G. BRUNELLI, G. CAZZETTA (eds.), *Dalla Costituzione "inattuata" alla Costituzione "inattuale"? Potere costituente e riforme costituzionali nell'Italia repubblicana*, Milan, Giuffrè, 2013, 40-49.

[7] Some scholars distinguish between "implementation" and "application" of the constitution – the former understood as a matter of legislation and administrative regulations, the latter as a judicial task (M. LUCIANI, *Dottrina del moto delle costituzioni e vicende della Costituzione repubblicana*, n. 6). The intended practical import of this distinction is that some constitutional norms are apt to (judicial) application, whereas other such norms are subject only to (legislative) implementation. In the interest of space, I will not expand on this point here, but I do think that this distinction is precarious at best. In the following, then, I will use "implementation" and "application" as synonymous.

idea somewhat anticipated by Hans Kelsen [8] – is now vindicated by "political constitutionalists", whose fundamental claim is that rights are better left to political debate and to the determinations of a democratically elected legislator rather than to courts. And, to this effect, they recommend also that the constitution be stripped of its properly legal character and confined only to the "political" realm. [9]

The opposite view is that the constitution is not just a political manifesto but a properly legal document – a proper source of law. [10] As such, the constitution is directly amenable to legal interpretation (as opposed to being confined to political debate), and constitutional norms are to be considered legal norms on all counts. The implementation, or application, of the constitution is not only a matter of sheer political choices to be adopted by the legislature, but also a matter of legal interpretation and legal reasoning performed by courts, with only rare exceptions. [11]

To be sure, in Italian legal culture the policy/mandatory norms alternative has now lost most of its appeal. As soon as the ItCC became fully operative, it claimed the power of enforcing – or at least of using in its legal reasoning – any kind of constitutional provision; as a consequence, Italian scholars became suddenly aware that the Constitution could and should be regarded as a proper source of law. Put differently, in Italian legal culture, the paradigm shift from a political-constitutionalist stance to a legal-constitutionalist one has been virtually complete and, as much as one may foresee, irreversible. [12]

---

[8] H. KELSEN, *The Nature and Development of Constitutional Adjudication* (1929), in L. VINX (eds.), *The Guardian of the Constitution: Hans Kelsen and Carl Schmitt on the Limits of Constitutional Law*, Cambridge, Cambridge University Press, 2015, 60. For a recent restatement of this very idea, G. WEBBER, *Legal Reasoning and Bills of Rights*, in *LSE Law, Society and Economy Working Papers*, No. 1, 1 (2011), 10: "Legislation [...] gives the various rights and freedoms affirmed in a bill of rights legal life. [...] Legislation does no more and no less than take the abstracted and reified affirmations of rights in a bill of rights and render them apt and cognisable in law by specifying their scope and content".

[9] See J. WALDRON, *A Right-Based Critique of Constitutional Rights*, in 13 *Oxford Journal of Legal Studies* 18 (1993); J. WALDRON, *Law and Disagreement*, Oxford, Oxford University Press, ch. 12; R. BELLAMY, *Political Constitutionalism*, Cambridge, Cambridge University Press, 2007; G. WEBBER, *The Negotiable Constitution*, Cambridge, Cambridge University Press, 2009, ch. 5.

[10] See S. GARDBAUM, *The Place of Constitutional Law in the Legal System*, in M. ROSENFELD, A. SAJÓ (eds.), *The Oxford Handbook of Comparative Constitutional Law*, Oxford, Oxford University Press, 2012 (contrasting "political", "legal", and "total" constitutionalism).

[11] The usual example is art. 4: "*The Republic recognises the right of all citizens to work and promotes those conditions which render this right effective*".

[12] Among the very few dissenting voices, A. PINTORE, *I diritti della democrazia*, Bari, Laterza, 2003.

Even those who insist that the courts should play a more limited role in the administration of rights – and conversely that the legislature should play a more central role therein – do not question the full-blown legal character of the Constitution and the importance of judicial review of legislation.

10.2.2. Constitutional rules, principles, and values

If constitutional norms are proper, mandatory legal norms and not just policy directions for future legislation, one may still ask what kind of norms they are. Here the relevant distinction is between rules, principles, and values. [13]

Of course, nobody would actually claim that the Constitution consists *only* of rules, or *only* of principles, or *only* of values. Rather, the point here is about the comparative importance of these different kinds of norms in the architecture of the constitution. [14]

In legal scholarship, "rules", "principles" and "values" are not always clearly defined, nor always used in a consistent manner. [15] For present purposes, we may rely on the following provisional definitions. Rules are norms that are relatively *precise* and *determinate* in both their scope of application and their normative consequences. Principles are norms that are relatively *generic* and *indeterminate* in both their scope of application and their normative consequences. Moreover, principles embody, or give direct legal expression to, some moral or political ideal; [16] accordingly, a principle

---

[13] On this distinction, as referred to constitutional norms, see R. ALEXY, *A Theory of Constitutional Rights*, Oxford, Oxford University Press, 2010, ch. 3; O. CHESSA, ***Libertà** fondamentali e teoria costituzionale*, Milan, Giuffrè, 2002, 357-393; G. ZAGREBELSKY, *Ronald Dworkin's Principle Based Constitutionalism: An Italian Point of View*, in 1 *I-CON* 621 (2003).

[14] In quite a similar vein, I think, but with different terminology, Jeffrey Goldsworthy distinguishes between a "positivist" and a "normativist" conception of the constitution, as two extremes of a spectrum that includes various intermediate possibilities. According to the former, the constitution consists of "a set of discrete written provisions" (i.e. rules), while according to the latter the constitution is "a normative structure whose provisions are, either explicitly or implicitly, based on deeper principles, and ultimately on abstract norms of political morality"; see J. GOLDSWORTHY, *Constitutional Interpretation*, in M. ROSENFELD, A. SAJÓ (eds.), *The Oxford Handbook of Comparative Constitutional Law*, Oxford, Oxford University Press, 2012, sec. 1. This choice of words, however, is rather unfortunate since "positivism" and "normativism" normally refer to two well-known traditions in legal philosophy, which are not even remotely related to specific viewpoints on the nature of constitutions.

[15] G. PINO, *Teoria analitica del diritto I. La norma giuridica*, Pisa, ETS, 2016, ch. 4.

[16] S. PERRY, *Two Models of Legal Principles*, in 82 *Iowa Law Review* 787 (1997), 788 ("*the explicit content of principles is value-oriented, whereas that of rules is action-*

is a norm that conveys a peculiar dimension of "importance". [17] Values are moral or political goods, conceived at an extremely high level of abstraction – equality, liberty, dignity, and democracy, are good cases in point.

Now, how is the rules-principles-values distinction relevant for constitutional interpretation? For one thing, when we talk about constitutional *norms,* we are assuming that some kind of interpretive job has already taken place: a norm is always the *result*, rather than the starting point, of legal interpretation. Before interpretation, there is no norm; there is just a text. The norm is the meaning (the semantic content) that is extracted from a source of law through interpretation. Accordingly, the possibility itself of framing constitutional norms in terms of rules, principles, or values is the outcome of a preliminary interpretive choice. Of course, the wording of the constitutional text provides some guidance to this effect. Accordingly, a sharply drafted provision will be easily interpreted as stating a rule, whereas a provision drafted in abstract, morally laden language will be easily interpreted as stating a principle (the case of values is different, as we shall see shortly). But the interesting point, here, is that *in principle* nothing prevents an interpreter from deriving a rule from a provision that is drafted in abstract, morally laden terms. And of course it is also possible to derive a principle from, or to read a value behind, a sharply formulated provision. Such interpretive choices ultimately depend on the background conception of the constitution adopted by the interpreter.

But there is more, of course. The "pre-interpretive" choice of framing constitutional norms in terms of rules, principles, or values, in turn, affects the next moves in the constitutional interpretation game – there are things that can be done (only, or preferably) with rules, things that can be done (only, or preferably) with principles, and things that can be done (only, or preferably) with values. Let's see.

If constitutional norms are framed in terms of *rules*, [18] they will be ex-

---

oriented"). See also N. MACCORMICK, *Legal Reasoning and Legal Theory*, Oxford, Clarendon, 1978, 234; M. JORI, *I principi nel diritto italiano*, in M. JORI, *Saggi di metagiurisprudenza*, Milan, Giuffrè, 1985, 301, 302.

[17] S. BARTOLE, *Costituzione (Dottrine generali e diritto costituzionale)*, in IV *Digesto delle Discipline Pubblicistiche* 288 (1989), 318; R. GUASTINI, *Teoria e ideologia dell'interpretazione costituzionale*, in LI *Giurisprudenza costituzionale*, 1, 743 (2006).

[18] Examples of a rule-oriented approach to the Constitution in Italian scholarship include: A. PACE, *Metodi interpretativi e costituzionalismo*, in XXI *Quaderni costituzionali* 35 (2001); A. PACE, *Interpretazione costituzionale e interpretazione per valori*, in G. AZZARITI (ed.), *Interpretazione costituzionale*, Turin, Giappichelli, 2007; M. DOGLIANI, *Il «posto» del diritto costituzionale*, in *Giurisprudenza costituzionale* 525 (1993); R. GUASTINI, *Diritto mite, diritto incerto*, in XXVI *Materiali per una storia della cultura giuridica* 513 (1996); L. FERRAJOLI, *Costituzionalismo principialista e costituzionalismo garantista*,

pected to provide clear-cut requirements applicable in an "all-or-nothing" fashion, and thus they will provide clear indications of what is constitutionally permissible and what is constitutionally forbidden. A rule, when applicable, is supposed to apply without exception. A rule-based constitution, thus, will provide interpreters with precise indications as to what is constitutionally permissible and what is constitutionally forbidden. Courts will enjoy little discretion in applying the constitution.

Interpreting and applying a principle-based constitution, [19] on the other hand, is an entirely different matter. As we have already seen, *principles* are characterized by a certain degree of genericity, indeterminacy, and importance. As such, principles cannot directly determine the outcome of a case. The application of principles requires a previous "specification" – a process that translates the original principle into a more manageable rule, or set of rules. Moreover, principles tend to conflict with one another: many principles may be relevant in a given case, pulling in different directions. And such conflicts are usually solved through a "balancing" exercise – an assessment of the respective importance of the principles at stake in the case in question. It is easy to see, then, that the interpretation and application of a principle-based constitution is bound to become a highly discretionary exercise – far more discretionary than the interpretation of a rule-based constitution. Specification and balancing are necessary steps for the judicial application of a principle-based constitution, and – precisely because of the indeterminacy and genericity of principles – there are many different ways of either specifying a given principle or of balancing competing principles against each other. From an abstract principle, or from two or more colliding principles, many different and alternative rules may be derived by way of specification or balancing. So, a principle-oriented understanding of the constitution brings to the fore the need for courts to engage in a highly discretionary interpretive exercise, as opposed to the alleged "automatic" precision that is supposed to characterize the application of rules. [20]

---

in *Giurisprudenza costituzionale* 2809 (2010); V. ANGIOLINI, *Costituente e costituito nell'Italia repubblicana*, Padua, Cedam, 1995.

[19] Examples of a principle-oriented approach to the Constitution in Italian scholarship include: G. ZAGREBELSKY, *Il diritto mite*, Turin, Einaudi, 1992; G. ZAGREBELSKY, *Ronald Dworkin's Principle Based Constitutionalism: An Italian Point of View*, n. 13; G.U. RESCIGNO, *Interpretazione costituzionale e positivismo giuridico*, in 1 *Diritto pubblico* 19 (2005); C. PINELLI, *Il dibattito sull'interpretazione costituzionale tra teoria e giurisprudenza*, in *Scritti in memoria di Livio Paladin*, Naples, Jovene, 2004, 1665.

[20] For this reason, some scholars maintain that it is the job of the legislator – and not of the judge – to transform abstract constitutional principles into judicially manageable rules: S. FOIS, *«Ragionevolezza» e «valori»: interrogazioni progressive verso le concezioni sulla forma di Stato e sul diritto*, in *Il principio di ragionevolezza nella giurisprudenza della*

Finally, constitutional *values* – a rather under-analysed concept in both legal theory and general legal discourse. Indeed, the distinction between principles and values is far from clear. Scholars and courts use these two terms more or less interchangeably, to refer to some exceedingly abstract normative standard imbued with moral or political significance.[21] Still, recourse to "values" gives a peculiar twist to constitutional interpretation (as we shall see shortly). While rules and principles certainly fit in the customary picture of the legal norm (in the sense that they are both *legal* and *norms*), the status of values is far less certain. On the one hand, a value is not normally thought of as a proper *norm*, but rather as the *foundation* of norms. On the other hand, the *legal* status of values is rather peculiar when compared to the legal status of an ordinary legal norm. Normally, values are not directly written into the text of the constitution,[22] and the individuation of values normally takes the interpreter far away from the text. Values are supposed to be inferred from the "spirit" of some

---

Corte costituzionale. Riferimenti comparatistici, Milan, Giuffrè, 1994, 103, 109; A. PACE, *Metodi interpretativi e costituzionalismo*, n. 18, 57-58; R. GUASTINI, *Ponderazione. Un'analisi dei conflitti tra principi costituzionali*, in *Ragion pratica* 151 (2006), 159; G. SCACCIA, *Valori e diritto giurisprudenziale*, in 1 *Diritto e società* 135 (2011); L. FERRAJOLI, *La democrazia attraverso i diritti*, Bari, Laterza, 2013, 133-137.

Similar concerns are also visible in constitutional scholarship in other countries: see M. NIMMER, *The Right to Speak from* Times *to* Time. *First Amendment Theory Applied to Libel and Misapplied to Privacy*, in 56 *California L.R.* 935 (1968), 947 ("[balancing] *may be criticized as a form of judicial lawmaking, and as such a usurpation of the legislative function*"); B. NEUBORNE, *Notes for a Theory of Constrained Balancing in First Amendment Cases*, in 38 *Case Western L.R.* 576 (1988), 578 ("*judicial balancing [...] licenses a judge to engage in overtly subjective decision-making that replicates and occasionally displaces identical thought-processes already carried out by a politically responsible official*"); P. DE LORA, *Tras el rastro de la ponderación*, in *Revista Española de Derecho Constitucional* 359 (2000), 367 ("*Esa tarea de los tribunales no dista mucho de la legislación*"); A. STONE SWEET, *Governing with Judges*, Oxford, Oxford University Press, 2000, 98 ("*A balancing jurisprudence not only gives the court great discretion, but it will inevitably cast the court into a more legislative style of deliberation and decision-making than would a jurisprudence of absolute rights*").

[21] Examples of a value-oriented approach to the Constitution in Italian scholarship include: A. BALDASSARRE, *L'interpretazione della costituzione*, in A. PALAZZO (eds.), *L'interpretazione della legge alle soglie del XXI secolo*, Naples, Edizioni Scientifiche Italiane, 2001, 215; M. CARTABIA, *Principi inviolabili e integrazione europea*, Milan, Giuffrè, 1995; A. BARBERA, *La Costituzione della Repubblica italiana*, Milan, Giuffrè, 2016. For a stark criticism of value-talk in constitutional interpretation see L. PALADIN, *Le fonti del diritto italiano*, n. 2, 143, and G. ZAGREBELSKY, *La legge e la sua giustizia*, Bologna, Il Mulino, 2008, 206-208.

[22] A. BALDASSARRE, *L'interpretazione della costituzione*, n. 21, 226. Among the scarce exceptions, one may point to art. 13 of the Italian Constitution ("*Personal liberty is inviolable*"), and art. 1 of the German *GrundGesetz* ("*Human dignity shall be inviolable*").

constitutional provision, or even from the whole constitution. The written provisions of the constitution may work as epiphanies of the constitutional *relevance* of a certain value, but the value itself will rest on some "objective," non-legal ground. More precisely, values are thought to be grounded in some objective moral system (or in some kind of natural law), [23] or in society, [24] or in a combination of both morality and society. [25]

Hence, the identification of values hardly qualifies as an exercise in legal interpretation – it is not constrained by the text of the constitution, and it is conceived as a kind of objective cognition of some moral reality.

10.3. Constitutional interpretation and conceptions of the constitution

The three approaches to the constitution (as rule-based, principle-based, and value-based) introduced in the preceding section embody different *conceptions* of the constitution – i.e., different conceptions of the na-

[23] An approach of this sort is conspicuous in German constitutional jurisprudence, whereby the German Basic Law is understood to incorporate an "objective order of values". See R. HERZOG, *The Hierarchy of Constitutional Norms and Its Function in the Protection of Basic Rights*, in 13 *Human Rights L.J.* 90 (1992), 91; D. KOMMERS, *German Constitutionalism: A Prolegomenon*, in 40 *Emory L.J.* 837 (1991), 851; D. KOMMERS, *Germany: Balancing Rights and Duties*, in J. GOLDSWORTHY (ed.), *Interpreting Constitutions. A Comparative Study*, Oxford, Oxford University Press, 2006, 203; M. HAILBRONNER, *Rethinking the Rise of the German Constitutional Court: From Anti-Nazism to Value Formalism*, in 12 *I-CON* 626 (2014); J. BOMHOFF, *Balancing Constitutional Rights*, Cambridge, Cambridge University Press, 2013, 103 ff. According to B. SCHLINK, *The Dynamics of Constitutional Adjudication*, in 17 *Cardozo L.R.* 1231 (1996), however, the "*Bundesverfassungsgericht's value orientation is a myth*" (at 1234). See also A. CHASKALON, *From Wickedness to Equality: The Moral Transformation of South African Law*, in 1 *I-CON* 590 (2003), 608 ("*The Constitution now contains an objective normative value system*"). For the use of value-arguments in American constitutional interpretation, see R. FALLON, *A Constructivist Coherence Theory of Constitutional Interpretation*, in 100 *Harvard L.R.* 1189 (1987), 1204-1209; P. BOBBITT, *Constitutional Law and Interpretation*, in D. PATTERSON (eds.), *A Companion to Philosophy of Law and Legal Theory*, Oxford, Blackwell, 1996. For a comparison between the German and the American approach to values in constitutional interpretation, see M. ROSENFELD, *Constitutional Adjudication in Europe and the United States: Paradoxes and Contrasts*, in 2 *I-CON* 633 (2004), 650-651, 661.

[24] A. BALDASSARRE, *L'interpretazione della costituzione*, n. 21, 226; A. BARAK, *Purposive Interpretation in Law*, Princeton, Princeton University Press, 2005, 381-382; G.J. JACOBSOHN, *Constitutional Values and Principles*, in M. ROSENFELD, A. SAJÓ (eds.), *The Oxford Handbook of Comparative Constitutional Law*, Oxford, Oxford University Press, 2012, 777.

[25] G. FASSÒ, *Il giudice e l'adeguamento del diritto alla realtà storico-sociale*, in XXVI *Rivista trimestrale di diritto e procedura civile* 897 (1972).

ture and function of the constitution in the legal and political system. It is in the light of a given background conception of the constitution that it makes sense to frame the normative content of constitution in terms of rules, or principles, or values.

In this regard, one can usefully distinguish between a "defensive" and a "foundational" conception of the constitution – or, somewhat more accurately, between a cluster of "defensive" conceptions and a cluster of "foundational" conceptions of the constitution.[26]

10.3.1. The defensive constitution

According to a "defensive" conception of the constitution, the constitution should be primarily, or even exclusively, regarded as a protective device against governmental intrusion into certain rights.[27] Under this approach, the constitution is limited in scope – it covers only a well-defined area of the social and political life of the relevant polity, and legislation is legitimate as long as it remains outside the area protected by the constitution. In other words, the legislature normally moves in a "constitution-free" area, and the content of a great deal of legislation is constitutionally irrelevant; the legislature must stop only in front of the gates of the constitutional fortress, guarded by the Constitutional Court. As a consequence, the constitution should work primarily as a checklist of "negative" validity conditions for legislation. Legislation may have any content whatsoever, as long as it does not clearly encroach upon the area protected by the constitution.

A defensive constitution, then, is premised exactly upon the possibility of clearly distinguishing between what is protected by the constitution and

---

[26] See G. TARELLO, *L'interpretazione della legge*, n. 1, 335-337. In slightly different terms, see V. ONIDA, *L'attuazione della Costituzione tra magistratura e Corte costituzionale*, in *Scritti in onore di Costantino Mortati*, Milan, Giuffrè, 1977, 501, and M. DOGLIANI, *Il «posto» del diritto costituzionale*, n. 18 (contrasting "defensive" and "expansive" conceptions of the constitution).

[27] This approach is usually associated to the mainstream American understanding of the constitution: see L. WEINRIB, *The Postwar Paradigm and American Exceptionalism*, in S. CHOUDHRY (eds.), *The Migration of Constitutional Ideas*, Cambridge, Cambridge University Press, 2007; M. COHEN-ELIYA, I. PORAT, *Proportionality and Constitutional Culture*, Cambridge, Cambridge University Press, 2013, chs. 5 and 6; J. BOMHOFF, *Balancing Constitutional Rights*, n. 23, ch. 5. The poster child of this attitude is of course the rule-like rendering of the First Amendment in the jurisprudence of the Supreme Court: see F. SCHAUER, *Freedom of Expression Adjudication in Europe and the United States: A Case Study in Comparative Constitutional Architecture*, in G. NOLTE (ed.), *European and US Constitutionalism*, Cambridge, Cambridge University Press, 2005.

what is constitutionally irrelevant – between the freedom of the legislature and the competence of the Constitutional Court. And this condition can be satisfied only if the constitution is designed as a set of (precise) *rules*.

All this has some interesting implications for constitutional interpretation. Under a defensive, rule-oriented conception of the constitution, constitutional interpretation should be performed with a good amount of self-restraint, with a view to preserving legal certainty and the distinction of competences between legislator and courts. To that end, textualism and originalism become the favourite canons of constitutional interpretation.[28] More generally, under this approach there is no meaningful difference between constitutional interpretation, on the one hand, and statutory interpretation, on the other. Constitutional interpretation requires the same interpretive canons that are in place in ordinary, statutory interpretation[29] – the constitution is just a statute that happens to be hierarchically superior to other statutes.

Finally, the defensive conception has implications for the role of courts vis-à-vis the constitution. Under this conception, the constitution is not supposed to be applied directly by ordinary courts in their ordinary adjudicative functions; rather, ordinary courts should limit themselves to "alerting" the Constitutional Court when they happen to stumble upon a constitutionally suspect statute. The Constitutional Court, in turn, should operate only as a "negative legislator" – its job is not to develop or implement the constitution but only to quash those statutes that are in clear contrast with the constitution.[30]

---

[28] M. DOGLIANI, *Il «posto» del diritto costituzionale* n. 18; A. PACE, *Metodi interpretativi e costituzionalismo*, n. 18; M. LUCIANI, *Interpretazione costituzionale e testo della costituzione. Osservazioni liminari*, in G. AZZARITI (ed.), *Interpretazione costituzionale*, Turin, Giappichelli, 2007, 48, and *Interpretazione conforme a costituzione*, in *Enciclopedia del diritto*, Annali IX, 391 (2016), 441; M. ESPOSITO, *In penetralibus pontificum repositum erat: brevi considerazioni sulla parabola discendente del diritto scritto*, in *Giurisprudenza costituzionale* 2995 (2004). More generally, on the link between originalism and a perception of the constitution "as a statute", see M. ROSENFELD, *Constitutional Adjudication in Europe and the United States: Paradoxes and Contrasts*, n. 25, 656-657.

[29] R. GUASTINI, *Interpretare e argomentare*, n. 1, 343-351; A. PACE, *Interpretazione costituzionale e interpretazione per valori*, n. 18, 95; M. LUCIANI, *Interpretazione conforme a costituzione*, n. 28, 441 (nevertheless acknowledging that the difference between constitutional and statutory interpretation may in fact be "in degree", rather than in kind); M. TROPER, *Constitutional Interpretation*, in 39 *Israel L.R.* 35 (2006); P. BOBBITT, *Constitutional Law and Interpretation*, n. 25, 127.

[30] The idea of the Constitutional Court as an essentially "negative legislator" was famously defended by H. KELSEN, *The Nature and Development of Constitutional Adjudication*, n. 8, and H. KELSEN, *General Theory of Law and State*, Cambridge, Harvard University Press, 1945, 268.

10.3.2. The foundational constitution

Under a "foundational" conception of the constitution, the constitution is seen as the foundation of the entire legal order: each and every norm of the legal system is valid only insofar as it is produced in accordance with the constitution, and is compatible with the constitution. Under this conception, the constitution is supposed to work *not only* as a set of negative limits but *also* – and most importantly – as a set of principles and values that call for implementation at both the legislative and the judicial level. Constitutional principles and values project their normative force upon the entire legal system. According to this conception, the function of the constitution is not only to *limit* governmental activities, but also to *direct* the actions of public authorities (including legislatures) towards certain constitutionally mandated objectives. Under a "foundational" conception, the constitution – far from being just a kind of statute – is a law of a peculiar kind, in virtue of its content and functions.[31]

As a consequence, the normative content of the constitution cannot be reduced to a set of fixed, stable, precise rules – the kind of norms we would expect to find in a statute. Rather, the constitution – the real content of the constitution, the most important part of the constitution – is seen either as a set of principles or as set of values. A foundational conception of the constitution, thus, may present itself either in a principle- based or in a value- based fashion.

A few interesting implications follow from this. First, under a foundational approach the constitution is not a separate field of the law, but rather it irradiates the entire legal order. Every area of the law is subject to the influence of constitutional principles and values. The entire the legal system has to be rendered fully compatible with the constitution, with no "black holes" or "constitution-free" areas.[32] The constitution, thus, becomes rele-

---

[31] G. ZAGREBELSKY, *La legge e la sua giustizia*, n. 21, 267; P. HOGG, *Canada: From Privy Council to Supreme Court*, in J. GOLDSWORTHY (ed.), *Interpreting Constitutions. A Comparative Study*, Oxford, Oxford University Press, 2006, 55, 77 (after the entry into force of the Canadian Charter of Rights and Freedoms, "the concept of the Constitution as a statute is well and truly over").

[32] This is sometimes referred to as the "constitutionalization" of the (entire) legal system. As far as I know this term, now widely used, has been first introduced in this sense by G. TARELLO, *L'interpretazione della legge*, n. 1, 337. Subsequently, see A. GAMBARO, R. PARDOLESI, *L'influenza dei valori costituzionali sul diritto civile*, in A. PIZZORUSSO, V. VARANO (eds.), *L'influenza dei valori costituzionali sui sistemi giuridici contemporanei*, Milan, Giuffrè, 1985, I, 5, 12; L. FAVOREAU, *Le droit constitutionnel, droit de la Constitution et constitution du droit*, in 1 *Revue française de droit constitutionnel* 71 (1990); L. FAVOREAU, *La constitutionnalisation du droit*, in J.-B. AUBY (eds.), *L'unité du droit. Mélanges en hommage à Roland Drago*, Paris, Economica, 1996, 25; L. FAVOREAU, *La constitutionnalisation de l'ordre juridique: considerations générales*, in *Revue belge de droit constitutionnel* 233

vant for any kind of legal, political, and social dispute – it is a "total" constitution.[33]

Secondly, under a foundational approach the responsibility to implement constitutional principles and values falls on every legal and political actor. Constitutional principles will be implemented – through specification and balancing – not only by legislatures but also by courts, no matter how much judicial discretion is involved in such operations.

Thirdly, under a foundational approach constitutional interpretation is perceived as different in character from ordinary, statutory interpretation. As a consequence, it resorts to interpretive methodologies that are specifically tailored to the constitution.[34] For instance, the peculiar normative content of the constitution – principles, values – is not amenable to a merely literal interpretation (hence the rejection of textualism), and requires to be frequently adjusted to the ever-changing factual and social circumstances (hence the rejection of originalism). Principles and values ask for a "generous," purposive interpretation (hence the rejection of strict constructionism). Moreover, given that the normative content of the foundational constitution is constituted by moral and political principles and values (such as liberty, equality, dignity…), the interpretation and application of the constitution will inevitably require some kind of "moral reading". Constitutional interpretation, that is, will necessarily be contaminated by moral arguments.[35]

(1998); R. GUASTINI, *La "costituzionalizzazione" dell'ordinamento italiano*, in 11 *Ragion pratica* 185 (1998); A. STONE SWEET, *Governing with Judges*, n. 20, 114-125 (analysing this phenomenon in Italy, France, Germany, and Spain).

[33] R. BIN, *Cosa è la Costituzione?*, in XXVII *Quaderni costituzionali* 11 (2007). See also M. KUMM, *Who Is Afraid of the Total Constitution? Constitutional Rights as Principles and the Constitutionalization of Private Law*, in 7 *German L.J.* 341 (2006); S. GARDBAUM, *The Place of Constitutional Law in the Legal System*, n. 10; M. COHEN-ELIYA, I. PORAT, *Proportionality and Constitutional Culture*, n. 27, 60 ("*in Germany, almost any legitimate individual or collective interest is grounded on a constitutional value and accorded constitutional status*").

[34] The idea that constitutional interpretation is a peculiar kind of interpretation, which is not reducible to the ordinary techniques of statutory interpretation, is probably the majoritarian view in current Italian constitutional scholarship; see C. PINELLI, *Il dibattito sull'interpretazione costituzionale tra teoria e giurisprudenza*, n. 19, 1666. In the international debate, see for instance A. BARAK, *Hermeneutics and Constitutional Interpretation*, in 14 *Cardozo L.R.* 767 (1993), 772; W. WALUCHOW, *Constitutional Interpretation*, in A. MARMOR (ed.), *The Routledge Companion to Philosophy of Law*, Abingdon, Routledge, 2012, 418-419.

[35] B. CELANO, *I diritti nello Stato costituzionale*, Bologna, Il Mulino, 2013; G. PINO, *Positivism, Legal Validity, and the Separation of Law and Morals*, in 27 *Ratio Juris* 190 (2014). The phrase "moral reading" has been famously coined by R. DWORKIN, *Freedom's Law. The Moral Reading of the American Constitution*, Cambridge, Harvard University Press, 1996.

The upshot of all this is quite straightforward: the foundational model acknowledges a wide range of interpretive discretion for the judiciary. Both constitutional and statutory interpretation become "activist" and "dynamic" enterprises, as opposed to the "restrained" and "static" approaches required by a defensive, rule-based model of the constitution.[36] Courts will routinely use constitutional principles and values, either by directly applying them to a case, or by using them "indirectly", as aid in determining the meaning of a statute. The Constitutional Court, in turn, will tend to perform judicial review mainly on an interpretive level, as it were. The Constitutional Court, that is, rather than quash a constitutionally suspect statute, will mostly strive to interpret it in a "constitutionally compatible way".[37]

Put differently, a "foundational" conception of the constitution recasts the role of both the Constitutional Court and ordinary courts in some important ways:

1) The Constitutional Court will not just be a "negative" legislator, but also a "positive" one: the Court will claim the power not only to quash statutes, but also to manipulate them in order to make them coherent with the constitution.[38]

2) The Constitutional Court will not only be engaged in a "validity check" on statutes, but will also play the role of an "interpretive agency".[39]

3) Due to the important and activist role played by ordinary courts in taking care of potentially unconstitutional legislation, the system of judicial review will tend to become a "mixed" one – both centralized and partially decentralized.[40]

---

[36] R. GUASTINI, *Teoria e ideologia dell'interpretazione costituzionale*, n. 17 (contrasting "activist" vs "restrained", and "dynamic" vs "static" approaches to constitutional interpretation). In a similar vein, see also P. CHIASSONI, *Tecnica dell'interpretazione giuridica*, n. 1, 159-161 (contrasting "traditionalist" and "modernist" approaches to constitutional interpretation).

[37] G. ZAGREBELSKY, *La legge e la sua giustizia*, n. 21, 261-262 (judicial review as performed by the Italian Constitutional Court is more concerned with issuing "constitutionally compatible" statutory interpretations rather than judgements on the constitutional validity of statutes).

[38] On this kind of judgments, see V. BARSOTTI, P.G. CAROZZA, M. CARTABIA, A. SIMONCINI, *Italian Constitutional Justice in Global Context*, n. 4, 86-88. See also D. ROUSSEAU, *The Constitutional Judge: Master or Slave of the Constitution?*, in 14 *Cardozo L.R.* 775 (1992), 778, on "constructive interpretations" rendered by the French Constitutional Council, whose role tends to become akin to a "colegislator" (783).

[39] For similar trends in other European countries, see A. STONE SWEET, *Governing with Judges*, n. 20, 71-73.

[40] See V. ONIDA, *L'attuazione della Costituzione tra magistratura e Corte costituzionale*, n. 26, 514; S. CASSESE, *La giustizia costituzionale in Italia: lo stato presente*, in *Rivista trimestrale di diritto pubblico* 603 (2012), 606. For some general remarks on this trend, visible

So far, I have pointed to some features that can be found in all versions of a foundational conception of the constitution. To be sure, within the foundational conception it is possible to find important variations, which depend on whether the normative core of the constitution is framed in terms of principles or of values. To these variations I now turn.

10.3.2.1. The principle-based model

As already noted, principles are norms that are characterized by a substantial degree of indeterminacy and importance. Constitutional principles, thus, do not have a precise scope of application. They display their normative force by generating more determinate rules or other – less determinate – principles. Now, if the normative content of the foundational constitution is framed in terms of principles, the general picture drawn in the preceding section may be enriched in the following way.

First, a principle-based constitution is pervasive – any kind of legal, social and even political issue may be "subsumed" under some constitutional principle. And, in this sense, the constitution is indeed a "total" constitution. But this does not imply that the constitution also provides *complete and precise answers*;[41] in fact, it is in the very nature of legal principles that they do not directly provide precise answers, exactly in virtue of their indeterminacy and genericity. A principle points in a direction: it "governs" – i.e., it is relevant for – a given subject-matter, without "regulating" it in a precisely detailed way. A principle-based constitution, thus, is not a blueprint but a compass – it allows for many "possible constitutional worlds".[42]

Secondly, in a principle-based constitution there is no fixed intra-constitutional hierarchy.[43] The several constitutional principles are generally

---

also in other European countries, see V. FERRERES COMELLA, *The European Model of Constitutional Review of Legislation: Toward Decentralization?*, in 2 *I-CON* 461 (2004).

[41] See D. GRIMM, *The Function of Constitutions and Guidelines for Constitutional Reform* (1972), in D. GRIMM, *Constitutionalism*, Oxford, Oxford University Press, 2016, 133; V. FERRERES COMMELLA, *The Consequences of Centralizing Constitutional Review in a Special Court: Some Thoughts on Judicial Activism*, in 82 *Texas L.R.* 1705 (2004), 1736. For a contrary opinion, see R. GUASTINI, *Applying Constitutional Principles*, in *Analisi e diritto* 241 (2016), 243 ("*since principles have no definite boundaries of application, the more constitutional provisions are treated as principles the more the constitution looks as "gapless" or "complete", in the sense that the constitution looks able to regulate any possible subject-matter whatsoever*").

[42] J.J. MORESO, *Legal Indeterminacy and Constitutional Interpretation*, Dordrecht, Springer, 1998, ch 4.

[43] G. ZAGREBELSKY, *Il diritto mite*, n. 19, 11, and G. ZAGREBELSKY, *La legge e la sua giustizia*, n. 21, 284; R. BIN, *Diritti e argomenti*, Milan, Giuffrè, 1992, 32-35; G. PINO, *Diritti e interpretazione*, Bologna, Il Mulino, 2010, ch 6.

on a par. To be sure, it is possible that some constitutional principle *presumptively* weighs more than some other principle. But even in these cases, principles do not escape the balancing game – indeed, a presumptively weightier principle may in some cases be less important than another competing principle. Consequently, a principle-based constitution makes room for the possibility – indeed, the inevitability – of intra-constitutional conflicts.[44] A related point is this: as a matter of course, it is consistent with the foundational model that constitutional principles are balanced and/or specified by both the legislature and the courts. But there's a wrinkle. When balancing/specification is carried out by the legislature, the result is a new piece of legislation. By contrast, when balancing/specification is carried out by a court – even by an ordinary court – the result is a new rule or principle that has constitutional "relevance", because it is supposed to derive directly from the constitution. The paradox, then, is that the implementation of the constitution performed by the legislature produces *legislation*, whereas the implementation of the constitution performed by courts produces *more constitutional norms*, albeit "unwritten" ones.[45]

Thirdly, as we have seen a principle-based constitution makes for a high degree of judicial discretion (supra, § 10.2.2). Supporters of this conception tend to countenance this with the development of rational – or at least controllable – ways to interpret and apply constitutional principles.[46] To that end, it is usually suggested that judicial balancing of conflicting principles should be consistent in time, i.e. that the Constitutional Court should respect its own precedents;[47] that "definitional" or "categorical" balancing should be preferred to "ad hoc" balancing; or that balancing should be performed not in a whimsical fashion, but in a procedural way with multi-

---

[44] G. ZAGREBELSKY, *Il diritto mite*, n. 19, 11, 16, 170-173; R. BIN, *Cosa è la Costituzione?*, n. 33; G. PINO, *Diritti e interpretazione*, n. 43, ch. 6. More generally on this point see R. DWORKIN, *Taking Rights Seriously*, n. 5; R. ALEXY, *A Theory of Constitutional Rights*, n. 13; L. TRIBE, M. DORF, *On Reading the Constitution*, Cambridge, Harvard University Press, 1991, 24-25.

[45] See S. BARTOLE, *Costituzione (Dottrine generali e diritto costituzionale)*, n. 17, 320; R. GUASTINI, *Applying Constitutional Principles*, n. 43, 248 ("*the judicial derivation of rules from constitutional principles develops and enlarges constitutional law*"); A. MARMOR, *Interpretation and Legal Theory*, Oxford, Hart Publishing, 2005, 142 ("*the main way in which constitutions change is by judicial interpretation*").

[46] L. PALADIN, *Le fonti del diritto italiano*, n. 2, 146-150; S. BARTOLE, *L'elaborazione del parametro e del protocollo delle argomentazioni*, in *Corte costituzionale e principio di eguaglianza*, Padua, Cedam, 2001, 35; R. BIN, *Diritti e argomenti*, n. 43, 5, 140.

[47] L. PALADIN, *Le fonti del diritto italiano*, n. 2, 146-150; G. ZAGREBELSKY, *Ronald Dworkin's Principle Based Constitutionalism: An Italian Point of View*, n. 13, 647-649, and G. ZAGREBELSKY, *La legge e la sua giustizia*, n. 21, 289-295.

ple steps, tests, or phases – thus transforming balancing into the ostensibly more structured "proportionality" analysis.[48]

Lastly, under a principle-oriented model constitutional interpretation is not different *in kind* vis-à-vis statutory interpretation. Rather the difference between constitutional and statutory interpretation is regarded as a difference *in degree*. This means that the same interpretive techniques are in place in both constitutional and statutory interpretation; however, in the case of constitutional interpretation, some such techniques (most notably, literal interpretation) are less used, while others are used more frequently, more visibly, and with a more intense exercise of value-judgements.[49] This, it should be noted, does not necessarily mean that the interpretive canons of statutory interpretation should also apply to constitutional interpretation (as the "defensive" conception, or the model of rules, would have it); rather, and more interestingly, under a principle-based model a sort of circulation of interpretive techniques takes place between constitutional and statutory interpretation. The quite "generous" interpretive techniques that are usually in place in constitutional interpretation – balancing, holistic interpretation, use of moral arguments, purposive interpretation, evolutive interpretation – will frequently be used also in statutory interpretation.

10.3.2.2. The values-based model

A different variation of the foundational conception of the constitution is value-based – it claims that the most important part of the constitution is represented by the host of moral and political *values* that it incorporates.

A value-based model of the constitution inevitably loosens the constraining role of the text. In fact, rare exceptions notwithstanding, values are not explicitly written down in the constitution – they can only be read

[48] This attitude is epitomized by Robert Alexy's "arithmetic" theory of balancing: R. ALEXY, *A Theory of Constitutional Rights*, n. 13 (see esp. the "Postscript"), and R. ALEXY *Constitutional Rights, Balancing and Rationality*, in 16 *Ratio Juris* 131 (2003). See also J.J. MORESO, *Ways of Solving Conflicts of Constitutional Rights: Proportionalism and Specificationism*, in 25 *Ratio Juris* 31 (2012).

[49] G. ZAGREBELSKY, *Appunti in tema di interpretazione e di interpreti della Costituzione*, in *Giurisprudenza costituzionale* 904 (1970); E. DICIOTTI, *Come interpretare la Costituzione?*, in 4 *Ragion pratica* 203 (1995); G.U. RESCIGNO, *Interpretazione costituzionale e positivismo giuridico*, n. 19; G. PINO, *Diritti e interpretazione*, n. 43, 116-117. See also O. PFERSMANN, *Le sophisme onomastique: changer au lieu de connaître. A propos de l'interprétation de la constitution*, in F. MELIN-SOUCRAMANIEN (ed.), *L'interprétation constitutionnelle*, Paris, Dalloz, 2005. This, in turn, squares well with the fact that the difference between rules and principles is itself a difference in degree and not in kind: see G. PINO, *Teoria analitica del diritto I. La norma giuridica*, n. 15, ch 4.

between the lines of the constitutional text. So, according to a value-oriented approach, the text of the constitution matters only in so far as it reveals the relevant underlying values. Constitutional interpretation unearths the underlying axiological texture under the body of explicitly stated constitutional norms, with the aid of philosophical speculation, social observation, and intuition.[50]

Moreover, supporters of this view tend to assume a cognitivistic and irenic approach to constitutional values. Constitutional values, that is, are supposed to enjoy some kind of objectivity (be it a moral objectivity, or a "social" objectivity, or both), and they coexist in perfect harmony.[51] And this produces some interesting consequences for constitutional interpretation.

First, under a value-based approach, conflicts among constitutional values are merely superficial appearances – on a deeper level, constitutional values constitute a harmonic whole. Thus, constitutional balancing is represented as an equilibrium-seeking enterprise – as a matter of discovering an objective equilibrium among the relevant values, rather than as a matter of choice and mutual sacrifice between the values involved. Balancing, and constitutional interpretation generally, are supposed to bring to light a sort of immanent harmonic ordering of constitutional values.[52] The magic word, here, is "reasonableness". Reasonableness becomes the guiding light of constitutional interpretation, enabling the interpreter to find the exact equilibrium between (apparently) conflicting constitutional values.

Second, in addition to projecting a cognitivist allure on balancing and constitutional interpretation generally, a value-oriented approach paves the way for a hierarchical ordering of constitutional values, whereby the value of human dignity ranks first, then life, health and liberty, then economic values, and so on.[53] Several constitutional values can coexist in a harmoni-

---

[50] See A. BALDASSARRE, *L'interpretazione della costituzione*, n. 21, 227.

[51] A. BALDASSARRE, *Interpretazione e argomentazione nel diritto costituzionale*, in 2 *Costituzionalismo.it* 6-7 (2007); R. NANIA, P. SAITTA, *Interpretazione costituzionale*, in S. CASSESE (ed.), *Dizionario di diritto pubblico*, vol. IV, Milan, Giuffré, 2006, 3215. This is particularly apparent in the value-talk of German constitutional jurisprudence: see for instance R. HERZOG, *The Hierarchy of Constitutional Norms and Its Function in the Protection of Basic Rights*, n. 23, 9 (and generally the literature referred to at n. 23 above).

[52] See P. HÄBERLE, *Die Wesensgehaltgarantie des Art. 19 Abs. 2 Grundgesetz*, München, C.F. BECK, 1962; D. KOMMERS, *German Constitutionalism: A Prolegomenon*, n. 23, 851.

[53] D. KOMMERS, *German Constitutionalism: A Prolegomenon*, n. 23, 860; E.-W. BÖCKENFÖRDE, *Critique of the Value-based Grounding of Law* (1990), in E.-W. BÖCKENFÖRDE, *Constitutional and Political Theory*, Oxford, Oxford University Press, 2017, 224.

ous way because they are not all on the same axiological level: according to this model, some constitutional values rank as "supreme" values and enjoy axiological priority over the other, "ordinary" constitutional values – the former entering the balancing game with a presumptively heavier weigh than the latter, and are immune from constitutional amendment.[54]

Third, the weight of a value cannot be appreciated in isolation; rather, it depends on the relation between that value and all the other constitutionally relevant values, rights etc. Constitutional interpretation, then, becomes a holistic enterprise. On the other hand, since values are extremely abstract entities, they will react in different ways when faced with different factual circumstances; as a consequence, the interpretation and application of constitutional values becomes a case-by-case judgement.[55]

In sum, under a value-based model, constitutional interpretation is an intuitive enterprise, sensitive to social mores, and case-oriented. Its fundamental methodological principle is "reasonableness". Constitutional interpretation is only minimally constrained by the text of the constitution (the wording of the constitution may be easily trumped by the appeal to some fundamental value, as long as it is "reasonable" to do so), and it is fully entitled to "discover" new unwritten constitutional rights, insofar as they derive from the underlying axiological structure of the constitution.[56] Moreover, constitutional interpretation is presented as a "cognitive" enterprise, inasmuch as it is meant to bring to light morally or socially immanent values. In this scenario, of course, the constitution requires forms and styles of interpretation that are completely different from the ordinary techniques of statutory interpretation: the difference between constitutional interpretation and statutory interpretation is really a difference in kind, and not just in degree.[57]

---

[54] See M. CARTABIA, *Principi inviolabili e integrazione europea*, n. 21. This idea is now widely shared in Italian constitutional scholarship, and has been adopted also by the ItCC in a series of important decisions: see V. BARSOTTI, P.G. CAROZZA, M. CARTABIA, A. SIMONCINI, *Italian Constitutional Justice in Global Context*, n. 4, 62, 98-99. On the idea of an intra-constitutional hierarchy of values (or principles) see D. KOMMERS, *German Constitutionalism: A Prolegomenon*, n. 23, 852, 860; Y. ROZNAI, *Unconstitutional Constitutional Amendments*, Oxford, Oxford University Press, 2017, esp. ch 2.

[55] A. BALDASSARRE, *L'interpretazione della costituzione*, n. 21, 225.

[56] R. NANIA, P. SAITTA, *Interpretazione costituzionale*, n. 51, 3217.

[57] A. BALDASSARRE, *Interpretazione e argomentazione nel diritto costituzionale*, n. 51; F. MODUGNO, *Interpretazione per valori e interpretazione costituzionale*, in G. AZZARITI (ed.), *Interpretazione costituzionale*, Turin, Giappichelli, 2007, 56.

10.4. Taking stock

The Italian Constitution fully belongs to the so called "postwar paradigm," or "rights constitutionalism".[58] Indeed, it has been a forerunner of this paradigm, at the very least for chronological reasons.

Constitutions that fit this paradigm all have some broad features in common: they are written and fully legal in character, they include a long and detailed Bill of Rights, they are protected by a system of judicial review, and they are difficult to amend. Moreover, these constitutions are supposed to last, they embody a broad project of social transformation in the aftermath of some traumatic event (a war, a civil war, a dictatorship, a revolution, etc), and they are inspired by the overarching value of social and political pluralism.[59]

These features of contemporary constitutions rule out the descriptive plausibility of both political constitutionalism and of a mere "defensive" conception of the constitution. In fact, contemporary constitutions are undisputably legal in character (which rules out political constitutionalism), and have a clear foundational function. Moreover, it is quite implausible that the normative content of a "postwar paradigm" constitution be framed essentially in terms of rules: the pluralistic character, the aspiration to last long, and the transformative spirit of this kind of constitutions require that constitutional provisions be drafted in generic, indeterminate, flexible terms. Of course, a political-constitutionalist or a "defensive" conception of the constitution may still be defended as projects of legal and political reforms that move away from the existing post-war model. I will not argue here on this. I will just note, without even trying to argue in favour of this position, that under the prevailing conditions of many contemporary societies, the foundational model seems, on balance, more likely to sustain a just society than its alternatives. The favourable attitude expressed in the text does not ignore, of course, that the foundational model may lead to exaggerations and aberrations in the exercise of judicial discretion, with costs in terms of legal certainty and democratic legitimacy. Nothing can prevent even a model that is fairly

---

[58] For these expressions, see L. WEINRIB, *The Postwar Paradigm and American Exceptionalism*, n. 27; L. PRIETO SANCHÍS, *El constitucionalismo de los derechos*, in *Revista Española de Derecho Constitucional* 47 (2004); G. ANDERSON, *Constitutional Rights after Globalization*, Oxford, Hart Publishing, 2005, ch 1; G. PINO, *Il costituzionalismo dei diritti*, Bologna, Il Mulino, 2017. See also A. SOMEK, *The Cosmopolitan Constitution*, Oxford, Oxford University Press, 2014 (on "constitutionalism 2.0").

[59] On the essential pluralistic character of contemporary, "postwar" constitutions, see G. ZAGREBELSKY, *Il diritto mite*, n. 19; E. DICIOTTI, *Come interpretare la Costituzione?*, n. 49; R. BIN, *Cosa è la Costituzione?*, n. 33.

good in its abstract formulation to go astray in its actual applications. Moreover, the comparative merits and demerits of each model cannot be assessed in purely abstract terms – they are contingent on the general institutional context. [60]

Be that as it may, and assuming that a foundational model appears to be both descriptively accurate and normatively desirable, one may still ask if such a model is to be preferred in the principle-based variant or rather in the values-based one. In my opinion, there are sound reasons for preferring a principle-based approach to the Constitution and to constitutional interpretation. These reasons essentially boil down to the following:

- A principle-based approach does not result in an implausibly "cognitivistic" picture of constitutional interpretation (one in which the normative content of the constitution is just discovered out of an immanent order of values). Quite to the contrary, it acknowledges the ineliminable margin of choice that is required by constitutional interpretation; and this choice, in turn, brings with it the need for accountability – first of all under the guise of a duty to give a complete and persuasive justification for the interpretive decision.
- A principle-based approach does not tie the meaning of constitutional rights to social values, which would make fundamental rights prey to majoritarian attitudes (thus betraying its pluralistic aspirations). [61]
- A principle- based approach makes for an evolving interpretation of the constitution, ensuring that the constitution does not become rapidly outdated.
- A principle-based approach acknowledges the space of democratic decisions, since it does not assume that the constitution contains the precise regulation of any social and legal matter. Rather, this model actually requires that in many instances the responsibility of balancing and specifying the relevant constitutional principles fall exactly on the legislature. [62] Even more importantly, in such a model no single authority – not the democratically elected legislature, not ordinary judges, not even the Constitutional Court – has the last word on the interpretation/implementa-

---

[60] See C. SUNSTEIN, A. VERMEULE, *Interpretation and Institutions*, in 101 *Mich. L.R.* 885 (2003); G. ITZCOVICH, *On the Legal Enforcement of Values. The Importance of the Institutional Context*, in A. JAKAB, D. KOCHENOV (eds.), *The Enforcement of EU Law and Values*, Oxford, Oxford University Press, 2017.

[61] Against the "social consensus" argument in constitutional interpretation, see A. MARMOR, *Interpretation and Legal Theory*, n. 45, 151 ff; G. PINO, *Diritti e interpretazione*, n. 43, 135-139.

[62] R. ALEXY, *A Theory of Constitutional Rights*, n. 13.

tion of the constitution. The normative content of the constitution, in this model, is supposed to be shaped in the ongoing interaction (be it in the guise of dialogue or of conflict) among several institutional actors.[63]

If these admittedly sketchy arguments are sound, then the theory of constitutional norms as principles seems better suited to the idea of a contemporary, pluralistic constitution, such as the Italian one.

[63] On this feature of contemporary constitutionalism, see G. ZAGREBELSKY, *Il diritto mite*, n. 19, 213; B. CELANO, *I diritti nello Stato costituzionale*, n. 35, 161-162; M. FIORAVANTI, *Legge e costituzione: il problema storico della garanzia dei diritti*, in 43 *Quaderni fiorentini per la storia del pensiero giuridico* 1077 (2014), 1092-1093; M. CARTABIA, *Diritto amministrativo e diritti fondamentali*, in L. TORCHIA (ed.), *Attraversare i confini del diritto*, Bologna, Il Mulino, 2016, 187; G. PINO, *Il costituzionalismo dei diritti*, n. 58, 46-49.

Chapter XI

THE RELATIONSHIP BETWEEN FORMS AND METHODS IN CONSTITUTIONAL INTERPRETATION: COMPARATIVE REFLECTIONS

Jeffrey A. Pojanowski

Sometimes a stranger can offer perspective on matters that appear invisible to others more familiar with the terrain – or, at least that is my hope, for I am a stranger here in two respects. First, I study the legal tradition of the United States. Second, I am not trained as a comparative lawyer, and am thus largely innocent of reflection or study on comparative constitutional law's purposes and methods.

Nevertheless, as a student of interpretive theory more generally, I hope I can contribute to a discussion on the Italian Constitutional Court's interpretive methodology. Luckily, Professor Giorgio Pino is an interlocutor whose work is clear, insightful, and a catalyst for deeper reflection on constitutional interpretation. Professor Pino's mastery of Anglophone jurisprudence and constitutional theory also builds a bridge between Italian legal thought and more parochial scholars like me. My contribution would not be possible without the entrée Professor Pino provides.

Professor Pino observes that Italian constitutional jurisprudence favors interpretation based on legal principles and objective values, and he contends that principle-based interpretation is more justified. As an observer of constitutional law in the United States, I would like to focus on one feature that stands out about Professor Pino's survey and argument, namely how formalist or originalist interpretation plays a more substantial role in constitutional jurisprudence in the United States.[1]

---

[1] By way of disclosure, I have elsewhere offered normative defenses of originalist constitutional interpretation. See, e.g., J.A. POJANOWSKI, K.C. WALSH, *Enduring Originalism*, in 105 *Geo. L.J.* 97 (2016).

I do not mean to overstate the difference. Although originalist constitutional interpretation was prominent in the United States until the beginning of the 20th Century, it retreated with the growth of the administrative state and the civil rights revolution. As a result, much of the Supreme Court's jurisprudence is emphatically non-originalist on its face and many of its doctrines involve balancing tests similar to proportionality review. Nevertheless, originalism has reemerged in recent decades as a respectable and influential, if not dominant, interpretive method.

That originalism is "on the wall" in the United States jurisprudence rather than "off the wall" is a substantial difference from Italian law and its notion of constitutional "relationality" emerging from the works of editors and authors in this volume. I will use this chapter for reflection on this distinction, some of its jurisprudential presuppositions, and broader implications.

11.1. Constitutional norms and interpretive choice

Professor Pino identifies three kinds of norms at play in constitutional law: determinate legal rules, legal principles, and values that transcend law. He contends, however, that before we can identify which kinds of norms reside in any particular constitution, we must first settle on an interpretive method for identifying them. This method, Pino contends, will turn on the interpreter's conception of what a constitution is and what it is for.[2]

This threshold choice of lens will affect what the constitutional investigator sees: a rule-based interpreter will be more likely to find rules; an aficionado of legal principles will engage in careful specification and balancing; and the value-focused interpreter will read the constitution as an instantiation of a transcendent, objective, and determinate ordering of ideal political morality. This Section will investigate these affinities and explain why Professor Pino is correct to identify the practical pull that interpretive method has on the content of constitutional norms.

Before evaluating the choices between rules, principles, and values in constitutional law, we should first consider this question of interpretive choice and its effect on constitutional norms. In an important sense, Professor Pino is correct that one's conception of what constitutions are for precedes and influences the search for a particular constitution's norms. Until a person picks it up, a written constitution is simply a collection of marks on a page, and even after one begins to read the document, one's purposes in reading it can affect the content. One could read a constitution

[2] Cf. L. ALEXANDER, *What Are Constitutions, and What Should (and Can) They Do?*, in 28 *Soc. Phil. & Pol'y* 1 (2011).

as a historical primary source or even, if one is so inclined, poetry or a coded prophecy about the future.[3] Reading it as a document that constitutes a state and speaks to lawyers, officials, and citizens about that order is a distinct enterprise that suggests certain modes of reading (to wit, the search for rules or principles or values) and excludes others (the search for insight about class structure and political alliances in 1948, irony, hidden numerological codes).

Thus, certain approaches to reading a constitution for legal purposes are plausible, others are plainly unacceptable, and interesting arguments go the merits of competing, plausible options. More complicated is the connection between interpretive choice and the particular forms of constitutional orders. Professor Pino correctly notes an affinity between originalist, formalist approaches to interpretation and "defensive" conceptions of constitutions. This connection, as Professor Pino recognizes, is more a matter of tendency than necessity. We can imagine a charter whose original legal content, understood via formal methods, contained "rules" establishing a foundational constitution in which judges were to apply legal principles or transcendent values as they best understand them (ordinary legislation notwithstanding). Originalists who seek to be faithful to the framers' choices would have little choice but to exercise such judgment to the best of their abilities.[4]

Thus, in the United States, Professor Jack Balkin's theory of "framework originalism" holds that many of the outputs of so-called "living constitutionalism" are faithful to a document whose original public meaning gives subsequent interpreters wide leeway to expound constitutional rights.[5] Similarly, Ronald Dworkin has argued that the framers' choice to include broad, moral language in the constitution indicates that judges are to undertake the principle-laden task of elaborating law as integrity.[6] Originalist research may or may not vindicate these arguments as to the United States constitution, but that is a contingent fact about the content of that particular legal instrument. An originalist reading of, say, the South

---

[3] For an example of esoteric readings in the non-legal, yet Italian, context, consider U. ECO, *Il Pendolo di Foucault*, Milan, Bompiani, (1988).

[4] See S.E. SACHS, *Originalism as a Theory of Legal Change*, in 38 *Harv. J. L. & Pub. Pol'y* 817 (2015), 821 ("The Constitution, and the Founders' legal system as a whole, was only as crisp and determinate as it actually was…[W]hy should we try to be more originalist than the Founders, or more Catholic than the Pope?").

[5] J.M. BALKIN, *Living Originalism*, Cambridge, Harvard University Press, 2014; see also W. BAUDE, *Is Originalism Our Law?*, in 115 *Colum. L. Rev.* 2349 (2015), 2376–86 (contending that many apparently non-originalist decisions are consistent with his theory of "inclusive originalism").

[6] See J. GOLDSWORTHY, *Dworkin as Originalist*, in 17 *Const. Comment.* 49 (2000).

African constitution, may lead to a more "foundational" understanding of the document than even a principled reading of its U.S. counterpart.

One can make similar moves with varying degrees of ease regarding principles and values. Imagine I believe, as a matter of political theory, that a defensive or political constitutional order is superior to a foundational legal order. Implicit in that position is a complex of beliefs about the nature of political rights and obligations, the proper role of courts and the political branches, democratic legitimacy, the division between the public and the private sphere, and, more generally, the proper extent of law's empire. In short, I would fear the total constitution,[7] and I would believe that discomfort is rooted in truths about political theory and moral reality.

Now imagine I am then given the Italian constitution to interpret. If I think that constitutional interpretation turns on objective values, and that the proper reading of a constitution integrates the document with the best understanding of those transcendent values, it is not hard for me to get to, say, a defensive legal constitution. For example: the true principles of republicanism and popular sovereignty in Article I are the interpretive keys to the document; negative liberties are enforceable and can override contrary legislation; and positive rights are programmatic, non-justiciable exhortations to the political branches. Principle-based interpretation may be a little trickier, but in the steady hands of a certain kind of Dworkinian, a jurisprudence weighing the competing principles of liberty, solidarity, and popular sovereignty could go a long way toward a defensive or even political constitution. And this would be so even if, as a historical matter, the framers of the Italian constitution understood their charter in terms of the post-war paradigm.

Now, the previous analysis has an air of unreality to it, and for good reason. As an historical matter, there has been an affinity between formal approaches and defensive constitutions, as well as between non-formal interpretation and foundational constitutional orders. It is, however, worth noting that as a theoretical matter, faithful application of a formal, rule-like approach gives constitution framers the most substantial power to choose a constitutional conception, whether it be political or legal, defensive or foundational. The originalist seeks to identify, if she can, the option the framers chose, whatever it is. Values-based interpretation, by contrast, is only loosely connected to the formal choice or text, leaving the true character of the constitutional regime subject to ongoing argument or discovery. Principle-based interpretation may constrain the pace of change away from

[7] M. KUMM, *Who is Afraid of the Total Constitution? Constitutional Rights as Principles in the Constitutionalization of Private Law*, in 7 *German L.J.* 341 (2006).

the original choice, but in a document of any complexity – which is most constitutions – internal antimonies and the necessity of individual moral judgment in resolving them will give the document an interpreter-inflected normative tilt. And the more judgments in favor of one of the competing principles over time, the more marginal its competitor(s) appear in the jurisprudential calculus.

Formal, rule-based interpretation gives framers the authority and flexibility to make enduring choices, both at the micro-level of particular constitutional provisions and at the meta-level of constitutional character (legal versus political, defensive versus foundational). This feature is a virtue to the extent one values the ability of constitutional framers and ratifiers to entrench durable political choices through legal norms. This is so even if the constitution leaves many substantive decisions unresolved while specifying which officials should exercise further choices down the road, as is the case with political constitutions (a choice in favor of political officials) or certain kinds of foundational constitutions (a choice in favor of constitutional courts).

Opinions will differ on the importance of constitutional framers being able to entrench constitutional norms, however. This helps explain why, notwithstanding the analysis above, interpretive choice plays an important role in determining the norms the interpreter finds in a constitution. For example, an interpreter who reads a constitution as a manifestation of objective, enduring value will be less inclined to care about the particular, contingent choices constitutional framers made – especially when those choices depart from ideal political theory. The original, historical constitution at best displays ultimate values through a glass darkly, and further jurisprudential revelation is needed to clarify and perfect the picture.

A practitioner of the principle-based model places more emphasis on the legal norms in the constitution, but, as Professor Pino notes, views such norms as a needle on a "compass", not a "blueprint" for governance. If one believes that framers' norms are gestures of general direction for a journey opening many constitutional worlds, one is unlikely to develop unwritten constitutional norms that identify concrete, historical instructions establishing a fixed hierarchy of principles or decisive rules. In fact, the relationship between the contemporary interpreter and the constitution's framers resembles the interaction between the court and the legislature in constitutional adjudication: both the framers and the legislature have input in the process, a kind of margin of appreciation, but lack conclusive power to determine the balance of principles at play.

It is also possible that the formalist, originalist approach to interpretation may increase how rule-like a constitution is as a practical matter. Even if the interpreter works in good faith to ensure she does not convert historically chosen standards into rules, in close cases a preference for rules may work as a thumb on the scale in favor of a rule. Similarly, the same preference for rule-like determinacy that inspires originalism may lead formalist interpreters, as a practical matter, to underenforce standards or treat them as political questions unamenable to judicial resolution. To be sure, departing from originalism in favor of rules over standards may be good normative formalism, but it is bad originalism – and American originalists have criticized Justice Scalia for demonstrating such a tendency.[8] Yet, with judges being imperfect human beings, it may be hard to for some to bracket their background reasons for originalism – determinacy, predictability, practical limits of adjudication – when originalist methods undermine those norms.

First, consider a jurist who embraces originalism for formalist rule-of-law reasons, but is confronted with a facially foundationalist constitution. In this respect, the dilemma of rule-formalism in ordinary law recapitulates itself at a meta-level. One standard defense of following rules is that even when a result does not square with the background reasons for the rule, following the norm reaps the benefits of coordination, notice, predictability, decision-making efficiency, and the expertise of the rulemaker.[9] Here, a rule-like approach to constitutional interpretation ("Find what the framers laid down, rather than have a roving constitutional convention by the courts!") discerns emphatically non-rule-like decision rules. The background reason for originalist interpretive method (normative formalism) clashes with its output (decision modes that lose the benefits of formalism).

On this ground, it is not surprising that those who are originalist because of the benefits of rule-based judicial decision-making may be inclined to read constitutional provisions in rule-like fashion or, alternatively, fill any gaps with fixed, rule-like precedents.[10] Nor might we blame them: there is something paradoxical about asking a person whose interpretive method turns on the benefits of rules to continually and perpetually apply standards for rule-like reasons.

A similar tension arises for those who embrace originalism for reasons

---

[8] See S. CALABRESI, G. LAWSON, *The Rule of Law as a Law of Law*, in 90 *Notre Dame L. Rev.* 483 (2014).

[9] See L. ALEXANDER, E. SHERWIN, *The Rule of Rules: Morality, Rules, and the Dilemmas of Law*, Durham, Duke University Press, 2001.

[10] This latter move may be consistent with originalism if the framers gave subsequent interpreters wide authority to implement the constitution to the best of their ability. The interpreter's best judgment would be that the polity benefits from rules. It is harder to square with originalism if the framers wanted the constitution to be implemented through continued, evolving application of legal principles or invocation of enduring values.

grounded in popular sovereignty or institutional competence. Constitutional adjudication in systems where judicial review is binding can close political discussion on particular issues and require courts to make complex, controversial normative decisions about human rights and the common good. For those who think the political branches should make such decisions for reasons of legitimacy[11] or institutional competence,[12] a polity's decision to delegate authority over such questions to the courts is at best unwise. Accordingly, such interpreters might give narrow readings to potential delegation of authority to judges in close cases or, less forgivably, sometimes even in not-so-close cases. Furthermore, when a constitutional provision contains a gap or is silent on questions of rights, such an originalist will prefer to defer to the political branches' resolution of such matters, rather than judicial elaboration of a total constitution.[13]

As the discussion above indicates, it is possible as a matter of theoretical structure for an interpretively formal originalist to recognize a living, foundational constitution. It is also possible for an interpreter who focuses on legal principles or constitutional value to read a constitutional document as a defensive and even political charter. As a scholar who values constitutional durability and stability, I view originalism's ability to respect framers' choices of constitution type – legal or political, defensive or foundational – as a mark in its favor. That preference, of course, is a normative one and other considerations compete with the legitimating and practical values of entrenched constitutional norms. There is the worry that the "dead hand" of the past will hold injustice in place or smother further progress. If so, the original constitution may be as much as a burden to overcome as an inheritance to transmit intact.

Curiously, however, when framed that way, such a concern about originalism seems to be a particularly American one. The U.S. constitution is old by contemporary standards and far more defensive and political in character than those operating in the postwar paradigm. From the perspective of many in contemporary social democracies, the dead hand of the American constitution has a far more ancient and restricting grip than their own charters. To be sure, an originalist reading of the Italian constitution might render many of the social rights nonjusticiable, though the Court's

---

[11] See, e.g., J. WALDRON, *The Core of the Case Against Judicial Review*, in 115 *Yale L.J.* 1346 (2006).

[12] See, e.g., P. YOWELL, *Constitutional Rights and Constitutional Design*, Oxford, Hart Publishing, 2018.

[13] See, e.g., K. WHITTINGTON, *Constitutional Construction: Divided Powers and Constitutional Meaning*, Cambridge, Harvard University Press, 2001.

"generally cautious approach" to such matters might minimize such a practical difference.[14] That aside, the Italian framing generation's fear of majoritarian tyranny and the document's ample language about human rights and dignity should lead any honest originalist away from any minimalist conclusions about the Constitutional Court's role. Compared to the United States constitution, the "dead hand" points to a far more active and dynamic role for the constitution and the court.

Hence, the puzzle is that originalism is a live option in a country where the dead-hand challenge is the most formidable, but is a rejected curiosity most everywhere else, including nations like Italy, with more recent and more easily amendable constitutions. Any explanation for this is likely to be complex and beyond my ability to provide, but that will not stop me from hazarding a few guesses. Part of it may have to do with the sense (fair or not) that officials' practice of "positivistic" legal interpretation abetted the atrocities of World War II.[15] Part of it may also be explained by the Anglo-American tendency to view constitutional law as a species of ordinary law that happens to be supreme,[16] whereas European expounders of constitutions seem more inclined to treat this domain of law as not just vertically supreme, but transcendent and meriting its own distinct methods – methods that may seep down to transform "ordinary law" as well.[17] The roots of this tendency may be as much institutional as theoretical, with the U.S. Supreme Court deciding questions of constitutional and ordinary law, rather than serving exclusively as a constitutional tribunal.

I also suspect a substantial part of the difference turns on the question of democratic theory. The more one views political legitimacy in terms of

---

[14] V. BARSOTTI, P.G. CAROZZA, M. CARTABIA, A. SIMONCINI, *Italian Constitutional Justice in Global Context*, Oxford, Oxford University Press, 2016, 114-150.

[15] The picture is of course more complex, with Third Reich jurists being encouraged to interpret in light of "healthy folk sentiment", not just the letter or original meaning of the law.

[16] See, e.g., M. WALTERS, *Public Law and Ordinary Legal Method: Revisiting Dicey's Approach to Droit Administratif*, in 66 *U. Toronto L.J.* 53 (2016). This tendency is obviously not unanimous, though the departures are instructive. Much, though not all, non-originalist U.S. constitutional theory in the past century regards the constitution as something emphatically different from ordinary law.

[17] See S. GARDBAUM, *The Place of Constitutional Law in the Legal System*, in M. ROSENFELD, A. SAJÓ (eds.), *The Oxford Handbook on Comparative Constitutional Law*, Oxford, Oxford University Press, 2012, 169. One sees this in Anglo-American legal systems as well, especially with respect to the "principle of legality", which requires clear statements from Parliaments before a court will recognize a legislative abrogation of basic rights, even those not explicitly entrenched in a constitution. See D. MEAGHER, *The Principle of Legality as Clear Statement Rule: Significance and Problems*, in 36 *Sydney L. Rev.* 413 (2014).

parliamentary supremacy or more direct forms of popular sovereignty, the more one will be suspicious of a total constitution administered primarily by courts. By contrast, the more we value a "culture of justification", in which popular voting and legislative deliberation is necessary but not sufficient, the more appealing one may find a system of constitutional law in which the political branches play a role in dialogue with a constitutional court. In the latter case, one can praise the system of proportionality review as a form of deliberative democracy, with the courts playing an aristocratic role in ensuring the political branches respect basic rights and overarching constitutional values. Here, the constitutional court plays a role similar to United States Senate (before its seats were opened to popular election) or the U.K. House of Lords (before it lost the power to nullify legislation).

This is not to say Anglo-American legal culture champions direct democracy or unadorned parliamentary supremacy. The United States has a written, counter-majoritarian constitution that divvies up power between the central government and the states and separates power in a way that makes federal legislation very hard to pass. Yet a significant strain of American legal thought strongly favors electoral political accountability. All three actors in the complicated dance of federal legislation are accountable by elections [18] and devolution of power to the states promotes more direct participation in governance. Even democracy-restricting constitutional amendments are subject to supermajoritarian ratification by Congress and the states. It is telling that a prominent, perennial headache in American constitutional theory has been the "countermajoritarian difficulty" posed by judicial review of legislation by judges with life tenure. [19]

No such neuralgia besets Italian constitutional law and politics. The Constitutional Court plays a prominent role in public affairs and, while individual cases briefly capture the public's attention, the appointment of justices does not, for example, play a substantial role in ordinary politics as in the United States. This suggests the "small-c" constitution – the Italian peoples' and officials' dispositions and political attitudes – embraces a model of democracy more deliberative and less direct than its counterpart in the United States.

That said, with the rise of populism in Italy and Europe more generally,

---

[18] The Senate by original design was supposed to be accountable to state legislatures, but in 1913 the 17th Amendment made Senators directly elected by the voters of their state.

[19] B. FRIEDMAN, *The Birth of An Academic Obsession: The History of The Countermajoritarian Difficulty, Part Five*, in 112 *Yale L.J.* 153 (2002); A. BICKEL, *The Least Dangerous Branch: The Supreme Court at the Bar of Politics*, New Haven, Yale University Press, 1986.

with persistent worries about the EU's "democratic deficit",[20] and with the increasing supervenience of ECJ and ECHR norms over Italian jurisprudence, one cannot help but wonder about the stability of that equilibrium. It is far from clear whether the Italian Constitutional Court will become engulfed in broader political disturbances. It is even less clear whether that should affect the Court's jurisprudence, let alone how it should; however, a reflection on Professor Pino's interpretive triptych and broader considerations of self-governance may nevertheless be useful.

11.2. Choosing among interpretive choices

As Professor Pino's contribution correctly recognizes, the threshold choice of interpretive method is normative. No book, let alone a chapter, can give the last word on such a choice. Professor Pino's elucidation of three models of constitutional interpretation, however, clarifies the choices facing a court. This section fleshes out the connections between interpretive method and higher values sketched above. By doing so, we can better grasp the normative stakes behind our choice and even appreciate some affinities that hide behind apparent methodological differences.

Although we usually understand rule- and value-based constitutional interpretation as polar opposites, they share a surprising structural resemblance. The rule model in its purest and perhaps caricatured form conceives of constitutional adjudication as the application of determinate legal norms – norms not of the judges' own choosing – to the case at hand. This may not often be a mechanical task, but it nevertheless aspires to be a search for authority, not an exercise in lawmaking or co-creation. To be clear, this model need not assume the original constitution is gapless. It simply, and more modestly, seeks to follow whatever authority it can find when it can find it.

Interpretation that regards the constitution as the instantiation of higher, ultimate values is emphatically less formal and historical as a legal matter but also has a parallel deductive structure. As Professor Pino's chapter suggests, for such an approach to be justified, it must presuppose (a) moral reality (b) that is determinate and accessible to the interpreter and (c) readily translated into adjudicative decisions. In this respect, value-based interpretation has a structure similar to rule-based interpretation; simply substitute something like natural law for the human positive law of the original constitution. One might even characterize value-based interpreta-

[20] Perhaps worries about the EU democratic deficit is Europe's version of the United States' concern about the countermajoritarian difficulty in public law.

tion as a search for authority of a higher kind. One substitutes the fixity of legal formalism for moral formalism.

Such an approach, of course, depends on strong claims about moral metaphysics and epistemology. This is one of the greatest challenges facing value-based interpretation – one that is compounded to the extent its practitioners do not grapple with those deeper commitments or even profess skepticism about them in other contexts. Furthermore, in its most robust form, it presumes controversially that non-judicial self-governance is excluded or marginal as an objective value. Rule-based interpretation, by contrast, avoids the baroque metaphysics of value-based interpretation. The challenges legal indeterminacy poses to formal interpretation pale in comparison to arguments about the competing demands presented by questions of human rights, the common good, and ideal political theory.[21]

This critique of value-based interpretation points to an affinity between rule- and principle-based approaches to interpretation: both seek to narrow the range of moral disagreement by rooting adjudication more closely to positive legal norms that exclude some set of reasons from consideration. To be sure, there are differences. Rules are usually conceived as providing on/off, exclusionary reasons, whereas principles have weight and merge with moral considerations. Nevertheless, legal principles also work to exclude moral considerations that do not pass a threshold level of fit with the positive law. In that respect, both rule- and principled-based constitutional interpretation allow previous, historical lawmaking acts to resolve cases even if the interpreter would choose a different outcome were she starting from scratch.

If we desire to exclude some domain of moral reasons from constitutional adjudication, the question remains whether rule – or principle-based decision-making is a superior approach. To say the debate and literature on this question are substantial is an understatement, so I will limit myself to a few observations.

A preference for rule-based, constrained approaches to interpretation need not entail moral skepticism. In fact, any plausible argument for such an approach will draw on arguments about political legitimacy, institutional

[21] A defender of value-based interpretation might seek to escape this critique by contending that values-based constitutional interpretation applies standards of "reasonableness" on a case-by-case basis, rather than engaging in formalist moral reasoning. Here, values-based interpretation looks less like Platonic moral deduction than the application of Aristotelian moral judgment. The escape leads to further questions. To the extent the case-by-case approach draws on related, prior cases, it is hard to distinguish it from the approach relying on legal principles. If not, it is fair to ask if courts are best suited to exercise this judgment, which is by often subject to reasonable debate given the uncertain character of the science.

competence, and the like. To be sure, formal, rule-based approaches in many cases preclude judges from weighing in on first-order questions of morality and justice. For example, a constitution that provides a clear rule on whether a legislative limitation on euthanasia is permitted may relieve a court from considering the justice of euthanasia. Nevertheless, the choice to treat such a discretion-limiting rule as binding, as opposed to suggestive of further, principle-based reasoning or as the manifestation of an objective moral value, reflects a second-order moral judgment about the proper, limited role of a constitutional court.

Normative argument on interpretive choice is therefore inevitable.[22] In this respect, we see connections between value-based approaches to interpretation and their principled and rule-based alternatives. The ultimate question is – given the nature of moral reality, the best reading of political theory, and questions of institutional competence – deciding the best way for a court to approach a constitution. The weakness of the value-based approach to interpretation, as Professor Pino suggests, is its unargued and controversial assumption that constitutions ought to be regarded as instructing interpreters to implement ideal morality directly in the context of adjudication.

Both principled and rule-based approaches recognize that rule-of-law values, which themselves draw on ultimate values, cut against a strong presumption that a constitution instantiates a system of ideal political morality. Both recognize that second-order considerations like respect for institutional history, coordination benefits, norms of equal treatment, and values of democratic self-determination preclude such a muscular judicial role in constitutional adjudication. Both constitutional framers and, to the extent a system values judicial precedent, constitutional interpreters should have the power to fix legal norms in ways that depart from subsequent interpreters' understanding of ideal theory. Even though those actors may make moral mistakes, there are good second-order moral reasons to give those actors the power to (at least sometimes) entrench those first-order errors. The disagreements between rule- and principle-based interpretation in any given legal system will turn on the comparative strength of first-order and second-order moral reasons in constitutional adjudication.

This judgment will, in part, turn on (a) how demanding our first-order theories of justice and morality are and (b) the moral character of a particular constitution as measured by ideal morality. The cost of rules is entrenching moral error. Their benefits are certainty, efficiency in decision-

---

[22] See, e.g., S. MACEDO, *The Inescapability of Natural Law*, in 5 *Benchmark* 117 (1993).

making, and any expertise conferred by the decisionmaker. Furthermore, when rules are chosen by the populace to constitute their republic, respecting those rules respects self-determination. Principles, by contrast, trade interpretive determinacy and efficiency while smoothing the rough edges of over- and under-inclusive rules and attributing to its framers the best moral reading available.

These tradeoffs are familiar, but I would like to underline their relationship to background moral and political theory. The more demanding the background theory – the more confidence we have in the determinacy of moral and political argument – the more likely we are to see errors in particular rules and therefore to find a principled approach more appealing. On the other hand, the more that we see first-order questions of constitutional structure, human rights, and the tradeoffs inherent in pursuing the common good as matters upon which people can disagree within a range of reason, the more appealing a rule-based approach to constitutional decision-making: it is possible the framers (or a legislature to whom the framers have given implementing authority) struck the wrong balance in crafting a rule, but to the extent we are uncertain, the rule of law and legitimacy costs of judicial supervision may outweigh the benefits of any fine-grained calibration the courts may offer.

The reverse is also true. The rule of law and self-governance, while important, are not unqualified human goods and different people may place different weight on them. If one thinks the moral goods of stability, predictability, and the like are comparatively weaker, or at least equally contestable as moral questions at issue in particular cases (e.g., the right to euthanasia, etc.), one would be more willing to engage in principle-based decision-making even when the answer on the first-order merits are uncertain.

A person who finds that many questions of human rights and justice fall within the range of reasonable disagreement, especially when rights conflict with rights, and who thinks that rule-of-law and self-governance values are worth defending so long as the constitutional system passes a threshold level of moral acceptability, will be more inclined toward rule-based interpretation. This is not moral skepticism – there is no moral obligation to uphold wicked constitutional orders – but rather a recognition that often such matters are questions of practical judgment not answered by neat deduction. Furthermore, there are reasons to question whether case-by-case adjudication by courts is the best way to resolve these practical questions. In this respect, we can find a defense of formalist originalism that combines Aristotle's understanding of phronesis, Aquinas's explication of *determinationes*, and more contemporary arguments about institutional competence and self-governance. In short, proportionality reasoning is not a science and it is not clear that jurists should exercise such final judgment.

Principle-based interpretation, embraced by Professor Pino and much constitutional theory outside the United States, suggests the opposite stance. It indicates a belief that first-order questions of justice are more determinate than the formalist concludes or, to the extent they present uncertain questions of practical judgment, those questions can and should receive ultimate resolution in the courts. Alternatively, or in conjunction, it suggests a comparative devaluation of any rule-of-law or self-determination benefits that formalism garners by treating constitutional (or delegated legislative) rules as excluding further judicial reconsideration.

It is in this respect that the value of *relationality* – highlighted by the authors of *Italian Constitutional Justice in Global Context* and many contributors to this volume – comes to the fore.[23] The relational orientation views the Italian Constitutional Court ("ItCC") as the organ responsible for (a) coordinating relations among the Italian courts, the Italian parliament, and other European legal institutions, and (b) interpreting the constitution in a manner that facilitates dialogue among the plural voices in Italian democracy. Implicit in support for the relational approach is the judgment that ongoing (ItCC-facilitated) deliberation between plural voices and institutions is the best way to pursue the common good through law. This contrasts with the judgment that it is better to seek authoritative, entrenched decisions by the political actors[24] or that apex courts should offer the final word on questions of value implicated in the constitutional order. Relationality presumes it is best to view the constitution as negotiable – neither fixed nor entirely up for grabs – and holds that the ItCC's role is to be a prime mediator, albeit one that also has its own views about the questions at issue.[25]

These normative presuppositions are plausible, yet contestable, as are the evaluations lurking behind arguments for competing political approaches to interpretation. Professor Pino's contribution identifies how those threshold value choices ground interpretive method and his defense of principled-based interpretation lays a foundation for a normative defense of the ItCC's relational jurisprudence.

---

[23] V. Barsotti, P.G. Carozza, M. Cartabia, A. Simoncini, *Italian Constitutional Justice in Global Context*, *op. cit.*, 235-39.

[24] "Political actors" here primarily refers to constitutional framers and legislators, though, depending on one's theory of adjudication, it can refer to judges given authority to lay down legal norms backed by stare decisis.

[25] Cf. G. Webber, *The Negotiable Constitution: On the Limitation of Rights*, Cambridge, Cambridge University Press, 2010.

11.3. Conclusion

Why are so few European constitutional law jurists and scholars originalists, and why do some of their counterparts in the United States entertain such ideas? Part of it may be a matter of intellectual history. Originalism was the lifeblood of the U.S. Supreme Court's approach to constitutional interpretation until the 20th Century and it is much easier to return to a lapsed tradition than to create a new one. Similarly, although the United States departs from the English tradition of parliamentary supremacy in important ways, its background conception of democracy and self-governance is closer to that understanding than that of continental European nations whose constitutional regimes sought to check mass totalitarianism.

Given this history, it will be natural for defenders of non-formal, counter – majoritarian constitutional interpretation to double down on the method when critics of Europe's "democratic deficit" are increasingly populist. For all I know, this instinct is sound. It is worth noting, however, that the leeway the ItCC has garnered in the past decades may become narrower in an era skeptical of centralized, non-democratic power. In the United States, an originalist court facing a countermajoritarian dilemma can try to point to a period of time in which a supermajority of the populace at one time chose to entrench a norm that remains good law under the system's rules of change.[26] As Professor Pino suggests, the present shape of constitutional argument in Italy does not give much reason to expect a strong originalist turn in the face of a democratic deficit.

To the extent a skeptical populace sees the ItCC as an elite institution excluding voices from political participation, a relational jurisprudence that limits legislation in the name of constitutional or transnational values might threaten the court's political capital. On the other hand, the ItCC might serve as a stabilizing mediator between established, centralizing institutions and a skeptical populace. Either way, contemporary events suggest that relationality will require careful judicial statecraft *and* a renewed defense of a non-formal interpretative mode whose mediation may be perceived as limiting popular participation in governance. Professor Pino's defense of principle-based constitutional interpretation and the various contributors' elaboration of relationality offer a starting point for both challenging tasks.

---

[26] The argument will not be persuasive to the extent the audience is concerned about the dead hand problem. Yet it is available when there is law on point.

Dialogue VI

NATIONAL CONSTITUTIONAL ADJUDICATION IN A TRANSNATIONAL CONTEXT

Chapter XII

THE ITALIAN CONSTITUTIONAL COURT IN THE EUROPEAN SPACE: AN EMPIRICAL APPROACH

Marta Infantino

SUMMARY: 12.1. A story of opening up. – 12.2. The quantitative experiment: process and caveats. – 12.3. A year in numbers. – 12.3.1. The demand side for europeanisation. – 12.3.2. Judicial encounters with European legal orders. – 12.4. European relationality at work. – 12.4.1. Pride and boundary-marking. – 12.4.2. Respect and sensibility. – 12.4.3. Persuasion and resistance. – 12.4.4. A qualitative test for dialogue. – 12.5. Conclusion.

Legal institutions and rules are never set for good. Nor do they live in isolation. These are truisms, which hold in every field of law, but also account for challenges posed to the study of the position of a national constitutional court in the European (multi-level, composite, pluralistic, dynamic, multi-dimensional, or however one wants to call it) constitutional space.

Such a study would require investigating how the national court's approach to the European Union's (EU) and the European Convention on Human Rights (ECHR)'s legal systems have changed over time. The study would also have to relate these changes to transformational developments and internal dynamics within the court itself. It would additionally require delving into the dialogues between national and European judiciaries,[1] into the mutable relationships between European supra-national bodies vis-à-vis states and their components, as well as vis-à-vis one another,[2] and into the local and global transformations in the understanding of the interplay between national sovereignty, constitutionalism, Europeanisation, fundamental rights, and the international legal order[3] – to mention just a few things.

---

[1] On the varieties of these dialogues, see, for all, A. MAZMANYAN, P. POPELIER, W. VANDENBRUWAENE, *Editors' Introduction*, in A. MAZMANYAN, P. POPELIER, W. VANDENBRUWAENE (eds.), *The Role of Constitutional Courts in Multilevel Governance*, Antwerp, Intersentia, 2013, 1-17; F. MAYER, *Multilevel Constitutional Jurisdiction*, in A. VON BOGDANDY, J. BAST (eds.), *Principles of European Constitutional Law*, 2nd ed., Oxford-München, Hart-Beck, 2009, 399-439.

[2] Think for instance of the scenarios that the EU accession to the ECHR would open up.

[3] Cf. M. DE VISSER, *Constitutional Review in Europe. A Comparative Analysis*, Ox-

Engaging in such an analysis as far as the Italian Constitutional Court (hereinafter: ItCC) is concerned would be daunting for a non-expert of constitutional law like me. For that reason, in this paper, I will rather rely on the masterfully summarised historical overview of the ItCC's attitudes towards EU and ECHR law offered in chapter 7 of the volume on 'Italian Constitutional Justice in Global Context'[4] to deal with a much more practical aim. The focus of this essay will be on the ItCC's activity only. Taking the last year (2016) for which a complete dataset was available at the time in which the research was carried out, the paper offers a critical review of all the decisions published that year by the ItCC on EU – and ECHR-related issues, in order to test 'in action' how the ItCC deploys its 'relational' style of adjudication when confronted with European law. To this purpose, I will start with a brief recap of the ItCC's current positions on EU and ECHR law. After some caveats about the methodology adopted, numbers and figures of the ItCC's EU – and ECHR-related case law in 2016 will be analysed. A survey of some of the Court's specific postures will follow, preceding the concluding remarks.

12.1. A story of opening up

As is well-known, the ItCC's approaches to EU and ECHR laws – and consequently to the Court of Justice of the EU (CJEU) and to the European Court of Human Rights (ECtHR) – have traditionally been distinct from one another.

This is partly due to the differences (both historical and current) in the institutional features of the two European legal orders, the quality of their supra-nationalism, and their degree of integration with national systems – in particular with the Italian one. These different reference frameworks clearly resonate in the ItCC's divergent attitude towards EU and ECHR legal orders. Moreover, since the constitutional reform of 2001, Article 117 of the

---

ford, Hart Publishing, 2014, 87-92, and H. KELLER, A. STONE SWEET, *Assessing the Impact of the ECHR on National Legal Systems*, in H. KELLER, A. STONE SWEET (eds.), *A Europe of Rights: The Impact of the ECHR on National Legal Systems*, Oxford, Oxford University Press, 2008, 677, 685-686.

[4] V. BARSOTTI, P.G. CAROZZA, M. CARTABIA, A. SIMONCINI, *Italian Constitutional Justice in Global Context*, Oxford, Oxford University Press, 2016, 205-230; see also D. TEGA, *I diritti in crisi. Tra Corti nazionale e Corte europea di Strasburgo*, Milan, Giuffrè Editore, 2012, 51-99; T. GROPPI, *La jurisprudence de Strasbourg dans les décisions de la Cour constitutionnelle italienne. Une recherche empirique*, in *federalismi.it*, No. 21, 1-46 (2016); G. MARTINICO, O. POLLICINO, *The Impact of the European Courts on the Italian Constitutional Court*, in P. POPELIER, C. VAN DE HEYNING, P. VAN NUFFEL (eds.), *Human rights protection in the European legal order: The interaction between the European and the national courts*, Antwerp, Intersentia, 2011, 261-286.

Italian Constitution ("Legislative power belongs to the state and the regions in accordance with the constitution and within the limits set by European Union law and international obligations") textually provides for a disparity between EU law and other international public law sources. Although the meaning of this article is far from settled, its new version has offered an additional basis for distinct treatment of the EU vis-à-vis ECHR law. As of today, the two evolutionary paths can be briefly summarised as follows.

On the EU side, the ItCC has long challenged EU primacy. Today, whilst preserving its ultimate authority on the national constitution, the ItCC recognises the primacy of EU over national law, and largely entrusts the task of upholding EU primacy to ordinary judges, who can directly submit requests for preliminary rulings to the CJEU and disapply national rules conflicting with EU law. However, the Court has retained the exclusive power to check the consistency of the Italian legal system with EU law in cases involving indirectly effective EU law and in the so-called direct proceedings.[5] It was indeed in the latter context that the Court, in a pioneering decision, ceased what was dubbed its 'self-exile' from (explicit) dialogue with the CJEU;[6] in 2008, the ItCC raised, for the first time, a preliminary question under Art. 267 of the Treaty on the Functioning of the European Union.[7] Three further important requests for preliminary ruling were lodged by the ItCC in incidental proceedings in 2013, in 2017 and in 2019.[8]

On the ECHR side, with its 2007 *révirement*,[9] the Court acknowledged that the ECHR, as authoritatively interpreted by the ECtHR, enjoys a higher status than domestic law, and that its rules are 'intermediate laws' or 'interposed norms' (*norme interposte*) which can be used under Art. 117 of the Constitution as a parameter of review of the constitutionality of national law. Yet the ItCC also maintains that there are constitutional limits to the application of the ECHR (and of ECtHR case law) in the domestic legal system. The Court keeps affirming its monopoly to review the compati-

---

[5] M. DE VISSER, *Constitutional Review in Europe. A Comparative Analysis*, *supra* fn. 3, 259; see also ItCC judgments 269/2017 and 20/2019.

[6] G. MARTINICO, F. FONTANELLI, *The Hidden Dialogue: When Judicial Competitors Collaborate*, in 8 *Glob. Jur.*, Issue 3 (Advances), Article 7, 1 (2008); G. MARTINICO, *Judging in the Multilevel Legal Order: Exploring the Techniques of 'Hidden Dialogue'*, in 21 *King's L. J.* 257 (2010).

[7] ItCC order 103/2008. At that time, only the Belgian, the Austrian, and the Lithuanian Constitutional Courts (respectively, in 1997, 1999, and 2007) have lodged preliminary references to the CJEU.

[8] Cp. ItCC orders 207/2013, 24/2017 (on which see below, esp. n. 7), and 117/2019.

[9] ItCC judgments 348 and 349/2007; see also, more recently, ItCC judgments 24 and 25/2019.

bility of national legislation with the Convention and its jurisprudence.[10]

This review of the ItCC's approaches to EU and ECHR legal orders gives a glimpse of the multi-layered and pluralistic character of contemporary constitutionalism. As with other European constitutional courts, the ItCC is caught between the need for constructively favouring European integration and facilitating the embeddedness of EU and ECHR laws in the domestic legal system, on the one hand, and the task of defending the norms and values underlying the domestic constitution, as well as its own institutional prerogatives, on the other hand.[11] The dynamic of this complex architecture of multilevel bridging is based on the varying relationships (of cooperation, accommodation, dialogue, mutual reinforcement, but also of defence, contestation, and resistance) between the ItCC and the other relevant subjects of the European legal space – from supranational courts and institutions to the domestic parliament, government, judiciary, and constituency. But how do these relationships concretely unfold, through what arguments, and how often? What role does the ItCC actually carve out for itself within the European legal space? The following statistical scrutiny of the ItCC's case law from 2016 aims to give us a picture that might help answer the above questions. Before getting to the core of the analysis, however, a few caveats are necessary.

12.2. The quantitative experiment: process and caveats

In recent years, the quantitative study of law, and of constitutional law in particular, has been burgeoning.[12] The beauty of numbers mostly lies – when they are not built to fit their producers' biases[13] – in their capacity to ease comparison, and to highlight patterns that otherwise would go unno-

---

[10] See, for all, T. GROPPI, *La jurisprudence de Strasbourg dans les décisions de la Cour constitutionnelle italienne. Une recherche empirique*, *supra* fn. 4, 5-12.

[11] On these functions, see A. MAZMANYAN, P. POPELIER, W. VANDENBRUWAENE, *Editors' Introduction*, *supra* fn. 1, 8-10; with specific reference to the ItCC, T. GROPPI, *The Italian Constitutional Court: Towards a 'Multilevel System' of Constitutional Review?*, in A. HARDING, P. LEYLAND (eds.), *Constitutional Courts: A Comparative Study*, London, Wildy & Sons Ltd, 2009, 145-147.

[12] It is especially so in the field of comparative constitutional studies. For a review of the literature, see A. MEUWESE, M. VERSTEEG, *Quantitative Methods for Comparative Constitutional Law*, in M. ADAMS, J. BOMHOFF (eds.), *Practice and Theory in Comparative Law*, Cambridge, Cambridge University Press, 2012, 230-257; R. HIRSCHL, *Comparative Matters. The Renaissance of Comparative Constitutional Law*, Oxford, Oxford University Press, 2014, 268-281.

[13] For a critical review, see M. INFANTINO, *Global Indicators*, in S. CASSESE (eds.), *Research Handbook on Global Administrative Law*, Cheltenham, Edward Elgar Publishing, 2016, 347-367.

ticed or underappreciated. Following the bright side of this trend, I will test how the ItCC positions itself in the European space by reviewing, through a quantitative (and qualitative) approach, all the decisions published by the ItCC in 2016.

For this purpose, I classified the 292 decisions delivered by the ItCC in the year in question according to ten variables (the nature of the proceedings, referring body, subject matter of the case, outcome of the case, etc.). I then selected and analysed the decisions implying a textual reference to either the EU or the ECHR law. The quantitative results obtained are described first, while the qualitative review of the selected cases follows. The entire dataset (which was created manually) is available at units.it/dircomp/infantino.htm.

It is well-known that, when applied to law, quantitative methodologies suffer from a number of intrinsic limitations.[14] While the simplicity of the study carried out here partially shields it from some of the most acute problems affecting quantitative legal research, at least three caveats are in order.

A first warning derives from the scope of the analysis. The one-year focus on ItCC's activity automatically excludes from consideration the role played by a variety of other actors (e.g., ordinary domestic courts) in influencing the way in which the ItCC has performed its functions in the European space. In a hybrid model of judicial review such as the current Italian one,[15] the ItCC's attitude cannot be properly understood without taking into account the constitutional postures of ordinary judges, who often contribute to setting the horizon for the ItCC's intervention. The one-year limit further narrows the scope of the research, providing a sample that might be too little to be meaningful. Finally, the representativeness of the year chosen adds another challenge, even though it has been noted that the ItCC's "European journey experienced some significant developments during 2016".[16]

Second, any numerical analysis of judicial activity requires determining the relevant variables and establishing their possible values. This implies making discretionary and overly simplistic choices regarding the variables and

---

[14] Among the many, R. HIRSCHL, *Comparative Matters. The Renaissance of Comparative Constitutional Law*, *supra* fn. 12, 268-281; M. INFANTINO, *Global Indicators*, *supra* fn. 5213, 360-362.

[15] V. BARSOTTI, P.G. CAROZZA, M. CARTABIA, A. SIMONCINI, *Italian Constitutional Justice in Global Context*, *supra* fn. 4, esp. 42-43; A. HARDING, P. LEYLAND, T. GROPPI, *Constitutional Courts: Forms, Functions and Practice in Comparative Perspective*, in A. HARDING, P. LEYLAND (eds.), *Constitutional Courts: A Comparative Study*, *supra* fn. 131, 1, 4.

[16] P. FARAGUNA, M. MASSA, D. TEGA, M. CARTABIA, *Developments in Italian Constitutional Law*, in R. ALBERT, Š. DRUGDA, P. FARAGUNA, D. LANDAU (eds.), 2016 *Global Review of Constitutional Law*, I·CONnect, 2017, 108, 110.

values to be considered. For instance, should one take into account the identity of the judge who wrote the opinion? What level of detail is appropriate for identifying the subject matter of the case? How should one categorise an ItCC proceeding where a direct recourse is merged with an incidental request? How can one classify the nuances of ItCC's interpretative decisions, or the cases where a request is at the same time partially upheld and partially rejected? One may answer these questions in many different ways, and each answer inevitably affects the data gathered and results achieved.

Third, it goes without saying that a citation study of the references made by the ItCC's decisions on EU and ECHR law provides only a partial and potentially misleading guide to the relationship between the ItCC and the European supra-national legal orders, since it does not capture the silent dialogues and unwritten dimensions underlying the ItCC's adjudication process. The ItCC notoriously takes into account academic debates and foreign law, but rarely – if ever – mentions them in its decisions [17] (in 2016 only two ItCC judgments, while examining ECtHR case law, briefly dealt with other states' approaches to the concerned issues [18]). A textual survey of the ItCC's quotation of scholarly and foreign materials simply fails to give a reliable picture of the informal, implicit and indirect inputs entering into its decision-making. Yet, it is true that (tracking judges' hidden references might prove a daunting task for anyone, and that) the textual references may tell us a lot about the styles, the patterns, the ideals, and the postures of the court expressing them. [19] This is why, notwithstanding the above caveats, I believe that empirical research might still add something to the picture – with the additional benefit of being more transparent, or, in other words, more verifiable than a non-empirical study. Below is the data from 2016.

12.3. A year in numbers

As already stated, in 2016 the Italian Constitutional Court published decisions (including both orders and judgments) in 292 cases. We will first examine the demand side: how many times, and in which cases, did the parties to the litigation ask the ItCC to consider either EU or ECHR law (or

[17] V. Barsotti, P.G. Carozza, M. Cartabia, A. Simoncini, *Italian Constitutional Justice in Global Context*, *supra* fn. 4, 80-81; T. Groppi, M.-C. Ponthoreau, *Introduction*, in T. Groppi, M.-C. Ponthoreau (eds.), *The Use of Foreign Precedents by Constitutional Judges*, Oxford, Hart Publishing, 2013, 1, 7, fn. 18.

[18] ItCC judgments 52 (on religious associations' rights) and 84/2016 (on in vitro fertilization).

[19] G. Frankenberg, *Comparing constitutions: Ideas, ideals, and ideology – toward a layered narrative*, in 4 *Int'l J. Con. L.* 439 (2006) (speaking about the text of constitutions).

both) when evaluating their claim for or against judicial review. To the limited purpose of this paper, the notion of 'parties to the litigation' will include the judge raising the constitutional issue and the parties to the original proceedings, the state and the regions, as well as interested parties submitting amici briefs (which are often non-governmental organisations).

We will then deal with the ItCC's own approach to EU and/or ECHR law, that is, the focus will be on the decisions in which the ItCC – more or less directly, and extensively – filled its opinion with EU and/or ECHR-related legal arguments.

12.3.1. The demand side for europeanisation

With some degree of approximation, parties' reliance on EU or ECHR law (or both) in Italian constitutional adjudication might be measured through the 'summary of the facts' opening the decisions.

According to these summaries, in 90 out of 292 cases, the parties to the litigation referred to European supranational sources to support their claims.

Of these 90 cases, 51 were incidental proceedings (started by judges raising doubts as to the constitutionality of a statute they were supposed to apply), while 34 were direct proceedings (made either by the state or by regions with regard to a piece of legislation allegedly infringing the constitutional division of powers). One case concerned a combined incidental-direct proceeding. Outside the judicial review function, parties made references to either EU or ECHR law in three cases involving a conflict of attributions between public powers, and in one case concerning the admissibility of a referendum.

Cases with EU-ECHR references made by the parties	
Incidental proceedings	51
Direct proceedings	34
Incidental-direct proceeding	1
Conflict of attributions	3
Referendum	1
Total	90

While focussing on the judicial review decisions, we must note that the 51 incidental proceedings cases where parties raised EU and/or ECHR-related arguments represented around 1/3 of the total incidental proceedings for the same year (51 out of 158). The great majority of these 51 proceedings were raised by civil and criminal courts (CCC), especially by first-instance tribunals, which alone were responsible for 30 out of the 38 cases stemming from CCC. While the geographic distribution of these tribunals was balanced across the peninsula, some tribunals were clearly more active than others (the tribunals of Bologna and Turin lodged 3 requests each, and the tribunals of Bari, Cagliari, Rome, Trento, and Treviso 2 each). A good fraction of cases (9) were raised by administrative courts (AC), especially, once again, by first instance courts (which alone lodged 7 requests). The remainder of incidental cases with EU/ECHR references (4) came from other kinds of judges: in particular, 2 claims were lodged by tax commissions, 2 by the Court of Auditors, and 1 by an arbitral tribunal.

Figure 1. Incidental Proceedings with Parties' Reference to EU/ECHR Law: Provenance.

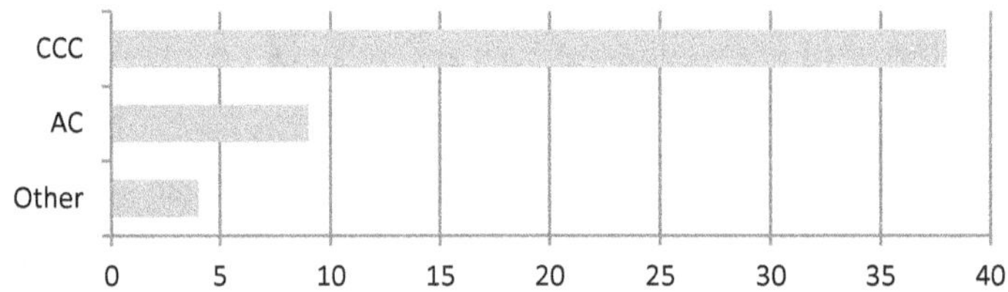

In some of these cases, parties made reference either to EU law (15) or ECHR law (24) only, while in others, references to EU and ECHR law were combined (13). Many cases concerned similar issues. For instance, there were 12 claims regarding criminal law and sanctions, while 8 involved employment contracts.

Figure 2. Incidental Proceedings with Parties' Reference to EU/ECHR Law: Issues.

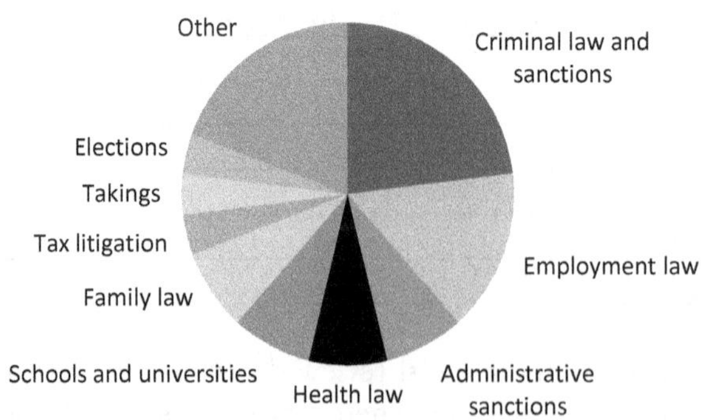

The 34 direct proceedings cases where parties made references either to EU or to ECHR law represented a little less than 1/3 of the total number of direct proceedings adjudicated in 2016, i.e., 104 (incidentally, as the large number of these proceedings shows, the Court is increasingly becoming more a "judge of political conflicts, and less a guarantor of rights").[20] While 20 of these claims were lodged by the state, 14 were lodged by the regions, with some regions clearly being more active than others. Half of these 14 cases were proposed by Veneto (7), whereas Sicily lodged 4 claims, and Lombardy 3.

Figure 3. Direct Proceedings with Parties' Reference to EU/ECHR Law: Provenance.

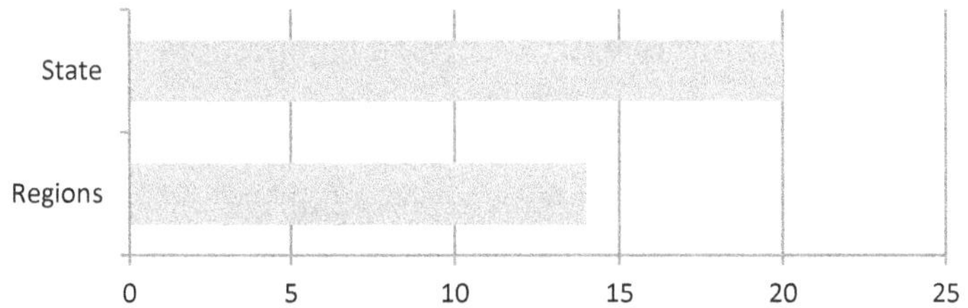

Only in one out of these 34 cases did the parties mention ECHR law. In the remaining 33 cases, the appellant exclusively referenced EU law (in two of these cases, the appellant demanded that the ItCC request a preliminary ruling from the CJEU). These claims largely concerned similar issues: for instance, 7 cases were about public expenditure, 5 on energy law, 3 each on competition law and on tax law.

Figure 4. Direct Proceedings with Parties' Reference to EU/ECHR Law: Issues.

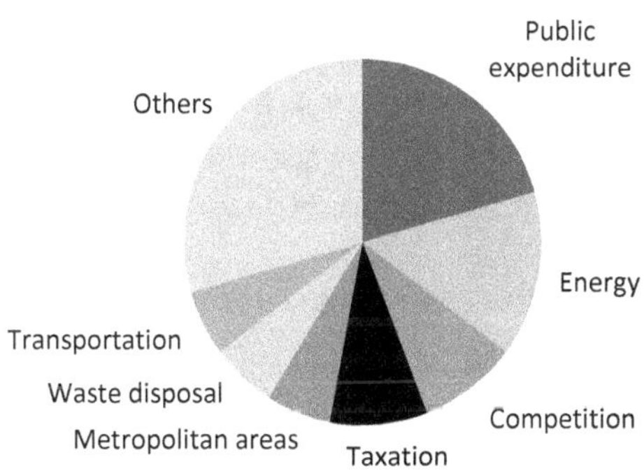

All of the above information makes clear that non-constitutional judges (especially first-instance ones), lawyers, bureaucracies on both the state and

[20] S. CASSESE, *Dentro la Corte. Diario di un giudice costituzionale*, Bologna, Il Mulino, 2015, 64, 199-200 (my translation); see also V. BARSOTTI, P.G. CAROZZA, M. CARTABIA, A. SIMONCINI, *Italian Constitutional Justice in Global Context*, *supra* fn. 4, 52.

regional level, as well as civil society (as represented by interested parties) have a heightened sensitivity to European supranational laws. In roughly one third of 2016's incidental and direct proceedings cases resulting in a published decision, at least one of the parties invoked either EU or ECHR law, or both. Yet, it should also be noted that, while parties to incidental proceedings relied extensively on both European legal orders, references to EU law dominated direct proceedings.

12.3.2. Judicial encounters with European legal orders

The above data depicts the demand for supranational-oriented judicial review. We should now focus on the ItCC's own approach to European legal orders, considering the decisions in which the ItCC referenced EU and/or ECHR law, their relationship with parties' arguments, and their rate of acceptance/rejection of the underlying claim.

The first point to be stressed is that, out of the 292 decisions (including orders and judgments) published in 2016, the ItCC mentioned in its reasoning – sometimes cursorily, sometimes at length – EU and/or ECHR law in 39 cases only. Of these 39 decisions which textually made references to European legal orders, 20 (of which 11 stemmed from direct proceedings, 9 from incidental proceedings, and 1 from a conflict of attributions case) looked at EU law only, mostly in the sectors of public employment (4), public expenditure (3), and public procurement (3). Seventeen decisions (of which 16 were incidental proceedings, and one a conflict of attributions claim) took into account ECHR law only, while two decisions (both incidental proceedings) analysed both EU and ECHR law. A great number (7) of the 17 decisions which referred to ECHR law only concerned criminal and administrative sanctions, which was also the subject matter of the two decisions where references to EU and ECHR law were combined.

Figure 5. Decision's References to EU/ECHR law.

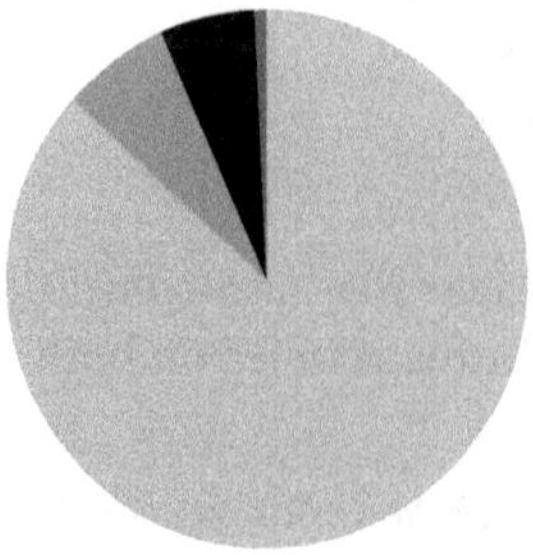

What is further interesting to underline is that in only six of the above 39 decisions with references to EU and/or ECHR law did the ItCC look at supranational legal orders autonomously – that is, without any hint from the parties in this regard. In the remaining 33 decisions, the ItCC responded to (some or all of) the parties' arguments on EU/ECHR law. Considering that parties invoked EU and/or ECHR in 90 cases, this means that in 33 cases the ItCC was willing to incorporate European-inspired reasoning in its decisions, while on 57 occasions it did not pick up parties' arguments on supranational law. The latter entered in the summary of the facts, but not in the judicial holding.

Figure 6. Case where Parties Argued about EU/ECHR Law.

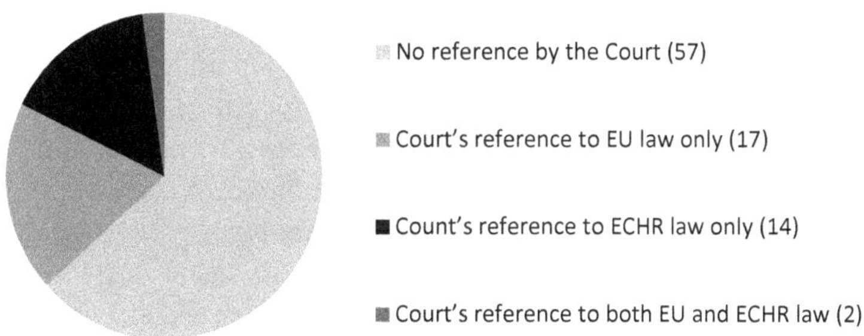

From the above data, one can infer that, within the ItCC, the stimuli for express consideration of EU and/or ECHR law largely come from external pressures – that is, from the European-inspired requests for judicial review lodged by the parties. In the absence of these pressures (and often in spite of them), the ItCC apparently seems eager to establish the self-sufficiency of the Italian legal system, discarding European-based arguments.[21]

The same tendency – that of affirming the autonomy of Italian law – emerges from the size and shape of the ItCC's references to EU and/or ECHR law. In many of the 39 decisions which mention either EU or ECHR law or both in the reasoning, the ItCC kept the mention limited to very cursory and brief allusions, for instance, evoking the generic need of 'abiding by EU-derived obligations'[22] or citing incidental ECHR provisions or ECtHR case law as a collateral support to arguments based on domestic

[21] The same point is stressed by G. AMATO, *Corte costituzionale e Corti europee. Fra diversità nazionali e visione comune*, Bologna, Il Mulino, 2015, 63, 70, 74-5.

[22] Cf. ItCC's judgments 43, 184, 188, 242/2016.

law.[23] Other decisions, after focussing at length on the Italian framework, dealt with EU and/or ECHR law at the end of the opinion only, coming to the conclusion that the European-based argument was either irrelevant under the circumstances, or already covered by the analysis of domestic law applicable to the case.[24]

All the above considerations apply equally to citations of EU and ECHR law. Interestingly, however, the rate of acceptance of judicial review requests (whereby acceptance includes – complete and partial – formal acceptance of the claim) seems to diverge depending on which European supranational law is considered. Of the 20 decisions which mentioned only EU law, 6 upheld the constitutional claim. Of the 17 decisions citing only ECHR law, the constitutional challenge was successful on 3 occasions. Of the two decisions with mixed EU-ECHR references, one resulted in a declaration of unconstitutionality. In other words, on average, the rate of acceptance for decisions quoting EU law was 30%, while the rate for decisions citing ECHR was around 17%. The latter rate falls considerably below the 2016 general average rate of acceptance for incidental and direct procedure (around 28%: in 2016, the Court upheld 74 cases out of the 261 incidental and direct procedure requests). The former rate is in line with that average, and slightly above it. This result might be related to the different degree of integration of ECHR, as opposed to EU law, in the Italian legal framework, but might also be the occasional outcome of the specific ECHR-related issues discussed before the ItCC in 2016. That year, as we saw, ECHR issues largely concerned criminal and administrative sanctions, a field in which – as we will see below – the ItCC displayed a considerable resistance to ECHR guidelines.

12.4. European relationality at work

What emerges from the analysis of the contents of these 39 decisions by the ItCC which resort to arguments based on EU and/or ECHR law is the variety of judicial postures towards European supranational laws. This variety, in 2016, ranged primarily from the re-affirmation of the autonomy of the Italian constitutional system to the deference to European guidelines, to a cautious resistance.

[23] Cf. ItCC's judgments 32, 84, 200, 203, 219/2016, as well as order 207/2016.

[24] Cf. ItCC's judgments 9, 23, 105, 109/2016 (as to EU law) and 204/2016 (as to ECHR law).

12.4.1. Pride and boundary-marking

The emphasis on the self-sufficiency of the domestic constitutional legal order vis-à-vis European ones is perhaps the most evident attitude running across the ItCC's 2016 case law.

While acting as a bridge between the domestic and European legal orders, the ItCC is always preoccupied with reminding its readership of the principal focus of the judicial review function, which is verifying the compatibility of the domestic legal system with the national Constitution – as it is in stressing its exclusive competence in this regard. Such a self-affirming penchant clearly emerges from the many decisions in which the ItCC underlines that, as far as the national constitution is concerned, it is the only body which can authoritatively adjudicate on the issue, even if this implies interpreting EU law or ECtHR's rulings.[25] For instance, with regard to the ECHR system, the ItCC recognizes that "ECHR provisions should be applied according to the interpretation given by the ECtHR", yet adds that "it is within the competence of this court to appreciate how and to what extent the interpretation offered by ECtHR fits the domestic constitutional order".[26]

The ItCC has other rhetorical strategies to downsize the centrality of European laws in domestic constitutional adjudication. In some decisions, the ItCC takes into account European supranational laws, but, rather than dealing with them *per se*, it reconstructs them through the lens of its jurisprudence on these very same laws. In judgment n. 39/2016 (concerning the constitutionality of a regional law, allegedly violating an EU Directive), the ItCC rejected the request for review because, inter alia, the examined law did not contrast with the rationale of the Directive as reconstructed by the same ItCC in its own previous case-law. In its judgment n. 132/2016 (in which the ItCC refused to uphold a claim challenging the constitutionality of a provision on employees' right to holiday, allegedly conflicting with the national Constitution and the ECHR), the ItCC reviewed many ECtHR decisions, especially the ones against Italy, through the medium of its own previous jurisprudence on the ECtHR's case-law.[27] In other words, in the ItCC's reasoning, 'European law' often becomes equivalent to 'European law as interpreted by me.' Hence, the consideration for the European legal order is actually turned into a re-affirmation of the ItCC's competence to interpret the laws that are relevant before it.

---

[25] ItCC judgment 187/2016, n. 11-12.

[26] ItCC judgment 193/2016, n. 3.

[27] The same reasoning underlies ItCC orders 165 (affirming the constitutionality of an electoral law) and 207/2016 (affirming the constitutionality of a criminal procedure law).

At other times, as we already saw, the ItCC reaffirms the boundaries of its exclusive competence by basing its entire reasoning – in spite of the parties' alleged violations of EU and/or ECHR law – on the Italian context only, relegating the analysis of European supranational laws to a concise passage at the end of the holding. One of the best illustrations of such a style of reasoning comes from judgment n. 12/2016, regarding the constitutionality of a provision of the Code of Criminal Procedure on the right of the victim of a crime to claim compensation from the tortfeasor in criminal proceedings. Although the constitutional challenge was partially grounded in the conflict between the Code's provision on the one hand, and EU and ECHR law on the other hand, the ItCC rejected the request on the basis of a lengthy discussion on the historical origins and actual developments of victims' rights in criminal trials under Italian law. It is only at the very end of the opinion that the ItCC briefly referred to EU and ECHR law, in order to concisely conclude that the alleged conflict did not exist.[28]

The same structure – implying an in-depth analysis of the Italian framework, followed by a collateral review of supranational rules – is common to many other decisions.[29] Still at other times, the ItCC avoids direct confrontation with European supranational laws, especially the ones stemming from the CJEU or the ECtHR, by engaging in a common-law-like, detailed distinguishing of precedents. The ItCC was thus able to put aside the issue of the alleged incompatibility between a statutory provision on public employees and EU Directive 2000/78/EC, as interpreted by the CJEU, in the name of the factual and legal differences between the case at issue and the one considered by the Luxembourg court.[30] Along the same lines, when requested to review the alleged conflict between article 649 of the Code of Criminal Procedure and the prohibition of double jeopardy under the Constitution and the ECHR, the court dismissed the ECHR-based challenge by concluding that, "to date, ECtHR case law, since it always remains related to the specificities of the cases it stemmed from […], does not allow to identify [sic] with certainty any principle […] that might help in evaluating the compatibility of Art. 649 C.P.P. with the Italian Constitution".[31] Similarly, when examining the constitutionality, in light of the ECHR, of a decision taken by the Prime Minister against a religious association, the Court refused to conclude that the decision was in violation of

[28] ItCC judgment 12/2016, n. 11 and 12.

[29] Cf. ItCC judgments 52 (esp. n. 5.1), 57, 90 (esp. n. 4), 95, 203/2016 (esp. n. 6.2 and 6.4, last sentences).

[30] ItCC judgment 133/2016 (on CJEU's judgment of 6 November 2012, C-286/12, Commission v. Hungary).

[31] ItCC judgment 200/2016.

the ECHR. The ItCC stressed that the ECtHR's case-law on freedom of religious associations invoked by the parties concerned states with a regulation of religious associations much more detailed than the Italian one; therefore, this case law was not relevant to the Italian context.[32]

12.4.2. Respect and sensibility

None of the above analysis means that the ItCC is only obsessed with its own self-affirmation. A parallel and equally clear tendency of 2016 ItCC case law shows the cooperative efforts put forth towards EU and ECHR law and institutions.

Cooperation is the key to understanding the active interaction with European courts engaged by the ItCC in specific instances. Good examples come from judgments n. 84 and 187/2016.

In the former, a tribunal raised doubts about the constitutionality of Italian law n. 40/2004 on in vitro fertilization (many provisions of this law have, in the past, been declared unconstitutional by the ItCC), with particular regard to the legal prohibition of using discarded embryos for research purposes. The point was that a similar challenge against law n. 40/2004 had been raised by a different claimant before the ECtHR, where the case was still pending. The ItCC therefore decided to suspend its own proceedings awaiting the ECtHR's decision. When the ECtHR finally issued its judgment (holding that states have considerable margins of discretion on how to regulate in vitro fertilization),[33] the ItCC followed suit, asserting – on the basis of a comparative overview of the approaches adopted in other European countries[34] – that the legislative choice, being discretionary and not arbitrary, was not reviewable by the Court itself. The decision is also interesting because, in spite of the circumstance that the law was attacked for its alleged contrast with the Italian Constitution only, the ItCC judgment autonomously and extensively relied on ECtHR's case law.[35]

The case of the other ItCC judgment – n. 187/2016 – is different. This case represented the continuation of a proceeding concerning the interpretation of an EU directive, on which the ItCC had filed, in 2013, a request for preliminary ruling before the CJEU (actually, it was the first request under Art. 267 TFUE ever lodged by the ItCC in an incidental proceed-

---

[32] ItCC judgment 52/2016.

[33] ECtHR, Grand Chamber, 27 August 2015, 46470/11, *Parrillo v. Italy*.

[34] ItCC judgment 84/2016, n. 9 and 11.

[35] *Ibid.*, n. 7, 9, 11.

ing).[36] In 2014, the CJEU delivered its judgment, finding that the Italian state had incorrectly transposed the Directive and was in breach of EU law.[37] Reinvested with the issue in 2016, the ItCC, after a lengthy examination of the CJEU's ruling,[38] abided by the CJEU's instructions but also stressed that it was still up to the ItCC itself to evaluate the consequences of Italy's violation of EU law. In the ItCC's words, "the primacy of EU law and the exclusivity of national constitutional jurisdiction, in a centralised system of judicial review, require a careful balancing [...]. The decision of the Luxembourg Court shows respect for the competences of Member States, to which it expressly recognises margins of autonomy. [...] These margins concern in particular the consequences of the violation of EU law. [...] On this point it is necessary to complement the CJEU's decision. Complementing the CJEU's decision cannot but be within the competence of this court".[39] At the end of the analysis, which included the appraisal of law n. 107/2015 (enacted by the Italian legislature to compensate those injured due to a breach of EU law by the Italian state), the ItCC established that the state had already adequately redressed the consequences of its violation of EU law.[40] The very same issue arose in two subsequent decisions, where the ItCC concluded that, under the circumstances of each case, it was for the judges who raised the constitutional challenge to re-evaluate the question.[41]

As these judgments show, the ItCC is often called to judge the compliance by the Italian state with specific instructions, obligations, or suggestions stemming from European legal orders. Indeed, judicial review requests frequently concern pieces of legislation enacted by the Italian state as an answer to an infraction procedure by the European Commission, to a preliminary ruling of the CJEU, or to a previous ECtHR judgment against Italy. For instance, in judgment n. 126/2016, the ItCC had to evaluate the constitutionality of a statutory reform of the 2006 Code on the environment (itself adopted to implement Directive 2004/35/EC), which had been enacted by the Italian state to remedy the defects denounced by the European Commission in an infraction procedure. In judgments n. 32 and 204/2016, the ItCC was asked to review the constitutionality of two statutory provisions that were revised by the legislature after an ECtHR's decision against

[36] See ItCC order 207/2013.

[37] CJEU, 26 November 2014, C-22/13, from C-61/13 to C-63/13, and C-418/13, *Mascolo et al.*

[38] ItCC judgment 187/2016, n. 4-10.

[39] *Ibid.*, n. 11-12.

[40] *Ibid.*, n. 19.

[41] ItCC order 194 and 195/2016.

Italy.[42] In both the judgments, the ItCC concluded that the new or revised statutory norms were in line, or could be interpreted as being in line, with the Constitution and with principles stemming from European legal orders.[43] Only in one instance – concerning a provision on the victim's right to compensation for the excessive length of judicial proceedings, adopted by the Italian state to allow the Italian legal system's conformity with ECtHR's guidelines –, did the ItCC hold that the challenged provision violated the instructions previously expressed by the ECtHR in its many judgments against Italy.[44]

In these cases, no matter whether the outcome is a declaration of unconstitutionality of the statutory reforms made by the Italian state to abide by European instructions, or their approval as constitutional, the ItCC always displays a meticulous attention in trying to strike a compromise between the costs and hindrances associated with conforming the domestic legal system to European requests, on the one hand, and the mandated deference to European institutions' pressures, on the other hand.

12.4.3. Persuasion and resistance

Besides pride and respect, there is a third posture that, although often intertwined with the other two, stands out among the ItCC's 2016 case law as distinctive. I am referring to the delicate but firm defence of the specificities of the Italian context – a defence which in some instances seems to inspire the ItCC's emphasis on the national space of autonomy within European legal orders, and on other occasions takes the tone of an open resistance, especially vis-à-vis the ECtHR.

From this perspective, we find many judgments in which the ItCC has emphasised the margins of discretion accorded to the Italian state by both EU and the ECHR law.[45] But we also find many decisions in which the ItCC engaged in a careful review of the ECtHR's case law against Italy to prevent too literal or generous an interpretation of these rulings to trump defensible (if not laudable) features of the Italian legal system.[46] The most

---

[42] ECtHR, 8 January 2013, *Torreggiani et al. v. Italy*.

[43] Cf. ItCC judgments 32, 126, 204/2016. See also ItCC judgment 219/2016 (affirming the constitutionality of a statute expediting the management of the financial consequences stemming from a condemnation of Italy by either the EU or the ECtHR).

[44] ItCC judgment 36/2016.

[45] As far as EU law is concerned, cf. ItCC judgment 133 (n. 4.2), 187/2016 (n. 11-12); on ECHR law, cf. ItCC judgment 84/2016 (n. 9 and 11).

[46] ItCC judgments 57 (where the Court carefully reviewed the ECtHR Grand Cham-

illustrative decision in this regard is perhaps judgment n. 193/2016, in which the ItCC had to verify the compatibility of the Italian general law on administrative sanctions (law n. 689/1981) with the ECtHR's case law (especially the one against Italy) according to which administrative sanctions of criminal nature can trigger the application of the ECHR's procedural guarantees (such as *ne bis in idem*) applicable in criminal matters.[47]

Although the judgment starts by stating that "ECHR provisions should be applied according to the interpretation given by the ECtHR",[48] the ItCC immediately specified that "it is within the competence of this court to appreciate how and to what extent the interpretation offered by the ECtHR fits the domestic constitutional order. The ECHR provisions, insofar as they complement Art. 117 of the [Italian] Constitution, enjoy constitutional status within the domestic system of legal sources [...]. It is within the competence of this court, in other words, to appreciate the European case law on the concerned provisions, in a way that should be substantially respectful of the ECtHR, but that should also include a margin of appreciation and adjustment allowing the court to take into account the specificity of the national legal order where the concerned provision is bound to apply".[49]

After engaging in a detailed analysis of the ECtHR's case law and of its possible application in the Italian context, the ItCC held that law n. 689/1981 was not in conflict with the guidelines laid down by the ECtHR. From the quoted passage, one can sense the clash between the wide interpretation given by the ECtHR to criminal law guarantees, and the traditional Italian understanding of the boundaries between administrative and criminal measures. Underlying this clash are the never-ending tensions in the field of fundamental rights protection between the advancement of rights and the risks of excessive judicialization of policy choices, as well as between the drive for uniformity and the need to respect local diversity.

---

ber's decision of 17 September 2009, *Scoppola v. Italy*, to affirm the constitutionality of an *ex post facto* criminal procedural law), 90 (the Court rejected a claim about the unconstitutionality of a provision on takings, arguing that the provision was in line with the ECtHR case-law against Italy on takings), 102 (declaring the inadmissibility of a challenge against a provision on administrative sanctions, since a declaration of unconstitutionality would have had no effect on the original proceeding), 132 (upholding the constitutional of a retroactive law on public employment, insofar as ECtHR's case-law against Italy did not exclude the adoption of retroactive laws for general reasons of public interest), 193/2016 (concluding for the compatibility of the challenged law on administrative sanctions and ECtHRs case-law against Italy).

[47] See esp. ECtHR, 27 September 2011, *Menarini Diagnostic S.r.l. v. Italy*; 4 March 2014, *Grande Stevens et al. v. Italy*.

[48] ItCC judgment 193/2016, n. 3.

[49] *Ibid.* (quoting previous ItCC's case law on the same points).

12.4.4. A qualitative test for dialogue

Looking for the ItCC's textual encounters with European laws in one year only clearly offers a limited view of the often unspoken, and often long-lasting, trajectories of the role of national constitutional adjudication in European legal orders. Yet, the reliability of the results just presented about the complexities of the ItCC's attitude vis-à-vis European legal orders might be complemented in many possible ways – for instance, by a comparison with similar stances taken by other European constitutional courts, and by a qualitative review of subsequent developments of ItCC's case-law.

While a comparative testing of the results herein highlighted is ingeniously performed by Patricia Popelier in her reply to this entry, the following pages provide a case-based qualitative review, showing how all the ItCC's approaches outlined above – pride, respect, and resistance – came into play in the ItCC's decisions on the so-called *Taricco* case, that is, ItCC orders n. 24/2017 and 115/2018.

The facts underlying the decisions are well-known. In 2014, an Italian tribunal lodged a request for preliminary ruling under Art. 267 TFUE concerning the compatibility with EU law of the Italian statute of limitation applying to criminal proceedings regarding VAT fraud. The underlying scenario was that, given the short limitation period provided by Italian substantive criminal law rules, and the long duration of criminal investigations and proceedings, charges for serious VAT frauds in Italy were often time-barred.

In its first judgment on the case,[50] the Grand Chamber of the CJEU held in September 2015 that national rules "prevent[ing] the imposition of effective and dissuasive penalties in a significant number of cases of serious fraud affecting the financial interests of the European Union"[51] are likely to undermine the effective protection of the EU's financial interests under Art. 325 TFEU. According to the CJEU, when confronted with rules of this kind (such as Italian rules on limitations in criminal law), national judges were expected to disapply them if their enforcement would result in preventing the Member State concerned from fulfilling its obligations under Art. 325 TFEU.[52] The CJEU further made clear that such a conclusion, even when referred to pending criminal proceedings, did not infringe on the principle of *nullum crimen sine lege praevia*, enshrined in both Art. 49 of the EU Charter of Fundamental Rights and Art. 7 of the ECHR. For the

[50] CJEU, Grand Chamber, 8 September 2015, C-105/14, *Taricco et al.*

[51] CJEU, *Taricco*, n. 66.

[52] CJEU, *Taricco*, n. 66.

CJEU, these provisions dealt with substantial criminal law and did not preclude the ex post facto modification of procedural rules, such as the ones regarding the statute of limitations.[53]

The CJEU judgment was received with much criticism. In 2015 and 2016, the Milan Court of Appeals and the Italian Court of Cassation resorted to the ItCC claiming, inter alia, that compliance with the CJEU judgment would have implied infringing Art. 25(2) of the Italian Constitution ("no punishment may be inflicted except by virtue of a law in force at the time the offence was committed"). According to a deeply rooted Italian interpretive tradition, the principle of *nullum crimen sine lege praevia* precludes ex post facto aggravations of the limitation period for criminal liability (which is considered as part and parcel of the substantive discipline of criminal offences), and mandates that criminal statutes be sufficiently clear and definite – which was not the case for the CJEU's instructions about a 'significant' number of 'serious' frauds.

Sharing many of the national courts' doubts as to the compatibility of the CJEU's judgment with the Italian constitutional order, the ItCC, with its decision n. 24/2017, for the second time in its history of incidental proceedings,[54] lodged a preliminary reference request under Art. 267 TFUE, demanding clarifications on how Art. 325 TFUE and the related CJEU's ruling had to be interpreted. The ItCC in particular asked the CJEU to clarify, through an accelerated procedure, whether the disapplication of national limitation rules imposed by the CJEU's judgment was mandatory, even when the effect of the disapplication would result in the infringement of fundamental principles of a Member State's national constitutional identity, as well as of EU and ECHR principles on the fundamental rights of the accused in criminal proceedings.

In light of the stance taken by the ItCC, the CJEU issued in 2017 a second decision,[55] where it rephrased its previous ruling, specifying that "Article 325(1) and (2) TFEU must be interpreted as requiring the national court, in a criminal proceedings for infringements relating to VAT, to disapply national provisions on limitation, forming part of national substantive law, which prevent the application of effective and deterrent criminal penalties in a significant number of cases of serious fraud affecting the fi-

[53] CJEU, *Taricco*, n. 54-57.

[54] The first time was with the ItCC order 207/2013, then followed by CJEU, 26 November 2014, *Mascolo et al.*, and by ItCC judgment 187/2016, on which see above, n. 5.1 and 5.2.

[55] CJEU, Grand Chamber, 5 December 2017, C-42/2017, *M.A.S. et al.* For a thorough commentary, see the papers collected in Riv. Dir. Comp., 1/2018.

nancial interests of the Union [...] unless that disapplication entails a breach of the principle that offences and penalties must be defined by law because of the lack of precision of the applicable law or because of the retroactive application of legislation imposing conditions of criminal liability stricter than those in force at the time the infringement was committed".[56]

Following this judgment, the ItCC ruled with its order n. 115/2018 that the claim of unconstitutionality raised by the Milan Court of Appeal and the Court of Cassation was manifestly unfounded.

Of the countless observations that could be made on the *Taricco* saga – from the limits of the EU modes of harmonization in criminal law, to the lack of comparative awareness in the European legal orders about divergences between national traditions –, what should be stressed for our purposes is the elaborate approach taken by the ItCC to disentangle, in its order n. 24/2017, the many conflicts arising from the case. The *Taricco* litigation actually involved not only a conflict between different sets of rights (those of the accused versus those of society at large in regard to the prosecution of crimes), but also a conflict between the interests of different actors (Member States' national sovereignty v. EU's financial interests), and between multiple normative systems (the domestic, the EU, and the ECHR ones).

Dealing with such complexity, the ItCC made use of all the argumentative styles and paths highlighted by our quantitative analysis. Order n. 24/2017 opens with the ItCC's commitment to deference to EU law and the CJEU, reminding readers that "recognition of the primacy of EU law is undisputed in this court's case-law",[57] and that "it is certainly not the task of this Court to give to Art. 325 TFUE a meaning other than that provided to it by the CJEU".[58]

Such assertions of respect, however, are immediately qualified by ItCC's careful but steady boundary-marking exercise. In the ItCC's words, "this court's case-law has always stressed that application of EU law in Italy is subject to compliance of EU law with the fundamental principles of the Italian constitutional order and people's inalienable rights recognized in the national Constitution. In the very unlikely case that, in a specific instance, such a compliance could not be assured, it would be necessary to declare the unconstitutionality of the national law ratifying the EU Treaties,

---

[56] *Ibid.*, n. 62.

[57] ItCC order 24/2017, n. 2. The decision was widely commented: see, e.g., D. TEGA, *Narrowing the Dialogue: The Italian Constitutional Court and the Court of Justice on the Prosecution of VAT Frauds*, in *Int'l J. Const. L. Blog*, Feb. 14, 2017.

[58] ItCC order 24/2017, n. 5.

insofar as (and only insofar as) that law would give rise to a non-compliance with the national Constitution in that specific instance".[59]

Once it clarified the extent and limits of the applicability of EU law, the ItCC then engaged in a detailed review of the place of the legality principle in criminal law within the framework of the Italian Constitution, the Nice Charter, the ECHR, as well as of the "constitutional traditions common to the Member States" under Art. 6(3) TUE.[60] In light of such a review, the ItCC highlighted the problems stemming from the interpretation of Art. 325 TFUE embraced by the CJEU. First, as to the ex post facto shortening of the limitation period mandated by the CJEU's judgment, the ItCC underlined that, under EU law, Member States are free to qualify statutes of limitations as either substantive or procedural rules, and to decide whether to include them within the umbrella of protection of the legality principle, eventually providing higher standards of protection than those found in EU law.[61] Second, with regard to the requirement of criminal law being sufficiently precise, the ItCC stressed that this requirement "is common to the constitutional traditions of Member States, and shared by the ECHR system, and therefore expresses a general principle of EU law".[62]

On the basis of such arguments, the ItCC formulated its position of resistance. "Under Art. 4(3) TEU [...], the relationships between the EU and Member States are inspired by the principle of sincere cooperation, which implies mutual respect and assistance. This also entails that the parties are united in diversity. [...] The legitimacy [...] and the force of unity in a legal order qualified by pluralism [...] are grounded in that legal order's capacity to respect that minimum threshold of diversity which is necessary to maintain the national identity reflecting the inner structure of Member States. [...] These ideas have always inspired the actions of both this Court [...] and of the CJEU [....]. Consequently, in principle, EU law and CJEU's judgments [...] cannot be interpreted as imposing Member States to relinquish the fundamental principles of their own constitutional order"[63] – that is, "the constitutional identity of the Member State concerned".[64] The

---

[59] ItCC order 24/2017, n. 2.

[60] *Ibid.*, n. 3-5, 8. For an overview of the meaning of the notion of "constitutional traditions common to the Member States" under Art. 6(3) TUE, see the papers collected in *Riv. Trim. Dir. Pubb.* 4/2017, as well as ItCC judgments 269/2017, and 20, 112 and 117/2019.

[61] ItCC order 24/2017, n. 4.

[62] *Ibid.*, n. 9.

[63] *Ibid.*, n. 6 (my translation).

[64] *Ibid.*, n. 7.

ItCC therefore asked the CJEU whether Art. 325 TFUE and the '*Taricco I*' judgment could be read in a way compatible with the Italian constitutional legal order.

The language was tactful, but the ItCC was conveying a serious message. As the subsequent CJEU's partial overruling of the '*Taricco I*' judgment makes clear, the CJEU listened to that message carefully.

12.5. Conclusion

All the above – the numerical survey of 2016 ItCC decisions, as well as the overview of the *Taricco* litigation – shows the ItCC's complex 'relationality' within the Euro-local space, where the ItCC is called to mediate among a multitude of actors and interests.

The concrete outcomes of these interactions are multifarious. The ItCC at times resists the Europeanisation pressures exercised from above and below, while on other occasions it spontaneously defers to its Luxembourg- and Strasbourg-based fellows. Sometimes European law provides an additional platform for solving disputes between domestic constituencies (e.g., between the state and the regions, the parliament and the courts), as well as for testing the solidity of local interpretive and political choices. At other times, European supranational law offers a leverage for criticising the internal state of affairs. Still at other times, facing European supranational legal orders gives the ItCC the opportunity to identify and defend national specificities.

What remains constant throughout these postures and discourses is the ItCC's effort to balance dialogue with tension. As in life, tension without dialogue would be dangerous, but dialogue without tension would be dramatically meaningless.

Chapter XIII

EUROPEAN RELATIONALITY IN THE EUROPEAN LEGAL SPACE: COUNTRY-SPECIFIC MIXTURES WITHIN ONE EUROPEAN STYLE

Patricia Popelier

13.1. Relationality in the European legal space: an Italian feature, or a European device?

Has the Italian Constitutional Court (ItCC) developed a specific, Italian style of adjudication, labeled 'relationality'? In her chapter, Marta Infantino substantiates this claim for the ItCC's position towards the European Court of Justice (ECJ) and the European Court of Human Rights (ECtHR). She describes the 'relationality' of the ItCC within the European legal space as a combination of 'pride, respect and resistance': an emphasis on the autonomy of its own jurisdiction, respect for European law, and resistance where European law interferes too intensely with the values and traditions of the Italian legal system.

Is this, however, a typical feature of the Italian Constitutional Court, or a device of all Constitutional Courts within the European legal space? The latter seems more likely, as studies have already revealed that both the ECHR and EU law play an important role in the case law of various European constitutional courts.[1] These courts have in common, as Infantino admits, that they are all confronted with the same problem of compromising between facilitating the implementation of EU and ECHR law in the national system,

[1] E. MAK, *Judicial Decision-making in a Globalised World: A Comparative Analysis of the Changing Practices of Western Highest Courts,* Oxford, Hart Publishing, 2013.

on the one hand, and protecting constitutional norms and values on the other. This compromising will sometimes result in a more deferential attitude, at other times in a more opposing one. In this mixture, the main accent may differ. Hence, some Courts, such as the German and some Central and Eastern European Courts, are at the forefront of a more oppositional movement, while others adopt a more 'Europe friendly' posture. Often, however, the most eye-catching judgments are referred to, whereby one more 'rebellious' judgment may outshine a more common stream of compliant judgments.

Where the emphasis is put may differ from one country to another. Within one country, this emphasis may evolve over time and may be different for relations with the ECJ compared to the ECtHR. Various factors may explain these differences within one legal system and across borders.[2] For example, courts in Central and Eastern European countries are often Strasbourg-friendly because, as post-authoritarian systems, they adopt standards for human rights protection which have been lacking in their own legal order; whereas, having only recently regained their sovereignty, they tend to be more critical towards the ECJ's efforts to establish EU supremacy. Whether the Constitutional Court may rely on its own legacy is also a matter of age. For example, the Belgian Constitutional Court, established only in the 1980s, does not hesitate to refer to the ECtHR to give legitimacy to its decisions, whereas the German Constitutional Court, having developed a high standard of fundamental rights protection throughout many decades, is more hesitant to do so. Attitudes are also case-specific. For example, it is reported that even the most Strasbourg-friendly countries turn against the ECtHR as soon as the latter interferes in sensitive social or cultural issues.[3]

Confirming that all European Courts display an attitude of 'relationality,' combining three different approaches, and explaining what determines the emphasis on 'pride,' 'respect,' or 'resistance,' require a comprehensive study, with empirical, quantitative and qualitative data over time for a large set of legal systems. Therefore, this article is confined to placing another example next to the Italian case study, to demonstrate that the 'relationality' approach is not unique to the Italian Constitutional Court. I select the Belgian case study for two reasons. One reason is that I have a large set of

---

[2] Several hypotheses to explain the different attitudes of states towards the European Court of Human Rights are identified in P. POPELIER, S. LAMBRECHT, K. LEMMENS, *Introduction: Purpose and Structure, Categorisation of States and Hypotheses*, in P. POPELIER, S. LAMBRECHT, K. LEMMENS (eds), *Criticism of the European Court of Human Rights,* Cambridge, Intersentia, 2016, 10-20.

[3] *Ibid* at p. 16.

data at my disposal. For another project, we have coded all (final) judgments of the Belgian Constitutional Court (BCC) in the period from 1985 (when the first decision was pronounced) until the end of 2015. Infantino analyses only one year, 2016, which is no longer recorded in our database. For the sake of comparison, I applied her analysis to the Belgian Court's decisions in 2016, but, as this is merely a snapshot, I will situate the results in the larger set of data, and with reference to earlier studies on the BCC's position towards the European Courts. Secondly, I selected the BCC because it is commonly regarded as a very Europe-friendly court.[4] Nonetheless, if my expectation is that all European Courts show an attitude of relationality combining the three different approaches, then even the Belgian Constitutional Court should display a more critical attitude in specific cases.

13.2. The Belgian Constitutional Court's approach towards the European courts in 2016

In 2016, the BCC was less active than the ItCC: it pronounced 170 decisions following either an annulment request (whether or not accompanied by a request to suspend the challenged act) or a preliminary question. It is relevant to note that the BCC can only decide on Parliamentary acts. Also, it has limited jurisdiction as to reference norms. Until 1988 it could only resolve disputes concerning the allocation of powers to the federal state or the state authorities (Communities and Regions). From 1988 on, it could also review Acts of Parliament against the equality and non-discrimination clause (currently Art. 10-11 of the Belgian Constitution) and the rights and duties concerning education (currently Art. 24 of the Belgian Constitution). As the BCC, through the equality and non-discrimination clause, covered all fundamental rights issues, its jurisdiction was, in 2003, extended to (most) fundamental rights clauses in the Belgian Constitution. The Belgian constituent deliberately excluded international acts as reference norms, as the Belgian Supreme Court (Court of Cassation) established in 1971 that all courts have the power to review Acts of Parliament against European and international norms with direct effect.[5] This, however, did not dissuade the BCC from indirectly reviewing acts against such norms, linked with the equality or non-discrimination clause or with fundamental rights provisions.

[4] According to M. Claes, *The National Courts' Mandate in the European Constitution,* Oxford, Hart Publishing, 2006, 641: it is 'the least protective and most *communautaire* of all constitutional courts'.

[5] Cass. 27 May 1971, *Pas.* 1971, I, 886.

For the sake of comparison, in what follows, this section adopts the structure of the Italian paper for a quantitative description of the use of European law in the case law of the BCC in 2016.

13.2.1. The demand side for europeanisation

In 74 out of 170 judgments, the requesting parties or the referring court claimed a violation of either EU law (9 judgments) or ECHR law (47 judgments) alone or both (19 judgments). At the level of pleas,[6] violation of EU law alone was claimed 22 times, ECHR law 91 times, and a combination of both 20 times. In 3 judgments, the requesting parties asked the Constitutional Court to refer a preliminary question to the Court of Justice, which was refused in all cases.

Hence, parties in Belgium are more inclined to turn to European law to support their claims, compared to Italian litigants (43,5% vs 31%). ECHR law is more often invoked than EU law (22% vs 35%). Two reasons may explain this. First, the Constitutional Court has for the large part turned into a fundamental rights court. This makes the ECHR a more obvious reference document. Increasingly, the Court invokes the EU Charter of fundamental rights. Invoking the ECHR, however, has the advantage of securing access to the European Court of Human Rights. Second, the application of EU law requires a cross-border element that is often not present in the case at hand.

Graph 1. Share EU/ECHR.

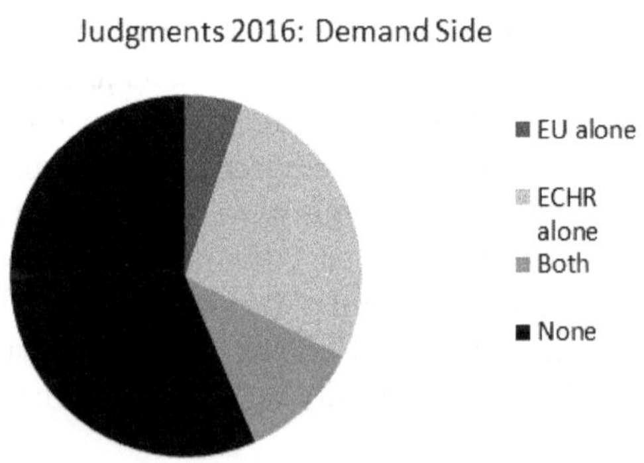

[6] Counted as (re)structured by the Court.

Of these 74 judgments, 39 were pronounced following an annulation request, 32 following a preliminary question, and 3 following a suspension request. Most of the preliminary questions were raised by first-instance tribunals (23),[7] followed by courts of appeal (11), with the Supreme Court (3), the Council of State (1) and another administrative court (1) rounding off the rest. The types of petitioners of annulation (or suspension) requests varied. In most cases (21), the petitioners were NGOs, followed by individuals (20). Business undertakings were petitioners in 8 cases. Finally, in 3 cases, the petitioners were decentralized public bodies: a local town, or an autonomous agency. Most often, they came in groups of 2 to more than 20. In several cases (18), the petitioners were a mix of types.

Graph 2. Petitioners.

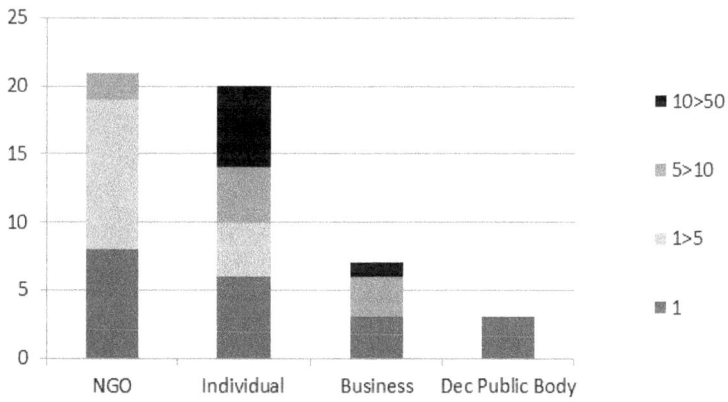

The domains are varied, with Labor and social security law on top (12) together with and Judicial organization and procedure, including procedures in administrative courts (11); followed by Tax law (9), Environment, energy, spatial planning and other administrative law (9), Substantive and procedural criminal law (8); Persons and family law (7) and Commercial and financial law (5); and at the tail Fundamental rights and privacy (4); the Law of property, special contracts and tort (3); Educational law (2); Public health (2); Migration law (1) and Animal protection (1).

[7] 17 courts of first instances, 3 labour tribunals, 2 criminal courts, 1 justice of the peace.

Graph 3. Domains.

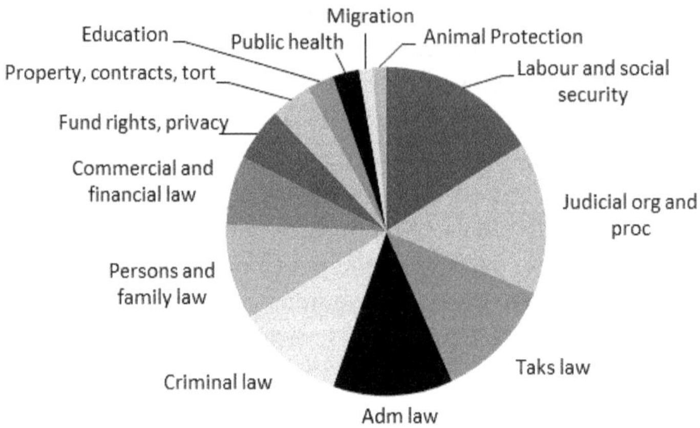

These figures depict a high sensitivity of European law in society and industry, especially with regard to the Convention system, to a lesser degree with regard to EU law.

13.2.2. Judicial encounters with European legal orders

Out of 170 judgments pronounced in 2016, the BCC used European law in its reasoning in 57 judgments – outnumbering the ItCC both in absolute numbers (57 vs 39 judgments) and in terms of percentage (33,5% vs 13%). Unlike the ItCC, the BCC referred to the Convention system more often than to EU law. EU law was referred to in 21 cases; the ECHR in 46. Of these, EU law and the ECHR were both mentioned in 8 judgments. The preference for the ECHR is even more salient at the level of pleas. The BCC referred to the ECHR in reply to 73 different pleas and to the EU in 29 different pleas; in 4 cases, EU law and the ECHR were combined in one plea.

Graph 4. Share EU/ECHR.

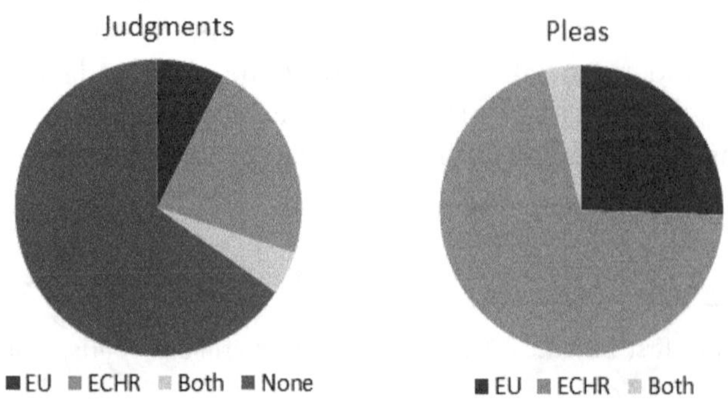

In 21 cases, the BCC did not respond to the parties' arguments regarding European law. Reasons are manifold: the case is already decided on the basis of one plea based on national law, so there is no need to respond to other pleas that refer to European law; the plea is answered on the basis of national law and using European law would not lead to a different reasoning; European (mostly EU) law is not applicable to the case; or the case is handled without judging the merits of the case. At the level of pleas, the BCC did not go into the claim that European law was violated in 46 cases out of a total of 143 pleas; in 9 additional cases of combined pleas, it only referred to either EU or ECHR law.

Conversely, in 7 judgments, the BCC used European law, even if the referring court or requesting parties did not (explicitly) refer to it. Sometimes European law only plays a secondary role in the reasoning. Often, however, the reference is more intense, including quotations from the ECJ (15 judgments)[8] or the ECtHR (40 judgments). In several judgments, more than 20 different ECtHR judgments were referred to.

Of these 59 judgments, the BCC decided on the merits in 55 cases. Of these 55, the Court found at least one violation in 25 judgments and no violation in 30 cases. The high level of findings of violations are somewhat nuanced when we look at the level of pleas: out of 99 pleas that invoked European law and led to a decision on the merits with reference to European law, 74 were rejected and 25 were considered well-founded . Hence, while the Court finds a violation in 45% of the judgments, it only finds a violation in 25% of the pleas.

Similar to the Italian experience, invoking EU law seems to improve the success rate at the BCC. Within the sample of 55 judgments, European law was invoked in 48. The Court found at least one violation in 4 out of 5 judgments where only EU law was invoked (80%); in 14 out of 31 judgments where only the ECHR was invoked (45%); and in 5 out of 14 combined judgments (36%). However, an analysis at the level of pleas within these 48 judgments moderates the picture. The Court found a violation in 5 out of 16 pleas where only EU law was invoked (31%); in 16 out of 67 pleas where only the ECHR was invoked (24%); and in 4 out of 16 combined pleas (25%). Here, the success rate is still higher when EU law is referred to, but less outspoken.

---

[8] Of which 2 concerned the ECJ's answer to a preliminary question asked by the BCC.

Graph 5. Outcome judgments.

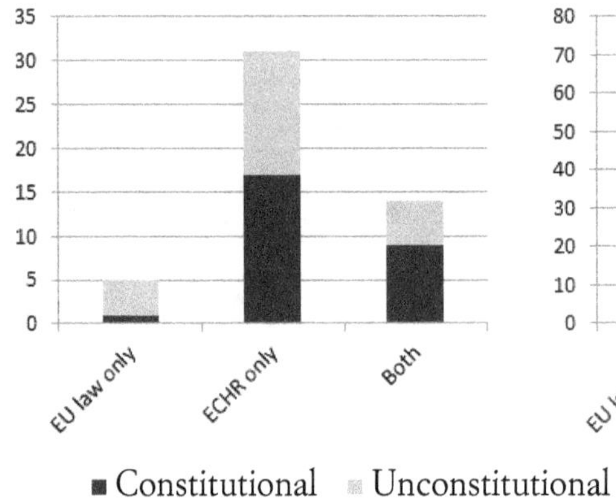

Graph 6. Outcome pleas.

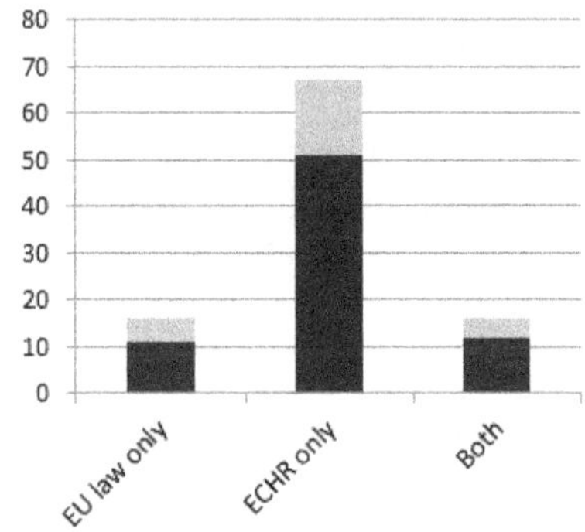

Interestingly, the BCC has a particular preference for turning to European law in salient cases. To identify salient cases, I used the three criteria developed by De Jaegere:[9] (1) media attention before the pronouncement of the decision (+1 press article); (2) parties involved in the litigation, including intervening and defending parties (+5 individuals or +2 types of litigants) and (3) referral to the full bench. In 2016, 5 cases met all three requirements and can therefor be labeled as highly salient.[10] The BCC referred to European law in all of them: the ECHR in all 5, EU law in only one. In 4 of them, the European Courts were quoted: all of these quoted the ECtHR, while one also quoted the ECJ. It seems, then, that the BCC considers European law as a tool to legitimize decisions and support their outcome in highly salient cases, when it expects not only the litigants, but also the press and the larger public to carefully scrutinize the judgment. The same observation can be made if we also include moderately salient cases, combining media attention with either party number or variety, or referral to the full bench: the BCC uses European law in 9 out of 11 (highly and moderately) salient cases. In most of the highly salient cases, the BCC rejects all claims; only in 1 case out of 5 did it find a violation. If we also include the low salient cases, the picture is different, with at least one finding of a violation in 4 cases out of 9. The latter figure aligns with the overall proportion of judgments where the Court finds at least one violation.

[9] J. De Jaegere, *Judicial Review and Strategic Behaviour*, Cambridge, Intersentia, 2019, 127-128.

[10] Constitutional Court Nos 2/2016, 12/2016, 53/2016, 130/2016 and 152/2016.

13.2.3. European relationality at work in 2016

What these figures tell us about the BCC 'relational' attitude in 2016 is that at the Belgian Court as well, a combination of 'pride, respect and resistance' can be found, but in a different order of relevance compared to Italy. While in Italy the Court is most anxious to point out the self-sufficiency of the Italian legal system, the Belgian Court is more open to engage with European law in a predominantly respectful way.

Respect – Considering the number of cases in which European law is used and the regular quotations of European case law, the BCC is clearly respectful of European law, in particular when compared to the ItCC. It is favorable towards integrating both European law and European case law into the national constitutional order, especially when deciding highly salient cases. In this way, the Court recognizes the multilevel nature of the Belgian constitutional order.

Pride – On the other hand, most cases are still decided without reference to European law. Moreover, in 38% of the pleas that invoke European law, the Court does not or only partially (in combined pleas) take that law into account. Also, the Court turned down the request to refer a preliminary question to the ECJ, arguing that it was able to apply the provisions of EU law itself without room for doubt. [11] This might indicate that the Court is also affirmative of the autonomy of Belgian law, although in a less explicit way compared to the ItCC. Moreover, in 2016, the Court for the first time explicitly joined the wave of European constitutional courts that uphold the constitutional identity doctrine. In one specific judgment pronounced in 2016, the BCC found the request inadmissible, but added in its reasoning that 'under no circumstances does Art. 34 of the Constitution allow discriminatory infringement of the national identity inherent to the political and constitutional basic structures or the core values that the Constitution confers to individuals.' [12]

Resistance – In 2016, no judgment was pronounced in which the BCC was openly critical towards the implementation of EU law or the ECHR. The reference to the constitutional identity doctrine, however, although only an *obiter dictum*, heralds the new, more combative position of the Belgian Constitutional Court towards European law that encroaches upon national values.

---

[11] Const. Court N° 125/2016, 6 October 2016, para. 39.1.

[12] Const. Court N° 62/2016, 28 April 2016, para. B.8.7.

As mentioned, the analysis of judgments pronounced in 2016 merely provides a snapshot. The question is whether the results fit in a more global attitude of 'European relationality.' This is considered in the next section.

13.3. The Belgian Constitutional Court's approach towards the European courts in the long-term

In what follows, we look for signs of respect, pride and resistance in the entire set of judgments, based on qualitative and quantitative analysis. The dataset which we established at the University of Antwerp for the period 1985-2015 was already analyzed and interpreted by Josephine De Jaegere for our project on the strategic behavior of the Belgian Constitutional Court. I refer to her results with regard to the BCC's quotation behavior.

13.3.1. Respect

The BCC started to refer to European law in 1990. This is linked with its jurisdiction: before that time, the Court was a Court of Arbitration, limited to intra-federal conflicts of competence. Despite the fact that the Court can only review directly against domestic provisions and only indirectly against international and European law, the BCC explicitly presented itself in one of its judgment as a 'guardian of EU law'. [13]

Still, until 2000, the BCC was rather reluctant to cite ECtHR and ECJ case law. A shift came first in 2000 for ECtHR case law and next in 2006-2007 for both European courts. Overall, in the period 1985-2015, the Court quoted the ECJ in 5% and the ECtHR in 10% of the cases. However, over time, the BCC increasingly refers to both European law and European case law. [14] By the end of this period, the ECHR was referred to in 40% and the ECtHR in 35% of the cases; EU law in 20% and the ECJ in 10% of the cases.

The ECtHR is most abundantly quoted in domains of persons and family law, criminal law and – less visible in the 2016 sample – migration issues, whereas the ECJ is mostly quoted in domains of environmental and energy law. [15] This, of course, is linked with the respective jurisdictions of the European courts. De Jaegere finds an additional explanation in the behavior of petitioners. Interest groups build their claims with references to the

---

[13] Const. Court No 151/2003, 26 November 2003.

[14] J. De Jaegere, *Judicial Review and Strategic Behaviour*, *supra* note 9, 246-250.

[15] *Ibid* 249-250.

ECHR, whereas business companies, often involved in cases concerning the environment and energy, are more likely to refer to EU law.[16]

De Jaegere also confirms the results of the 2016 sample with regard to highly salient cases. In these cases, the Court takes more care of substantiating its reasoning with references to advisory opinions of the Council of State, political agreements and scientific evidence, but also to case law of the European courts: the ECJ and the ECtHR are cited three times as often as in regular cases.[17] In almost all these cases, the scrutiny against European law was demanded by the litigants.[18] Even the factor of deliberation in plenary session alone, already leads to a higher reference rate to European courts and especially the ECtHR.[19] Reversely, if parties invoke EU and ECHR law, the Court is more likely to refer the case to the plenary session.[20] This means that the Court not only tends to quote European Courts more often in politically salient cases, but also in cases that are salient from a purely legal point of view: if petitioners refer to European law, judges may prefer a broader legal deliberation.

Another indication of the Court's commitment to European law is its referencing behavior. The Belgian Constitutional Court refers the most preliminary questions to the ECJ compared to other constitutional courts – 28 in the period 1985-2017 –, and was the first of its kind to do so.[21]

Finally, specific examples chronicle the Court's positive attitude towards European law as well as the European Courts. For example, the BCC reversed its jurisprudence following the ECtHR's case law, adding a proportionality test where earlier it argued that the legislator may freely determine the amount of a criminal or administrative fine.[22] In a doctrinal article, Paul Martens, then President of the BCC, noted that the Court 'without even the slightest inclination to resist' reverses its case law if necessary to comply with the ECtHR and has already suspended its decision to await the outcome of a pending case before the Strasbourg Court.[23]

---

[16] *Ibid* 249-250.

[17] *Ibid* 274.

[18] *Ibid* 274.

[19] *Ibid* 271.

[20] *Ibid* 155.

[21] See Court of Justice of the European Union, *Annual Report 2016 – Judicial Activity,* Luxembourg, 2017, 109-111.

[22] Compare Const. Courts No 60/2002, 28 March 2002, No 138/2006, 14 September 2006 and No 8/2007, 11 January 2007 with Const. Court No 81/2007, 7 June 2007. For another example, concerning the inclusion of social security rights in the notion of property: Const. Court No 8/99, 28 January 1999.

[23] P. Martens, *L'influence de la Cour européenne des droits de l'homme sur la Cour constitutionelle*, in *Chroniques de Droit Public* 350 (2010), 356.

Specific examples also show how the BCC tries to link domestic and European constitutional law. For example, while the BCC considered inadmissible requests to review Acts of Parliament against the EU Charter of Fundamental Rights (linked with the equality clause in the Constitution) as long as the Charter did not have binding force,[24] it did take into consideration that document in so far as it confirmed values shared by both the EU and the national constitution.[25]

13.3.2. Pride

The BCC, however, is not always as inviting towards European law. Regularly, it mentions European law because it was invoked as a reference norm but fails to elaborate on it. In particular, when it mentions EU law or the ECHR as a reference norm, it does *not* quote the ECJ or the ECtH in, respectively, 63% and 58% of the cases.[26] Also, in several cases it has refused to send a preliminary reference to the ECJ as requested by the litigants. Scholars have held that requests were turned down even in cases that did leave 'scope for any reasonable doubt.'[27] Added to that is the appeal to the constitutional identity doctrine, as mentioned in the overview of the year 2016, to safeguard domestic constitutional values.

Moreover, the BCC refers questions to the ECJ not only on the interpretation of EU law, but also on its validity. In 8 out of 28 preliminary references, leading to 13 (out of 80) different questions, the validity of EU law was questioned. In one case, the ECJ confirmed that the EU directive in question violated the principle of equal treatment of men and women.[28] Hence, the Courts' preliminary reference behavior is not always an indication of compliance; instead, it is sometimes used as a defense against EU law.

Finally, including European law in the constitutionality test is sometimes part of a 'bringing rights home' strategy. By avoiding subsequent appeals before the ECtHR, an external court that is less familiar with national specificities and sensitivities, the assessment of national legislation remains within the control of the BCC. Also, if the national decision carefully bal-

---

[24] Const. Court No 10/2008, 23 January 2008; No 58/2009, 19 March 2009.

[25] Const. Court No 167/2005, 23 November 2005; Const. Court No 101/2008, 10 July 2008.

[26] See J. DE JAEGERE, *Judicial Review and Strategic Behaviour*, *supra* note 9, 275.

[27] P. VAN NUFFEL, *Het Europees recht in de rechtspraak van het Arbitragehof* (European law in the case law of the Constitutional Court) in A. ALEN (eds.), *20 jaar Arbitragehof*, Antwerp, Kluwer, 2005, 43-45.

[28] C-236/09, *Belgische Verbruikersunie Test-Aankoop*, 1 March 2011.

ances rights and interests in conformity with ECtHR case law, the Strasbourg Court will use more restraint in its own proportionality test.[29]

13.3.3. Resistance

While the BCC positions itself as a very Euro-friendly court, signs of resistance show on particular occasions, although in guarded terms.

On some occasions the BCC refers to an ECJ judgment but does not actually comply with the judgement. One example is the Money Laundering Case, where the Constitutional Court asked the ECJ to rule on the validity of the EU Directive in the light of the right to a fair trial, enshrined in Art. 6 ECHR.[30] The Constitutional Court quoted the ECJ's ruling,[31] concluding that the Law was in conformity, but deviated from the judgment by following the Advocate General's Opinion: it tested the act against Art. 6 as well as Art 8 ECHR and found it in conformity only in so far as it was interpreted in a specific way, that was broader than the interpretation provided by the ECJ. Additionally, it annulled the Law on another point as contrary with art. 6 ECHR, although that provision was also a (not literal) transposition of the EU Directive but had not been included in the preliminary question.[32] Some scholars read a preference for constitutional law over secondary EU law in this judgment.[33] A more explicit objection can be found in the *Bressol* case on access to higher education, where the BCC, in its judgment following a preliminary reference, disputed the ECJ's argument that the risk for disproportionate costs for the financing of higher education was not a decisive factor for treating students differently on the basis of nationality and could therefore not play a role in the justification.[34]

With regard to the ECtHR, deviations are even more covert, but they occur nonetheless. For example, the BCC has complied with the ECtHR *Koua Poirrez* judgment regarding nationality requirements for enjoying so-

---

[29] *Sukhovetskyy v Ukraine* [App No No. 13716/02] 28 March 2006; *Axel Springer AG* [App No 39954/08], 7 February 2012 (Grand Chamber); *von Hannover v Germany (n° 2)* [App No 40660/08, 60641/08] 7 February 2012; *Animal Defenders International v UK* [App No 48876/08] 22 April 2013.

[30] Const. Court No 126/2005, 13 July 2005.

[31] Case C-305/05, *Ordre des barreaux francophones et germanophone and others* [2007] ECR I-5305.

[32] Const. Court No 10/2008, 23 January 2008.

[33] E. CLOOTS, *Het Grondwettelijk Hof en de toetsing van secundair Unierecht aan fundamentele rechten*, in A. ALEN, J. VAN NIEUWENHOVE (eds.), *Leuvense Staatsrechtelijke Standpunten*, Bruges, die Keure, 2008, 50-52.

[34] Const Court No 89/2011, 31 May 2011.

cial security rights regarding aliens registered in the population register, but not concerning aliens registered in the register of foreign nationals.[35] In an article written by a judge of the BCC and two law clerks, it has been pointed out that to this point, the BCC has not felt that its effectiveness was jeopardized by Strasbourg case law,[36] which suggests that the BCC's position towards the ECtHR might shift as soon as this happens.[37]

Finally, as mentioned, the explicit reference to the constitutional identity doctrine holds the potential for more defiant behavior were European law to infringe upon sensitive domestic constitutional values.

13.4. Conclusion

The European relationality approach is presented as a mix of approaches taken by the Constitutional Court towards European law. These approaches range from a respectful attitude, over the concern for the autonomy of domestic law, to resistance. In this reply, I hold the assumption that this mix, in varying degrees, is present in all European constitutional courts and I used the Belgian Constitutional Court as a case study. While the Belgian Court is clearly a Europe-friendly court, it also safeguards the autonomy of domestic constitutional law and it even conceals the seeds for resistance. Key in the European 'relational' approach is a commitment to enter into dialogue with the European Courts. This does not necessarily imply subordination to European law; on the contrary, as was argued in the paper, it can be strategically used to avoid interference by the European courts.

The reason why the emphasis is on 'respect' in one country and on 'pride' in another, can be explained by a combination of structural, political, cultural and institutional reasons. For example, the Belgian Constitutional Court was established only in the 1980s and had to position itself amongst pre-existing national and European courts. The use of European law empowered the Belgian Constitutional Court, whose jurisdiction was very limited in its initial years. A study showed that structural factors such as population size, willingness to litigate, and Member State compliance

[35] Const. Court No 92/2004, 19 May 2004; Const. Court No 153/2007, 12 December 2007.

[36] A. ALEN, K. MUYLLE, W. VERRIJDT, *De verhouding tussen het grondwettelijk hof en het Europees hof voor de Rechten van de mens*, in A. ALEN, J. THEUNIS (eds.), *Leuvense Staatsrechtelijke Standpunten – Deel 3,* Bruges, die Keure, 2012, 16.

[37] More elaborated on the BCC position towards the ECtHR: P. POPELIER, *Belgium: Faithful, Obedient, and Just a Little Irritated*, in P. POPELIER, S. LAMBRECHT, K. LEMMENS (eds), *Criticism of the European Court of Human Rights, op. cit.*, 117-128.

with EU law partly but not entirely explain variations in reference behavior to the ECJ.[38] In another study, already mentioned in the introduction to this paper, we explained the different attitudes of countries towards the European Court of human rights, from Strasbourg-friendly to Strasbourg-suspicious, on the basis of several factors, such as familiarity with constitutional review, historical legacy, the behavior of the European Court in sensitive domestic issues, political power relations, the tradition of rule of law, and the perceived legitimacy of the European Courts.[39] Probably, similar factors also explain why one court is more open towards the influence of EU law and more willing to enter into dialogue with the ECJ compared to other courts. For example, invoking ECJ case law and referring preliminary questions to the ECJ is only useful as a strategy to give legitimacy to the Constitutional Court's ruling and safeguard compliance if in that country the public is supportive of the EU.

In this mixture of attitudes, Constitutional Courts have become crucial agents to find a balance between autonomy claims and the need for efficiency and coherence, between differentiation and integration.

---

[38] M. BROBERG, N. FENGER, *Are Structural Factors (Part of)) the Explanation?*, in 19 *European Law Journal*, No. 4, 488 (2013).

[39] P. POPELIER, S. LAMBRECHT, K. LEMMENS, *Introduction: Purpose and Structure, Categorisation of States and Hypotheses*, *op. cit.*, 10-20.

CONCLUSION

Chapter XIV

POWER IS PERFECTED IN WEAKNESS: ON THE AUTHORITY OF THE ITALIAN CONSTITUTIONAL COURT

Armin von Bogdandy and Davide Paris *

SUMMARY: 14.1. The idea of "strength in weakness". – 14.2. Limited access. – 14.3. Low profile. – 14.4. Adverse environment. – 14.5. Playing poker.

14.1. The idea of "strength in weakness"

"That is not how we expected it to turn out" – so the first Federal Chancellor of Western Germany, Konrad Adenauer, reportedly said when observing the very first years of the German Constitutional Court's operation.[1] These words succinctly express a peculiar feature of the German Constitutional Court. A direct confrontation with the political power was the foundational moment of the Court's authority – a confrontation in which the Court achieved a shining victory that let it emerge as a counterbalance to the ruling majority. In 1952 and 1953, two events marked this confrontation in a particular way.[2] First, in the battle over Germany's rearmament, the Court was thrust into center stage with regards to the highly political question of whether ratification of the European Defence Community Treaty required a previous constitutional amendment. The Court was able to resist political pressure from the ruling majority and the opposition, whi-

---

* We had the opportunity to discuss some of the ideas expressed in this paper in the research meeting "Relationality and Hierarchy in Constitutional Justice: *Bundesverfassungsgericht* and *Corte costituzionale* as Two Models of Constitutional Courts?" at the Max Planck Institute for Comparative Public Law and International Law in Heidelberg, 9 July 2018. We would like to thank all participants, and in particular Justices Marta Cartabia and Peter M. Huber, for their valuable insights. Many thanks to Desirée Schmitt and Lucas Humbel for language editing. The usual disclaimers apply. The research leading to this paper was supported by the German Research Foundation (DFG) in the context of the Gottfried Wilhelm Leibniz Prize.

[1] Original: "Dat ham wir uns so nich vorjestellt", see C. SCHÖNBERGER, *Anmerkungen zu Karlsruhe*, in C. SCHÖNBERGER, M. JESTAEDT, O. LEPSIUS, C. MÖLLERS, *Das entgrenzte Gericht*, Berlin, Suhrkamp, 2011, 26.

[2] C. SCHÖNBERGER, *Anmerkungen zu Karlsruhe*, *supra* note 1, 21 ff.

ch both had to accept at great costs that the Constitutional Court could not be used for political purposes. Second, the Constitutional Court was able to break the administrative dependence on and supervision by the Ministry of Justice in the "status-battle": it became acknowledged as a constitutional organ alongside the Federal President, the *Bundestag*, the Federal Government, and the *Bundesrat.*[3]

Things went differently in Italy. The foundational judgment 1/1956 – the "Italian *Marbury v. Madison*"[4] – was not a direct challenge to the political power: the time for direct confrontation with the political power would come about 40 years later. After all, judgment 1/1956 struck down a fascist statute limiting the freedom of expression. The ruling majority at the time was probably happy to continue to silently take advantage of this and similar pieces of repressive legislation, but it certainly would not have openly defended an illiberal fascist provision. Instead of challenging the political power, judgment 1/1956 was a straightforward challenge to the authority of the Supreme Court. On the one hand, the Constitutional Court held as unconstitutional a statute that the Supreme Court had previously upheld under the Constitution, thereby validating the lower "rebelling" courts right. On the other hand, it swept away the two core doctrines of constitutional review that the Supreme Court had developed in previous years. First, the Constitutional Court rejected the doctrine that pre-constitutional legislation escapes the jurisdiction of the Constitutional Court, stating that all statutes are subject to its review no matter whether enacted before or after the Constitution. Second, it rebutted the distinction between prescriptive and programmatic norms, stressing that both can serve as a yardstick for constitutional review.

The authority-building paths of the German and the Italian Constitutional Court, however, do not only differ with regard to their respective main contender – the highest political or judicial powers[5] – but also with regard to

---

[3] For a historical account of these two foundational confrontations see U. WESEL, *Der Gang nach Karlsruhe. Das Bundesverfassungsgericht in der Geschichte der Bundesrepublik*, München, Karl Blessing, 2004, 54-82. In English: J. COLLINGS, *Democracy's Guardians. A History of the German Federal Constitutional Court 1951-2001*, Oxford, Oxford University Press, 2015, 9-28.

[4] V. BARSOTTI, P.G. CAROZZA, M. CARTABIA, A. SIMONCINI, *Italian Constitutional Justice in Global Context*, Oxford, Oxford University Press, 2016, 30 (but see also 236).

[5] To be sure, the German Constitutional Court too had to face a strong confrontation with the Supreme Court in the first years of its existence, in particular in the battle on the *Stellungnahmeverfahren* (see A. FARAHAT, *Das Bundesverfassungsgericht*, in A. VON BOGDANDY, C. GRABENWARTER, P.M. HUBER (eds.), *Handbuch Ius Publicum Europaeum. Band VI. Verfassungsgerichtsbarkeit in Europa: Institutionen*, Heidelberg, Müller, 2016, 92). However, this does not seem to have had the same foundational meaning for the Court's identity as the confrontation with the political power.

the outcome. There is no doubt that by issuing judgment 1/1956, the Italian Constitutional Court scored in the confrontation with the Supreme Court. But less than ten years later, in the so-called 'first war of the courts', the Constitutional Court failed to achieve another victory over the Supreme Court. At stake was the Constitutional Court's attempt to make its own interpretation of the law accepted by the Supreme Court. In the end, this attempt was unsuccessful, and the Constitutional Court was forced to back down. The Court justified this result with the new doctrine of the "living law".[6] Essentially, this means that the Constitutional Court must review laws as interpreted by the Supreme Court and cannot replace that interpretation with its own.

On that occasion, the Italian Constitutional Court experienced its own weakness in the clearest manifestation: unlike other constitutional courts, the Italian Constitutional Court has to share and bargain its authority with the ordinary courts, on which both its activity and its effectiveness are conditional. Indeed, the Court's most important power – the concrete review of legislation – depends on the willingness of the ordinary courts to refer questions of constitutionality to it. Similarly, the success of many decisions of the Constitutional Court is contingent on their acceptance by the ordinary (including the administrative) courts.

However, what appears to be the Italian Constitutional Court's main weakness if compared to its German counterpart, is perhaps the Court's most remarkable feature. Its institutional weakness led the Italian Constitutional Court to establish a well-functioning cooperation with the ordinary courts. This "interjudicial relationality" can be considered the most defining strength of the Italian system of constitutional adjudication, as the book by Vittoria Barsotti, Paolo Carozza, Marta Cartabia and Andrea Simoncini illustrates.[7]

The phrase "power is perfected in weakness"[8] captures this essential feature of the Italian Constitutional Court. The logic of 'power in weakness,' however, goes beyond the Constitutional Court's relationship with the ordinary courts. In the following sections, we try to provide a reading of the Italian Constitutional Court according to the *fil-rouge* of weakness that turns in-

[6] See judgments 11/1965 and 52/1965 as well as judgments 127/1966 and 49/1970.

[7] V. Barsotti, P.G. Carozza, M. Cartabia, A. Simoncini, *Italian Constitutional Justice in Global Context*, *supra* note 4, 236.

[8] 2 Corinthians 12:9. Readers familiar with the Pauline epistles are likely to object our use of Saint Paul's words in this chapter because the meaning of these words in the original context clearly diverges from the one that we attribute them here. However, we decided to pick up this formula for its ability to convey like no other a clear concept on the relationship between weakness and power in a very succinct way. But the analogy does not go any further than this and any other comparison with the original text exceeds the authors' will.

to strength, which binds together the topics that have been discussed in this book by Italian scholars and external observers.

With regard to access to the Court, the Court was able to overcome some limits of its constitutional regulation in a way that now raises the question of whether a constitutional amendment would still be desirable. The Court's rather minimalist style of reasoning and its overall low-profile standing in public opinion seems, at first sight, to be a weakness, but in reality it may not be, for these features present some advantages, too. The weakness of the political context in which the Court operates, and notably the unresponsiveness of the legislature, could have been an obstacle to the Court's power. But in the end, it pushed the Court to become more activist and to surpass the role of a "negative legislator". Finally, the dynamic of "strength in weakness" can be applied to interaction with the European courts as well: despite several limitations, the Court was able to gain a significant role in the European legal space.

Throughout this contribution, the German Constitutional Court will frequently serve as the main comparative reference, as it already did in this introduction. Even though the Italian and German Constitutional Courts share the status of being among the oldest constitutional courts in Europe, as well as having a similar historical background (both courts were established as post-authoritarian institutions), the German Constitutional Court seems to represent a very different – if not opposite – model. Both in the way they built their authority and in their relationships with other authorities, at the domestic as well as at the European level,[9] the two models strongly differentiate themselves. Thus, comparison with a contrasting approach will help to better grasp the essence of the Italian way.

This chapter shows the remarkable way that the Italian Constitutional Court built its authority on a weak legal basis, which is particularly visible when compared with its German counterpart. However, this is not meant to be an acritical defense of the Italian Court: our purpose is to stress some characteristics. Furthermore, one should not forget that the path from weakness to strength can be reversed. This is a realistic scenario in Europe, as the Hungarian Constitutional Court has demonstrated.[10]

[9] In this way, this paper responds to Marta Cartabia's suggestion to move towards "a new taxonomy of constitutional courts [...] elaborated on the basis of their general attitude towards other actors": see M. CARTABIA, *Of Bridges and Walls: The "Italian Style" of Constitutional Adjudication*, in 8 *Italian Journal of Public Law*, Issue 1, 37 (2016), 43.

[10] See L. SÓLYOM, *The Rise and Decline of Constitutional Culture in Hungary*, in A. VON BOGDANDY, P. SONNEVEND (eds.), *Constitutional Crisis in the European Constitutional Area. Theory, Law and Politics in Hungary and Romania*, Munich-Oxford-Baden-Baden, Beck-Hart-Nomos, 2015, 5 ff.

14.2. Limited access

The lack of direct constitutional complaint to the Italian Constitutional Court amounts to its most apparent weakness: it renders the Court's authority contingent upon the cooperation of the ordinary courts. This forced cooperation may be difficult to grasp for a German constitutional law scholar. In Germany, the concept of "judicial dialogue" refers to the interaction of the Constitutional Court with the European Courts, and not, as in Italy, to the relationship with the ordinary courts as well.

Since its seminal *Lüth* judgment, [11] the German Constitutional Court does not, in principle, *cooperate* with the ordinary courts but rather *corrects* them. This is a conscious decision. The procedure under Art. 100 para. 1 of the Basic Law (*konkrete Normenkontrolle*) is very similar to the Italian incidental method of judicial review. However, the German Constitutional Court set the bar for raising a question of constitutionality so high that it discouraged all courts from making use of it. [12] The underlying logic is that it wants to be at the top of the judicial system. The constitutional complaint (*Verfassungsbeschwerde*) is foremost a complaint against a judgment (*Urteilsbeschwerde*), in which the Constitutional Court reviews whether ordinary courts, by their application of the law, violated the fundamental rights enshrined in the Constitution. [13] Additionally, there is no advantage for rebelling courts to not follow the jurisprudence of the German Constitutional Court: this might lead a Chamber of the Constitutional Court to quickly quash the decision for its arbitrariness, something that hardly any judge is willing to have on his or her track record.

To be clear, this does not mean that ordinary courts' judgments are mostly reversed. The German Constitutional Court only reverses a tiny percentage of the ordinary courts' decisions. [14] However, it is the general attitude towards ordinary courts – correction vs. cooperation – that illustrates the difference between the two Courts. Whereas the Italian Constitutional

---

[11] BVerfGE 7, 198 (15 January 1958).

[12] See J. LUTHER, *Die italienische Verfassungsgerichtsbarkeit*, Baden-Baden, Nomos, 1990, 82 ff., stressing the more flexible interpretation of the requirements to raise a question of constitutionality in Italy than in Germany.

[13] According to the *Annual Statistics 2017* (available in English at www.bundesverfassungsgericht.de), 5.231 of the 5.456 constitutional complaints proceedings terminated by the Court in 2017 were directed against a judicial decision (95.88 %).

[14] See M. JESTAEDT, *Verfassungsrecht und einfaches Recht – Verfassungsgerichtsbarkeit und Fachgerichtsbarkeit*, in *Das Deutsche Verwaltungsblatt* 1311 (2001), 1311-1312; and M. JESTAEDT, *Phänomen Bundesverfassungsgericht. Was das Gericht zu dem macht, was es ist*, in C. SCHÖNBERGER, M. JESTAEDT, O. LEPSIUS, C. MÖLLERS, *Das entgrenzte Gericht*, *supra* note 1, 94.

Court speaks essentially to the referring courts, the main addressee of the German Constitutional Court's judgments is the individual. The former protects the individual's rights *alongside the ordinary courts*; the latter protects them *from* (among others) *the courts*. The proverbial German expression "Going to Karlsruhe" (*der Gang nach Karlsruhe*).[15] Which refers to finding justice by bringing one's case to the German Constitutional Court, captures this orientation towards the individual in German constitutional justice.

The contribution by Elisabetta Lamarque to this book clearly explains how the Italian Constitutional Court was able to turn this ostensible weakness into an opportunity for a cooperative relationship with the ordinary courts. She also documented how it managed to redress the shortcomings of the limited access to the Court and to fill the most evident gaps in judicial protection without the need for constitutional amendment.

Besides shaping the relationship with the ordinary courts into one of cooperation rather than correction, the lack of constitutional complaints also awards the institutional organization of the Italian Constitutional Court one of its most characteristic features: its collegiality. Always deciding as a whole – "the Constitutional Court" – and having all judges equally and fully involved in every single case help to strengthen the legitimacy of the Court, the consistency of its jurisprudence, and the deliberative and inclusive nature of its adjudication. But this is only possible because the Court deals with some hundreds of references annually. The same level of collegiality would be impossible for the German Constitutional Court, which deals with roughly 6,000 constitutional complaints per year.[16]

In sum, the Italian Constitutional Court built its authority upon a weak competence to the point that a constitutional amendment introducing the individual complaint procedure can nowadays be seriously questioned – as Elisabetta Lamarque and Victor Ferreres Comella do, following the opinion of Roberto Romboli. The expected gain (a more comprehensive protection of individual rights) might not balance the certain losses (collegiality and the cooperative relationship with the ordinary courts).

It is important to note, however, that the restrictions in access to the Italian Constitutional Court are not confined to the lack of a constitutional complaint procedure. The Constitution even frames the abstract review of legislation in a rather strict way, as parliamentary minorities cannot bring a statute before the Court. Abstract review is confined to the controversies

---

[15] U. Wesel, *Der Gang nach Karlsruhe. Das Bundesverfassungsgericht in der Geschichte der Bundesrepublik*, *supra* note 3.

[16] In 2017, 5.784 new constitutional complaints proceedings were brought to the Court: see *Annual Statistics 2017*, *supra* note 13.

between the State and the Regions. It seems that this limitation was due to an intervention by the then head of the government, Alcide De Gasperi.[17] Apparently, he did not want the Constitutional Court to be a direct counterbalance to the Government and its majority.[18] Hence, abstract review of legislation should, in principle, mainly concern the distribution of legislative power between the State and the Regions and should not interfere with major political questions.

In his contribution to this book, Victor Ferreres Comella advances good arguments which call for introducing standing for parliamentary minorities.[19] Even in this case, however, one can seriously doubt whether the lack of direct recourse by parliamentary minorities is a weakness or a strength of the Court.

Recourse by parliamentary minorities comes at a price. When a statute is challenged by a parliamentary minority, the constitutional court is subject to the highest political pressure because its decision – whatever that might be – can easily be criticized for being politically biased by the party that lost the case. This poses a serious threat to the constitutional court's legitimacy, especially when dissenting opinions are allowed. Therefore, if a well-functioning system of incidental review allows the contested statutes to reach the Court despite the lack of parliamentary recourse, one may argue that a lack of direct challenge mechanism on behalf of parliamentary minorities is not significantly harmful. This is especially true in a highly fragmented political context that lacks a shared constitutional culture, as is the case in Italy today. In short, it seems that even in the case of abstract review of legislation, an apparent (and planned) weakness of the Court has proven not to be a critical weakness and possibly even a shield for the Court's legitimacy and authority.

14.3. Low profile

The authority of a court depends not only on the substance of its decisions but also on the way in which they are reached and on how they speak to their audience. "Impressive" opinions at the end of an inclusive and public-

---

[17] See E. LAMARQUE, in this book.

[18] This does not deny, however, that the very existence of the Constitutional Court is due to the Christian Democratic party (of which De Gasperi was the undisputed leader), which supported the creation of a constitutional court with the strongest conviction from the very beginning, overcoming the skepticism of the Socialist and the Communist parties.

[19] See V. FERRERES COMELLA, in this book.

ly-followed proceeding certainly contribute to consolidating a court's authority and prestige, both domestically and abroad. After all, a constitutional court's jurisprudence can be seen as the best introduction to a nation's legal culture because one can expect that a legal order's most sophisticated doctrine is produced by its highest court. From this perspective, dissenting and concurring opinions can serve as an important tool to foster the court's authority. Separate opinions, as Diletta Tega stresses in her contribution, can help to produce a clearer, more coherent, and transparent reasoning, which in turn simplifies dialogue with other institutional actors as well as with society.[20] The same applies with regard to direct engagement with legal scholarship: by quoting scholarly opinions in its decisions, a constitutional court shows that it is cognizant of academic debate and that it might even engage with the critical voices of its legal culture, which, ultimately, can strengthen the legitimacy of the institution itself.[21] Maybe, it is not a coincidence that justices of the two most authoritative courts on both sides of the Atlantic – the U.S. Supreme Court and the German Constitutional Court – write separate opinions and engage explicitly with legal scholarship.[22]

From this perspective, the Italian Constitutional Court does not shine at first sight. Neither dissenting opinions nor direct quotations of legal scholarship are at its disposal, or the Court has not yet resorted to either of those tools. Furthermore, proceedings before the Italian Constitutional Court are rather closed as far as third-party interventions and *amici curiae* are concerned. This is partly because of the procedural rules governing constitutional litigation and partly because of the Court's own volition.[23] In principle, this tends to insulate the Court from public debate and limits its grounding in society, whereas a more inclusive approach in principle bolsters a court's authority, as Maartje de Visser notices in her contribution to this book.

It should not come as a surprise, then, that the very names of the Constitutional Court's justices, including the Court's president, are essentially unknown to the public. From this perspective, there could be no greater contrast to the United States, where the health conditions of a single justice can be top news in the media and gather the interest of common citizens.[24]

---

[20] See D. TEGA, in this book.

[21] See P. PASSAGLIA, in this book.

[22] On the link between the lack of separate opinions and the quotation of legal literature, see P. PASSAGLIA, *supra* note 21.

[23] See T. GROPPI & A.M. LECIS COCCO ORTU, in this book.

[24] See, for example, the titles of some articles in the major U.S. newspapers on 8 No-

The public visibility of the Constitutional Court is also far higher in Germany than in Italy. When exiting the Karlsruhe train station, there is no need to instruct a taxi driver on the address of the Constitutional Court, whereas this might be the case when exiting the station of Roma Termini, a result that does not solely depend on the different sizes of the two cities.

However, one should not ignore the other side of the coin by underestimating the advantages of a less visible power. Being unknown to the public certainly does not contribute to the legitimacy of the Court, but "judicial ego" can harm a court equally, if not more. The lack of dissenting opinions surely curtails a justice's freedom of expression and makes it difficult for that justice to become a public character. But it protects all justices, and, more importantly, the Court as a whole, from accusations of political biases, thereby supporting their independence. While hiding single personalities, collegiality strengthens the anonymous Court. In his famous dissent in *Obergefell*, Justice Scalia questioned the legitimacy of the Supreme Court's decision with these impressive words: "Today's decree says that [...] the Ruler of 320 million Americans coast-to-coast, is *a majority of the nine lawyers on the Supreme Court*".[25] This objection, however, loses part of its grip in a legal system like the Italian one, where "constitutional justice is a function carried out by a body, not by fifteen persons".[26]

Not quoting legal scholarship has some advantages as well. As Paolo Passaglia suggests, the authority of a decision can be jeopardized if references to legal scholarship are incomplete or imprecise.[27] Furthermore, following the legal opinion of a certain law professor not only exposes the Court to the risk of being criticized for choosing a certain opinion over another, but also makes the judgment's authority contingent, to a certain degree, on the fortune of the author's opinion. This can be avoided by a "furtive" use of legal literature, as Marc Verdussen puts it.[28]

Similar considerations apply to the openness of the constitutional proceedings. The practice of the Court described by Tania Groppi and Anna Maria Lecis Cocco Ortu – that is, paying attention to third-parties' arguments and *amici curiae* despite their inadmissibility – has advantages. In

---

vember 2018: *Justice Ruth Bader Ginsburg Hospitalized With 3 Broken Ribs* (The New York Times); *Supreme Court Justice Ruth Bader Ginsburg Hospitalized with Fractured Ribs* (The Washington Post); *Justice Ruth Bader Ginsburg Is Hospitalized After Fall* (The Wall Street Journal).

[25] U.S. Supreme Court, *Obergefell v. Hodges*, 576 U.S. ___ (2015) (Scalia, J., dissenting); emphasis added.

[26] D. TEGA, *supra* note 20.

[27] P. PASSAGLIA, *supra* note 21.

[28] M. VERDUSSEN, in this book.

this way, the Court is able to consider the broader interests that arise from society while it avoids placing the constitutional process at the center of the public's attention, thereby relieving the judges from the pressure of public opinion.

All in all, the lack of separate opinions and of a direct dialogue with legal scholarship, combined with relatively closed constitutional proceedings, render the Court and its justices less visible to the public. But there are good reasons to think that no direct relationship exists between the visibility and the authority of a court. In the Italian case the opposite might be true. Especially during the last two decades, the Italian Constitutional Court was able to withstand a harsh confrontation with the political powers; but one could ask the question whether this happened *despite* its rather low-profile approach or *because of* it.

The Italian Constitutional Court's style of reasoning also reflects this general approach and shares the advantages and disadvantages thereof. The forms and methods of constitutional interpretation that the Italian Constitutional Court deploys are not peculiar. As Giorgio Pino explains in his contribution to this book, the Italian Constitutional Court favors principle-oriented and value-oriented interpretation,[29] as do most constitutional courts in Europe. On this side of the Atlantic, neither the courts nor the scholarship value Originalism, which Jeffrey Pojanowski sees as quite paradoxical when considering the younger and more easily amendable European constitutions.[30] Nevertheless, the way in which the judgments of the Italian Constitutional Court are phrased differs considerably from the style of its German counterpart.

In writing its decisions, the German Constitutional Court exhibits a scholarly approach, which is best expressed in its famous "paragraph C.I".[31] In this paragraph, which starts the decision on the merits of the case, the Court instructs the legislature (and the society as a whole) on the guiding constitutional principles in a certain subject area, making clear what is allowed and not allowed under the Constitution. In its tone and abstractness, paragraph C.I is closer to a constitutional law paper than to a traditional judicial decision, providing a general and comprehensive picture of the limits set by the Constitution. The actual decision of the case is presented as an application of such broad reasoning. Sometimes its reasoning even re-

[29] G. PINO, in this book.

[30] J.A. POJANOWSKI, in this book.

[31] For a strong critique of the structure of the German Constitutional Court's decisions see O. LEPSIUS, *Die maßstabsetzende Gewalt*, in C. SCHÖNBERGER, M. JESTAEDT, O. LEPSIUS, C. MÖLLERS, *Das entgrenzte Gericht*, *supra* note 1, 161.

sembles sermons celebrating the Constitution, essays on political theory, or public pedagogy.

By contrast, the style of reasoning of the Italian Constitutional Court very much corresponds to the U.S. Supreme Court Justice Alito's description of the minimalist approach: "We decide the case before us and leave broader issues for another day".[32] An example of this is the so called "absorption-technique" that is applied on a daily basis in the Italian Constitutional Court's case law. When there are several pleas of unconstitutionality and the Court believes that one of these pleas suffices to strike down the impugned law, the Court examines the easiest plea first and declares the other pleas "absorbed" without reviewing them in substance.[33]

This minimalist approach certainly testifies to the Court's unwillingness to perform a pedagogical function towards the legislature and society. At the same time, as Sarah Harding stresses in her contribution following Cass Sunstein's reflections, minimalism is also a form of dialogue with other institutions – notably with the legislature – because narrow decisions can be "important avenues for legal development".[34] Moreover, it must be noted that, in this dialogue, the Italian Constitutional Court enjoys a rather favorable position, as the two judgments on the immunity from criminal proceedings of the State's highest officers of 2004 and 2009 prove.[35]

In 2003, the ruling majority adopted a statute that suspended the criminal prosecutions pending against the state's five highest officers. One year later, the Constitutional Court held the statute to be unconstitutional, pointing out that the law required all criminal proceedings to be suspended regardless of the accusation, and that the suspension was subject to no time limit. However, the Court did not address the question of whether, in general, laws expanding constitutional immunities must be adopted as constitutional amendments. This latter plea was considered to be absorbed by the aforementioned unconstitutionality. In 2008, the same majority replaced the unconstitutional statute with a second one of similar content, which this time took into account the remarks of the Court's 2004 judgment. In a courageous judgment of 2009, the Court struck down the second statute as well, stating that the extension of judicial immunities for political authorities is only possible through a constitutional amendment.

This minimalist approach is certainly open to criticism. After all, the

---

[32] U.S. Supreme Court, *NASA v. Nelson*, 562 U.S. 134, 148 (2011).

[33] See A. BONOMI, *L'assorbimento dei vizi nel giudizio di costituzionalità in via incidentale*, Naples, Jovene Editore, 2013.

[34] S. HARDING, in this book.

[35] See judgments 24/2004 and 262/2009.

Court could have already said in its first judgment that a constitutional amendment was necessary, thereby preventing the legislature from enacting a second law that was again unconstitutional. But it must be acknowledged that this careful strategy of not playing the highest card until it is strictly necessary – a strategy mostly alien to the German Constitutional Court – gives the Italian Constitutional Court a significant advantage in the dialogue with the legislature and avoids, to a certain extent, the need for the Court to have to reckon with difficult precedents in the future.

14.4. Adverse environment

The powers of a constitutional court, and the way in which they are exercised, cannot be assessed in isolation; rather, one must take into account the "external" conditions of the political and institutional context in which the court operates.[36] In particular, the relationship between the constitutional court and the legislature, and notably the "responsiveness" of the latter to the "requests" of the former, strongly affects the Court's powers.

Often, a mere declaration of unconstitutionality not only fails to eradicate a flaw of unconstitutionality, but also risks making matters worse. This is the case, for example, when a law grants a right to certain categories of persons but excludes others in a similar situation; or when a law grants insufficient protection to a certain (social) right. Merely striking down the contested law would aggravate the situation of unconstitutionality when what is required to redress the law's unconstitutionality is an extension or increase of the law's benefits, not a denial of those benefits for those who already enjoy them.

In such situations, the effectiveness of constitutional review depends on the responsiveness of the legislature. When a court believes that the legislature will quickly respond by passing a new law in conformity with the constitution, it will be more willing to exercise its power of striking down legislation. But when the court cannot rely on a responsive legislature, it will probably refrain from striking down the law, because imperfect legislation is usually better than no legislation at all. Put differently, the extent to which a court can exercise its powers significantly depends on its counterpart: a reliable legislature allows the court to exercise its powers with more

[36] See S. Cassese, *La giustizia costituzionale in Italia: lo stato presente*, in S. Cassese, *Dentro la Corte. Diario di un giudice costituzionale*, Bologna, Il Mulino, 2015, 304, pointing out the weak support given to the Italian Constitutional Court by the other State-powers.

freedom, whereas with an irresponsive legislature some of the court's power may remain only on paper.

Even from this perspective, one may observe a dynamic of strength in weakness to the advantage of the Italian Constitutional Court. In Germany, the Constitutional Court could generally count on a responsive legislature, which, when asked by the Court to amend or replace unconstitutional legislation, would respond within a reasonable time.[37] This prompted the German Constitutional Court to develop a particular type of decision to address those abovementioned situations in which it cannot simply declare unconstitutional the provisions at stake because a new, more comprehensive regulation is necessary to overcome the situation of unconstitutionality.

These are the decisions of mere incompatibility (*Unvereinbarkeit*) with the Constitution.[38] The contested law is not declared null and void but merely incompatible with the Constitution, and the legislature is given a deadline to pass a new law in conformity with the Constitution. Until the legislature intervenes, the German Constitutional Court either allows the unconstitutional provision to be still applicable,[39] or (less frequently) dictates itself a provisional regulation,[40] or (still less frequently) requires pending proceedings to be suspended to wait for the legislature to act.[41] In these decisions, the Court's instructions are sometimes so precise that one could question whether any political choices remain for the legislature in passing the new law. In principle, however, the German Constitutional Court respects the separation of powers, and, notably, the domain of the legislature. Even when the Court itself dictates a regulation of the subject matter, this is always conceived as a *provisional* regulation that expires as soon as the legislature intervenes. This is possible because the Court can rely on the

---

[37] In 1991, the German Constitutional Court held unconstitutional the automatic assignment of a man's surname to his wife following marriage if the couple cannot reach agreement on their surname (BVerfG, order of the First Senate of 5 March 1991 – 1 BvL 83/86). Through this *Unvereinbarkeitserklärung*, the German Constitutional Court declared the relevant provision of the civil code incompatible with the Basic Law and called on the legislature to amend it. The reform of surname regulation was passed on 16 December 1993 and entered into force on 1 April 1994. In a similar case, things went very differently in Italy: see *infra* note 43.

[38] See K. SCHLAICH, S. KORIOTH, *Das Bundesverfassungsgericht*, 10th ed., München, Beck, 2015, 295 ff.

[39] See, e.g., BVerfG, judgment of the First Senate of 10 April 2018 – 1 BvL 11/14 on property tax.

[40] See, e.g., BVerfG, judgment of the First Senate of 18 July 2012 – 1 BvL 10/10 on social benefits for asylum seekers.

[41] See, e.g., BVerfG, order of the First Senate of 10 October 2017 – 1 BvR 2019/16 on third gender option.

responsiveness of the legislature. Indeed, it is currently discussed in Germany to what extent the recent fragmentation of the political parties' system, which has led to weaker coalition governments, will diminish the power of the Constitutional Court.[42]

Historically, the Italian Constitutional Court has been confronted with a much more fragile political and institutional context. The Court could reasonably expect its appeals to the legislature to amend or replace unconstitutional law to fall on deaf ears.[43] This weakness of the political and institutional context could have strongly curtailed the potential for constitutional adjudication because it is not reasonable for a constitutional court to strike down an imperfect law in anticipation of a better law that may never come. The Italian Constitutional Court, however, reacted the opposite way. Confronted with the lack of a responsive legislature, it decided not to retreat, but rather to raise the stakes by developing the so-called "additive" and "substitutive" judgments.[44]

Through these judgments, the Italian Constitutional Court declares a law unconstitutional "to the extent that it does not regulate something", or – in rarer cases – "to the extent that it stipulates something instead of something else" that the Constitution mandates.[45] In so doing, the Court *re-*

[42] C. SCHÖNBERGER, *Anmerkungen zu Karlsruhe*, *supra* note 1, 58.

[43] Consider, for example, the case of the automatic assignment of the father's surname to a married couple's child. Already in 1988, the Constitutional Court, while acknowledging that it is for the legislature to regulate this issue, stated that "it would be possible, and probably in keeping with the evolution of the social conscience, to replace the current rule [...] with a different criterion that affords greater respect to the autonomy of the married couple" (order 176/1988). In judgment 61/2006, it considered this rule "a legacy of a patriarchal conception of the family" that was no longer compatible with the constitutional values of moral and legal equality between man and woman. However, since several options were at disposal to the legislature, the Court considered the choice to be for the legislature, and not for itself. Finally, in 2016, since no reform was passed in the meanwhile by the legislature, the Constitutional Court decided to declare the relevant provision unconstitutional "insofar as it does not permit the married couple to attribute also the mother's name to the child by mutual agreement at the time of birth" (judgment 286/2016).

[44] See V. BARSOTTI, P.G. CAROZZA, M. CARTABIA, A. SIMONCINI, *Italian Constitutional Justice in Global Context*, *supra* note 4, 86.

[45] For example, consider law of 25 February 1992, n. 210, providing monetary compensation for those suffering irreversible diseases as a consequence of vaccinations. The law's initial version granted compensation only for a limited number of vaccinations and to a limited number of beneficiaries. However, by no less than 7 additive judgments (see, lastly, judgment 268/2017), the Constitutional Court extended compensation to other vaccinations and to other beneficiaries in the name of the principle of equality. Although the legislature left the law untouched, its scope of application expanded significantly through the Court's additive judgments.

places the legislature. In theory, the legislature could re-regulate the whole subject matter in a different way by means of an ordinary law; but this is neither necessary nor does it frequently happen. Far from limiting the Constitutional Court's powers, the weakness of the Italian political context prompted the Court to be active and regulatory.[46]

A comparison of the recent jurisprudence of the German and the Italian Constitutional Court is very telling in this respect. The German Constitutional Court has a long tradition of deep judicial review of the electoral law.[47] In 2012, the Court made a particularly "risky" decision when it not only declared that the electoral law was incompatible with the Constitution in so far as it does not properly redress the "negative voting weight effect",[48] but also declared part of the law null and void, all the while assigning the legislature a strict deadline to pass a new law. By doing so, the Court made the electoral law incomplete such that, if elections were to be held before the intervention of the legislature, no applicable law existed to assign the seats.[49]

It is safe to say that the Italian Constitutional Court would have never taken a risk like this or, at least, it never took it. The guiding principle of the (more recent but no less remarkable) jurisprudence of the Italian Constitutional Court on the electoral law is that the legislation remaining in force following a declaration of unconstitutionality by the Court must guarantee the renewal of the Parliament at any time.[50] This limit, however, did not push the Court to refrain from exercising its review of the electoral law. Instead, it prompted it to a bold (and rather free) rewriting of the electoral law that was found unconstitutional in judgments 1/2014 and 35/2017. Little remains of the idea of a "negative legislator" in these two judgments. But this creative attitude by the Court does not have its roots in the Court's

[46] Notice, however, that the Court resorts to additive and substitutive judgments particularly in the field of social rights, in application of the principle of equality. In other domains, notably in criminal law, the Court exercises self-restraint and avoids replacing the legislature.

[47] For an overview in English, see D.P. Kommers, R. Miller, *The Constitutional Jurisprudence of the Federal Republic of Germany*, 3rd ed., Durham and London, Duke University Press, 2012, 238 ff.

[48] This is a complicated mechanism in the German federal electoral law that, in particular circumstances, allows an increase in the number of votes to lead to the loss of a mandate, or a loss of votes to lead to winning a mandate.

[49] BVerfG, judgment of the Second Senate of 25 July 2012 – 2 BvF 3/11. See in particular para. 162: "As a consequence of this finding, there is a lack of valid regulation of the procedure for allocating seats in the elections of the German *Bundestag*" (translation by the authors).

[50] So, for example, judgment 1/2014.

will to extend its powers, but rather in a realistic appreciation of the weakness of the political context.[51]

14.5. Playing poker

The power logics examined in this paper at the domestic level can also be observed in the interaction between the Italian Constitutional Court and the European Courts. For reasons of brevity, we will confine our analysis to the relationship with the Court of Justice of the European Union.

Patricia Popelier stresses in this book that, in principle, all constitutional courts in Europe – and not just the Italian one – are part of an inter-relationship with the European Courts that reflects attitudinal elements, which Marta Infantino calls "pride, respect, and resistance".[52] Surely, in the European legal space, "relationality" is a "device" of all constitutional courts, rather than a peculiar feature of the Italian Constitutional Court. If we look at the way in which this interaction takes place, however, it seems to us that a specific "Italian style" can be singled out. Once again, the comparison with the opposite "German style" can help to capture these features.

It is worth noting that the Italian Constitutional Court enters the European judicial dialogue with a significant handicap. Unlike the German Constitutional Court, and most of the constitutional courts in Europe, it does not have jurisdiction to review the constitutionality of international treaties, including EU Treaties, before their ratification. This means that the Italian Constitutional Court cannot express *ex ante* its general view on the constitutional limits of European integration. There is no *Maastricht* or *Lisbon* decision in the Italian constitutional jurisprudence. Unlike the German Constitutional Court, the Italian Constitutional Court cannot interfere with European treaty-making; it can only step in when a concrete conflict between EU and constitutional law arises before a court, and only when this conflict finds its way to the Constitutional Court.

Despite this limit, the Italian Constitutional Court was able to carve out a significant role in the European judicial dialogue on fundamental rights, as the *Taricco* saga has recently made clear. The latter can be taken as the best example of an "Italian style" of multilevel dialogue. But let us first examine the "German style", so that the Italian one will become clearer.

---

[51] Already G. ZAGREBELSKY, *La Corte costituzionale e il legislatore*, in P. BARILE, E. CHELI, S. GRASSI, *Corte costituzionale e sviluppo della forma di governo in Italia*, Bologna, Il Mulino, 1982, 118, suggested that sometimes the replacement of the legislature by the Court testifies to the weakness of the Court rather than to its arrogance.

[52] See P. POPELIER and M. INFANTINO in this book.

When confronted with an actual or foreseeable conflict between EU and constitutional law, the German Constitutional Court tends to instruct the Court of Justice clearly on the limits within which it is prepared to accept the primacy of EU law. The German Constitutional Court sets the boundaries, and the Court of Justice should not overstep those boundaries.

Consider, for example, the reaction of the German Constitutional Court to the broad reading of the Charter's scope of application in *Åkerberg Fransson*.[53] Two months after the Court of Justice's judgment, the German Constitutional Court, in an *obiter dictum* to its judgment on the counter-terrorism database, spelled out the following: "[*Åkerberg Fransson*] must not be read in a way that would view it as an apparent ultra vires act or as if it endangered the protection and enforcement of the fundamental rights in the Member States [...] in a way that questioned the identity of the Basic Law's constitutional order [...]. The decision must thus not be understood and applied in such a way that absolutely any connection of a provision's subject-matter to the merely abstract scope of Union law, or merely incidental effects on Union law, would be sufficient for binding the Member States by the Union's fundamental rights set forth in the [Charter]".[54] The German Constitutional Court leaves little room for interpretation: *Åkerberg Fransson* must be interpreted narrowly, otherwise it will be declared *ultra vires*.

A similar approach marks other judgments of the German Constitutional Court as well. The detailed catalogue of the State powers that cannot be transferred to the EU in the *Lisbon* judgment immediately comes to mind,[55] as well as the judgment on constitutional identity of 15 December 2015, in which the Court set out the minimum standard mandated by the Constitution to allow extradition in the context of a European Arrest Warrant.[56] The German Constitutional Court's preliminary reference in *OMT* can rightly be considered the peak of this approach.[57]

In *Taricco*, the Italian Constitutional Court followed a different approach. Undoubtedly, in its order of reference 24/2017, even the Italian Constitutional Court somehow threatened the Court of Justice: it made clear that it was likely to use its most powerful weapon, the "counter-limits", if the Court of Justice had upheld its unacceptable *Taricco* judgment. However, unlike the German Constitutional Court, the Italian Con-

---

[53] Court of Justice (GC), Case C-617/10, 26 February 2013, *Åkerberg Fransson*.

[54] BVerfG, judgment of the First Senate of 24 April 2013 – 1 BvR 1215/07.

[55] BVerfG, judgment of the Second Senate of 30 June 2009 – 2 BvE 2/08.

[56] BVerfG, order of the Second Senate of 15 December 2015 – 2 BvR 2735/14.

[57] BVerfG, order of the Second Senate of 14 January 2014 – 2 BvR 2728/13.

stitutional Court did not sketch the decision it wished from the Court of Justice but confined itself to stating the existence of a conflict between a judgment of the Court of Justice (*Taricco*) and a supreme principle of the Italian Constitution (legality in criminal matters). The Italian Constitutional Court did not dwell on the scope of the principle of legality in criminal matters, such that what the Italian Constitutional Court considers acceptable is not clear in the order of reference.

This seemed to be a strategic move in its confrontation with the Court of Justice. By not stating the scope and the limits of the supreme principle that prevents compliance with the *Taricco* judgment of the Court of Justice, the Italian Constitutional Court retains the ability to respond when the case comes back to it after the former's decision. It is as though the Italian Constitutional Court played a first very open move waiting to see the reaction of the Court of Justice.

Both the German and the Italian approaches can be effective. The Court of Justice not only overruled *Taricco* following the preliminary reference of the Italian Constitutional Court,[58] but it also softened its *Åkerberg Fransson* jurisprudence[59] and enhanced fundamental rights protection in the execution of a European Arrest Warrant in *Aranyosi and Căldăraru*,[60] in both cases following the "suggestions" of the German Constitutional Court.

If one had to visualize the style of the Italian Constitutional Court, one might say that it is a poker-player. Poker games last a while, and it is essential to observe how the other players react to one's move. The Italian Constitutional Court does not put all its cards (its core arguments) on the table in a single move. Rather, it announces only one of them at a time – not necessarily the strongest – and waits for the reaction of its contender. When playing poker, even a player with weaker cards can ultimately win, if he (or she) plays them skillfully, as did the Italian Constitutional Court in *Taricco*.

---

[58] Court of Justice (GC), Case C-42/17, 5 December 2017, *M.A.S., M.B.*

[59] See Court of Justice, Case C-206/13, 6 March 2014, *Siragusa*; Case C-265/13, 27 March 2014, *Torralbo Marcos*; Case C-198/13, 10 July 2014, *Julian Hernández*.

[60] Court of Justice (GC), Joined Cases C-404/15 and C-659/15 PPU, *Aranyosi and Căldăraru*.

INDEX

G

H

I

J

P

Q

R

T

U

V

W

X

Z

For Product Safety Concerns and Information please contact our EU
representative GPSR@taylorandfrancis.com
Taylor & Francis Verlag GmbH, Kaufingerstraße 24, 80331 München, Germany

www.ingramcontent.com/pod-product-compliance
Lightning Source LLC
LaVergne TN
LVHW011116300926
849160LV00008B/406

* 9 7 8 0 3 6 7 6 1 7 7 2 1 *